£39.95

BAUDY
THE ANIMAL MAN

The Biography of Robert Baudy
with Sandra Thompson

RAINBOW BOOKS, INC.

LIBRARY OF CONGRESS CATALOGING-IN-PUBLICATION DATA

Baudy, Robert, 1923-
    Baudy, the animal man the biography of Robert Baudy / with Sandra Thompson.
    p.   cm.
    ISBN 1-56825-033-9 (hardcover) (alk. paper). -- ISBN 1-56825-032-0 (trade softcover : alk. paper)
    1. Baudy, Robert, 1923-   . 2. Animal trainers -- Biography.
I. Thompson, Sandra.   II. Title.
GV1811.B325A3   1996
636088'8'092--dc20   95-41123
[B]   CIP

BAUDY, THE ANIMAL MAN
Copyright ©1996 by Robert Baudy and Sandra Thompson

All rights reserved. No part of this book may be reproduced or transmitted in any form or by any means, electronic or mechanical, including photocopy, recording, or any information storage and retrieval system, without permission in writing from the publisher. All inquiries should be addressed to Rainbow Books, Inc. P. O. Box 430, Highland City, FL 33846-0430.

Baudy, The Animal Man
By Robert Baudy and Sandra Thompson
Design by Marilyn Ratzlaff
Cover Art and Design by Sandra Thompson
Photographic Images/Pepito, Tampa

Printed in the United States of America

to south Florida to a locale more accessible to visiting Robert. They also left their wild animals behind.

When Ed and Jodi asked if I would be interested in doing another biography — the life of Robert Baudy — my interest was piqued. A date was set to journey north to central Florida where Robert had settled years before to raise and breed exotic cats and other wild animals at the Savage Kingdom and the Rare Feline Breeding Center.

I was most anxious to visit the man in the environment that had become home to him and his cats in the middle of a Florida oak hammock. The encounter would afford the opportunity for me to get a feel for the man, the place, and the possibility of working with him to help tell his story.

On the appointed day, Jodi and Ed pulled into our drive in their handsomely equipped van for the three-hour journey into the "wilds." It was to be quite an adventure in itself, and who knew where it would ultimately lead? The day was bright with a cloudless, vivid blue sky. We talked all along the way of what was ahead as we approached "Robert's compound." When we pulled off the turnpike north of Orlando to head west, I could sense what the appeal was to a man who needed open space away from human population to pursue a livelihood so completely wrapped up in his love for and knowledge of exotic cats and other animals.

Driving further inland, the passing panorama held fewer houses as we seemingly left civilization behind — at least civilization that we had become accustomed to, where multitudinous dwellings and dense population covered manicured grounds dissected by roads carrying rapidly moving traffic. We drove until there were few houses and little traffic. The ground seemed to rise and fall slightly with oak trees cutting the horizon above pasture land. Animals grazed peacefully, in what seemed a place far removed from the tropical lushness and frenzied congestion of south Florida. Soon we saw a weather-beaten sign that read "Savage Kingdom," in peeling and faded white letters, giving the appearance of a bygone era — a business enterprise no longer viable — a magical animal habitat driven into oblivion. How false was the impression.

Ed turned down a dirt road which accessed the back entrance to Robert's place. We drove in and out of oak hammocks as we

INTRODUCTION

I had heard about Robert Baudy, the cat man, as I enjoyed, along with David, some compelling conversations with Ed and Jodi Schaffer. Ed had known Robert for over thirty years. Ed and Jodi were new neighbors who became aware that we had just published a book about Dave's early years in Palm Beach. The book included several chapters describing his involvement in World War II as a member of Patton's Army. Perhaps it would interest a French animal trainer who also fought the Germans as a member of a French Division serving under Patton.

Ed and Jodi had regaled us with stories of their own where zoo animals were concerned — animals which they owned and raised on 47 acres outside Indianapolis. Years ago in Indianapolis, Dr. Ed, an orthopedic surgeon, was called upon to treat a Siberian tiger visiting the area as part of an animal act. The owner of the sick cat was Robert Baudy, renowned animal trainer and breeder, who was at the time performing a circus act with his cats on tour throughout the United States. Since a local veterinarian was not available, Ed was called upon to diagnose the cat in what to him was a total departure, but fascinating challenge for an orthopedic surgeon. Ed and Robert formed a unique relationship in which many common interests and diverse backgrounds were shared and related. Through Robert, Ed became more knowledgeable about the world of wild animals and began raising several different species on his Indianapolis acreage — animals purchased through Robert. When Ed retired from medical practice, he and Jodi moved embrace. Instantly, I realized that my left hand was paralyzed, the animal's razor-sharp claws imbedded in it. Simultaneously, the first crushing bite went through my right wrist, immediately followed by another massive attack on the forearm, and a third broke through my biceps. I heard skin, tendons, muscle and bone being torn and crushed like paper and yet, felt absolutely no pain. Survival instinct made me scream the animal's name, "Chilly," and, almost miraculously, the furious predator released his hold and retreated to the other side of the arena where he began to pace back and forth — neck expanded, growling menacingly.

Slowly I arose, searching for the steel training fork and hickory stick. I looked down at my left hand — it had been brutalized. The lacerated skin hung over the forefingers. My eyes focused on the pacing, enraged animal as I groped and finally was able to retrieve the fork with my left hand. I was not able to find the wood stick laying somewhere on the ground to the right. My right hand felt absolutely numb. A quick glance revealed the extent of mutilation. The forearm had been broken, the lower part hanging useless with the two major bones protruding from an open wound — the pulsating artery squirting a powerful stream of blood.

When I entered the arena, I had a helper outside the exit door. The huge 300-pound fellow, according to his references, had worked as a doorman for Clyde Beatty. A quick look over my shoulder to the door revealed that the helper was gone, which meant I had to try with a crippled left hand to operate the vertical double-latch bar controlling the exit door. Facing the tiger, I slowly backed away from the bloody center of the arena, dropped the fork, and finally managed to open the door halfway — struggling with my back to the exit — eyes constantly focused on Chilly. When half my body was through, the tiger sprang wildly into the air and hit the door like a Mack truck, sending me flying backwards, and miraculously closing the self-locking device on the gate . . .

Welcome to my world/ Je l'invite dans mon Monde.

ROBERT BAUDY

Something had gone wrong. For six months the individual training of each of the eight tigers had taken place almost like an assembly line. Each day from sunup to sundown, animals were gradually trained, first to recognize their permanent pedestals, then to go to a specific location in the center of the 40-foot steel arena. The session lasted about 15 minutes per specimen, and then my outside helper would open the door and within seconds send another cat through the entrance. The next step was to rehearse two animals at the same time. When the two were absolutely synchronized in their routine, a third cat was then introduced, and then another, and another, and so on. On this fateful day of September 20, 1960 — which was my 37th birthday — three seconds of life crystallized in my memory and will follow me to the grave.

Boris and Chilly, two enormous male Siberians, were my present students. Chilly, for some unknown reason, refused to do the return jump from one pedestal to another 17 feet away, so I prodded him gently with the tip of the whip, which was the extension of my hand. It is impossible to have direct human contact with a mother-raised specimen due to potential violent reaction and danger ever present. As I watched Chilly, I knew that he was out of control. Suddenly, without warning, he turned and 500 pounds of ferocious tiger was airborne coming straight at me, dilated eyes focused with fury; his wide-open mouth displaying four menacing ivory fangs.

As our bodies met, the impact floored the two of us in a lethal

25.	Florida — 317	
26.	Back On Tour/ *Retour en la Route* — 337	
27.	Tigers and Other Animals/ *Les Tigres et Autres Bêtes* — 348	
28.	New Animals, New Marriage/ *Nouveaux Animaux, Nouveau Mariage* — 364	
29.	Mr. and Mrs. Baudy On Tour/ *Monsieur et Madame Baudy en Tournée* -- 374	
30.	Gerard — 388	
31.	Many Dramatic Changes/ *Beaucoup de Changements Dramatiques* — 404	
32	Women / *Les Femmes* — 413	
33.	Savage Kingdom/ *Le Royaume Sauvage* — 426	
34.	Movies and Other Dramatics In The Kingdom/ *La Cinéma et les Drames au Royaume* — 443	
35.	Exposure/ *Sous la Lumière* — 454	
36.	Life In The Savage Kingdom/ *La Vie au Royaume Sauvage* — 467	
37.	Kathy — 480	
38.	Honors and Recognition / *Les Honneurs et la Reconnaissance* — 499	
39.	Breeding/ *L'Élevage* — 509	
40.	Life and Death/ *La Vie et la Mort* — 534	
41.	Addendum By Sandra Thompson — 548	
	About the Author, Sandra Thompson — 557	

TABLE des MATIERES

Robert Baudy — 7
Introduction — 9

1. The Young Hunter/ *Le Jeune Chasseur* — 21
2. Home To Le Vesinet/ *Retour au Vesinet* — 32
3. St. Nicolas — 45
4. New Business and Sex Education/ *L'Occupation Nouvelle et l'Education Sexuelle* — 52
5. War On The Horizon/ *La Guerre à l'Horizon* — 62
6. War/ *La Guerre* — 65
7. German Occupation/ *L'Occupation Allemande* — 78
8. Leaving Le Vesinet/ *Départ du Vesinet* — 86
9. Escape To Fegreac/ *L'Echappement vers Fegreac* — 89
10. Life In The Forest/ *La Survie en Forêt* — 99
11. Escape To Marseilles/ *L'Echappement vers Marseilles* — 108
12. Return To France Via Spanish Hell-hole/ *Retour en France par l'Enfer Espagnol* — 119
13. The Free French/ *Les Forces Libres* — 124
14. Chasing The Germans/ *La Poursuite des Allemands* — 151
15. Freedom / *La Liberté* — 172
16. Marriage To Odette — Period Of The Carrots/ *Le Mariage, Odette, et les Carottes* — 179
17. Circus Fame and A Baby Boy/ *L'Etoile du Cirque et Papa* — 199
18. Early Tour Engagements/ *Le Début sur la Route* — 211
19. European Acclaim/ *Le Succès en Europe* — 229
20. American Tour Begins/ *Le Début en l'Amérique* — 248
21. New Tour and Freedom / *Les Nouvelles Libertés* — 265
22. Charlotte — 280
23. Manhattan — 299
24. Great Danes/ *Dressage de Danois* — 311

MESSAGE FOR FUTURE GENERATIONS

A mission must be sacerdotal in essence.
What is called for is a common
religious commitment to preserve
and prolong a disappearing heritage.
Without this global mystique everything will be lost,
including our souls.

— Robert Baudy

I dedicate the writing of *BAUDY* to two men:
To Robert, whose life has never been easy but in sharing it — the joys as well as the pain — he reveals an invincible, intrepid spirit and a true animal lover . . .
and to David, whose patience, support and love is sustaining through an obsessive process.

worked our way through dappled sunshine to a closed barbed-wire entry that Ed opened and then closed behind the van once he had driven through the enclosure. The dirt road continued past a large field where deer and exotic horned animals grazed in a muted, green-beige, luxuriant pasture that could have been in Africa, or the Wild Animal Park in San Diego, or any number of other locations in the world where deer and antelope play in natural environs.

Soon a deeply shaded hammock appeared before us, containing a long concrete building painted yellow ocher and fading badly. Jodi explained the building was Robert Baudy's residence. We had been told that the man lived among his animals in an accommodation which had been shared with many different people over the years. Ed and Jodi spoke with such affection and esteem for the "Cat Man" that anything initially rustic or unattractive about the surroundings would soon totally fade in the wonder of what we were about to witness.

As the van pulled alongside then circled to the back of the housing, we moved out of the sunlight and into heavy shade. I saw wire-enclosed cages intermingled with huge 100-year-old oak trees and a family of goats grazing close by in the open. We were met by a curious, prancing Doberman and saw Robert standing not far from where the van finally settled. The Doberman moved around the van with guard-dog curiosity, but never barked once — perhaps because he recognized friends in Ed and Jodi. When the van doors were opened, the first sensation was the strong odor of animals that quickly filled the van and my nostrils. The smell, not unpleasant, would diminish in the next three hours.

We were introduced to Robert — firm handshake and blue eyes intently focused on his guests and me, as possible helpmate in writing his story. The deeply tanned face etched with a generous smile enhanced his easy manner and obvious enthusiasm. Our gracious host was dressed in pale off-white dungarees, well-worn cowboy boots, and a multi-blue plaid shirt that contrasted with his tanned skin and dark hair, white at the sideburns. He wore a thick-banded watch on a muscular arm. His physique was that of an athlete, a dancer, a performer who has had to stay in shape to handle and supervise the care and raising of crafty, sinuous, dangerous cats that now filled the many penned areas we were about to visit.

I looked beyond Robert into the hammock, then more deeply

to the dark but dappled reaches, where the rays of sun played on massive tree trunks as they found openings in the leaf canopy. I then brought my focus closer to a mother goat with three babies learning to walk on slender, shaky legs. The goats were after hay that had been dropped on the deck of a wood structure with an open-beam, pitched roof housing on one end and an open deck on the other. The goats, startled by our intrusive arrival, peeked out from behind the slatted housing as we stood for several minutes talking to Robert. Finally, after watching and being watched, they felt secure enough to come onto the wood planking to munch the hay. The babies were darling, perfect miniatures of their mother. It was a precious introduction.

For the next three hours, we walked and listened and observed as Robert guided us around and through the hammock from one heavy wire mesh enclosure to another. In one, two baby snow leopards wrestled in kittenish playtime. They tumbled and pounced and withdrew to advance again and roll together in a frolicking ball of speckled fur. The temptation to put a hand between the bars to pet the darling, sweet-faced kittens was great, but Robert warned that their claws could cause serious scratches and bleeding.

As we stood by one enclosure that seemed to be empty, we looked toward the darkly shaded recesses where a wood housing had openings two feet by three feet. We could see the dark head and shiny eyes of a full-grown leopard. All of a sudden, as we stood quietly, the large cat emitted a menacing snarl and hurtled through the air, crashing against the heavy mesh in an attempt to break through to us.

The drama of sight and sound was real, unplanned, and natural, all a part of Robert's world — his all-encompassing passion. We were experiencing a truly unique and fascinating environment where a man of great courage and passion lived alongside some of the most dangerous, beautiful, and bloodthirsty beasts. They looked so regal and elegant as they languished on wood planks, the limb of an oak tree, or sauntered haughtily with eyes always focused on the enemy. It was an incredibly provocative interlude.

As we walked and talked, I observed the many different cats and listened to Robert's explanation of their origin and habits — all the nuances of each species and the purpose for which each existed, whether for breeding or for sale to a particular zoo or private collector. I also managed to snap some photographs. At one enclosure, Robert opened the door for me to step inside behind him to take a photo unobstructed by bars or mesh. As Robert entered, I watched him being watched so closely by the cat, which began to slap at the metal prod he carried to ward off attack. The cat took me into his sights as I carefully watched his strong and subtle movements, his keenly focused eyes , his body poised to leap. I had no desire to walk into the enclosure even with Robert as shield and protector. I declined his offer, feeling more secure with the wire mesh between me and cat.

While watching the different cats move slowly and majestically through their pens, then suddenly direct their gaze and crouch, ready to attack, I realized how quickly and lethally the victim would be put down and how assuredly there would be no escape without terror and life-threatening injuries. I had confidence in Robert's ability to control his cats, but I did not want to put him to the test on my behalf simply to capture a photograph. I was able to place the camera inside the openings of the mesh to achieve adequate focus to simply capture a bit of the color and aura of the cat-filled hammock.

I apologized for my cowardice and told Robert I appreciated his attempt to provide security for me, but I also listened to his impartation on the lack of loyalty in the beasts and the innate characteristic to attack. There was no desire to give any indication of confidence, although I felt it in Robert as I continued to watch the man interact with his animals. I knew that he possessed a tremendous amount of talent. He was a consummate performer, and as I continued to listen, I knew that he did indeed have a unique story to tell, a wonderful story, and I wanted to be a part of the telling.

As we continued through the maze of enclosures in the shaded hammock containing snow leopards, tigers, Florida panthers, jaguars, bobcats, and monkeys with various birds moving freely, I listened to Robert's commentary — suddenly broken by his apologetic excuse, to return to one of the enclosures where a fight was occurring. I had not heard any of the sounds to which Robert was so finely attuned, but he knew all the subtle nuances and fully realized that he was needed to break up an altercation that, if left unattended, could be very costly. He walked quickly back to where two tigers, sharing a large enclosure, were having a heated physical battle. Along with a female helper, Robert separated the animals with a prod and water. There was blood from a head wound on one cat, strongly contrasting the white fur of the magnificent beast. Robert pulled open a door which had been cleverly engineered to operate from outside the enclosure. As the heavy separating door slid open, Robert used the prod and audible persuasion to inspire one of the cats to go through the opening and into the adjoining compartment. With disaster diverted, he introduced me to Lily Lehman. Lily, a pretty, dark-haired, diminutive girl, was obviously a key player on the compound.

As we continued to stroll through the hammock, it was apparent that Robert was very much at home and in control as he gave us statistics on how many panthers, leopards, tigers, and other rare species he had bred in captivity. He had raised and supplied cats to various zoos, both foreign and domestic, for more than 30 years at the Rare Feline Breeding Center. I listened, fascinated by the tale, and watched Robert as the cats observed our every move.

In one enclosure was a young tiger which had been raised by Lily. Robert asked her to enter the enclosure to demonstrate her ability to make the cat perform. Before Lily entered, it was obvious the cat recognized her, and there was an affectionate interplay as she put her hand through the mesh and rubbed the cat's fur and let the animal nuzzle her cheek, giving her a generous kiss. Once inside, as we watched, Lily used a prod to entice the cat up on its hind legs to wave its front paws in the air. But as the cat performed, I could feel the tension, the lack of trust, and could see that Lily was always aware of her escape route, if it became necessary to exit quickly.

My enthusiasm for what I was witnessing and hearing grew with each utterance from the cat man as he described his experiences. I warmed quickly and assuredly to the possibility of composing Robert's memoirs as I began to imagine what his past contained to bring him to this place. His was a unique, specialized expertise as one of the world's leading authorities occupied in raising and breeding captive exotic cats and other animals. I knew that I was about to embark on a wondrous adventure.

Robert referred to a phone call he received that morning

from a rancher in Wildwood who had a horse to be put down. Robert did not get an accurate address from the rancher and knew that another call would come requesting the horse be picked up. Robert or an employee would drive to the farm to fetch the animal for slaughtering, as they were frequently called upon to fill the need for 2,000-3,000 pounds of raw meat required daily to feed the cats and other animals on the compound.

As we walked, I saw large bare bones that had been picked clean, giving evidence of the enormous demand in time and labor involved every day to maintain the 60-plus cats that filled the cages in the oak hammock. It was obvious that each cat was a magnificent specimen being cared for with a depth of knowledge, compassion, and understanding which Robert explained was information being sought by several universities as well as government agencies. They contacted him for documentation on the care and breeding of many cat species — some of which were endangered and nearly extinct.

Robert's house had been a topic of conversation on the trip to Center Hill. As we approached the heavily-treed hammock, its outer appearance gave no clues whatever to the treasures within. Before we were to leave for home, it seemed appropriate to tour the house to enhance my perception and to further understand the man in view of the accumulated possessions that were so much a part of his life. Upon entering a screened area at the end of the housing, I left any trace of sunlight as I walked through the porch into the living room darkened by heavy drapes covering the windows. A couch and chairs upholstered in dark fabric were covered with animal skins of various colorations. He explained that he preserved the skins as the only thing he could to physically maintain a part of each animal that had been important to him.

The walls contained many photographs and paintings. Robert proudly directed my gaze to several oil paintings of cats in natural habitat that he had painted with a great deal of mastery. There were copies as well as original art of cats rendered by world-renowned wildlife artists who had worked directly with animals at the Breeding Center.

Above the paintings on one wall was a massive snake skin mounted on a firm backing. The skin was nearly a foot in width and about 17 feet long. Robert explained that the skin was from a boa constrictor similar to one that lived in the attic for months. He further explained he was perfectly happy to have a boa live in such close proximity, since the snake kept the rat population down dramatically. When a visiting reptile authority advised that the boa could and possibly would eat the small child living in the house at the time, Robert made the decision to rid the attic of the dangerous predator. He captured the boa and preserved the beautifully decorated skin as a memento to remind him of the great rat hunter that lived under the eaves.

As I looked through the maze, there were treasures everywhere. Fine bronze statues on tables and pedestals were abundant as well as shelves containing small animal sculptures. Along the floor against the walls were piles of magazines, books, and papers. Amidst the clutter were several wonderful heavy pieces of marquetry furniture which had found their way from Europe many years before. One wall contained a collection of daggers and other military weapons, each of which had a special story connected to its history and to Robert's acquisition. While the handsome and valuable antiques seemed incongruous in the Florida cement block building, they fit beautifully and naturally in the living space of an eloquent and worldly man.

As I explored the remaining rooms, I found the kitchen tidy enough for a bachelor, but cluttered, as was the bathroom and the rest of the house. There was much memorabilia acquired over many years by a man who had traveled and collected extensively and finally settled into quarters too small to house all that was important and meaningful. Robert was living alone at the time of our visit, but he often shared his domain with many guests and visitors over the years.

Robert told of a recent interview he gave to the German magazine, *Stern*. A writer and photographer were sent on location to capture the man in what was his place in the sun after all the dynamic fame first attributed to the European tours. His fame was further enhanced by his success in the States, all of which led to the legendary role of leading authority on captive breeding of exotic felines.

As he continued to entertain with wonderful anecdotes, he spoke of a *Playboy* magazine shoot at the compound. A crew arrived to do location photography with a nude model posing with a cat. In one pose, the model was lying on a tree limb while the cat was directed to walk over her. After a long rehearsal, the nervous model was soothed and relaxed by Robert into posing with a rhapsodic expression. Suddenly a llama appeared in a nearby clearing which caught the cat's attention. With four powerful, flowing leaps, the cat had the llama in its mouth and in little time had mauled and killed the victim while the stunned model, photographer, and crew looked on.

Our man was center stage and obviously enjoying the rapt audience as he continued to tell how Marlin Perkins wanted to film a segment for his "Wild Kingdom" show depicting the capture of a Bengal tiger in India. Marlin, an old friend, called Robert requesting the use of the compound and some animals in Central Florida to complete the segment after the crew returned empty-handed from location in India. The colorful episodes recounted during the brief time we shared gave further credence, importance, and interest to what I visualized as a life filled with an extraordinary variety of adventure.

The art of Drout, one of many original bronzes in the collection.

As we stood in the living room I asked Robert to tell me about his most life-threatening experience where an animal was involved. Without hesitation, he told the story of the attack by Chilly. I did not ask any questions as he seemed to relive the terror he felt in what could easily have been his final performance; however, the tape recorder that we brought to leave with Robert was not turned on. I knew that I should be recording the episode, but I didn't want to interrupt his performance to retrieve the recorder left in the van. I was so enthralled as I listened to the words and watched his body move as he described all the bloody details of Chilly's brutal attack. He experienced again every agonizing moment of the drama. As I watched him, I did not listen to or retain the details. I was totally captivated by the performance. When he was through, I asked him to use the recording machine to reenact just what I had witnessed, pretending that I was still standing in his presence. Then he was to send the tape to me, and I would begin working. He agreed with the arrangement, and I was exhilarated in anticipation of a uniquely exciting opportunity.

My excitement seemed to mirror his genuine enthusiasm. He kissed me after we shook hands — a sweet and tender gesture that seemed to express his sincerity and also his acceptance of me. We autographed a copy of *Palm Beach From The Other Side Of The Lake* for him to read to gain a perspective on what he could expect from me in a similar effort on his behalf. As we pulled away from the oak hammock and returned to the main highway, I felt deeply gratified with the meeting and anticipated sharing an adventure that I sensed held great privilege. I was stimulated by the encounter and anxious to begin the labor.

Soon after returning to south Florida, I sent off self-addressed bubble envelopes to Robert. I included a rather comprehensive outline of material I required pertaining to his birth and early years in France. When I felt certain that Robert had ample time to do some recording, although I knew that he would only be available to work in the evenings after putting in many hours of daily labor, I asked Jodi and Ed if they had heard from their animal man. They in turn contacted Robert. Robert told them that he found reading the Palm Beach book most enjoyable and was able to relate well to the chapter pertaining to the War. He explained that he and Dave had been only 30 miles apart as they battled the Germans.

Robert informed Ed Schaffer that he was anxious to have his story told, but was experiencing difficulty relating to the tape machine and had resorted to writing down his thoughts in answer to my list of questions. I knew that would be a labor that he could not and would not sustain very long. We would have to find another method to communicate his thoughts. The best way would be for me to talk to him, draw him out just as I had with Dave, to prod his memory. One answered question would lead to another and another and slowly, starting from the beginning, we would build the story.

Before his written material arrived, I decided to write the lead-in "Chilly" attack as I imagined it. Robert would amend it to capture the drama and his imagination, but I would gain some momentum in proceeding with the work. Robert would read and change my translation, and from there we would go forward.

When Dr. Ed informed me that Robert had composed some thoughts as a result of my initial contact and request for material, I chose a time to phone him to begin our dialogue. I purposely telephoned him at 7:30 in the evening in the hope that I would not interrupt his dinner hour. He said that his Lean Cuisine was cooking and that he would phone me back. He explained that he had just worked a 13-hour day, which was not atypical. He had a horse to butcher, a cat to capture after it escaped its confines, and many other details to accomplish in what was just another day at the Breeding Center.

Robert read me his description of the "Chilly" attack after informing me that he was quite pleased with my effort and my plan to use the attack as the opening piece in his story. As he read to me, I realized more fully his potential to tell a wonderfully entertaining and unusual story.

I told Robert that I would hunt for a recording device so that I could question and record future conversations and free him of the need to use the tape machine and send tapes to me. His daily routine was complicated enough without having to talk into a machine, remove the tape, and mail it. I wanted to accommodate his schedule. He answered my queries pertaining to his birth, parentage, and early childhood. I was quite enthralled as I listened to the voice, heavily accented in French, describe his early impressions of a culture so totally foreign and colorful and knew that his talents as a performer were going to be more fully utilized and appreciated through our work.

Robert described his early years and the exposure to animal training demonstrated by his father and performed with his help. I was fascinated by his experiences and recall and knew that it held so much depth of color — a palette of many hues. As I listened to

Robert, I was intrigued with the vivid details of a bygone era recalled and recaptured by a marvelous photographic memory that revealed emotional responses to early life experiences.

We completed one telephone session, the first of what would be many dialogues, and it was filled with compelling descriptive content. I knew if these were his early years, there were many wonderful facets to follow. It needed only a voice to question, an ear to listen, and hours on the telephone and at the old Olympia — but I was ready, and Robert, too, seemed eager. The time had finally come for him to go back in time and retrace the journey once again. I could hardly wait.

I taped the second telephone session, until the tape became jammed and twisted with Robert's voice becoming a slow drone totally undecipherable and then stifled. I became angry and frustrated by the seeming inadequacies of the recording device. In my frustration and disappointment, I left the project to return hours later to unravel the tape and rewind it back to the beginning and then, joyously, realized that I did have Robert's voice loud and clear. I was exhilarated knowing that we finally had a working arrangement and a beginning.

As I listened, I could picture Robert standing in the midst of his animal compound. He stood about five feet nine, erect and ruggedly handsome with narrow hips, tight flat stomach with broad shoulders, dark wavy hair, white as it hit his shirt collar. His sideburns deeply contrasted the tanned skin that bore scars from too many close encounters with cats and other dangerous animals over the years. His many life-forming encounters, relationships, and emotions which began in a Paris suburb 69 years earlier, were carefully described in heavy French accent.

As I listened, I was again fascinated with his words and would try to capture the phraseology in the composition. I would pull from Robert all that I could in the limited time available in each session. As Robert answered my questions, I was entertained by his natural showmanship and his performance in formulating and coloring an extremely unique life. He seemed to relish accessing his memory, easily and eagerly placing himself back in time to where it began. We were starting the collaboration of a lifetime.

Sandra Thompson

1

THE YOUNG HUNTER
Le Jeune Chasseur

I was born September 20, 1923, in my parents' hotel in Bois-Colombes, a suburb of Paris, to Emile and Berthe Baudy. It was the custom at that time to give birth at home. Shortly after my arrival, the hotel was sold and we moved to a newly purchased hotel near Le Vesinet.

Father, born in 1884, was 13 years older than Mother. It would be several years before I fully appreciated the industrious team, my parents, always working to provide the many services associated with running a hotel and restaurant, limousine service, and other occupations near the beautiful, exclusive Paris suburb. I have no early recollection of the first hotel in Bois-Colombes or of the hotel in Le Vesinet, having been sent soon after birth to live with grandparents residing in an ancient monastery located in the Nièvre area of central France.

Father, the better educated of my parents, was raised in Brittany in a well-to-do family and spoke five languages fluently. It was the custom in the prominent, predominantly Catholic families to send a child to be trained as either a priest or nun. The strongly held belief was that if at least one child was so trained, it would be some sort of guarantee that if the other children did not turn out well, at least one would be "in good with God." Father was the chosen one in his family and was sent to study at the seminary in Vitre.

Years later, I drove past the school where he lived and received his training for the priesthood. It always sent chills through me to look at the dark granite-walled fortress, ominous

Father in army uniform.

and foreboding, in its secluded setting so apart and different from the commerce and industry that existed in other areas of society. As I looked at the stone prison, I was grateful, in spite of the superior education proffered, that I, as an only child, was not sent off to fulfill the long-held custom and repeat what Father experienced. I can only imagine his emotions, his fear, as he first approached the austere building, realizing that he had no choice but to spend the rest of his life sequestered in a way that I knew would be intolerable. Possibly he was caught up in the honor and privilege of being the "chosen one" in his family. But I looked with utter horror at the somber prison which contained and influenced him and would ultimately be an influence in my life, be it vicariously, through his behavior and philosophies largely formed by years in seclusion.

Father was close to being ordained when, in 1910, he was called upon to perform compulsory military duty in the French Army. About the time when he had completed his stipulated tenure, the First World War began, and he was shifted from noncombat to the trenches of Verdun, the primary battleground of the war in France, as an active member of the Army. As an aside, Father told me proudly years later that he performed his military duties alongside the American, Harry Truman, the man who would become President of the United States.

During four years of noncombat and then four years of active duty, Father was a member of the artillery in an army entirely mechanized by horse power. As a result, eight years of his young adult life were spent on horseback, first in training and then in the heat of battle, mixing and associating with ordinary people both in military as well as civilian life.

The unique exposure so far removed from life in the seminary influenced his thinking profoundly, and a decision was made that angered and disappointed his family — he would not become a priest. The decision was further confirmed by a six-month period in Italy following the war, where he realized that beautiful ladies and good wives were also very important in life.

It was at this juncture that he became involved in the banking business, working for the largest banking firm in France — the Banque Generale. As a young representative, he was sent to Germany, where he spent time in Frankfurt, and then to North Africa. Upon returning to France, he sold insurance in Paris and through friends became acquainted with Mother, who was working as a maid for a wealthy family in the beautiful city. I do not know the details of their courtship, but after they married, they bought the hotel in Bois-Colombes.

Berthe Archambault was one of ten children raised in a poor farming family. Her formative years were shared with parents, sisters, and brothers in a 500-year-old monastery close to Nevers, located approximately 250 miles south of Paris. Her education was limited, but her nature and disposition were that of a saint. I never saw my mother do anything wrong or ever impart a lie or deception on another person. She possessed boundless compassion and unselfishly dedicated her life to helping others. She was a very dear and precious person to my way of thinking, and I adored her.

Father chose civilian life as a banker after the war.

Looking back, I realize that she brought compassion and tolerance to the marriage, governed by the overriding precept of all French marriages — once married you stay married. Divorce was not only difficult to obtain, but it was also not tolerated in the staunchly Catholic society.

I was raised as an only child after a first sibling, Lisette, died of double pneumonia when she was 18 months old. I know nothing of the emotional trauma at her passing, but can only imagine Mother's anguish at the tragic loss, and in retrospect, the anguish suffered with the need to send me, her baby, off to live with grandparents on a farm so very far from Le Vesinet.

I remembered little of the first year in the monastery. When I returned for special visits to the provincial place of my earliest recollections, I more fully appreciated the many nuances of a lifestyle devoted to hard work performed in methods that did not yield to change — methods dictated not only by ancient tradition and custom, but by the total lack of any progressive, outside influences. The early impressions were etched deeply to guide, enrich, and influence my life as I observed and then interacted with grandparents, aunts, uncles, and cousins in the 500-year-old monastery and environs located near the idyllic River Allier, an affluent of the Loire, its rivulets entwining the lush countryside of central France.

The ancient monastery was constructed of native, irregular-shaped stones finely joined to support an enormous slate roof over a storage attic. There were three large bedrooms, all furnished with heavy wood beds, each supporting a handmade mattress and pillows. I rarely slept alone as cousins also lived in the house, and other young people stayed for overnight visits.

There was a pantry filled with Grandmother's preserves with cherries, plums, pickles, and other savories, cooked and sealed just waiting for an appreciative audience. The pantry, a small room, was close to the kitchen and adjoining dining room — dark but massive in scale. There was a wood-burning stove and a huge fireplace in the kitchen. Beside the fireplace was a cast-iron plaque showing the year 1501 in Roman numerals. I remember Father expressing a strong desire to remove the ancient plaque to take it to the hotel at Le Vesinet. That never came to pass.

Beneath the living quarters' four-foot walls was a cellar where the temperature remained cool year-round regardless of outside conditions. The cellar was gained by stone steps that led to a heavy oak door opening to arched recesses below. It had been the winery and was Grandfather's domain where he made wine and apple cider. My trips into the black cellar were always scary. I used an oil lamp to illuminate the passage, creating wavering shadows cast by the large barrels and iron rings imbedded in the stone walls to hold the monk's torches as they labored over the wine production. The ceiling was totally black from years of smoke and mildew; but when the weather was stifling, we always found blessed relief in the dark confines beneath the house.

There was a three-acre garden filled with fruit trees and vegetables of many varieties. My grandparents labored for hours each day in the garden. I learned later that when Grandfather bought the property, the most chal-

The monastery dating from the 1400s where I spent my very early years.

lenging job he encountered was attempting to plant the garden. As they began the task of digging, they found bones everywhere in what had been the cemetery where bodies of monks had been interred for the hundreds of years of life and death in the *monastère*.

My grandparents, short by American standards, were built like most farmers in the area; both were stocky, Grandfather a bit taller. They were not unlike my parents or Father's family, all sturdy of build with curly dark hair. I came by my eventual strong build, modest height, and coloring quite naturally. Grandfather wore a handlebar mustache and I remember well watching him shave using a *blaireau* (badger) shaving brush to mix and apply the foam from homemade soap. He used a straight-edged razor, and I was fascinated to watch as he sharpened the blade with a leather strop usually talking to Grandmother during the process, and taking care not to touch his mustache.

There was no such thing as electricity in the old monastery, where each day before daybreak, Grandmother worked by oil lamp to prepare vegetable soup, coffee and bread. She was a

Grandma and Grandpa on the left. Aunt Marie Louise is holding me.

wonderful cook, creating the most compelling aromas which filled the kitchen as she constantly labored. When I awakened each day, I went to the kitchen for a large mug of coffee and a piece of French bread. Grandfather, already fed, would be working in the garden. I enjoyed the activity of digging from time to time, and I, too, unearthed long-buried bones as I eagerly joined in the important labor.

The abundance of produce attracted many birds to the garden. Grandfather was not a hunter and I remember his sentiments, "The birds are part of our world, and we must grow for them as well." Grandmother did not share his magnanimity where the winged marauders were concerned, and I watched as she hung all sorts of pans in the plum trees to noisily ward off the thieves, but the birds adapted to her methods and continued to enjoy the bounty.

One of my chores, when I was older, was to fetch water from the deep stone well. Water was a vital resource used for coffee, soup, and other cooking, as well as for bathing and laundry. It was a continuous activity. I lowered the wooden bucket into the 60-

foot-deep well, then cranked it to the surface, and carried it into the kitchen. Laundry not done in the monastery was taken to the small village of Meauce. The *lavoir*, located very near the farm, attracted local women who arrived wearing the traditional black dresses and carrying wicker baskets of laundry atop their heads. I accompanied Grandmother to the *lavoir* for the social outing where the kids played while the women chattered and scrubbed.

Two of Mother's brothers lived near the farm — Uncle Emile ("Mimil" for short) and Uncle Adolph. Adolph was the more attentive when I was old enough to go on hunting forays into the neighboring countryside. Built like a gorilla with large hands and massive chest, his rugged face topped by a heavy mass of Archambault dark curly hair, Uncle Adolph worked as a laborer laying track for the railroad when he was not hunting. He was a wonderful companion who made toys for me and willingly shared his expertise as we ventured into the forest and along the river bank to capture the wily game and fish. I was enthralled watching him catch fish with his bare hands. He caught live partridges and cleverly trapped rabbits and other fascinating animals so abundant in the surrounding fields and neighboring estates. I watched as he set snares and was absolutely thrilled when he taught me to make the simple traps.

There were many animals, both large and small, but the most striking domestic animal was the Charolais cow. The huge, snow-white, 3,000-pound animals dotted the landscape. For a period of time, Grandfather was the foreman on the neighboring farm owned by a wealthy landowner who raised the Charolais. Years later when I saw in the 1960's stud book papers listing bulls exported from France into the United States, I was filled with a sense of pride when I realized they came from the very farm Grandfather ran. But I am jumping way ahead of my story.

Grandmother was a fine looking woman, her face open and honest, her eyes always moving from one activity to the next. She never was idle with so much work to do every day beginning before daybreak until late in the evening. She always wore black, and even when the weather was freezing cold, she worked in the garden with little to protect her except a black sweater thrown over her dress. Her hands were strong, toughened by manual labor yet capable of preparing the most delicious food and mending the finest clothing if necessary.

Food preparation was labor-intensive with game caught or domestic animals raised for the household being butchered and cleaned. I watched the butchering process with horror at first. In addition to chickens and rabbits, there were always several hogs raised to provide pork for the family. At the appropriate time, it was traditional to have the neighbors participate in the kill. The hog, after being cornered and tethered by ropes, was slaughtered using a very sharp knife to cut the jugular vein in each side of its neck. The poor animal, left to bleed thoroughly to produce white meat, screamed and struggled as the torture began. I hated to witness the whole process, but learned to accept it as part of my initiation. When the animal was sufficiently bled, it was scorched in a straw fire to burn off the hair, and then placed on a table where everyone participated in scraping the body clean.

The hog kill was not the only violence that I found upsetting. When Mother came to visit, she was not shy about going into the chicken coop, as I had seen Grandmother and Grandfather do many times, grab a capon, fattened for the table, and using a chopping block and sharp knife, decapitate the poor innocent bird. While I was horrified with the routine slaughters, I soon learned that the very acts were an integral ongoing farm activity, and I became inured somewhat to the deaths.

Grandmother was too busy to watch me constantly, but there were some escapades, highly unpopular with her, that tempted and challenged me. The railroad ran close by the farm, and every day the old wood-burning locomotive noisily belched black smoke on its journey. I was completely captivated by the passing marvel and ran to stand by the tracks for a close-up view. If I was caught in this pursuit, Grandmother switched me. She was afraid that a stone thrown by the passing train might injure her inquisitive charge.

Her instruments of torture to mete out physical punishment were the thorny nettles growing beside the house. For serious misdemeanors, she grabbed a handful of the prickly plant and pulled down my pants to thrash my bare behind and legs. This did not occur often, but I did manage to raise her ire by what I felt were perfectly innocent pursuits.

I loved to go into the chicken coop and pull eggs from under the hens. Then using a nail, I poked holes in each end to suck them. Eggs were an important source of income as well as food for the family.

Another highly unpopular activity further jeopardized her culinary largesse. There was a wall four feet high surrounding the property. It was the original monastery wall made of ancient crumbling stones. There were always snails clinging to the rough surface and seeking shelter in the moldy, dark crevices. I enjoyed hunting the shy mollusks, the *escargot*, regarded as a delicacy to be collected and cooked for family reunions. My fun was in capturing the small shelled creatures and moving them to other walls on neighboring farms. How quickly I learned how much snails were coveted.

With little monetary wealth and no access to material goods, many items were handmade. In addition to preserving all sorts of food and making soap, mattresses were manufactured. Many hands were required in the process using a carder, which had teeth that worked the wool back and forth, separating the rough particles after the fibers had been washed and bleached. Carding made the wool homogeneous, ideal for fine, well-crafted mattresses.

In growing aware of my surroundings, I realized that for the adults, work was what occupied nearly every hour of every day with little time for leisure. As a child there was time for play, but I was being imbued with a work ethic that could not be denied. The humdrum of constant labor was broken only by special occasions when visitors arrived or when the family gathered. Then there was a festive air permeating the monastery.

When my parents were expected, the anticipation and the actual visit formed a pattern that became more pronounced as the years passed. I always knew when a reunion was imminent. The occasions only occurred several times a year with the initial greetings warm and welcoming with hugging, kissing, and much laughter. Soon a sumptuous meal was served with everyone enjoying the camaraderie.

After the early meal, Father would steal off with me in tow either for an automobile ride shared with Mother, or to go into the woods to set traps to capture birds. I enjoyed the excitement of riding in the shiny automobile or the quiet of the woods waiting for the bait to attract innocent little birds. As the afternoon ended and dinner time approached, I learned that the evening would always build to an explosive crescendo.

The Archambaults, while not members of the Communist party, found the party line appealing to assuage the frustration of laborers, the *bourgeoisie*. Father's success as a businessman, coupled with his political philosophy, was so diametrically opposed to those of Mother's family. When vehemently expressed, it only fueled the flames of contention after a few bottles of wine served with dinner. Mother became more nervous as the evening proceeded with Uncle Adolph's firmly held opinions castigating the governing forces, "The existing system is designed to extract blood from the working man."

Dinner was ended with the traditional *pousse café* followed by strong cognac and a continuing heated diatribe. It was at this juncture when the kids would ask permission to leave the table and the house to seek solitude in climbing trees or playing games in the garden, darkly shadowed by the old monastery walls which enclosed the loud bickering of my family.

When bedtime came and quiet returned to the monastery for the night, the routine was as predictable for the following day. When the time came for my parents' departure, it was unsettling to see Mother cry, but soon they would leave, and life on the River Allier would return to normal. I watched my grandparents do their labor and participated in many facets of the provincial lifestyle, eager to learn, and very happy with my position in the family. I cherished the unbridled freedom even as a small boy, and never indulged thoughts of leaving the farm, of living anywhere but in the old monastery, where I was secure in the love of my grandmother and stimulated by wonderful adventures with Uncle Adolph.

However, at three and a half years of age, my parents deemed it provident that I live with them at the hotel in Le Vesinet. How could I leave Grandmother and Grandfather? How could I leave Uncle Adolph and my cousins — the people whom I loved dearly? I would miss the adventures on the river as I swept along the currents in the small red boat, the river defined on the far side by the green cliff that rose dramatically to support the grand castle on the Schneider estate.

On future visits to the farm, I would more fully appreciate the beauty of central France and begin to understand more of the fullness of the life-experience as I accompanied Uncle Adolph on forays onto the fringes of the Schneider estate to capture and trap rabbits and the large red deer so prevalent on the massive preserve. Only then would I learn that the activity was illegal — my uncle was a poacher. But I learned as well that every fish, every rabbit, every partridge and deer caught was utilized either to provide food for the table or income from sales to local merchants or other farmers. Nothing was captured for sport.

As a very young hunter, it was perfectly natural that I hunted snails and helped myself to the eggs, that I found snakes, rabbits, birds, and deer stimulating to enhance youthful incursions. Leaving it behind was beyond my imagination.

But I would never fully leave it behind. The examples set by my grandparents — hard work and stoicism — and by my hunting companions, or as I wandered freely engaging in many adventures would all serve to deepen sensitivity to my environment and influence every twist and turn of my life. Only in time would I fully realize how uniquely precious were my formative years in Nevers.

Uncle Adolph taught me to hunt at an early age.

2

HOME TO LE VESINET
Retour au Vesinet

*T*he day dawned like previous days with absolutely no indication that this day would be so different. My parents were coming to visit, and that was a rare and wonderful occurrence. The drive from Le Vesinet took over three hours, and their involved lifestyle running the hotel and restaurant so thoroughly occupied them every day, seven days a week, leaving them little time for holidays. I remembered previous visits and looked forward to their arrival with no more importance placed on this particular occasion. They would come and they would go. They were my parents, but I knew little about them. I was not yet four years old.

When I awakened, I heard all the familiar sounds of a farm rousing to a new day as animals outside and in the chicken coop stirred. From the kitchen came food preparation noises and aromas that filled the old monastery. The activities held the same level of commotion as before, but this day would mark a very important transition in my young life.

Ordinarily when Mother and Father came, I would perhaps go on a bird hunt or be taken out in whatever vehicle they brought, be it the commercial van or the city car — a Citroen. Since there was no car at the farm, the novelty of riding as a passenger in the motorized vehicle was quite extraordinary and also very frightening if the weather turned foul. I was always very excited to ride in the car and watch the window-filled scenery change rapidly. But if there was a storm with lightening splitting the sky and booming thunder echoing around the small moving target, tears would well up in eyes frightened by the drama, fearful that I would not be safely transported back to the sturdy confines of the monastery.

On this day Mother and Father arrived in the shiny black Citroen; the elegant car driven proudly by my father gained much attention. In time I would more fully realize just how important were Father's automobiles.

Along with my grandmother and grandfather, I welcomed my parents. Father wore a suit but no tie. He was not tall, but strongly built with a serious demeanor under curly dark hair and a neatly trimmed mustache; his expression and attitude commanded respect. He became jovial as the day went along. Mother wore a beautiful print dress, her curly hair softly framing a pretty face, with light blue eyes and a generous smile exuding love and kindness. All indications pointed to this being a typical family gathering when Grandmother would satisfy culinary yearnings with her wonderful meals, including the relished escargot if my hunting hadn't diminished the crop too badly. If a car ride was in the plan, I would journey with Mother and Father through the Nièvre countryside and enjoy their pleasure in sharing the time with me at their side in a holiday atmosphere, or I would hunt birds with Father. As the day turned to evening, I would listen to the family political exhortations. Then when their visit ended, they would say their goodbyes with Mother's tears always punctuating the sad time. But I did not place too much store in their routine appearance.

This day was indeed different. Mother and Father did not remain for the usual length of time. There was no motor trip into the country, and my clothing and cherished possessions had been gathered. There were toys that had been made by Uncle Adolph, simple toys that gave much pleasure to entertain myself or playmates. One toy was a hollowed-out willow branch that held a wooden piston or plunger to create compression. I watched as Uncle Adolph took sheep's wool to form a compact, hard, round ball to be placed in the branch and then come popping out in a loud and startling explosion that was great fun to work. Another toy was a trumpet made of tree bark. Uncle Adolph cleverly cut the bark at an angle to wrap into a spiral. It took less than an hour to complete the instrument using a chicken bone inserted in one end as the mouthpiece. The sound emitting from the small trumpet carried for over a mile. I also had slingshots crafted specifically

With my mom.

for my use which gave credence and importance to my hunting prowess.

When the time arrived for departure, it was Grandmother who cried. Instead of staying with her, I was leaving and Mother was not crying as she embraced Grandmother to comfort her. I do not recall being upset as we drove away from the farm, although I hated to see Grandmother cry. It all seemed like a wondrous new adventure to me, although I remember well, soon after arriving in Le Vesinet, the wet trickle of tears staining and stinging my cheeks as I lay in bed alone in the hotel with thoughts of Grandmother and of my uncle and the carefree days spent exploring and roaming freely about the farm and neighboring estates and playing with my cousins. I would feel particularly sorry for myself if Father felt the need to reprimand me, but I had no choice in the matter. Apparently the time had come when my parents decided I was old enough to join in their industry of running Les Charmettes. I had grown to the age and size to be trusted on my own and even to be a help.

In spite of missing Grandmother, I was soon surrounded by the love of my mother and the domination of a strict and demanding father. He demonstrated his caring in the time spent tutoring me which became a total commitment.

I settled into the hotel, a four-story, stucco-covered stone building with 20 guest rooms on the upper floors over the lobby and kitchen, and a dining room that accommodated 25 tables. I soon found the activity and commotion constant and stimulating. There was little time for self-pity.

The hotel was situated 20 miles from Paris, surrounded by farmland and a quarter of a mile from the small village of Le Vesinet. The village to this day is a very fashionable suburb of Paris, nestled in a magnificent country setting which, in former times, dating back to Louis XIV, was nothing but a wooded area used as hunting grounds by royalty. There was a circle at the junction of four paved roads marked by a 15-foot high statue of a deer in bronze on a rock mount. It was the very place where the nobility met with their hounds and where present-day nobility still seek a more leisurely pace from the hectic city life. Le Vesinet sits picturesquely on a slender tributary of the Seine, as the fabled river bends and twists through Paris and in many directions into the neighboring countryside.

While I missed the freedom I enjoyed at the farm, I found much that was fascinating and totally different in my new home, with many demands made and restrictions enforced. Father had been educated by the Jesuits just like his father and grandfather, and he seemed intent on being my tutor. In his own manner, he applied a crash course to make up for the three years that I had been on the farm, away from and out of his influence. He wasted absolutely no time, and while the demands of the many businesses owned and managed required many hours a day, he made certain that a good deal of time was devoted to me. I accompanied him as he went about performing the myriad of duties — his daily diet.

I often went on business trips in one of the various vehicles to be drilled with a repetition of syllables, or on the mechanization of the vehicle, or a lengthy discourse concerning some other worthy block of information to fill mind and senses. If the lesson was to understand the operation of the engine of the vehicle, he explained its components and had me repeat every detail. At five I could recite, "It takes four essential fluids to make a vehicle run: gas, oil, water, and transmission fluid." Father kept feeding me information and asking me to repeat over and over again in sessions that lasted for hours. If I tired and rebelled at the bombardment, my protestations were ignored.

Life had taken a severe turn, and obviously my days of going off with Uncle Adolph and watching him set snares and swimming in the River Allier, of hunting snails and sucking eggs were gone as new adventures and new demands unfolded daily. With each day I became tougher and drew on lessons that served me well. I had learned from Uncle Adolph to never fear the unknown. I had watched him catch fish with his hand and was thoroughly exhilarated as I followed his example extending my arm into the cold river waters, working my arm and hand into the dark recesses along the bank to where the fish sought safety. I gently and smoothly wiggled my hand into position and then quickly grasped the fish, feeling it struggle to gain freedom, and then released it back into the water. I felt very brave and very proud to be so agile. I was learning to have respect for all creatures in nature and developing a love for animals that would strengthen and affirm a strong commitment to be sustained throughout my life.

With memories of the farm secure, comforting, and ever present, I began to add experiences and encounters. There were new sensations and much to keep mind and body occupied. Through Father's diligent tutelage, I could read the newspaper fluently at four and a half years of age. Father took great pride in the fact, and when there were visitors or family gatherings, he took great delight in throwing a paper into my hands and saying, "Robert, how about reading what happened yesterday." I had a rapt audience as I proceeded to demonstrate my absolute skill in being able to read any and all of the latest news. Although I did not thoroughly understand the content, the words and sentences were clearly and correctly enunciated.

In between chores and while in the car or van, or whatever conveyance, the barrage of information was continuous. Father could have been a professional teacher and I was his student body. There were times when I tired and refused to repeat what was proffered and requested, and then I would fully realize how strict he was. He was simply duplicating the manner in which he was taught at the seminary in Vitre. If I didn't cooperate, I was given two verbal warnings, then a punishing swat. He was a tyrant in a way, but he knew no other method for imparting all that he knew. I later recognized that his fervor was based on the great deal of love he felt for his only son and the need to make up for the years I had been away from his influence.

One of my most striking early recollections of life at the hotel was in the very early morning hours. I wakened before daylight to the clamor and commotion of the heavily laden wagons arriving in the courtyard below as the local farmers gathered for their brief respite on the way to market. The fields for miles were cultivated with produce that was hauled to the central market in Paris. The farmers grew carrots, beets, and other vegetables that were conveyed by horse-drawn wagons. I heard the hooves of the huge draft horses on the road and then on the compacted yard. The wagons clattered and groaned and rolled over the rutted entry into the yard with all the cacophonous sounds associated with the labor. The horses were drawn up and the wagons pulled to a halt. I heard the muffled sounds of bridles and reins dropping and being tethered and the horses snorting and whinnying as they settled temporarily to feed before continuing the journey. As I watched the farmers secure their rigs, I was completely captivated by the activity so dramatically played against the dark and quiet of my sleep in a symphony of rich and wondrous sounds and sensations. I smelled the strong aroma of beef soup and strong coffee wafting into my bedroom above the kitchen. The farmers were stopping at the hotel for the breakfast prepared by "Madame Baudy," consisting of freshly cooked soup, hot coffee, and plenty of wine. Even at four in the morning, the farmers wanted their two glasses of red wine to sustain them for the cold, damp ride into the old market place of Les Halles.

As the farmers dined, I quietly left my room, clad only in pajamas. The clandestine adventure was brave in combating not only the cold, but also Father's strict orders. But I had a mission to accomplish. I stole down into the yard and walked between the wagons and the horses. The animals were impressive not only in size, but handsome and well-maintained, each with a small sack of oats tied under their noses. As they munched away, I stealthily went from horse to horse to carefully cut or pluck hairs from their tails, using scissors. Father had agreed to make a wooden horse for me, and I said at the time, "I want the horse to have a real tail and a real mane." He did not realize how I was gathering the horse hairs.

I suppose there was danger of being stepped on or even crushed if the horses were startled by my intrusive marauding. If I was caught in the act by Father, I was reprimanded severely. If I escaped safely back to my room undetected, I watched from the window as the wagons and teams of horses, sometimes as many as 25, pulled away. Their groaning, creaking, and snorting sounds as they left, one behind the other, to form a caravan, reminded of scenes from the American Western movies. They lumbered off in the dark, etched against the brightening horizon, to continue their journey to Paris.

My nocturnal escapades paid off. I ultimately gathered many

hairs and presented them to Father. I waited patiently for Christmas. Sitting under the tree was a wonderful wooden horse with handsome thick mane and long flowing tail. Father made other toys for me, but he also bought toys from time to time that had to be assembled. His reasoning was they would stimulate my intelligence and also my imagination and enhance mechanical ability.

As I think back on my life, I have so much for which to thank Father, but I also appreciate the fact that I have been witness to the passage of the age of the horse to the landing on the moon.

Airplanes were another early fascination. There was a small private airport near the hotel. The most amazing sight was to watch the contraptions made of canvas flying overhead. There were steel bi-planes similar to the present-day planes used for crop dusting. One day a plane crashed a mile from the hotel. It created quite a sensation, and Father took me to the location to see the broken remnants. After the inspection and with the permission of the owner of the field, Father collected the parts he wanted in order to use them or to study them to increase his knowledge of the intricate mechanisms. He removed the cables and turnbuckles as I watched his delight in the unique opportunity. Father was a fine mechanic with a thirst for knowledge and curiosity which he willingly shared, obviously desirous that I, too, benefit and learn from every experience.

I was told when I first arrived in Le Vesinet that I was not to cross the road unassisted. There were automobiles that passed from time to time; and since the hotel was located on a main highway, both Mother and Father insisted that I obey the rule. There was a wooded area covering six acres across from the hotel owned by a neighbor and enclosed by fencing that I would compare to modern snow fencing. Mother actually locked me in what seemed a huge cage albeit very large and wooded and filled with many natural adventures. It contained and occupied me within sight of the hotel. I felt the security of the proximity although the arrangement was in strong contrast to the complete freedom I experienced at the farm. Father even placed a bell around my neck and admonished that if the bell was removed or lost, I would be punished. I hated that bell, but I never lost it.

My parents were keen that I be protected from all harm. There were other children who came to play with me — all boys

— and we had a wonderful time investigating the far reaches of the wooded area by exploring, hunting and capturing the animals that lived in the unmolested forest. We spent hours in the enclosure playing cowboys and Indians. Even as French children, we had been exposed to the American West via black and white movies shown at theaters in Paris. Father drove me into the city from time to time to see the Westerns that piqued imagination and inspired American war games.

Wildlife was abundant with plenty of red squirrels and various types of snakes. There were vipers that sunned themselves. While I knew they were dangerous, I had lots of practice in dealing with snakes through wanderings with Uncle Adolph. I had handled snakes enough to know that I could use a stick placed behind the viper's head, and in that way capture the dangerous snake by holding it firmly behind the head and squeezing to force the snake to open its mouth and expose its fangs. The other kids always wanted to kill the vipers, but I was far more fascinated holding the snakes, particularly when I saw the strong reaction the activity induced in my playmates. Mother and Father were horrified when they witnessed me holding the venomous snake, examining its mouth and fangs as it struggled slashing about my arm to gain freedom. Even at five years of age, I had a positive feeling that the poisonous vipers should be left to live. I found Father's antipathy for snakes a curiosity. He loved animals but saw the snakes as a potential danger as predators to the birds that he captured and sold. He particularly disliked the *couleuvre* snake which grew to an impressive size in its emerald green skin and frequently raided the birdhouse.

My father was an amazing man who could do anything and who operated many businesses at the same time. He saw the potential of the old hotel in Le Vesinet located in a beautiful and prosperous area where rich and famous Frenchmen and expatriates had homes and country estates. He and Mother worked hard to refurbish the old lodging during the time that I was with my grandparents on the farm. I did not witness any of the labor involved in taking an old, run-down establishment and turning it into the active and successful business that it became by the time they came for me, but I soon was aware of their industry and of the affluence in and around Le Vesinet.

An enterprise that Father could see a need for was the limousine business. The hotel, in the midst of the exclusive Parisian suburb, was surrounded by political figures, artists, and stage and movie personalities residing in the neighboring residences and estates. There was Mr. Sarrault, Minister of Finance for the French Government; Josephine Baker, the American movie star who lived in a palace made entirely of pink marble; and the famous dancer Mistinguett. Maurice Chevalier had a home close by as did the painter Utrillo.

Father was elegant in uniform when he performed his driving service behind the wheel of the custom-made, 6,000-pound Delahaye limousine, similar to the American Dussenberg, with its plush grey velvet interior. One of the outstanding features of the magnificent automobile was the *Lalique* crystal bouquet holders and radiator cap. I still have the crystal cap in my possession to remind me of the handsomely appointed car and the many prominent persons who solicited Father's services as they were driven into Paris for dinner, theatre or business.

Father wore many hats. He raised and bred guard dogs. He was the first person in the area to import Doberman pinschers and German shepherds. There was a kennel in back of the hotel where as many as 15 to 20 dogs resided at any one time. There was constant turnover as the wonderful breeding stock became much in demand. Father was knowledgeable, very particular about choosing and purchasing the dogs, and diligent in the training process. He worked with them along with some of the hotel employees who were pressed into dog-training detail in their spare time.

There was also a professional trainer from Belgium who, as a partner in the enterprise, worked with the dogs. I, too, got into the act and was particularly keen to be working when the professional trainer was present. The pro from Belgium was purported to be the finest dog trainer around Paris in those years. A man in his fifties, while working for my father, he would regale us with stories involving clients. My ears were always attuned to his colorful tales. Apparently for years, he trained dogs for a Frenchman who smuggled tobacco across the Belgium-French border. The smuggling activity, according to our authority, had been ongoing for over 300 years due to high taxation. Since the Belgian Government did not tax tobacco, the French version was at least 35 percent higher. It was a lucrative occupation to train dogs to carry the contraband under the cover of darkness.

Our trainer gave a detailed explanation of the covert operation. He explained that often customs officers were encountered while crossing the border, and they used trained dogs as well. The smugglers used a decoy dog to walk the specified trail ahead of the tobacco-carrying dog. At no time would a human be directly involved. The initiator on the Belgian side of the border released the dogs from a location five miles distant from his French counterpart. The job of the decoy dog was to make certain the chosen route was clear in order to make way for the German shepherds to pass through carrying waterproof tobacco-filled pouches that weighed about 30 pounds each and were strapped to each dog's back. The decoy dog was further trained to ward off any attack or alert the carrying dog and its escorts of any problems that might arise. It seemed to me, as I listened intently, that it was impossible to train a dog to perform with such keen sensitivity to every nuance of the illegal heist.

He continued to explain that if the lead dog went through the designated trail without being detected, the shepherd carrying the pouches would follow accompanied by five or six protector dogs. If a customs agent attempted to interfere, armed with a gun and also trained dogs to aid him, the smuggler dogs were gruesomely equipped to succeed. As I continued listening, my eyes widened like saucers and my mind pictured everything he so vividly described. He went on to explain that when a customs agent arrived on the scene, the smuggler's dogs were trained to first attack or run off the agent's dogs and to then quickly surround the agent and race in rings around him so that he could not draw a bead on the rapidly moving dogs. They were further trained to attack the agent from behind with his upper thigh as their target. The smuggler's attack dogs were equipped with steel fangs to induce immobilizing, crippling wounds to the victim. The razor-sharp fangs sent the agent into a paralysis as the dogs proceeded to cross the border.

The account was grizzly and I was relieved after hearing the story to realize that Father's business was legal and profitable without subterfuge or steel fangs. A well-trained, well-bred dog, after hours and hours of repetitive training, was worth the equivalent of $15,000. The price seems very high, but the training process was lengthy and Father never sold a dog that was not exceptional.

The Belgian trainer often arrived at the hotel accompanied by his own Doberman. The man put the dog through its paces and one day demonstrated a miraculous maneuver. The trainer had a large piece of plate glass set in place and commanded the Doberman to jump through the glass. The dog did not hesitate but on cue left the ground with his front paws extended to hit the glass in such a way that the glass broke clean and the dog's body went through the opening without getting cut. It was impressive.

Another enterprise was the reason Father held such strong enmity for the *couleuvre* snakes. It was legal in France to catch migratory birds. Nightingales and red robins (different from the American robin) and other song birds were common and popular. During March and April, Father set traps for the birds which ultimately found homes in clubs or in private homes. Wealthy estate owners and nightclub owners kept the caged birds in semi-darkness to affect a natural song-inducing environment. No two nightingales sing the same song, and it was common to sell several birds to each owner to provide a unique symphony. When autumn arrived, the birds would be released to again migrate. The ongoing business continued of trapping and selling the birds for the enjoyment derived for a season before the birds were turned loose, and then the trapping process would again commence. It didn't make much sense to me that a purchaser would pay the equivalent of $1,000 for a little bird to release it after several months; but Father had a loyal clientele, and it was a lucrative business.

Trapping the birds was another adventure in which I shared. Father designed his own traps. I still have some of them; and as I look at the intricacy of design and manufacture, I appreciate his expertise and patience. I vividly recall the hours spent helping him trap the little birds. The traps are masterpieces of workmanship with natural silk netting and a wonderfully crafted tripping system. Mother accompanied us on the bird trapping forays into the forest of Fontainbleau outside Paris.

After we had judiciously placed and set 15 traps I settled into the shadow of a tree and remained perfectly still as I watched and listened to Father's performance. He called in a unique way until the male bird responded, and then others would follow. Each trap was carefully placed in a location where the sun's rays peeked through the forest canopy to catch the bait — a meal worm which had a hard shell that glistened as it reflected the sunlight, its yellow-gold color shimmering and twisting in the light accompanied by Father's bird calls. Apparently the combination was impossible to resist, and we never left the forest without three or four captive birds to be transported to the hotel and into the aviary located in a building behind the main building. The room was about 30 feet long and 50 feet wide — one wall stacked with cages to hold and contain the birds in an ongoing symphony that changed as the birds' songs changed.

There was much to learn as I watched, listened, and interacted with the many people and animals who came to the hotel each day and in the many fascinating jaunts with Father. He tutored me well in reading, and I loved to read whatever I could get my hands on, even at a very young age.

I was more than ready academically when, at five, I attended formal school, which was a nonreligious civic school, located three miles from the hotel. There was no form of transportation provided. Regardless of the weather, I walked to classes each day. I was just a little guy and I remember well how miserable I was to be pulled from under the warm covers on cold and rainy day, as I set out to do what duty called and what my parents absolutely insisted. I had no choice. I would have preferred to stay within the confines and warmth of the hotel where there was so much of interest to hold my imagination and involved me physically as well. I developed early on a resentment to being forced to leave each day in what appeared to be a dull regimentation. And that feeling, strong in me at five, was deeply etched long before I was shipped off to boarding school.

The Catholic religion was the dominating religion in France and most assuredly the religion of my parents. I remember being taken to church by Mother most Sundays, but not every Sunday, unless the activity at the hotel permitted her to be absent for several hours. On those days when we would attend, I was dressed quite handsomely in short formal pants and a dress shirt. All of my youth was spent in short pants, which was the typical costume of the day for French children. I have a picture of me in my first communion dress outfit.

I also dressed appropriately for weddings and funerals and even burials attended at the church. The association of death, burial, and the cemetery made a very strong impression. I realized that in Le Vesinet there was only one cemetery. It was beautifully maintained, but was strictly provided for and open only to Catholic burials. If you were not Catholic, you were buried in the "other cemetery," a horrid place possibly likened to a dump where only the disenfranchised, the outcasts, the stray dogs, so to speak, were interred in a dreadful setting. I am certain to this very day it was, in large part, why 99 percent of the French population professed strict adherence to the Catholic faith, whether or not they were predisposed to attend church regularly. There was a very real dread of being "dumped" at death and not having a decent burial in the Catholic cemetery.

Paris, in almost every way, always seemed to be a separate entity from the rest of France, apart from the Provinces. As a young person, I certainly did not know much about the large, sophisticated city. I only witnessed the behavior and customs of the residents of Le Vesinet and was greatly impressed by the complete, unwavering, and unquestioning faith in which dogma was laid down by the church and blindly obeyed and adhered to by almost every French citizen I encountered.

I became a tough little boy with strong feelings and opinions and began to question authority. I maintained a firm and abiding admiration and respect for my parents as I watched them labor, and labored alongside them in sharing a very full, active, and productive life. While Mother seemed determined to see to my religious training, I noticed that Father, in spite of and perhaps because of his Jesuit education, did not attend church. This enigmatic behavior evoked many questions that I dared not express to him. He never went to Mass and only occasionally attended any formal ceremonies at the church. I knew that his absence was, in part, due to the many-faceted business demands, but it spoke eloquently to my young mind of a free spirit and also a different approach to life. I know that it influenced my thinking and my attitude where dogmatic tenets were laid down and found to be, by me, reason for questioning and a lifelong search for answers — answers that were rarely proffered by the formal educators of my day.

3

ST. NICOLAS

In my ninth year, I was transferred from the local school to St. Nicolas, a boarding school located in deBuzenval, 15 miles north of Paris. The school, contained in a huge forbidding building, was set on a prominent hill. The dormitory gave access to an impressive view, particularly at night, of the lights of Paris. That view was perhaps the warmest and kindest attribute that I could give to my new surroundings, which were harsh, completely uninviting, and totally intolerable to me. So like the seminary at Vitre where Father was incarcerated, St. Nicolas was a semimilitary Catholic school where we were required to wear uniforms with stiff, stand-up silhouette collars (which I hated.) Imagine me, a little guy, not tall in stature but rough and tumble, accustomed to wearing shorts and a sweater most of the time, being forced to dress every day in a damned uniform with a stiff collar. It was a prison within a prison, and I absolutely hated every aspect of the new school and the miserable pall that suddenly pervaded every aspect of my existence.

There was no such thing as heated water or even heated rooms at the school, which I shared with 700 other boys. The austere setting of grey walls closed in on me so profoundly that my initial reaction was to rebel and lash out at my incarcerators. I could not understand how Father, who had told me often of his Jesuit training at Vitre and the harsh and inhumane treatment he suffered at the hands of the priests, could place me in a similar circumstance. Unlike the seminary, the Jesuits at St. Nicolas wore no robes, but their methods and their strictures were equally cruel. I have to believe that the reason I was sent off to this horrific place was to temper and discipline a tough boy who was rough on the kids who lived near and around the hotel and whose Mother and Father could not, or did not, have the time to supervise or discipline. Like an unbridled horse or an untamed tiger, I had to be handled in a special way, and they knew no other way. I quickly learned how a caged animal must feel.

The discipline at the civic school had been severe, but nothing to compare to the Catholic boarding school. Of course, my rebellious nature and lack of respect for doctrine induced unusually harsh and bloody measures. After a certain period of time, there was the possibility of going home weekends if there were no points against my record. I managed to have a lot of points against me, and so my weekends often were spent restricted to the school. I did receive visits from Mother and Father, who were informed of my unruly behavior which must have been a source of embarrassment. I was required to attend church every morning, chapel every evening, and two Masses on Sunday were mandatory but did nothing to quell my questioning and skepticism. I would sit in class and ask my teachers for proof concerning theology — making them livid. My questioning was irreverent and tedious. The teachers could not nor did they even attempt to supply adequate answers to impertinent and blasphemous rhetoric. While the other students displayed shock and incredulity at my outbursts, the teachers, after menacing stares, attempted to ignore my queries. It was some time later that an opportune time would present itself, and then the manner of punishment was extreme.

I asked one priest, "Sir, you mention to us that there are 75 major religions in the world. They all proclaim to be the right one, and they all proclaim to be the only good one, including ours. How can we be sure that we aren't wrong?" I would continue in this vein as the whole class looked at me like I was some crazy anarchist — The Antichrist. The equally horrified teacher did not react using physical punishment in class, but would wait until I was caught out of line or failed to perform a math problem correctly (math was not one of my strong subjects) and then if discipline was meted, I was always hit the hardest or treated with the most severity.

One time as we were filing into the refectory, I was caught talking against the rules. A teacher came up from behind, grabbed hold of my left ear, and twisted it so hard that it actually separated in part from the side of my head, ripping the skin and creating a great deal of pain and bleeding. That was only one such incident.

The measures were incredibly extreme, which served to toughen me further and deepen my resolve to question a religion that could permit such harsh, unreasonable punishment. I hated the school, I hated the teachers, and I was not overly fond of many of my fellow students; nor did I ever really settle in or adapt to the strictures. However, I did realize that I wanted to spend weekends back at the hotel. Mother and Father were horrified at my behavior, but also with the extreme penalties administered, and were very happy when I was given the okay to leave the dreaded school for the brief respite afforded by a weekend spent in Le Vesinet. The times away from St. Nicolas were blessed events.

Perhaps as a reward for good behavior or to quiet some guilt in sending me off to what he fully realized to be a torturous environment, Father began teaching me to drive an automobile. I had ridden with him for years in all of the vehicles and watched as he shifted gears, cautiously started and maneuvered the large machines, and stopped them very carefully. It was with the same care, not only for the machine but also for the passengers, that I was taught to drive the Citroen. I was never given the privilege of driving the limousine, his pride and joy and not the sort of vehicle used in driver training. But driving the city car and also the van was exciting enough. My tutor was very demanding as he placed a glass of water on the dash and had me start the car and put it into gear and then have it advance and stop without spilling even a drop of the water. In this way, he pointed out, I was able to always have the confidence of any passengers and to provide a smooth, safe ride.

Soon after I mastered the art of driving, the Government passed a new ruling granting drivers licenses. The political situation between France and Germany was deteriorating, and drivers were drafted into the army to drive motorized vehicles. The age to qualify for a license was dropped to twelve, and I qualified for my license while I was attending St. Nicolas.

Academically, I would consider the education at the boarding school excellent in spite of the harshness of the living conditions. Each day began at 5:00 a.m. with very little time allotted for washing. During the winter months, the temperature was sub-zero in the bleak, cold darkened dormitory. With only cold water for bathing, it was a brutal and rude awakening. After washing quickly we filed silently down to the refectory for breakfast. Each morning we could smell the odor of thick, stinking, burned-out soup. Thank God, Mother and Father supplemented the food situation when they visited, which was against regulations, but the contraband was relished. Mass followed the early meal, and then we attended classes. Every meal was preceded by prayer. We seemed to spend a great deal of time on our knees.

When I discussed school with Father, he was honest in relating to me all that he experienced, so much of which was my daily experience. He told me that he had gone to church every day of his life beginning at age six until he was 21. The seminary training required that he also serve Mass three times a day and in the evening; and he, too, spent a good deal of time bowing in prayer while kneeling on a wooden support similar to the rounded two-by-four oak supports at St. Nicolas. He was well acquainted with the occupational hazard — enormous calluses on the knees.

I formed several friendships while at St. Nicolas, but they were rare and with the few others who, like me, were rebels. I was the most outspoken, which drew disfavor from most of the other students, boys from well-to-do families who looked upon me as some sort of swine. They either seemed afraid to express any opinion that was counter the dogma or were content to go along day in and day out blindly following the regimen and strictures as they were set down and enforced.

When I did qualify to go home for a weekend and during the three weeks of summer vacation, I kept very busy at the hotel helping with dog training, caring for the birds, trapping song birds to fill the cages in the aviary, and also driving one of the automobiles. Over a period of time, Father had several different models of the Citroen, which was considered a very fine automobile in those days. He first had a *dix Cheveaux,* and then he owned a *quinze Cheveaux,* which was an 11-horsepower model, and then he moved into a 15-horsepower. Those automobiles were a breakthrough in automotive design as the first front-wheel drive vehicles sold in

France. They created quite a stir in Le Vesinet, and I enjoyed the hell out of driving the handsome vehicle through the village and gained the attention of some of the girls. I noticed them as well.

There were vacation trips to visit my grandparents on the farm, either on my own or in the company of Mother and Father when we would join the rest of the family and enjoy peaceful days away from the work and demands of the hotel and of school. But as my interests and responsibilities expanded, it became more compelling to remain in Le Vesinet.

I enjoyed spending any free time with a good friend of the family, Paul le Royer. Paul, an animal trainer about 20 years my senior, came from a wealthy family and traveled in high society with the upper-crust families of Le Vesinet. He was an elegant, handsome, cultured gentleman who encouraged me to spend time at his home and animal compound where he trained many different animals. Paul lived in a mansion, was related to nobility from Brittany, and purchased his first trained dog from Father. They became good friends, and I became absolutely fascinated by the training that I witnessed. Paul had bears, ponies, three leopards, monkeys, and four chimpanzees as well as various dogs and birds. He was a wonderful trainer discovered by the motion picture industry to provide animals for innovative roles.

It had become the rage to feature animals in movies performing all sorts of human-like behavior, and Paul trained his animals to do many amazing acts. He trained one of the bears to enter through a door, sit down at a table, and open a bottle of champagne. That does not seem quite so extraordinary in this time and place, but at that time it was startling.

I watched in awe and admiration as Paul worked by the hour with horses and even leopards. It was like going to a circus, but better than any show I had ever attended.

In addition to the hours of entertainment, I pulled extra duty cleaning out the animal cages and cutting up the raw meat fed to the animals. Paul even demonstrated and gave me lessons in the use of the whip. The compound was absolutely fascinating and fun and such a departure from the confines of school and the labor of the hotel.

Having a driver's license at 12 was impressive, but a far more meritorious honor was bestowed in my twelfth year. There was a compulsory student examination administered to obtain the "First Degree" which was called the *Certificate d'Étude*. All students from the department, which would be the equivalent of four or five Florida counties, were required to compete for the state degree. All students from public, private, and religious schools competed equally, although the Catholic school education at that time was considered to be superior. While my grades at St. Nicolas were not so great, I was usually confined to my quarters three weekends out of four and spent a lot of time studying and reading. When the state exam was commenced under the auspices of the non-Catholic government bureaucrats, I was just one of nearly 600 competitors.

Lo and behold, guess who came in first in the state oral and written tests . . . Robert Baudy! That was really quite an accomplishment and also a gauge to the type of education obtained at St. Nicolas. It also demonstrated my avaricious reading habits and retention of information. I came away with the highest number of points in spite of the strict state-appointed monitor who stood watching over every ten students, governing every phase of the exam in the politically volatile atmosphere where the Catholic school students were least favored. I was first in composition, first in art, first in natural history, and I even did well in math.

After the prestigious award and honor (for which I was given a standing ovation when the test scores were repeated in class,) I detected an immediate change in attitude toward me. I had one year remaining at St. Nicolas and found in the final year that I received more respect, better treatment, and also improved grades. Those were positive signs.

But still, at the end of the year a decision had to be made. Another school had to be chosen, and Mother and Father were hearing from friends and relatives that since I was built like a fine athlete, I should be placed in a school situation where the curriculum would train and prepare me for a more physical avocation. On the other hand, there was a similarly vocal group who disagreed totally and stated that, "Robert is an intellectual who loves to read." Both assessments were correct.

My reading habits developed at a very early age, and I grew up reading anything I could get my hands on, particularly technical books and journals. I was a speed-reader who devoured a book a night and became imbued with a craving for culture and history, facts and details. I must admit that in my lifetime I have only read a dozen novels due to my thirst for knowledge of what is real. But I also knew well that physical activity is important to body and soul. I was an outdoorsman, a rugged individual, and I hoped that the next school would fulfill all of my attributes and interests.

Father made the final decision. I was enrolled in a technical school in St. Germaine, located 15 miles west of Le Vesinet. I biked the 30 miles each day to the new school where my courses were directed toward the printing business. I learned to set type and also to use various machines to produce fonts. I was not overly enthused with the new courses which required so much time producing writings rather than design and actual manufacture. But there were compensating factors. I was at least home each evening and available to help Father in his newest business enterprise.

4

NEW BUSINESS AND SEX EDUCATION
L'Occupation Nouvelle et l'Éducation Sexuelle

*F*ather was always looking for ways to make money. I was 13 when he purchased a meat market in Le Vesinet. When he fully realized how lucrative the business could be, he sold the hotel, Les Charmettes, for a substantial profit over what he initially paid for the old, run-down hotel years before. With the money he decorated the market lavishly in imported marble from Italy and other elegant accoutrements befitting the prestigious Paris suburb. Our new residence was on the second floor behind the market on Le Thiers Street, the most exclusive area in Le Vesinet. The clientele were the well-to-do residents in the neighboring streets as well as the wealthy estate owners and celebrities who lived in the surrounding area.

Father retained an interest in the dog training business moved by the Belgian trainer to a location away from the hotel. The Delahaye limousine service, so carefully and proudly provided for the dignified clientele, was also sold.

As a part of the new enterprise, it was my job to ride with Father in his small van, a *Camionette,* to the centralized slaughterhouse in Paris. The *La Villette,* which in French means "small city," was filled with seemingly hundreds of acres of forbidding stone complexes called *abattoirs,* each designed for processing either beef, sheep, or hogs. It was built by Louis XIV in the late 1600s for the sole purpose of slaughtering animals at a time when French law prohibited slaughtering in the provinces.

I remember my first visit well. There was a bronze, lifelike statue of a bull standing prominently at the enormous entry gate, a railroad terminal active day and night with animals being brought from all over the country into the central facility. As I stepped into the sprawling *abattoir* for the first time, the combination of smell, sight, and sound was completely overwhelming and riveting. My first reaction was to the change in temperature. It was freezing outside, but in spite of the lack of a heating system inside on the killing floor, the body heat from dozens of freshly eviscerated animals created a palpable, thick, steamy cloud which hung around each carcass — a fog of death!

Hundreds of sounds mixed to form a cacophonous symphony from hell. The desperate bellows of beasts about to die, the muffled thud of dead bodies hitting the bloody floor, the killers yelling to each other, the rattling of steel shackles, all mingled to tell the horrible story being enacted before my eyes in the huge den of death and suffering. I was totally riveted as Father shook me to my senses. I looked with utter horror at the frenzied scenes of brutality.

Father had verbally prepared me before we stepped through the narrow, heavy oak door, built small to prevent any loose animals from escaping. His words could not begin to describe all that was contained in the confines of hell. I was first repulsed by the smell of urine, manure and blood that permeated the cavernous buildings. Immediately, I was caught up in the commotion, noise, and gore as I watched, eyes wide and focused, as the cows ran frantically down the many shoots from the holding pens to the slaughter stall or killing floor.

The process of killing the cows was performed swiftly as each animal was met by a muscular man wielding a wood-handled hammer contraption called a *merlin*. One end of the sturdy hammerhead was square; the other held a hollow pointed piece of steel. With one forceful blow to the skull, the animal fell instantly. It was immediately skinned and then shackled to a winch to be further processed. I was impressed by the dexterity of the butchers who began the cutting producing blood gushing from the carcass.

I felt sick but was distracted by the industry as I watched the large men wearing rubber boots or wooden *sabots*, their torsos bare with only a large leather apron with a chain belt that held five or six razor-sharp knives, each of them designed for a specific purpose, along with the shiny sharpening steel.

Two men were working on each carcass with such speed that in minutes the carcass was skinned on the floor, lifted by a winch, and quartered with surgical precision. Every move and stroke of the knife was orchestrated. After each carcass was processed, the floor was washed; and the men, whose milky white bodies had the pallor of inside labor, contrasting sharply and dramatically to the fresh blood, wiped the gore from their arms and torsos.

As I watched, a bell signaled the routine ten o'clock break for the *casse-croûte,* a steaming bowl of soup and huge sandwich downed with deep gulps from a bottle of red wine to sustain for the ongoing slaughter.

As we moved on to the hog *abattoir,* I soon realized there was a common procedure for killing, and also unique methods for dealing with the smaller animals. As many as 15 of the squealing 500-pound hogs were let into a ring, approximately 100 feet in diameter, where a muscular man stood at the opening of the shoot. He held a six-foot long wood-handled sledge hammer ready to meet each hog as it came down the narrow passage. With unbelievable precision and strength, the *tueur* hit each hog once between the ears, the thud of impact by the massive iron synchronized with the animal falling. Immediately, two young helpers bled each animal, and in less than a minute all the hogs were similarly dispatched. The attendants then brought armfuls of wheat straw, covered each carcass, and set fire to the straw to burn off the hair. It all brought vividly to mind Dante's Inferno. I stood in the middle of a killing field, violent and bloody where life was being terminated on all sides.

In the sheep *abattoir,* the bleating animals were corralled in a 50-foot square area containing low benches about two and a half feet high. Two young men picked up one animal at a time, their hands under the belly, lifting and carrying the defenseless sheep upside down to a bench, head dangling. There the dispatcher, an older man with gray hair carrying a number of razor-sharp long knives, with a single stroke, decapitated the animal. I watched, wide-eyed at all that I was witnessing, absolutely hypnotized, in a state of shock, as I watched the heads dropping from bodies, seemingly without pain. For the first time, I had serious, lingering thoughts of mortality. My life, too, could be over with a single stroke.

Our mission at the La Villette was to purchase meat. Father taught me as we went along how to properly select the different cuts. One of the major items sold in our shop was the lamb or sheep testicles, which was and still is considered a delicacy by the French. This prime part of the animal was referred to as the *yo-yo* for obvious reasons; and with Father's tutelage, it was my job to go from stall to stall where the animals were being processed to go through the large steel vats where the various body parts were thrown in search of the best looking *yo-yos*.

Mother in front of market where yo-yos and other fine meats were sold.

One visit to La Villette held a viewing of the kosher *abattoir*, which was located in a remote section of the slaughterhouse. Jewish religious tenets, in order to fulfill long-held dietary restrictions, required that animals to be consumed be bled alive. In the case of the 2,500-pound Charolais bull, the huge animal was driven into a narrow chute, not killed instantly, but its front feet shackled to an iron ring embedded in the concrete floor, the hind legs shackled and attached to a powerful winch, the body, stretched taught like a bow-string as it bellowed in agonizing pain. A Rabbi entered the torture chamber and removed from his carrying case a sacrificial razor-sharp, prayer-engraved, long-bladed knife. As he began slowly slitting the throat of the huge animal, I had to look away.

I heard the Rabbi recite the ritual prayers to the accompaniment of the animal's grotesque, muffled death gurgling.

Fortunately, there were diversions in my life to take me away from the horror of the slaughterhouse experience. I found escape and great pleasure in my time spent watching healthy, living animals being trained by Paul and his assistants at his compound.

I also became fascinated with women. That newly discovered awareness would stay with me always. I was not tall at 14, but had attained most of the height that I would ultimately gain. I was strong, good-looking, and one of the few boys of my age driving a car, an impressive car at that. I did not have any trouble attracting girls. The only problem I had was accommodating my sexual fantasies with school every day and work taking up the remainder of the daylight. The only time to pursue my lustful incursions was at night, and I began to sneak out of my bedroom after retiring early for the evening under the guise of having to study. Occasionally after slipping down the drainpipe outside my bedroom window, my absence was detected, and Mother became upset particularly if I stayed out until four or five in the morning. I became quite delinquent but could not deny myself the pleasure of this new adventure. I was not happy at the technical school where I studied for nearly two years. Father and Mother also realized that the school did not provide the proper education or atmosphere for me in St. Germaine.

Prostitution was legal in France at that time, and there were two very exclusive bordellos located just a block from the school. Under French law, the houses were supposedly watched and supervised by the police and no minors under the age of 18 were to enter the premises. I estimate that 75 percent of the student body from the technical school frequented the houses and were rarely turned away. The house that I preferred was lavishly decorated with heavy red velvet drapes and upholstery. The girls employed were checked by the government health department. As students, we were not the most desirable clients as we were broke most of the time. The drinks alone were very expensive, but the appeal was great and the accessibility also more than ample with many houses dotted all over St. Germaine.

I had lost my virginity before I began frequenting the houses. My first sexual encounter, other than the casual dating of girls in Le

Vesinet, was with a good friend of my parents. The lady who taught me so much about sex was a singer and dancer who performed under the theatrical name of La Esmaralda. Her specialty was Spanish Flamenco dancing. She was a beautiful woman of about 30 or 35 when I became involved with her. I was 14 at the time and apparently had gained enough physical maturity to appeal to the mature woman. I think I was ready for the explosion.

La Esmaralda was married to an American named Chester Kingston, who moved from Brooklyn to France after the First World War. Chester was also a performer, an acrobat and contortionist. My parents took me to see both the beautiful singer-dancer and also the acrobat perform on separate occasions. I enjoyed offstage encounters with Chester primarily because I found his unique Brooklyn-American accented French very funny. I must give him credit for trying to speak the language, but how he did massacre it. However, his talent as a contortionist was quite exceptional. During his performance, he utilized an ebony box that was quite small. I would estimate its size to be two feet by four feet. The box was black with gold oriental decorative trim. Chester wore a Chinese costume and worked along with a muscular male assistant who moved the shiny box to a table located stage center. The house lights dimmed dramatically as the oriental strains accompanied floodlights which changed colors and highlighted the box. Slowly the box opened, and the six-foot tall man magically snaked himself out of the small enclosure.

Chester's act was full of wizardry onstage. Offstage he was a green-thumb gardener who demonstrated his hobby in lush, beautiful gardens surrounding the cottage he shared with La Esmaralda. Chester also collected oriental art books. La Esmaralda had the additional talent of being an amateur artist. She worked in a studio on the beautifully flowered property where still-life flower arrangements were painted. I visited the cottage and the studio with my parents as guests of the performers.

There were theatrical engagements and contracts that took the artists away from Le Vesinet. Chester signed commitments that required leaving La Esmaralda for months at a time. She remained in Le Vesinet to fulfill her own performing schedule at the Moulin Rouge or at Le Gaumont Palais located on la Place de Clichy. The Palace was the French equivalent of New York's famous Radio City Music Hall.

As the family friendship developed, I felt very comfortable in the presence of Chester and La Esmaralda and thought nothing of stopping to visit occasionally on my own. One day I stopped, expecting Chester to be present. I shall never forget that warm summer day and what it held for me. Chester was away on tour. I was made welcome by La Esmaralda and went into the living room. I pulled one of the books from the shelf. The book was a handsomely illustrated edition of the Kamasutra. As I settled on the couch, La Esmaralda joined me and together we looked at the provocative reproductions depicting the many varied positions of foreplay and sex, which evoked some commentary, which in turn evoked some very strong stirrings in me and also in the lady who was sitting so close to me. Before I knew what was happening, she led me to her bed, and we were wrapped in an embrace that exploded every sensual nerve in my body.

I had had erotic dreams and fantasies and had touched the bodies of the girls I dated, but nothing could have prepared me for the exquisite sensation experienced that day in the cottage with La Esmaralda. As I felt her soft skin, smelled her perfume, and felt her hands exploring my body, we joined together in a rhythmic motion of strength that filled me with a depth of physical and emotional stimulation unlike anything I had ever felt before.

It was a wonderful, exciting introduction to sex and the beginning of an obsessive relationship with a very beautiful and quite extraordinary lady. I was completely captivated by her and filled with the most glorious thoughts as I left her that day to return to what was ordinary and routine in my young life, a life that would never again be quite as ordinary or routine.

Fortunately, I had many other obligations that kept me from being totally consumed by La Esmaralda. She, too, had a full commitment to her career and also to Chester when he returned to Le Vesinet, and, I presume, to other gentlemen as well. I returned to the cottage whenever Chester went out of town, and I felt no guilt but rather great excitement, pleasure, and anticipation.

I look back at the episodes, the arousal of sensitivity that was induced, and feel very fortunate that I was with a mature woman who was knowledgeable and taught me what should and should not be done sexually and what gave pleasure to a woman. That was a beneficial lesson. Without her as teacher-lover, I was definitely on course to contract a sexual disease that could have been devastating. I view the encounters with a great deal of nostalgia and gratitude.

It was not long before Mother sensed the depth of my involvement. My truancy became a problem as far as she was concerned. She took me to a specialist, a woman psychoanalyst who was a friend of the family. After several sessions, the analyst told Mother, whom I overheard tell Father, that she didn't think that my appetite for beautiful women would or could be curbed and would probably be with me until I died. I appreciated hearing that! I had a mandate to continue my quest. The analyst also advised that the best my parents could do was see to it that I was knowledgeable enough to protect myself and know the facts of life so that I would not get hurt or hurt others.

Imagine my parents, raised in the strict Catholic theology, knowing their son was a young philanderer. It had to be so totally abhorrent, particularly to Mother. She even resorted to locking me in my bedroom after I turned in for an evening of studying. I then used the window and slid down the drainpipe to gain access to the ground below and freedom. Quietly, I would hop on my bike for the ride to the cottage. One night I left for a rendezvous and on the return trip got my pant leg caught in the bike chain. I worked for nearly an hour with nothing to pry the sturdy fabric free. The result of my frustrated pulling was to tear the pant leg. That produced incriminating evidence and also made the trip up the cold drainpipe hazardous.

One sexual dalliance to St. Germaine sticks out prominently in my memory. It occurred at a time when La Esmaralda was away from Le Vesinet, and I joined a couple of other boys to drive the 15 miles to the bordello to fulfill lustful yearnings. It was a blustery, cold winter day with snow on the ground as I recall. We arrived in St. Germaine and parked away from the chosen house, not knowing if we would be welcomed by the Madame. Business was apparently slow, and in spite of our not being of legal age, we were admitted.

There was a front door and a back door. We had parked at a distance, but worked our way to the front door carefully watching for the *gendarme*. It took very little time for us to become busily engaged in the activity at hand, buck naked, and enjoying the

A young Tarzan discovered women and they discovered me.

pleasures enormously when the house was suddenly raided. We could hear the commotion of the marauding police officers as they worked their way from room to room. We all left the rooms quickly and headed for the back door. We exited the house and found ourselves out in the snow. We had escaped arrest, but our clothes were in the house as we stood, shivering, at the back door. There was no alternative to freezing except to get to the car and home. We ran, darting like hunted animals attempting to hide our nakedness, but too cold to see any humor in our plight. The car gave a certain refuge; however, it was bitter cold, and with no car heaters in those days, the drive was bleak with no protection whatever from the elements or the bitter reaction of parents. We could not think of an appropriate alibi, but we did learn our lesson well. On future trips to St. Germaine, we made certain that a second set of clothing was stashed in the alley at the back of the house before entering.

I continued to be a trial to Mother. In my youthful quest to experience every adventure, some of which I really did attempt to keep from my parents, I should have known better. I was naive in thinking I could keep anything from Mother's scrutiny. While not formally educated, she had a wonderful sense of detail and a photographic memory. I can recall the *gendarmes* coming to see

Mrs. Baudy at the hotel seeking information concerning rough characters who had come through the area or seeking information concerning events that had occurred months prior to the inquisition. She was a marvelous source and through her valued intuition and recall, she was instrumental in many people being arrested by the police for a variety of crimes. My mother was well-respected and became acquainted with the Captain of the gendarmes. That was a significant relationship. Since the local constabulary witnessed some of my misdemeanors, it was good that I was the "son of Mrs. Baudy."

With Mother, deeply concerned about the activity occupying me so late after classes, and my after-dark liaisons, she was most supportive of my decision to quit the technical school in St. Germaine to move on to loftier education. The new school chosen, Nicole Estienne, was located in Paris. I was ready to move on.

5

WAR ON THE HORIZON
La Guerre à l'Horizon

*T*he Paris school was excellent. I was learning bookbinding and lithography and was actually doing some creative finished art that I found stimulating and exciting. I had found my niche, at least for the time being, and was quite content. I was operating as an adult on many levels, and it was most gratifying to me. We had been residing behind and above the meat market for some time, and my daily routine was to go by commuter train into Paris where I switched to first one and then another subway in order to gain access to the art school. The school was government-run and the first school in my experience that suited me. I enjoyed the exposure to fine arts and hoped to continue attending in spite of the startling news reports that sent ominous signals through every strata of society.

While my personal life was serene and happy, there was background music that was hardly soothing. Hitler and Germany became the main preoccupation and the centerpiece of news reports and written articles concerning Europe's future with threats and incursions and diabolical incantations. They created unrest and trepidation in government chambers and at public and private gatherings.

In September, 1939, Hitler sent his forces into Poland. The sorrowful Neville Chamberlain proclaimed a state of war between the British Empire and Germany. Edouard Daladier, then Premier of France, within hours of hearing the proclamation, declared his country's allegiance to its former ally, of a quarter century before, against the same enemy. In so doing, he committed France to a cause which held much controversy within its quavering borders. In August, 1940, with word of the Russian/German pact, Parisians left the city as the lights went out and the transportation system became immobilized in an attempted mass exodus. The Government was thrown into chaos, and the military took over to defend the country behind what was thought to be an impregnable and ingenious Maginot Line.

All during the earlier threats and then the actual incursions, Father listened daily and religiously to the radio broadcasts, particularly to reports concerning the diatribes attributed to the Nazi leader. Before dinner he would have his *aperitif*, and as he enjoyed his wine, engage anyone who would listen to what he predicted as the fate of France.

My father was a staunch ally and a wonderfully loyal Frenchman who was becoming more upset by the day with what he saw as a darkening cloud moving over the entire continent. He had served eight years, including four years of combat, fighting for France during the First World War. His predictions of what was now occurring were complete and utter doom for France, the continent and the world. He spoke so eloquently and so knowledgeably, but not always to a sympathetic audience. He understood the political climate well and was becoming more upset by the broadcasts and by the complacency being demonstrated by so many of his fellow countrymen. He became so critical of the French people as well as the government in realizing the extent of the malaise that he lashed out over and over again in conversations with anyone who would listen and those who did not want to listen.

Customers who came into the market heard his rantings, and many were liberals who did not share his views. Even Father's ideological loyalties were being questioned, which was absolutely shocking for me to witness. But I, too, was guilty of tiring from listening to the repetitious commentary, the arguing, and the obsessive ranting.

Father would not leave the radio alone as he devoured every news broadcast. Since speeches were broadcast in German, I was unable to understand them. Mother, too, was upset as well as bored by the constant level of hysteria and Father's insistence that I listen to his translation so that I would be completely informed. Hitler was being concise and candid in informing the whole world just what his game plan would be to take over first the European countries and to become, ultimately, the leader of the world. There were friends and even family members on the left side of the political spectrum who became intolerant of Father and even labeled him a collaborator — a friend of the Germans — when they heard his expletives describing the existing level of ignorance and his disappointment in his own government, his own people.

Father a collaborator! Preposterous! He was anything but. He had lived in Germany after fighting against the Germans and knew them well. He could see the salient concerns and wanted France to be alert to the extreme dangers. His ongoing harangue held the blind French people at fault for not standing up to the threats nor realizing the gravity of the situation.

Finally, all that he had predicted for so long came tumbling painfully and truthfully around us in the very pattern that Father had prophesied for months. My school, along with every industry and activity, came to an abrupt halt, and darkness fell on the City of Lights.

6

WAR
La Guerre

There were many visits to the farm over the years since that fateful day when I was nearly four years old, and Mother and Father took me away to live with them in Le Vesinet. I remember the visits as holding many peaceful and also wild adventures in the midst of a loving and caring family.

Grandmother was the matriarch who held forth as her family would come and go, each in their own endeavors. Mostly the memories were of summer idylls, playing with the snails and the snakes, and going off with my uncles and my cousins as we watched and also participated in the hunt.

There were visits when Mother and Father accompanied me; and there were times when I would make the trip alone by train to be picked up at the station by one of my uncles, or I would walk the eight miles from the train station to the farm near the River Allier. There were days when I would spend many hours on my own venturing out to swim in the river or to drop a line and fish or play with the fish that sought shelter in the dark cool recesses along the bank. I remember going off in the little red boat that so smoothly floated me along the river.

There were so many excursions in the all-encompassing security of a peaceful, provincial lifestyle provided stoically by the ancient monastery and the good and kind people who labored in their secure, lifelong patterns. There were many festive and noisy family gatherings with much laughter, and I was often the brunt of teasing about my spankings when Grandmother would

Paul le Royer working with a leopard.

thrash me with the thorny nettles after my snail hunts or a raid on the hen house. And I have wonderful memories of the food that Grandmother prepared and served, of the marvelous aromas wafting from the old kitchen. I learned to enjoy eating the *escargot*. I was growing older and wiser.

As the years went by, I was involved with school and chores, and my interests expanded to include time spent helping Paul le Royer with his animal training. Visits to the farm became less enticing. I had other types of hunting trips behind the wheel of one of the hotel vehicles. After we sold the hotel, I became involved in Father's meat business and in life in the midst of Le Vesinet, where the maids who worked on the large estates began catching my eye, and then there were cottage idylls that held so much allure.

But then came Hitler and everything changed. There was so much that would be different, and yet, as a 17-year-old, how could I possibly know the extent of what Father spoke when in May, 1940, after months of listening to him and to the many voices that seemed to conflict with his views, all that he predicted during an emotionally unstable time for every Frenchmen became reality as each one of us immediately and intimately were drawn into the heart of the conflict, the war to save France from a madman.

We heard reports of the terrorizing that the Germans reputedly perpetrated as they went first into Poland months before, then Holland, Luxembourg, and now had broken through the Ardennes Forest. The history books report that there was no doubt that they were marching *"Nach* Paris" flanking the Marginot Line to attack the Allied Armies from the rear. The French were galvanized with fear, knowing that the pending battle was the very battle they had been expecting and fearing for the past months. With the latest news, all of France became chaotic as frenzied hoards filled the village lanes, streets, and then the highways to escape the dreaded juggernaut.

I was in the market when a customer rushed in looking for Father. The British lady who lived in Le Vesinet was extremely agitated. She explained her plight to me. She was married to a high-ranking military intelligence Colonel. She had not heard from her husband for weeks and was frantic to leave Le Vesinet quickly with important documents she felt had to be kept from the Germans. She wanted to hire Father to drive her west to deposit the papers in Rennes about 300 miles distant from Le Vesinet. My parents were not at home at the time. The lady was frantic to escape and asked if I could drive her. I did have my license, and she offered to use her own car, a fine automobile I might add; and I became caught up in the excitement of the mission. She also offered to pay me what amounted to the sum of $3,000. I told her that I would have to ask my parents, which I did before the day ended. They were totally against my leaving and performing what appeared a highly dangerous mission, but I persuaded them that I would return to Le Vesinet immediately after successfully depositing the woman, her young son, and the cartons of classified documents in Rennes. My parents, like everyone else making an exodus in front of the German invaders, were in a quandary but decided they would leave Le Vesinet to head south.

We lost very little time exiting Le Vesinet for the drive to Rennes. As we journeyed toward the main highway, the roads were congested with hundreds of French, civilians as well as military convoys, making their escape from the invading troops. The woman's automobile was a 15-horsepower luxury sedan not easy to maneuver through all the people and conveyances glutting the roadway. Arrival at our destination would ordinarily take most of a day, but this trip took two-and-a-half days. There were few stops, but many restrictions. All communication was shut off. We did not have access to information of the German troop movements and were startled upon arriving in Rennes to realize that the enemy was directly behind us.

As a hired driver, I took my directions from the woman. She decided we should head southeast toward the central part of France. We drove in our continuing flight to Decize, near Nevers, 20 miles from my grandparents farm. In order to get to Nevers, we had to cross the River Loire using one of several stone bridges. As we approached the first bridge, a span of 900 feet, we were again right in the midst of retreating French troops and civilians. They carried whatever possessions they could manage, pushing wheelbarrows, riding bikes, and struggling, overburdened with packages, crushing forward away from the enemy in a frightened horde that made the automobile awkward, obsolete, and a menacing obstacle.

I attempted to keep from hitting the crazed mass of humanity. I was becoming impressed with the seriousness and reality of the invasion although I knew nothing of war except for news broadcasts and Father's impassioned tirades. I continued to maintain a certain cynicism in witnessing my fellow countrymen fleeing in panic from an enemy that I had yet to see. I could not fully appreciate the gravity of the circumstances as my parents could, having lived through one war with Germany. The horror, witnessed firsthand particularly by Father, who fought and blessedly survived the battlefield, was going to be repeated. Not wanting me to leave them to drive the lady to Rennes was perhaps totally justified. I was an innocent, invincible at that; I had a great deal to learn.

Before we reached the bridge, a German Air Force plane flew over strafing our position. I could see, to my total surprise and horrified enlightenment, people hitting the ditch beside the road. They fell in every direction seeking shelter from the blistering assault. Some did not succeed. The plane continued on, but the bodies in the ditches and the hysterical screaming brought quickly and assuredly into focus the total justification for the panic all around me and the fear expressed by my parents in the final hour before I left Le Vesinet.

My senses were assaulted as I heard and then saw artillery shells falling on the bridge. I pulled at the wheel and set the car on course to drive on to the second bridge in order to secure our safe arrival in Nevers. At the very moment of our ascent, I did not know if there was a safe place, but we had to continue searching. We were engulfed in confusion and congestion with the screams of people hit by enemy fire echoing in my ears and by the sight of those people not hit running and shoving in a crazed mass. I could only move the car slowly as we were buffeted by pedestrians and then another strafing sortie.

When we were two miles from Nevers, I heard more planes coming and could see that we were in their line of flight. I stopped the car, commanded the woman to open the passenger door, pushed her out along with her boy, and then jumped as we fell together into the ditch beside the road. We heard the roar of the Stuka bomber and the fire hitting all around, huddled closely, tightly, and prayerfully as the ground and our bodies shook. We hoped that we would escape the flying rapid fire. We were dead center in a nightmarish scene of murder and destruction, reacting instinctively to the horror unlike anything I had ever experienced before.

When the planes flew on, I gratefully realized that I was not hit nor were my two passengers. The car was not so fortunate. It was full of holes. Bullets had hit the engine block, which put an end to our automobile transportation into Nevers. The decision was made that we would separate. The lady, along with her son, joined a military convoy and went off carrying the documents and suitcases. I never saw them again.

As I watched them go and then continued on, walking toward the second bridge to cross the river, I could see Mother's face, pinched in anguish. I could hear both Mother and Father express the fear that we might never again return to Le Vesinet. All of the horror, all of the morbid predictions of what Father bespoke were being enacted on every side and I was one of the featured players. Could this be a dream? No time for thinking. I had to press on. As I walked, the heavy strafing continued. I reached the bridge and felt somehow that being on the solid span gave some sort of security in the mass of pushing, shoving bodies that surrounded me.

The noises of bullets and explosions continued as flak from artillery fire rained down on the bridge filled with stampeding, screaming humanity. I didn't waste any time looking up to see if it was German or French fire that was falling. The French had more vested interest in blowing the bridge as the river would form a natural boundary. As soon as I had safely and miraculously reached the far side of the river and managed to struggle away from the target toward Nevers, I heard a tremendous explosion and knew the bridge was gone.

I made a hasty retreat into Nevers and went to Aunt Marie Louise's apartment to find it recently evacuated. I investigated a friend's apartment on the first floor of the building, and found that

Madame Bergin and her daughter Paulette were also gone. As I headed for the railroad station two miles from downtown, I was surrounded by shelling. As I approached the station, I saw on the siding a train overloaded with refugees and displaced persons seeking asylum from the barrage of invasion troops and planes. The train was nearly invisible with people sitting on top and hanging from the windows of cars crammed to overflowing. The train would be the last one to leave Nevers with its destination Clermont Ferrand in the south to be gained by crossing over the Loire on the last stone bridge still standing.

I climbed the dirt embankment and pushed my way through bodies crushed together in a tight, molded mass that did not welcome the intrusion. Almost immediately upon boarding the train, I miraculously met Uncle Michel, Aunt Marie Louise and my cousins Guy and Claire. They were huddled together with Madame Bergin and Paulette and another neighbor from Nevers, a Mrs. Simons and her three children. It was absolutely astounding, in the hundreds of escapees crushed together, to meet relatives and friends in the frenzied flight. It was a relief to know they were alive and that we were together in spite of all that was uncertain and dangerous. I'm sure they, too, were grateful to have another male family member present.

As we pulled slowly away from Nevers, the train labored hard to move along the narrow track toward the last remaining bridge before it, too, was blown. The train crawled south, pulling overloaded cars bloated with humanity. The trip was further imperiled by the constant threat of German strafing.

We arrived in Gimouilles, approximately ten miles from Nevers, and saw billowing, acrid smoke pouring from an enormous fuel storage complex — another grim and threatening testimony to the destruction being leveled at our country. I recommended leaving the train to go to the farm, but my compatriots overruled me. They felt that leaving would expose them to further danger. They preferred to stay on the train which would ultimately deliver us to a safe haven somewhere in the south. As the train continued on, we received more strafing near La Ferte Hauterive by Italian Air Force planes. The damaged train was temporarily disabled. Nearly everyone exited the train to raid some boxcars positioned on a nearby siding loaded with large metal drums thought to contain military combat rations. It was speculated that the 50-pound drums would hold bacon and other precious foodstuffs. The desperate crowd, pushing and shoving, erupted into fist fights in the fray for food. I took some blows to the face, but managed to get hold of one of the drums which I excitedly returned to my family and friends. The slow forward motion continued as we pried open our treasure. What gross disappointment to find the drum filled with spicy mustard. All the melee achieved was two black eyes, but no food.

I am at the top of group of refugees escaping German invasion.

The next stop was Riom where we all exited carrying our meager belongings. Those who left the train swelled our small group to 14 filthy, exhausted, famished adults and crying children. We continued on foot searching for shelter, too tired to feel the fear blurred in the need to survive.

We walked for miles on a rough mountain road to a dilapidated farm called La Faye. We all caved into the hay in the huge barn for much needed rest. I became the designated food purveyor. Everyone was starving. I rested briefly before foraging for animals that would sustain us. I managed to snare some partridges, rabbits, and hare, and also captured a viper, which I took back to the barn much to the consternation of my family who were terrorized by the poisonous snake.

Water was the only liquid available, and that was not easy to obtain. There was a well, ancient and abandoned, about 85 feet deep filled with debris collected over years of disuse. I was lowered into the well to clear the thick, foul residue polluting the vital resource. Some of the other kids participated in this labor, which required using a pulley made of wood to run buckets down and then up to first remove the stagnant water. We emptied nearly a hundred buckets of fetid, murky water before we began getting any that could be safely drunk.

I proceeded in the following weeks to work 12 hours a day hunting to provide enough food for the group. In addition to the animals snared, I was able to forage for fruit and vegetables on farms in the area. The living conditions and sleeping conditions were barely adequate. I did manage to find some comfort in sharing the darkness with Paulette.

Paulette was a married lady whose husband had joined the military forces months before. There had been no word from him and no way of knowing how long we could continue to live in the barn or when we might be discovered by the Germans. With so many unanswered questions and the constant threat of death at the enemies hands or from starvation, we sought comfort and pleasure in one another. Paulette's mother knew of the relationship, but she also appreciated that I was the person working each day to provide food for the table. We were all victims in isolation not knowing how or when we might escape, when we could return, if ever, to the safety of our homes.

After several weeks, I decided I must work my way back to Le Vesinet. It was not easy leaving the desperate group knowing that survival would be more difficult without me, but I felt I had to return to my parents. My grandparents' farm was my first destination. I had only the clothes on my back which marked me as a refugee. I left on foot heading north.

The first city en route, which was a welcome sight after a night of walking, was Riom. Tired and hungry, but without any money I sought a job, work of any kind, but there was no labor to be had. I was approached on the street by an obese, well-dressed gentleman who looked to be in his early fifties. He said, "I see you are one of those young men in trouble."

He was correct and my appearance confirmed his opinion, but I replied defensively, "I'm not in trouble. I'm trying to reconnect with my family."

The man spoke with compassion and invited me to have a meal with him in spite of my ragged appearance of clothes worn for weeks and not properly washed. I too was unwashed. During the course of the meal, for which I was most hungrily grateful, the gentleman informed me that he was a local judge at the courts of Riom. When he offered me hospitality, I was again so grateful to have a place to stay and did not question the reason for his generosity.

We went first to his chambers; I was impressed with the diplomas and other furnishings that gave credence to his position of authority in the city and also to his financial ability to help a young man in trouble. We moved on to his residence, a beautiful home on the outskirts of the city. I was introduced to a friend of the judge, a handsome man, tall, blond, and cordial as he, smiling curiously, looked intently at the young derelict standing before him.

It did not take long for me to fully understand the situation. I knew enough about homosexuality to pick up some of the vibes that I recognized in the manner of speech and in the actions that I witnessed in the two men. I quickly realized that if I were to remain in the house, I would have to be on guard.

The judge directed me to what would be my bedroom for the period of time I stayed there. I badly needed a place to stay. The room on the second floor was appointed with fine art and a French armoire. There was a maid to prepare and serve the food, accompanied the first night by wine and champagne. I had been raised drinking wine as was the custom of all French people, but I never overimbibed. On this occasion with elegant surroundings, it seemed festive, a sort of celebration of survival; and I drank more than normal, but recognized it as routine for my dinner companions.

I retired, exhausted and unsteady from the alcohol, to my upstairs bedroom and slept well that first night in the luxurious comfort of the home in Riom. What a departure from the cramped, smelly train and the run-down, abandoned farm where I shared the obscure accommodations with Paulette and family members. I thought of them and felt guilty in being safe in a place of such opulence. The house was filled with art, paintings, carved ivory statues, and other fine demonstrations of the wealth and position of the owner, my host. I appreciated the decor, but I appreciated more the food and safe haven.

After a day spent investigating my surroundings, I again joined my host and his companion for dinner and then, retired to my room. It was warm and I slept naked with the window open. I was sleeping when suddenly I heard the door open and was startled to see the judge, naked, standing in the middle of the bedroom. He moved to the bed and sat beside me. Shocked, I hardly knew what to say. I stuttered a bit to say the words to let him know that I was not at all interested in what he seemed to propose. I was damned scared in my vulnerable position as I lay, naked, in his house, in his bedroom, with him lustfully looking at my body. I saw that he was drunk and was further horrified as my eyes left his face and moved to the milky white roles of flesh, a body that repulsed and disgusted me. The corpulent stomach nearly covered his hand holding an erection and then, suddenly, he reached for me. I jumped out of bed and threatened, "You touch me and I'm going to hit you!"

Rejected and bleary-eyed, he looked pleadingly for what seemed a long time, then stood up and left the room. When the door closed, I fell into bed and soon off to sleep. The last thoughts filtering through a very active mind were of Mother and Father, wondering where they were and knowing that so much of what they feared was true. I might never see them again, but I had to press on.

The next morning I was up early and downstairs before the judge wakened. His blond companion was also downstairs. I told him I didn't know what his relationship was to the judge, but that I was not at all interested in having sex with the man and I would not stay in the house any longer.

The handsome fellow was quick to point out that I was damned lucky to be housed and safe in a part of France that the Germans had not discovered or at least not occupied. If I went off to return to the north, I would find myself thrown into the middle of the German-held territories where I would be in grave danger. He convinced me that I would do well to remain where I was — that he would talk to the judge and persuade him to leave me alone. The blue-eyed Adonis told me he was sleeping with the judge, that he was bi-sexual.

None of the information placated me in the least. During the following days, I preached to the young man about his wonderful attributes, questioning his reason for prostituting himself when he could do so much better on his own if he would leave the influence and affluence of the judge. I must have made an impression. After four days, I told him I was leaving Riom. He decided to leave with me.

With the decision made, we had to realize the judge was not going to condone our departure and had the power to have us arrested by the local *gendarme*. We planned our escape to follow a full dinner and made certain the judge had enough wine and champagne to induce near unconsciousness before we walked out of the house and out of the city.

We continued walking through the night and into the following day. Occasionally, we hitched a ride with a local farmer engaged in moving produce by horse-drawn wagon. We finally reached the demarcation line separating the north of France from the south. The border was heavily patrolled. Every bridge and every road was monitored. We encountered a farmer in one of the villages near the line who told us that if we went into his field, located ten miles off the highway, we could watch the patrol pattern for an opportune time lapse to break into the northern area. The guards were all armed with weapons as well as with dogs.

The farmer accompanied us to the wheat-filled fields and pointed out the line separating the "free" from the "occupied" side. With our co-conspirator, we watched as one guard walked about 500 or 600 hundred yards where he met a comrade, then they would separate and return, each to meet another guard in the opposite direction. There was approximately five minutes to make our escape. My traveling companion had money that he perhaps had received from the judge. He gave the farmer some of the money to demonstrate our gratitude for showing us the access route and for spending so many hours pointing out the hazards involved in bolting across the line. The farmer had tears in his eyes as we bade him farewell. Perhaps he knew more than he was telling. He knew that our chances were slim and that we would face torture and death if we were detected.

We decided not to make the run together, but for me to go first. From our vantage point we could see two hills in the distance, one was two or three kilometers from the other. We planned to rendezvous on the second hill.

My friend had been carrying a sack with a blanket and other articles. I would travel with no impediments. We waited, lying in the wheat field, watching as the guards came to their meeting place, turned, and went in separate directions. As the day faded to dusk and I felt the dogs would not hear me, I moved as fast as possible keeping my body low so that if the dog did bark and the field glasses were directed toward me, I would be able to fall to the ground quickly. I managed to get safely to the first hill and stopped to look back. Undetected, I moved on to the second hill.

I remained there for the remainder of the night, slept fitfully and waited into the next day, but my friend did not come. I was upwind and could not hear gunshots, but I suspected that he must have been captured or worse. I left the rendezvous spot and moved on to search for a road to orient myself for the trip back to Nevers.

As I worked my way through fields and finally found a highway, I encountered German convoys of light reconnaissance vehicles. I remember being struck by my first up-close view of German soldiers: handsome, imperious, and self-assured. I was also struck by the professional appearance of not only the men, but also of their equipment. And I was gratefully impressed by their seemingly oblivious reaction to me.

I soon realized that I was very near my grandparents' farm. What a blessed relief to arrive in familiar surroundings as I approached the place of my early childhood. How wonderful to be met in an emotional embrace by Grandmother and to further realize that due to their remote and isolated location, they were untouched by what was occurring in many parts of their beloved country. Their daily living situation did not seem changed or greatly affected by the occupation except that two of my uncles, Louis and Mimile, were serving in the army and had not been heard from in some time.

I did not stay in the old monastery for long, but left feeling secure in the knowledge that my grandparents were safe. They even told of having German soldiers come into the area, young men starved for food just as so many French citizens were starved. They found the soldiers to be polite and appreciative of anything the farmers would sell to them. This was the dichotomy of war that in mutual suffering there was sympathy or at least a humanizing emotional response.

There were no phones or any other forms of communication operating from one part of France to another. Transportation was also in complete disarray. Grandmother told me that when I left Le

Vesinet with the woman and her child to head west to escape the Germans, Mother and Father also left to head south. Father was quick to realize that the fleeing French crowds and the congestion on the roads made travel nearly impossible. He knew from past experience, that by running they risked eventual capture by the German military and even execution. They made a U-turn and returned to Le Vesinet.

I left the farm to walk to Nevers where I caught a train heading north. That alone was quite an accomplishment and also extremely fortunate as the trains had been taken over by the enemy to transport soldiers. I was on the final leg of my journey toward Paris and home.

When I walked into the market, Mother looked at me — pale blue eyes wide in disbelief, as if seeing someone who had returned from the dead. She cried out, "My God, my God, you listened to my prayers," and held her arms out to receive her son. We embraced for a long time. Even Father, stoic and unemotional in most instances, displayed how deeply touched he was by my safe and miraculous return.

It took Mother two days to recuperate from the shock of my survival. In their minds it was truly a miracle that I had lived after hearing reports of strafing and of the many lives lost as the German forces attacked the refugees moving west, the direction in which I began the dangerous mission carrying secret documents to Rennes. As they listened intently to the BBC, the only source of news available at that time, they became completely and tragically convinced after months of not hearing of me or from me that I, too, had fallen to enemy fire or worse — slow torture by the hands of the Gestapo.

7

GERMAN OCCUPATION
L'Occupation Allemande

Life in Le Vesinet had taken a dramatic turn. Nearly half the population had fled. One of the most noticeable changes was the abandoned estates. The wealthy had the money and the connections to leave the country. The pink palace of Josephine Baker had been left empty except for a caretaker. There was no sign of La Esmaralda or Chester. The Germans were quick to scour every city and village in their search for Americans, British, and Jews held as the targets of their purge. Because Chester was American-born, he was a prime suspect; I'm certain that he went into hiding along with La Esmaralda. Those who were left in the village were business people and other French citizens, many of whom had turned their allegiance to the left — Communists — and some few loyalists like my parents.

The Germans settled in as they began taking over the large estates and any and all other facilities that they pressed into service and use. They had taken over the exclusive private Ravegot Hospital. Located in the middle of a wooded area the hospital was run and maintained for the political elite of France. As the war proceeded, German officers, including Rommel, were treated in the luxurious environs of the well equipped facility.

Life in Paris, as in most parts of the country, had also changed dramatically. The school was open, but classes had been disrupted. The transportation system was chaotic, operating under the pall of occupation and confusion created by the left-wing takeover. Mother, in talking politics, spoke of the "right thinking"

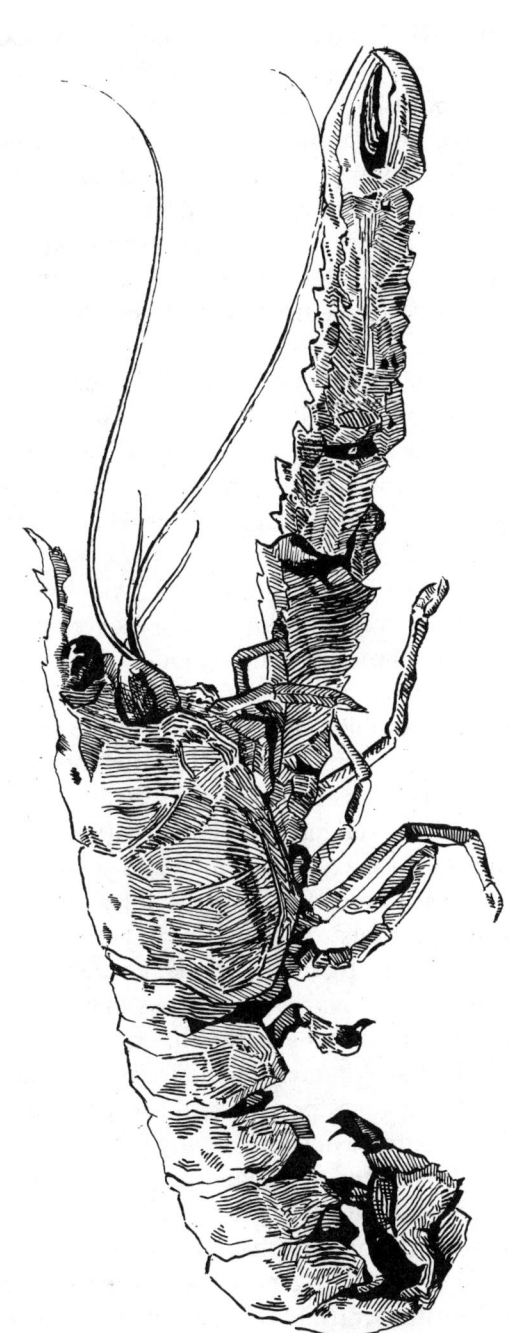

BAUDY

Nicole Estienne, School of the Book, inspired an ink drawing. One of many assignments.

conservatives who stabilized and strongly countered the Communists, but they had fled, many to be shot down. We were left in the middle of a hotbed of politically and militarily powerful French and Germans who were philosophically and in every other way opposed to my father's thinking and who Father had openly argued against before the Occupation. In addition to his political views being opposed, his success as an entrepreneur was another mark against the whole family. "Mr. and Mrs. Baudy," facetiously and contemptuously spoken, were treated as aliens not only by the Communists, but also by the locals who had lost everything. In this volatile atmosphere, Father found himself in the position of having to deal with these people in the market and to accept the "funny money" that the new regime all seemed to have. It further embittered him to do business with the enemy. But his hands were tied. It was no longer possible or prudent to speak out against the opposition that surrounded him.

I attended classes when I could get to Paris, which was rare. I began spending more time working with Paul le Royer. Paul was a strikingly handsome man who always had good-looking women in his employ as a part of his performances and to help train the animals.

When France began mobilizing its troops at the time of the German invasion of Poland, Paul was called into the army as a noncommissioned officer and assigned to the cavalry which was, in contrast to the mechanization that had occurred after World War I, a horse division similar to the *Spahis* which had served in North Africa years before. As *Marechal des Logis*, Paul wore a uniform with blue *Képi* and elegant custom-made, high riding boots. He made a most imposing military figure. However, against the modern tank and artillery warfare, the cavalry proved less than effective. In the first encounters with the Germans under Hitler, many lives were lost. His unit was smashed in a dramatic demonstration that the days of the "Great Charge" were gone forever. Paul escaped capture and suddenly materialized, in tattered uniform, totally demoralized. However, his return to Le Vesinet and to his animal compound was met with a popularity which was quite unexpected.

When Hitler emerged from the shadows inciting the throngs with Nazi propaganda and holding political rallies to enlist the masses, he was not permitted initially to use state buildings for his political advances. He arranged to speak publicly at circus performances in order to address the many people who enjoyed the state-run entertainment. As his following increased, he rented the large circus tents for the rallies. His early association with the circus and with the people involved, animal trainers, etc., served to elevate and give them special favor amidst the Nazi rise to power. As a result, when the Germans settled into their full occupation of France, Paul's professional performances were highly sought, and he left for weeks at a time to travel throughout the country entertaining and performing with his animals under the full support and authority of the new government regime.

Paul was involved at the time with a beautiful — spectacular might be a better description — blond named Maguy, which was short for Margueritte. Maguy worked for Paul as an assistant helping care for the animals at his compound and also was intimately involved with Paul as his mistress.

I spent a lot of time at Paul's home, which was large and very beautiful, located not far from the marble palace of Josephine Baker. There was a huge basement divided by large cages to contain the animals. The second story had been transformed into a training arena with a special floor to support the animals as they were led upstairs from the basement into the training area. Since I was spending so much time at the compound, and Maguy, too, was there much of the time, I became very aware of her and of the relationship she shared with Paul.

Maguy was tall with long blond hair and a fashion-model figure. Her body was beautifully proportioned, and it was sheer pleasure to watch her move through the training process with the various animals. She was sexy even in the work clothes that did not hide the many female attributes of which she too was well aware. When she dressed to perform in the arena, she was absolutely sensational.

Since there were engagements that took Paul away for weeks at a time, not always requiring Maguy, she would remain in Le Vesinet at the compound. I, too, would stay in the mansion overnight so that I could more easily feed and care for the animals early in the morning. The circumstances of shared quarters between a beautiful lady and a young man full of life became more than I could or wanted to contain. I began sharing Maguy's bed in what became a mutually stimulating and passionate affair. She was a magnificent partner. I felt some guilt over this indiscretion with Paul's lady in Paul's home, but Maguy was willing and available; and we could not resist temptation in what had become a highly volatile and uncertain world.

One day Paul approached me and said, "Robert, just between the two of us, you are like a son to me. I have to ask you a question." He caught me off guard as he continued, "I have a sneaky feeling that you and Maguy are lovers!"

I looked right at Paul and without hesitation said, "Yes." Then I paused, shaken by my disclosure, and went on. "It was not planned; there was no premeditation. The fact that we work together . . . and sometimes when I had to stay overnight because the animals had to be taken care of early in the morning . . . one thing led to another . . ."

Paul's reaction surprised me. He said that my answer was honest and I didn't try to lie. He appreciated my candor and since Maguy had said nothing to him and I could have lied, he accepted my answer and my explanation. I continued to work for Paul after the encounter, and I continued to spend some wonderful nights of love-making with Maguy although time and circumstances would soon change all that.

With the German take-over, the Nazis quickly re-organized the Government. They had a stronghold over the northern portion of France and began putting into power French citizens who were loyal to Germany and had been loyal for a long time prior to the invasion. This fact was nearly impossible for me to believe, but Father had been predicting all that was coming to pass. I gained even more respect for his knowledgeable foresight and assessment of the evolving debacle.

It was shocking and revolting to see how many native French turned out to be bona fide left of the political spectrum — people who would be shot or imprisoned by the thousands after the liberation. I could hardly believe what was occurring. There were so many prominent citizens who had obviously been paid and set up long before who were moved swiftly and directly into power positions, which only further traumatized the loyalists and created greater alienation between the many differing factions. The pro-Germans among us were referred to as the Fifth Column or *Collaborateurs*.

Because the French had so many paid people in their camp,

GERMAN OCCUPATION

I was entirely happy at the art school and produced some watercolor work.

the transition to a German-supported government went very quickly. Before we knew what was happening, many loyalists were jailed. Another shocking result of the Occupation was the carefully planned and executed round-up of Jews and other anti-German groups. Anti-Semitic propaganda was widely circulated, and the Jewish population of Le Vesinet, wealthy business people, were vanishing.

On several occasions I witnessed firsthand the blatant anti-Semitic activity. One day I had gone into Paris to attend school. Before I entered the building, I heard the rumblings of trucks. Suddenly 25 or 30 German Army trucks pulled in to seal off ten blocks near the school. The soldiers exited the trucks and placed a solid cordon completely around the area. Then the soldiers thoroughly and methodically questioned every citizen and requested individual IDs.

As I watched from a distance, some of the detainees were directed to stand to the left and some to the right as they were scrutinized and channeled into segregated lines. Then, those gathered on one side were forced into the trucks. I saw this activity from time to time and heard reports of many such incidents but was always caught off guard by the sudden arrival of the soldiers with very little warning — no sirens — no signal of pending doom. The trucks would arrive and seemingly innocent people were soon herded away. We knew what was happening but were powerless to thwart the vile, shocking, inhumane activity.

To contrast the crude and rough behavior of the Gestapo, when I was on the train or in the subway, I watched my fellow passengers. If there were German officers aboard and the train was full, the officers would rise to offer their seats to a lady when she entered the crowded train.

Even in Father's shop the Germans, as customers, were polite. It was a strange, dichotomous evil that took hold of my country and its inhabitants. But all of what was happening had been predicted by Father, and he became more embittered when he had to deal with the hated oppressors as they came into the shop. Because he spoke fluent German, he could communicate in their language and that produced a strong reaction from our neighbors, who actually labeled Father a *bourgeois* collaborator.

I, too, became a victim of the highly volatile situation. There was a group of boys in Le Vesinet from families that were Communist sympathizers. One day I was riding my bicycle through the village when I saw four of these young toughs on their racing bikes coming toward me. I turned and tried to out-run them by riding down the narrow winding streets, but their bikes were faster than mine and the bullies cornered and jumped me. I was in pretty damned good physical shape, having received excellent training and conditioning when I was involved in the pre-army training school in Rueil. The school, called the Caserne, was designed as a boot camp where every weekend some boys from well-to-do families in Le Vesinet would pile into a car and attend the tough army training classes. We were taught sharp-shooting as well as boxing because it had to do with reflexes in the use of the bayonet.

When the toughs jumped me, they got a surprise. I landed some significant blows in the battle, but I still took a good beating.

The same ambush-type activity targeted toward me took place on another occasion in addition to rocks thrown through the market window. Even our delivery van sustained damage with tires slashed and a heavy metal implement run down the side of our car creating a deep, ugly gash. The incidents were in retaliation for our opposition to the Germans or to strong feelings by locals who felt Father was a collaborator when he seemingly pandered to the German officers' requests. Actually, he obviously despised the Nazi bastards, but could not express his total and complete contempt without risk of being shot.

It became increasingly dangerous for us to remain in Le Vesinet with so many enemies on our doorstep every day. Father decided that we must change our living situation to escape the dangers and to leave the stormy political climate that existed in and around Paris. He was totally frustrated, but more than that, fearful that I would be picked up by the Germans and pressed into slave labor, never to be seen again. His fear drove us from Le Vesinet.

8

LEAVING LE VESINET
Départ du Vesinet

I accompanied Father on two occasions to Brittany. His plan was to reacquaint himself with the area of his early years. Clementine, his widowed and recently retired sister, lived in a beautiful home near Rennes. The house set atop a cliff overlooking a valley with broad vistas that, on a clear day, took in 20 miles of rolling countryside. His idea was to find a country home away from Le Vesinet where we could safely reside until the Occupation ended and conditions for living again in the Paris suburb improved.

Aunt Clementine had lived outside Paris after a rather interesting career in the city. She was raised in the large city and attended nursing school. She married a wealthy man who made it possible for her to open a clinic engaged in a specialized field of medicine, to care for pregnant women. The clinic, situated in Auteuil, in the Sixteenth Arrondissement, the finest residential area of Paris, was equipped and staffed to house Aunt Clementine's patients to stay for the duration of their pregnancy.

The mansion, situated off the main street, had lush shrubbery in front and a carefully attended entrance which did not attract attention or stand out as being different in any way from the other mansions in the exclusive neighborhood. My aunt's clients, ladies from very wealthy families, were pregnant out of wedlock or for whatever other reason did not want their conditions known to family or friends. They disappeared from their homes under the guise of going on "vacation" or an "extended trip" to spend months in the clinic. They became well-acquainted with my aunt and her staff where fine service and care were administered for a very substantial fee.

From time to time, I went into the city from Le Vesinet to visit Aunt Clementine and to work at the clinic doing maintenance work and whatever labor was necessary. On one visit, I was busy scrubbing down the spiral stairs that led to the third floor when I heard screams coming from one of the bedrooms above. I was startled by the commotion in what was usually a quiet, serene atmosphere and headed up the stairs to find my aunt and a young nurse beside the bed of a patient who had given birth five days earlier and who had just died of an apparent heart attack. In those days it was common after giving birth to remain in bed for two weeks. It was not so common for the patient to die.

I was shocked. I had never seen a dead person or witnessed the degree of emotions displayed by my aunt and the nurse who was hysterical. I had no idea of the seriousness of the event except to feel shock as I looked, wide-eyed, at the still body in bed. Aunt Clementine and the nurse were reacting to the sudden death, but they also knew fully what was ahead in having to inform the family of the deceased and to contact the French authorities who would order an inquiry within 24 hours.

I never did know the outcome of the unfortunate occurrence, but apparently it did not deter Aunt Clementine from remaining in the business of providing fine care for women in trouble for a number of years after the incident. She became wealthy in her own right as a result of the exclusive service rendered. When she retired and then was widowed, left with a large inheritance, she sold the mansion and moved to Brittany. There she purchased the country house and a farm which she did not operate herself, but owned on the basis of receiving 50 percent of any profits derived from the enterprise.

In driving through the surrounding countryside, Father found property fragmented into three parcels near the small village of Fegreac. One piece of the property, about 20 acres, was located a mile from the ten-acre parcel that held the main house, and another parcel, also about 20 acres, held an apple orchard. The stone house with stucco finish stood two stories above a huge basement and had a slate roof over an equally large attic. Situated on one of two hills, the view spread across rolling country to the charming village of Fegreac, the steeple of the 800-year-old church standing prominently in the center. It was a spectacular setting, like a fine landscape painting.

When Father made the decision to buy the properties, offered to be sold together, he dealt with the owner, a local businessman. My father told the man that it would be a cash sale. The monetary situation in France was in a state of flux due to much uncertainty about the value of money in circulation. The owner requested he be paid in gold.

My father said, "What about 50 percent gold and 50 percent cash?"

That was an acceptable offer to the seller. What surprised and impressed me about the transaction was the gold. I had no idea that Father had so much gold. Apparently many French people at that time held gold somewhere in reserve, stockpiling it in preparation for the unstable currency situation that prevailed with the threatened invasion and corruption in government prior to the Occupation.

9

ESCAPE TO FEGREAC
L'Echappement vers Fegreac

As we left Le Vesinet for Brittany, the weather was as bleak as it had been on each of the prior trips. The weather seemed to mirror the circumstances, gloomy and threatening with many strong and diverse political factions clouding the skies over France. And there was great imminent danger. As a young man, in excellent physical condition, I was a prime target and particularly vulnerable. The Germans were picking up young people to press into slave labor. We hoped the situation would not be as volatile as we headed away from Paris and Le Vesinet into the Provinces.

My reaction to leaving Le Vesinet was resignation in knowing there was no safe place for me in the village where I had grown to manhood. The Germans were suspicious of young people who threatened their effectiveness by going underground and forming resistance groups. In addition, there was the very real possibility of being picked up and sent off to Germany where most of the healthy and strong young Germans had been pressed into military service. This created a dangerous paucity in the labor market to perform the many skilled and labor-intensive military support jobs and to work on the farms in the Fatherland.

Although the channels of communication had been cut and were soon monitored and supervised by the invaders, we knew from past history that the methods of cruel and inhumane treatment assuredly followed each incursion into a foreign country. Then we began to witness firsthand all that had been threatened. Everything that had occurred in Poland and the Netherlands, Belgium, and Luxembourg was happening in France. Thus my father felt pressured to hide me in order to save my life. I left Le Vesinet still self-assured and with a feeling of naïve invincibility; but as time went by, I knew that his fears were well-founded.

Father turned the meat business over to a manager, Mr. Oliveaux, a fine, hard-working man in his mid-thirties, and his wife. Father, in the meantime did not remain idle. He became actively involved in several business ventures. He had the apple orchard and an established delivery business that he purchased from the man who also sold him the property outside Fegreac. The new business included a delivery van and routes that had been established in Fegreac and throughout the neighboring isolated villages. He delivered produce as well as material for clothing. I helped Father work the route for a short period of time but soon realized that I had to maintain a low profile. I was not interested in either the grocery business or farming or for that matter, the meat market back in Le Vesinet. My interests were hunting, working with animals, and enjoying beautiful women, all of which would become controversial involvements in the future. However, my skills at hunting would serve me well very soon.

Les Bossettes (small hills) was the name of the farm. My father retained the services of one of his brothers who was retired from his work in Paris and had escaped the city when the Germans invaded. Uncle Gauthier and his wife had fled to Brittany, and Father provided a small house on the property for them.

My uncle was a handsome man with wavy white hair, and I recall he always had a cigarette in his mouth. He became engaged in caring for the three-acre garden behind the house, which was planted in many varieties of vegetables. He also cared for the apple orchard, which required an enormous amount of time pruning and harvesting the crop and making cider. Uncle Gauthier also performed maintenance chores on the main house. His presence was a comfort to my father and mother at a very difficult time in all their lives, and his labor freed Father to deliver his route.

The route became increasingly difficult to maintain with fuel rationing. The Germans cut off access to gasoline to civilians except for the known collaborators. The delivery business was temporarily discontinued until Father geared up with a newly developed system called gasogene. A heavy boiler was installed and welded onto the vehicle and was fueled by burning green wood. The boiler was connected to the power block. The bulky power source must have weighed a thousand pounds with a supply of wood a permanent part of the load to stoke the boiler every 20 miles.

The system resembled a locomotive. All gas-driven civilian vehicles were similarly converted with the result that traffic was slowed tremendously as the weighed-down conveyances lumbered along the narrow country lanes.

Father's new business put him in contact with the local residents as well as the French governing officials. His new associations did not ameliorate his fears for my safety. He soon realized the volatile political climate existed in the small village of Fegreac, just as in Le Vesinet. There was no escape. And there was no way anyone could remain neutral. We were again surrounded by many factions. We had to choose our friends wisely. The intense fear that we felt permeated all areas of society.

The Germans had taken over most businesses and imposed strict rules on farming whereby all growing and distribution of produce was regulated, and all butchering of animals done in controlled and guarded circumstances. If there was any activity discovered, deemed illegal by the occupational authorities, hostages were taken. Those people found guilty simply disappeared. The level of fear and mistrust prevailed at every turn.

The possession of firearms was illegal and guns of every description were to be turned over to the authorities. Anyone found with a gun or weapon was taken out and shot on the spot. Or, if an example was to be made, the "criminals" were tortured at the hands of the Gestapo for information prior to deportation or death.

The methods of torture were cruel, with hanging the most common. Hanging was often by the tongue using two small bicycle-type cables attached to the small organ which nearly always required amputation if the victim survived. Electric shock was also used in addition to forced lack of sleep for days by poking the victim and disrupting any and all attempt to slumber. The Gestapo were feared and hated for the many atrocities being perpetrated against good, hard-working people who felt the heavy hand of oppression and total dominance.

In spite of the extreme danger, I made several trips back to Le Vesinet. The shortages of food caused by strict rationing necessitated subterfuge and created increased value on certain commodities. Butter was as valuable as gold. I was able to get butter from Aunt Clementine's farm. Then I would pack a suitcase with the precious cargo to take to my friends. I particularly missed seeing Paul and Maguy and participating in the wonderful adventures at the training compound.

When I left on the clandestine journeys from Fegreac with my cache of butter, I had no idea which trains would be searched. I had developed a pretty good intuition and sense of preservation over the years by surviving encounters with dangerous snakes and animals as well as jealous husbands and lovers, and most recently with strafing bombers and political traitors. I attributed my sensitivity to Mother who, while not formally educated, possessed a wonderful awareness, and this would serve me in good stead. If I felt in jeopardy, I jumped off the train one or two stops before Paris to await the next train. It was incredible, but on two such occasions I found out later that my gut reaction did bode well. The train that I exited had been boarded on arrival in Paris where I would have been arrested on the spot with no questions asked, and carried off to be enslaved, or if the Germans had found the butter, I would have been shot.

The Mayor of Fegreac, Mr. DuDresnay, a member of French nobility, was married to a lady of equally noble ancestry. They resided in a beautiful castle outside the village. Mayor DuDresnay, a lean, ascetic man, was trilingual. His wife spoke German fluently, and by their speech and their manner, it was clearly evident they were in favor of the collaboration.

One day my father returned home after having a serious discussion with the Mayor and came to me, extremely upset. Also in Mother's presence he declared that he, "Would not, under any circumstances, permit Robert to report with two blankets and a suitcase to City Hall to please Mr. DuDresnay!" We had already been informed that at least 25 young people from the area had been solicited to report, not under threatening conditions, but under the guise of performing "volunteer" duties, and every one of them had disappeared. Father was feeling the pressures of the danger in the small provincial village, so peaceful in its pastoral setting, but so volatile in its politics.

There was a strong resistance group, the French Underground,

Hunting became my occupation.

living in the huge forest of Rennes. I was approached by kids my own age to join the group, but I knew that 90 percent of the Resistance members were Communists. Their politics did not bode well with my father's extreme conservative loyalties, which had influenced my ideological choices as well. The Resistance was well-armed and, of course, Father was well-acquainted with the risks involved in bearing arms. Whenever the collaborators flushed any members of the Resistance out of hiding, they were quick to torture or execute or both. There were many extreme examples set to deter any activity which was counter the new regime.

I became acquainted through Mayor DuDresnay with another nobleman, a Mr. DePioger, owner of a small estate where he raised dogs to perform his great passion — hunting. He owned about 15 small fox terrier-type dogs, and asked if I would assist him with his dogs, recognizing that I had a great deal of exposure to animal training. Mr. DePioger was actively engaged during the winter months in the business of going, upon request, to various estates with his dogs as a guest for several days to hunt and catch the foxes and badgers that were ravaging the gardens and marauding the hen-houses. Mr. DePioger enjoyed the hunt enormously, and as his assistant, introduced me to other members of the local nobility.

I began, on the side, raising a few dogs of my own and soon after my initial introduction, was invited, along with my dogs and my own assistant, to perform the hunting service in place of Mr. DePioger. Apparently there was clannishness and jealousy in the upper echelons of the nobility, and I was flattered to be given such an honor. When Mr. DePioger became aware of my incursions into his special domain, he was incensed. The focus became increasingly dangerous for me.

During this time I began raising ferrets as well as the dogs. Keeping firearms was absolutely illegal and hunting was also strictly monitored, so the animals became a valuable asset to perform the illicit activity. I was also preparing for a time when I might have to sustain myself away from the protective cover of my parents' home. A daily reminder came in the newspaper, a list printed in very small type giving the names and ages of French hostages who had been executed the day before for violating any martial law or in retaliation for German soldiers killed. There were many reported incidents of Germans being stabbed in the back in Paris — ambushed — and then the automatic gathering of hostages to be summarily executed. Each day revealed the gruesome details of the pending, constant danger.

But in spite of the danger, I raised the ferrets in my parents' basement. I had a breeding pair and soon, the prolific animals produced enough offspring to sell at a very good profit. I raised albino ferrets with pink eyes and brown ferrets that looked like minks. The small furry animals had been raised and used for hundreds of years in France for the purpose of hunting rabbits.

The European rabbits became a vital source of food in the meat-rationed economy, and the successful hunting of rabbits depended on the dexterity of the ferrets. The rabbits lived in extensive underground colonies. I would find the exit holes and block them with nets which were supported by two pieces of wood stuck securely into the ground. When the ferrets were turned loose in the dark passages, they chased the rabbits that in turn, came speeding out of their holes into the nets, which closed down around them. I quickly grabbed the rabbits, rolled up and struggling as they became enmeshed in the netting, and put them in a sack.

At one of the hunting gatherings, I was introduced to another nobleman, a Mr. DuPlessis. I became friendly with the pro-German gentleman who admired my abilities with the dogs and with the hunt, and who was also well aware of my tenuous circumstances. In spite of his political posture, he demonstrated compassion and seemed to want to secure my situation so that I would not be picked up and sent to Germany. He explained that if I took a job in the slaughterhouse in St.Gildas, near Abessac, a village 20 miles from Fegreac, I would be safe at least for the time being. I discussed the offer with my parents. We all agreed it seemed like a positive move.

A priority of the German Occupation was to take over and regulate the slaughtering of animals. No slaughtering was to be done by any individual farmer. All cattle to be slaughtered were sold at auction under strict, controlled supervision of the Germans. A small portion of the animals remained in France — the bulk of the cattle was shipped live to Paris to be slaughtered and then shipped on to Germany. This created a short supply of meat and meat by-products in France, which in turn guaranteed a continuing market for my animals to satisfy. But the activity was no longer safe, and I was forced to leave the hunt to work in St. Gildas.

My new position placed me in direct contact with the oppressors. The slaughterhouse in St. Gildas was small as compared to the La Villette. However, there was too much that was the same, and in my new position I became an active member of the slaughter team. I had been repulsed and traumatized by the blood, gore, and violence of the industry as witnessed in my youth. In my need to survive, I would see it from a different view, and it would serve to protect me from the enemy, at least for the present. At the smaller facility the concrete floor and walls contained a corridor from the receiving and holding pens that led to shoots that ran to the killing floor. I was one of five young men working the bloody floor.

There was a Gypsy in our ranks, which was most unusual in itself. The Germans held the Gypsies in such enmity as their pattern of living was uncontrollable and threatening to the Occupation. The Gypsies moved from place to place, setting up their tents, the women reading fortunes, and the men robbing everything in sight. In addition, the Gypsies had their own language, foreign to the Germans and the French. Since the unscrupulous vagabonds were targeted along with the Jews for extermination, it was shocking to have one working alongside me. I was immediately impressed with the handsome, powerful young man. He was the most perfect male specimen that I had ever seen. He was reminiscent of Hercules in his musculature, which had not come to him by lifting weights. He was magnificently built and a hard worker, which helped secure his temporary safety in the industry so vital to the German cause.

As the animals came down the shoot one by one onto the processing floor, they were attached, each to a ring mounted in the concrete floor, where one person, using a *merlin*, wielded the pointed side of the heavy sledgehammer through the skull of the cow to penetrate the bone and the brain, instantly killing the animal. I had witnessed the procedure from afar at La Villette where my job was to sort through the animal parts to find perfect *yo-yos* for our customers in the market in Le Vesinet. Now I was directly involved in the gruesome, bloody murdering process as it protected me from being slaughtered. What a hellish, diabolical turn! I had no choice but to continue seeking shelter as the nightmare continued.

Immediately after the animal fell to the floor, the carcass, turned upside down by a winch, was skinned by two men then hoisted up, quartered, and the fat carefully removed. All of the procedure was closely watched and scrutinized as the fat was then placed in steel barrels. Beef fat was used for cooking, but also by the Germans to make soap and as a lubricating oil for their weapons. The meat was a highly valued commodity as well, but the fat was treated as particularly precious and governed under a separate statute. The French also valued the fat as something very rare and desirable since butter was scarce.

As we removed the fat and placed it in the waiting barrel watched by an armed guard, we sought methods for surreptitiously acquiring a portion of the bounty. At the end of the day an inspector in uniform came to check the amount of fat rendered to be weighed and then sealed in the barrel. We waited until the sentry left briefly during the day for a trip to the bathroom, to secret a large chunk of the solid fat which we quickly hid under the animal's skin on the floor. We often worked 18 hours a day at this labor. It was dark when our work was done, the barrels sealed, and the sentry relieved of his duty. At that time in the dark, we would uncover the precious fat, strip off our clothing and encase our bodies in a layer of beef fat. Dressed with winter coats to shield us from the cold for the bicycle trip back to our respective quarters, we were successful in our heist; and the fat protected me for the 20 mile ride from Abessac to Fegreac. Eventually, the Germans detected they were not getting as much fat as they knew was being processed.

One night, as three of us were on our bikes heading for home in the pitch dark, a roadblock suddenly appeared. We each carried a bag containing the steaks that were permitted — one per person. Fortunately, the sentries did not look further than in our bags for the missing fat. We continued the thievery undetected for months. If we had been caught with the fat, we would have been shot on the spot with our bodies displayed as examples of firm measures meted to anyone who broke the strictures of the governing bastards who were merciless in their on-going endeavor to rout and expose any resistance to authority.

I worked in the slaughterhouse for months until one day when I was at home in Fegreac. I was upstairs when I saw in the distance flatbed trucks on the road heading from the village to our home. As the trucks drew closer, I saw the occupants clearly enough to know that I must hide. There were many young armed men. I left the house through the back door and sought shelter in the woods behind the garden, fortunately undetected by the members of the Resistance who forced their way into the house. I learned later they backed Father against the wall in the living room at machine-gun point. The demand was made: "Where is Robert? Where is your son?"

Father replied, "I don't know. He left yesterday!"

The spokesman further demanded, "Where did he go?"

"I have no idea. We had an argument and the kid took off." The toughs proceeded to search the house from top to bottom, leaving not a single room or potential hiding place unscrutinized before retreating to their trucks and leaving the property. If I had hidden in the attic, which was my initial impulse to their sudden intrusion, I would have been found and taken away. My intuition again saved my life.

I stayed in the woods and moved away from our property to a

The dogs were fine companions in the forest.

small farm about ten or 15 miles from our home. I stayed at the farm, where some of my young companions lived, for two days. Then I returned to my parents' home. The way the house was situated was ideal for sneaking in and out undetected. The house faced the village with the back acreage planted in a huge garden abutting the forest. I could approach the house from the forest, run through the garden where a hedgerow provided excellent shelter, and enter the house from the rear.

There were two other boys, whose parents were farmers, who did not want to join the Resistance, totally controlled by the Communists, and who did not support the local government of the collaborators. We formed our own intimate neutral group. I realized that my time at home was running out with the threat of more unannounced invasive searches by the enemy. I had to put me and my parents out of danger, free them of the harassment. I had to go into hiding. I left the house, joined by my two compatriots and three dogs, to live in the forest. I did not know if or when I would return.

10

LIFE IN THE FOREST
La Survie en Forêt

Having made the decision to leave home, I was determined that I would not be caught by the Germans nor by the Resistance. Father was not totally supportive of my leaving, but he fully realized the dangers inherent in my remaining in the house as long as the Germans and their puppets were in control.

Before the Germans invaded France, there was much corruption in the Government. This only produced in many French citizens the hope that the German take-over would eliminate the festering criminality and actually improve the political situation. This, along with the centuries-old antipathy towards England, only served to solidify the French collaboration. And then there were the Communist-controlled resistance groups and the underground, anti-German forces all totally fanatical in their own right. Our enemies wore many hats with everyone suspect.

Mother was worried sick about my leaving. As long as I would escape for a day or two and then return, she was secure in knowing that I was still alive. When I left to hide out for an unspecified period of time, she was gravely concerned, and rightfully so, that I might never again return.

The forest behind our house was large and dense. It must have been 300 or 400 acres. It would become home to me and my companions who shared my fear of the governing forces as well as the Resistance forces — both of whom wanted very much to capture us for their own, albeit differing, purposes.

We faced having to live off the land except for forays onto

neighboring farms from time to time to obtain butter, so rare and coveted, and eggs, fruit, and vegetables. We carried no guns due to the noise element that would gain undesired attention and possible exposure. Hunting animals was important for our sustenance, and my past experience came into play as we set snares to trap the many animals that lived in the forest.

We stuck together most of the time, and each had duties to perform. One was responsible for lighting the fire for cooking. We used very dry wood so that there would be a minimum of smoke. Someone was always the lookout. We had to remain alert at all times and plan every move. There were spotter planes that flew low over the forest looking for smoke, the sign of a pocket of resistance to be flushed out.

Red squirrels, rabbits, and even red foxes were our prime source of meat. With the help of the dogs, I eventually caught over 300 European badgers.

As time went on, we risked an occasional visit home. My compatriots would stay with the dogs when it was my turn to leave, and I would carefully work my way through the woods to see if the way was clear. As I moved stealthily through the garden behind the hedge rows and right to the back of the house during the day or night, I was able to arrive and leave with certain impunity. My clandestine visits of an hour served to reassure my parents, fearful for their son's survival. They told me the first time I arrived without warning, that the Resistance members had returned several times to barge unannounced into the house to look for me. I knew that I could not remain for more than an hour. I returned to the forest with butter and other food-stuffs and the knowledge that my parents, at least for the time, knew that I was well. I stowed a bike at the edge of the woods, well-concealed, to provide a welcome conveyance if the need arose.

We moved from place to place, never wanting to set any pattern or establish any permanent campsite. If the weather was very cold, we occasionally stopped at a friendly farm and sought permission to stay in the shelter and warmth of the hay loft in the barn. We never stayed for more than a night, but enjoyed the luxury of the indoor shelter. If we were particularly fortunate, we ate hot food prepared in the farmhouse by compassionate hosts who risked their lives by harboring criminals.

One day when the weather was particularly cold, we built a fire, then soon heard the sound of an airplane. We quickly put out the fire and worked our way through the thick woods to a hill for a better view of the surrounding terrain. We saw many trails, some of which led to a major highway about two miles distant from our location. Suddenly, we saw German trucks mobilizing in a surrounding maneuver to seal off the area. Watching just long enough to see the troops jump from the vehicles, we knew that only our quick retreat and knowledge of the forest would save us. The Germans used trained dogs to sniff out scents that made hiding extremely difficult. We took to a stream to break the scent. While this very same activity occurred frequently during the two years we remained in the forest, our little dogs, our trusted companions, were always with us and never barked once while the enemy was in pursuit. They performed obediently and effectively in helping us survive.

One of the dogs was a crossbred Airedale, a barkless dog. One of the terriers was a very small animal particularly useful in entering the dens of the baby foxes. The forest was infested with European hares which were a prime target in the hunt. Our method, learned years before as I watched my uncles, was to place nearly a hundred snares in a ring around an area about two miles in diameter. The snares were comprised of a loop made of copper wire twisted very delicately into a hanging knot. The snares had to be smoked to eliminate all human scent. We hung hundreds of the twisted copper snares over a smoking fire made of wet leaves. Left for more than an hour, we removed them after rubbing our hands in mint or some other strong-smelling grass, and then attached the snares to heavy string. Then they were attached to a flexible limb, so that when the animal hit the well-designed trap, it bounced back over the animal's head, neck or foot, the noose closing over the struggling, screaming animal setting the snare.

After we had the area surrounded with the small sturdy traps, we led the Airedale out, especially when the moon was full, to better see our prey. After releasing the dog in the middle of the trapped area, he began his performance of sniffing out the hare. He did not bark but made a sound like a fox as he searched out the scent of the furry animals and then drove them, frantically seeking escape, into one of our traps. It was a tricky maneuver because if improperly set, the snares were useless.

We managed to catch many hares to sustain ourselves and also to give to farmers in exchange for the use of their barns or as barter for cider, vegetables, and fruit. Our bounty was welcome at a time when the farmers, living in fear of harsh disciplinary measures being applied for any misdemeanors, could not perform their lifelong natural pursuit of hunting. When we visited a friendly farm where a hot meal of soup was so deliciously and appreciatively received, we gladly offered a few hares, a fox, or a bird to demonstrate our gratitude before leaving the shelter in the hope that our presence would not be detected. Our hosts, realizing the dangers, were desperate for the food we offered in return.

My clothing was simple. I carried a couple of pieces of protective clothes and wore boots. The chosen lifestyle was tough as we ranged through the woods, never settling in any one place for long. I was particularly surprised one day when we came upon a cache of British uniforms and boots that had been dropped by British paratroopers. It appeared as though the British were dropping the clothing to help support the Resistance. I was excited to get a pair of the black combat boots and lost little time placing them on my feet. But I soon realized the boots were not an asset. They gave evidence to my being a part of the Resistance if I was ever picked up on the rare occasions when I rode my bike outside the forest.

I did not venture forth often, but when I did I made certain that I carried a substantial bag of produce which gave validity to my mission. The Germans looked the other way if I innocently appeared to be involved in delivering a package. On the other hand, if I was ever caught walking without a parcel, I would definitely risk being picked up. It was better to remain in hiding.

We came upon other Resistance members from time to time as we moved through the forest. Whenever we met with any of the other forest dwellers, they tried to feed us their own particular brand of propaganda to get us to join up. Most of those we met were Communists. They had a convincing argument when they implied that it was totally unpatriotic for us to remain neutral when our country had been invaded. They also argued, when we had lost one of our compatriots who chose to return to his home, that two of us trying to survive would be far more successful and more secure if we banded together with their forces. However, I felt quite differently. I knew that two of us with the dogs were less encumbered and could move more quickly to avoid contact with any unfriendly groups and to escape the frequent German searches.

One day, miles from any roads or trails, deeply set in the middle of the forest, we came upon old stone foundations indicating habitation at one time many, many years prior to our discovery. There was an old hermit living in a small hut in the middle of the ruins. We found him cooking over a fire in the crudely furnished hut. There was a piece of furniture that stood apart and made such a strong impression on me. Sitting in the middle of the living area was a solid block of granite with concave areas set in the top to hold food. It was prehistoric, perhaps dating back to the Druids who knew only the barest necessities. The old man was hospitable and offered to share with us the hare that he was cooking. I am certain we were not the first humans who had come across the isolated hut, but he would not have many visitors. He seemed anxious to have us share his largesse as we dined at the old table, encrusted with food residue that had been worked into the cracks by centuries of use.

On one trip to my parents, I met a very beautiful girl named Simone living near Fegreac with her parents who were refugees from St. Nazaire. The Germans had set up U-boat manufacturing and a base in St. Nazaire, which became a target for British air raids to eradicate the dreaded submarines that so effectively cut off British supply boats. The constant bombing of the port city left it an empty shell. Its inhabitants sought shelter inland. When I first saw Simone, I was captivated by her beauty and her innocence. I had little time to spend with her, but whenever I returned from the forest for my brief, clandestine interludes at home, I always tried to visit with her.

After several unplanned meetings which had been friendly opportunities to indulge in thoughts and emotional reactions to what was happening all around us, I realized that my thoughts while away from her were only of her. I knew that I desired to be with her as often as possible. She was a virgin and I was feeling nearly celibate since my trips to Le Vesinet were a thing of the past with Maguy and love-making only a palpable, lovely dream.

I would meet Simone at a designated location. When my

parents became aware of my latest liaison, they were incensed. They knew Simone's parents were Communists and felt that I was compromising my ethics as well as my safety in such a relationship. At the same time, Simone's father was adamantly opposed to our meetings. He did not want his daughter seeing the son of a Fascist. I could not deny his allegation. Following the First World War, a political party was formed under the leadership of Colonel LaRoque whose politics were extreme right. I remember, as a young boy in Le Vesinet, attending some of the party gatherings along with Father, who wore the party insignia and took on all the tenets laid down by the ultraconservative, right-wing party. Simone's father was so violently opposed to me that while arguing with her not to have any further contact with me, he struck her in the face. I saw the marks left and was shocked and embittered by the assault, which was an attempt to curtail our continuing relationship.

In spite of parental abhorrence, we became more closely bonded and more determined to continue the rendezvous plans whenever I felt I could safely move from the protective cover of the forest. I would sneak from the woods about four or five miles south of my parents' place. Simone, too, would ride her bike to the special place atop a hill with woods on either side.

One day I arrived at the appointed place at the agreed upon time, but did not see Simone who, ordinarily, would be waiting. I pulled my bike aside, sitting on it to wait, when suddenly, her father burst out of the covering behind me. He had studied our meeting pattern. Without a word, he jumped, knocking me from the bike, and landed heavily on top. He was a large powerful man, about six-foot-two and in his mid-forties, but I struggled mightily and freed myself from his grasp, then turned on him in a vicious attack. I punched his body with strong, rapid blows to his midsection.

I was furious to think of what he had done to Simone. When I tired, I left him on the ground, stunned. I grabbed his bike, smashed it against a tree, and angrily threatened, "This way you are not going to be able to follow me or follow Simone." And with that I took off on my bike. It was a brutal encounter which fully indicated the depth of hatred he felt for me and I for him. However, I saw Simone again in a week, and we made a decision to meet under different circumstances. We were falling in love and to keep us apart would not be possible as long as there was life in me.

She lived with her parents in a house on the edge of a highway not far from Fegreac. There was a wooded area near the house on the same side where her bedroom was located. The ground sloped up and away from the house, which gave access from the woods to her window on the second floor. As I stood on the hill, about 200 feet from the house, I could communicate with her by sign language. Through this new method, we signaled where we would meet later that day. We kept changing our rendezvous locations.

As I approached the hill one day, close to the house to wait for her shutters to open and our message to be conveyed, I saw her father sitting where I would ordinarily stand. Fortunately, he did not see me as I silently approached from the cover of the woods, moving like an Indian as I had been so well-trained years before by my uncles. I was able to withdraw undetected. It was a result of my training to watch every step for twigs that could break or anything else that would make the least sound. He had a shotgun and I'm certain he wasn't hunting rabbit. I slowly reversed my steps and escaped but did not stay away from Simone.

It seemed the more adamant my parents became against the liaison, the stronger I felt for the beautiful young lady with the long flowing hair and the beautiful, angelic face. She, too, reacted to her father's violent disapproval with a deepening devotion toward me. We still had not consummated our relationship. Our times together had been so brief, and I knew she was innocent. I did not want to violate her trust or her love for me until she wanted me fully. We had flirted and touched one another, embraced and kissed which aroused me, but I managed to suppress my physical desire. One day when we met, I knew that the time had come when we would make love.

We were in the woods. It was quiet, free of sound or activity as we began embracing one another. I was mindful that she was without experience in the intimacy of what was to come. I had been well-taught and tenderly introduced to my first intercourse by La Esmaralda. I, too, wanted very much to be tender, caring, and sensitive to the beautiful young lady when she asked if I would take her for the first time. I had learned well how to stroke and guide her into an all-encompassing embrace to fulfill the depth of our yearnings. It was a very beautiful interlude with her body moving against mine so strongly and then the deep satisfaction we both felt as we lay together breathless with pleasure. I left Simone that day filled with beautiful thoughts of what had been and in anticipation of future love-making. I did return often to meet with her and to be fully with her. But soon I would have to leave Simone and the forest to find some other place to hide from the ever-present enemies.

The months of living and hiding in the forest, with brief visits to my parents and wonderful but too-brief encounters with Simone, lasted nearly two years. I never knew when I might be discovered and taken away by the Germans. There were increasing incidents as the Germans began to send truck loads of paratroopers into the forest to search out encampments of the underground groups that shared our densely wooded shelter. We came upon an area where maybe 25 or 30 members of a resistance group had set up camp. It was a mistake to put down any sort of permanent encampment.

If discovered, the Germans shot on the spot any members who were found and then would hunt down any escapees. We didn't actually see any bodies of the victims left at the campsites as we were not about to wait around when imminent attack was threatened and we knew better than to return to the scene any time soon. The Germans either took prisoners to demonstrate their methods of discipline to the local townspeople, or they left bullet-ridden or tortured bodies to be used as bait to further entrap any surviving members who might return late at night to retrieve their lost comrades. The brutality of punishment became greater with sometimes 300 or 400 German troops storming through an area. Even the French *gendarme* were engaged in flushing out the Resistance.

As the intrusive searches became more frequent and more intense, a decision had to be made to further protect my family. It became absolutely imperative I not be found. No longer were the Resistance members rounded up for slave labor. They were taken to a Gestapo Center and tortured. Then the families were arrested and also tortured and murdered. With examples of horror increasing, I had to leave the forest and leave Fegreac. When I spoke to my parents of the perilous situation, it was decided that I should leave Brittany and go to my grandparents' place in Nièvre. Making it across the boundary into the south of France would not be easy, but I had to try.

Saying good-bye to Simone was torture itself. I did not know if I would see her again. We made love for the last time and promised to love one another always.

11

ESCAPE TO MARSEILLES
L'Échappement vers Marseilles

Going to my grandparents' farm would only place them in the very same danger my parents faced with searches, threats, and even imprisonment or death for harboring a refugee. I wondered if there was a safe place for any of us. But I had to leave Fegreac and I had to change my identity to take the onus from my family, in case I was picked up. I obtained forged I.D. papers from a friend in Redon. When departure time came, I rode my bike to catch the train out of Redon, leaving the bike for Father to pick up on one of his delivery trips.

I boarded the train for the first leg of the journey to cross the boundary and seek refuge in the south of France — the "Free Zone." I did not stand out conspicuously as I traveled alone. There were young people traveling from place to place, laborers employed in factories or businesses under German control engaged in the war effort. But there was always the danger of being searched or questioned with most trains boarded and all passengers forced to produce proper identification. My papers were good as long as I remained in the occupied areas, but in order to cross the boundary I would have to possess a *Laissez-passer* (a passport) granted only to those persons politically loyal to the new regime or people in authority. I had some comfort in knowing that if stopped and my identification papers checked, by traveling under an alias, my parents and family would at least be protected. I was totally on my own with no place to go except forward, never knowing what the next stop held. However, tragically, I was not alone. There were refugees of all ages attempting to escape the *merlin,* the axe hanging perilously overhead, like cattle in the shoots at the La Villette frantically running toward the unknown in a frenzied search for freedom.

I was in contact with members of my family in Paris who did nothing to reassure me. The situation in the city had become increasingly dangerous with the Germans feeling the pressure of the strengthening Allied Forces. I caught the train out of Paris determined to reach Marseilles. I purchased a ticket to Moulins just north of the border. There was no choice as the ticket agent could not sell me a ticket to cross the boundary without proper identification.

The trains in those days were comprised of three classes: first, second, and third. There was a walkway alongside the compartments, and each compartment had sliding doors with glass windows giving visual access to the separate passenger areas. I purchased the least expensive ticket for third class and then proceeded to walk the length of the train to find a place where I could settle safely for the trip south. I saw in one car, in first class, a lady alone in a compartment with books on the seat surrounding her. She was a distinguished, fine-looking woman, perhaps in her sixties, and I decided that her compartment would also be my compartment. I stood outside the door as the train began moving. With my back to the compartment, I looked at the passing panorama as city became suburbs, then country landscape, and the train picked up speed in its southerly journey toward Moulins and hopefully Marseilles.

Each car on the train had a bathroom and I realized that my "companion" would eventually leave the compartment to use the facility at the end of the car. At that time I would make my move. As expected, she did get up to leave the compartment, designed to seat eight passengers, and I quickly slid into the first-class accommodation and crawled underneath the seat covered with books. I was soon very tightly encased looking out at the grey material that covered the seat above. The area was not designed to conceal a body and was cramped, but it had the benefit of a heater which felt good initially against the cold.

Soon the lady returned to take her seat and resumed reading, never noticing that she had a companion in the compartment. The train was not crowded as it proceeded, making several stops on the journey south. I remained perfectly still for several hours looking at the lady's ankles. The space that contained me was no more than 18 inches deep, which quickly became a small, hot torture chamber that compressed and prohibited movement. I did not dare even a heavy breath for fear of being detected.

After stops for the boarding and exiting of passengers, we pulled into the station at Moulins. The train was boarded by the French Station Master along with a member of the Gestapo, a German officer, and two German soldiers. The inspection brigade walked from one car to another, one compartment to another as they demanded to see each passenger's I.D. I could hear the French being translated into German and vice-versa. All of a sudden, I heard a commotion followed by the heavy steps of the soldiers' boots as they led some passengers out of the train. I was able to sneak a look from under the seat to see the uniformed invaders: a hated Gestapo officer in long black leather overcoat, and another German officer in full dress uniform sporting shiny, long jackboots. I shuddered at the sight of the hated blue-eyed officer in a black leather coat. Witnessing the activity was torturous enough without the existing conditions of being totally contained for three hours, unable to sneeze or cough or move while being roasted by the heater pressing against my body. I felt like a pig on a spit, but the spit was not turning.

Soon the inspectors returned to the compartment adjoining ours, and I heard too clearly the pattern of their inquiry. They questioned the occupants, and while talking I heard what sounded like the German officer running his riding crop under the seats to check that the hidden areas were clear, or if not clear, to search through the cases that may be riding there. I envisioned, with horror, that my cramped journey was about to end in arrest. I was cooked in more ways than one.

My initial reaction was to come out from under the seat and give myself up. Quickly, I reasoned that I was not politically involved with the Resistance and my family was not going to be implicated. Nor was I carrying a weapon or any contraband. Aside from being deported, I felt that I would not be shot for my misdemeanor. But then I decided to remain in hiding and wait to see what occurred when they entered our compartment.

I heard the boots approach, then saw them as the officers stepped into the compartment. The voices communicating in German were met with German responses from my "companion." Soon, in checking the lady's *Laissez-passer* a discrepancy was detected. It seemed her papers had not been stamped by the *Kommandantur* in Paris. The lady was politely requested to accompany the soldiers to the station master's office. As I watched from below, all I could see were boots, then the lady's shoes as she, too, left the compartment. I was expecting that the detainee would be booked for illegal paperwork, but I was wrong. I did not move. She returned to the compartment along with her interrogators who apologized profusely and then left the compartment — without having run the riding crop under any of the seats. It was a miracle! I released a heavy deep breath closing my eyes in utter relief.

I had escaped a very close encounter, which for some horror-filled minutes took my mind off my cramped, hot containment. I continued to be cooked and miserable as I waited nearly an hour for the train to begin moving through the countryside south of Moulins. I could not appreciate its visual beauty, but I felt it and was grateful for every mile, every turn of the wheels as we gained the ultimate destination — Marseilles.

As the train traveled south, I took a very small instant of comfort in realizing that I had crossed the boundary and was in "Free France." However, there was no comfort to be had in my present position. The physical pain of my incarceration became completely intolerable after more than five hours without being able to move except for the blinking of my eyes.

I thought that my compartment companion was asleep when I began slowly and quietly to extricate my charley-horse cramped body from the confines of the narrow berth. I was hoping I could remove myself totally from the compartment without arousing attention. As I crawled from beneath, blackened from the soot of the engine heater that had been accumulating under the seat for perhaps years, I was a frightening visage. The lady was not sleeping soundly enough. One look at me and she screamed uncontrollably. I could not blame her. I was black and compressed from too many hours of immobility as my body twitched and jerkily reacted to muscle spasms.

I knew the train inspector would come to make his rounds,

and I had no alternative but to take my dirty hand and close it over her mouth. I explained that I was not a thief nor was I a criminal, just a young Frenchman leaving the Occupied Territory and that she was perfectly safe with me but to please stop screaming. I managed to convince and calm her before I left to go into a third-class compartment for the remainder of the trip after a brief visit to the lavatory to clean up and stretch my body and legs in blessed relief.

By the time I reached Marseilles, I had the feeling that with the changing military situation of the Allied Forces more strongly threatening and countering the Germans, that the Occupation might not be permanent — that some day France might be returned to the loyal French. It was a feeling to be nurtured and believed in spite of the continuing threats and inhumane treatment that I began to witness even in the so-called Free Zone.

I quickly realized that southern France, under the Vichy Government headed by General Petain was completely controlled by the Germans through the French *gendarme* and the French security force. Every refugee was in the same circumstance trying to hide from slave labor or from being taken hostage. There were daily reports of at least 20 German soldiers killed each day by civilians. Under martial law, the penalty was to round up ten French hostages for every German killed and to shoot them in retaliation. The names of the French victims were then published in the newspaper. My "safe haven" did not appear from the onset to be safe.

Marseilles was an ancient seaport with many old and forbidding areas. I began exploring the city of refuge. One of the first nights after my arrival, I walked in a section with poor lighting. As I worked my way through the cobblestone alleys, I heard a woman's screams in the distance. As I continued, the shrill screams became louder. I noticed movement coming from an alley and suddenly saw a well-dressed man actively engaged in beating a lady. There was much brutality in the way he was slapping her. As I got closer, I became aware that the assailant was well-dressed in a fine, light colored suit and alligator shoes — quite out of character in his behavior and in the rough environs of the depressed area. I closed on the two of them. By this time the man had the lady on the ground. She, too, was nicely attired wearing an evening dress and high-heeled shoes. I approached and tapped the man on the shoulder as he continued the beating. He turned and directed one fist toward me. I reacted defensively, threw a punch, and then we exchanged blows until I suddenly heard a click and knew the familiar sound of a switch-blade. The lighting was poor. I could not see his weapon but knew that I was in trouble as the tall, well-built man seemed braced to attack. I had no weapon. My thoughts went to the military training school where I was trained in the art of jujitsu. I knew the basic defense move and knew that it was my only chance to survive the life-threatening knife. I quickly stepped to the side and then moved alongside my attacker. With lightening speed, I managed to administer a powerful blow to the back of his neck — a karate chop with all my strength. He crumbled, and the knife dropped from his hand. He regained himself and tried to get up. I hit him again and he fell back.

I was about to go after him when I felt sharp blows to my back and the back of my head. In the darkness I could not see who my assailants were, but knew there had to be more than one. The blows were sharp, quick, and painful. When I turned, I discovered that it was the beaten lady attacking me with her high-heeled shoes and screaming, "Stop killing my man!"

Her violent attack left me cut and bleeding, and I quickly left the scene as her accusatory epithets became muffled. I was bewildered by the whole scene. I felt like I was being a white knight, a John Wayne coming to the aid of a woman in distress. I learned a good lesson that night in Marseilles: Never get in the middle of a domestic quarrel, no matter how violent. The lady was perhaps a prostitute and the man her pimp. I left them, bloodied, but wiser.

Marseilles was a teeming city. There were hundreds of young people in the very same circumstance, broken away from family searching for a way to survive the Occupation and the displacement. I struck up an acquaintance with another guy, and we joined forces to seek some sort of work. It was not possible. There were too many of us to be sustained in the overcrowded, glutted city. Starved, we wandered about looking for work and for food.

The two of us were on the outskirts of the city when we saw a tree loaded with cherries. We took turns climbing the tree to harvest the crop to fill our empty bellies. When we had eaten all that we could, we left the tree and began to walk back toward the city. Two French *gendarmes* riding bicycles materialized and stopped to question us. We were not carrying anything, not even evidence of our cherry heist. But our rape of the fruit must have gained the attention of the farmer who reported the incident.

We were arrested and taken into custody to be jailed. The jail was not unpleasant nor unclean, but we were not there long before a representative of the Vichy government-sponsored youth camp came to pick us up. Our next incarceration was a camp compound, a designated holding area for young people ages 16 to 20, where we became a part of the military routine of daily flag raising to honor our savior General Petain as we were forced to sing, "*Maréchal nous voilà tes enfants devant toi le sauveur de la France.*"

We listened to rhetoric expressing the hope that the new regime would "put an end to the corruption of the governments of Western Europe and return discipline to a country that needed it badly." Our duties while in the camp were to go out in groups each day to cut down trees and chop wood. I am certain the ultimate goal was to whip us into shape to be mobilized for active duty. I did not want any part of the forestry activity, and I certainly did not want to take part in the war effort if it was to participate as a member of Petain's military offering. His puppet regime for the Nazi hierarchy had overrun our country and had destroyed every vestige of freedom. I had to formulate yet another escape.

Very soon after being pressed into forestry detail, I managed to have a brief period which was almost like escape, almost a vacation. I was in the forest splitting trees, and accidentally hit myself in the testicles with an ax handle. The blow nearly caused me to pass out — the pain was excruciating. I was not attempting to gain attention and was damned stoic. I bore the intense pain and continued cutting wood. However, after a miserable night of sleeplessness and pain, I could not walk the following day. My testicles were badly swollen, and there was blood in my urine.

The camp infirmary was run by a nurse who just happened to be quite beautiful and who was the mistress to the camp commander. I had to remain in bed in the infirmary with a small piece of plywood propped under my testicles. My penis had to be irrigated which was less than pleasant and even embarrassing. The beautiful nurse administering my treatments compensated, to a degree, for the discomfort and embarrassment. It was extreme luxury to languish in a clean bed, in spite of the pain, and the scenery was damned pleasant.

The camp commander became very upset by the nature of my malaise and the treatments his lady friend administered. He came to the infirmary, and I could feel the hatred in the man as he looked down at me while his lovely friend checked the wood brace and examined my penis. I was tempted to ask him if he wanted to change places with me, but I hesitated to aggravate the situation further. I was in no condition to perform physically any of what he feared. His mistress was quite safe.

After my release from the infirmary, I returned to the forest knowing fully that I did not run away from occupied France to serve General Petain, the Collaborator, and the other pro-German authorities. The camp was not well guarded nor were there fences to keep us in. We had taken an oath of allegiance and signed an agreement to fulfill a commitment to ultimately serve a cause opposed to everything I believed in. Our housing was a farm house near the forest, and I left during the night.

I left with nothing but the clothes on my back — no money and no food. The following day I found another cherry tree and helped myself to the fruit. I was on the run again when I was picked up by a *gendarme* who had a warrant for my arrest based on breaking my oath of allegiance, which was a mockery. I had signed the paper only to secure my situation temporarily. I needed time to plot the next move. My allegiance was not to Petain or to the Vichy Government, but to a truly free France.

I was put in jail in a small village outside Marseilles. The cell was clean, painted white with black bars on the window and the cell door. The *gendarme* brought my food into the cell. I was grateful for the sustenance and for the cleanliness and for the attentiveness of the lady who prepared the food, the wife of one of the *gendarmes*. It became obvious that my captors were not vindictive. They knew that I was not a criminal, just a young person separated from family and running, searching — a victim.

The second day of my imprisonment dawned and breakfast arrived. When it came time for lunch, the lady and a *gendarme* delivered the meal which, under normal circumstances, is a lengthy two-hour break. When they left the cell, I ate the food and then stood to stretch. I walked to the door. When I leaned on the door, it opened. I could not believe what was happening. I looked out and saw no one. Then I ventured further and still saw no one. I was surprised and puzzled for an instant. I did not want to be a jail escapee and actually began looking for the *gendarme* to alert him of the error. Soon I realized that my release was planned. The way was clear for me to escape. I left the jail and the village.

I headed north, away from Marseilles, not really knowing where I was going. I was again arrested by the *gendarme*. There were no questions asked. I was one of many young people wandering in the Free Zone and the orders must have been to pick up all refugees. I was taken to a prison. This time my lockup was not white nor clean. The heavy door clanged securely, locked by a Corsican guard who shoved me menacingly into the dark, dank confines.

The prison, in Aix-en-Provence, about 20 miles north of Marseilles, was like a fortress, a God-awful looking facility that I later learned had been the stables for thousands of horses during the reign of Louis XIV. The walls were six feet thick, and the enclosures within were dark and musty with no windows. There were no toilet facilities except a crude shower arrangement in one corner of the dungeon.

After a routine check, I was thrown in with five other young men, all in their mid-to-late twenties, clean-cut and in good physical condition. I soon learned they were all locals and members of the Communist Party. At that time all Communists were either underground or in jail in both the north and south of my divided country. The guards were Corsicans and obviously full of contempt for any and all Frenchmen. The ingrained hatred, developed over centuries of French rule, burying any hope for Corsican independence, produced treacherous prison guards totally lacking compassion. The food was less than meager; a small tin cup of thin soup for breakfast, another cup of soup with beans at lunch, and the same offering at dinner. It was a horrific subsistence. My cell mates were better cared for with food brought to them by their families. I had no one but the dreaded guards to serve up the watery, foul soup.

I slept on a thin mattress on the concrete floor. The second day I was on the mattress when suddenly two of the guys came out of the shower naked, one of them had an erection, and the two jumped me.

I fought like hell to prevent the rape and was able to kick and struggle free of their grasp when the other cell mates joined in. The intense battle with arms and legs flailing, mine moving against their restraints, created a loud commotion. I fought wildly in my determination to ward off the attack. I know the guard heard the noise, as we fought and groaned and rolled around the cell. There were muffled cries of pain as I managed to land some blows. Finally, I heard the keys clanging in the lock as the door opened and the rapists became subdued. I lay back on my mattress, exhausted.

As the days passed, my assailants left me alone and the days became weeks. Fortunately, their attack came at a time when my strength and stamina were substantial enough to fight them off. It did not take long before my physical condition deteriorated and along with it my morale. Hell could not be worse.

Prior to the dark, stinking stables, I had been busy attempting to stay alive, too busy to feel sorry for myself or to dwell for long on my circumstance. I was on the run to escape from what was behind, driving me toward an unknown goal. I was focused as long as there was a train to catch or a buddy who needed support as we worked together to seek food and shelter, always trying to keep away from the authorities.

Now, as my physical condition weakened, all that I tried to keep in focus became blurred. I was in a vile prison with the threat of fellow prisoners attempting to violate me. There was no where to run, no escape, parents so far away, no friends, and no food. I became totally depressed as I witnessed other prisoners, corpses in emaciated skeletal condition, bodies exposed, on flat pieces of wood, carried by other prisoners. I began to think that I, too, would be removed from the ancient stable to be dumped as a body unidentified and unclaimed. No Catholic burial in the well-maintained cemetery. No last rites. No ritual. No honor. Simply an emaciated form dumped with other emaciated forms into a random heap of waste. I was pathetic and had given up any hope for survival when all of a sudden an angel came into my life.

There was a system in Aix-en-Provence whereby a social worker came into the prison to inspect conditions and to visit detainees to offer assistance. After listening to my plight and my story, the lady was clearly appalled by my appearance. I had no way of seeing myself and had given up even caring, but her contact and her compassion was a spark, a small measure of hope.

My merciful advocate was about 30-years-old, attractive and filled with genuine caring.

She listened and said, "Starting today I am going to make application for a *liberté provisoire*." This meant that she would apply for me to be released on parole until my trial. It took several days for my petitioner to fulfill her promise, but finally she came for me. I was released into her custody, a walking skeleton who had not seen the light of day, with weak body and emaciated legs unaccustomed to use. But I walked with her to the Palais de Justice Building to sign papers. That done, we left and walked some distance before she turned to me, tears in her eyes, and took my hand in hers. She said, "Don't look. You can feel money in your hand. I want you to take the money and leave here as soon as you can. Disappear. God bless you."

I, too, had tears in my eyes as I left the lady and departed Aix-en-Provence. She had given me enough money to live on for a couple of weeks. I was too weak to go far that first day. I found a farm where sympathetic peasants generously provided food and shelter. I remained in their barn for a week resting and exercising my legs and being nourished, gaining the strength needed to move on and away from the nightmare of the ancient stable prison.

Hitching a ride would be dangerous. As I left the farm, I walked south, away from the road, until I was back in Marseilles. Soon after arrival in the teeming old port, I met some guys who shared my quest for freedom. We decided to band together and head for Spain. The word was that if we crossed the border and the mountains to reach the French consulate in Madrid, we could get to Morocco, and from there to North Africa and freedom. We stayed close to the highway cautiously seeking rides on horse-drawn farm wagons until we reached the French border abutting Andorra.

12

RETURN TO FRANCE VIA SPANISH HELL-HOLE
Retour en France par l'Enfer Espagnol

*T*here was no problem crossing into Andorra. We skirted the independent country that straddles France and Spain as we worked our way through the mountains. It was winter and there was snow on the peaks. I was wearing a coat, welcome against the cold. My experience living in the Rennes forest was very resourceful as we worked our way closer to the Spanish border.

Our information held that Spain, under Franco, rejected the Axis Pact affiliation and offered only lip service to Hitler. Spain, determined to maintain a neutral stance, kept its borders tightly guarded against invasion from the north since Germany was capable of taking over all of France. The Spanish armed forces were very evident as we reached the border. There were troops in full battle gear everywhere. We stayed away from the highway, working south toward a point where we could cross the heavily patrolled border.

When we did finally cross into Spain in an area of rough, unprotected terrain, we felt that our ultimate destination was more firmly in view. We moved closer to a highway in the hope of finding a farmer transporting produce who would drive us toward Madrid. Unfortunately, the Spanish *gendarme* found us first. The officers in their Napoleonic uniforms with the black *papier-mâché* hats stood out noticeably, and we tried desperately to avoid capture, but it was unavoidable. We were only a small handful of the many thousands of French expatriates invading Spain in search of freedom and escape from tyranny.

The arresting officers were not cruel but had their instructions. We were taken to a prison. I cannot recall the name of the prison or its exact location, but it was an ancient fortification made of stone and housing hundreds of French refugees in overcrowded cells, another dungeon.

We were thrown into a cell with 25 other lost souls, who informed us that they had witnessed some of the detainees, after a couple of months, being released to the custody of the French Consulate in Madrid. At least the horror of the putrid cell held a glimmer of hope. It was something positive to hold onto, something to help maintain sanity.

The Spanish guards demonstrated their intense hatred for the French as they roughly forced us into the dark, filthy hell-hole and grudgingly delivered our food — watery soup with beans and occasionally pieces of dark bread. We humans were not alone. There were rats living in the stone walls. The furry rodents lived in the deep, dank crevices between the stones until dark when they came out in search of scraps of bread and spilled soup.

There were cell mates who had developed a way to start a fire. They were also avid hunters. As a rat appeared from one of the recesses and worked its way along the floor, a quick firm strike stunned the vermin, but often at the expense of being bitten sharply on the hand. However, being bitten was a small price to pay and did not deter my hungry cell mates starved for meat. They strangled the rats and cooked them in a small fire made using stone-age methods. A small piece of stone worked rhythmically against another set off sparks to ignite a bit of cotton, which in turn set fire to the straw from one of the thin mattresses that served as our beds.

I refrained from eating the meat, but knew well the physical and emotional deprivation that created the craving for food. Again I witnessed skeletal bodies being removed from the jail as guards crudely demanded that prisoners carry the corpses of their fellow inmates.

"Move the rotten meat."

Hope was again ebbing. Thoughts of family and home were

painful when one day, with no forewarning, my compatriots and I were released from the stinking, rat-infested prison. We had not been detained more than two weeks when we received papers of intervention from the French Consulate guaranteeing our safe deportment to Madrid.

I relished release, but had decided that if I did survive the jail, I would not go to Madrid. I had other ideas. I was sickened by the running, by the constant fear of the unknown as I continued to race like the hunted rats in the cell, scurrying to find a crumb to sustain. I no longer wanted to be away from France and felt a compulsion to return and actively participate in the battle being raged in my beleaguered country. My thoughts and memories flooded over me of family and friends as I seemed further and further away seeking what? Freedom? How could I ever find it without them, without that which was the very essence of Robert Baudy? I had to go back. I had to reverse my tracks. I left along with one companion, and we began the long trek home. I had had enough experience crossing borders to do it well without being detected.

As we crossed through the heavily guarded Spanish border through mountainous Andorra and reentered the south of France, I was determined to stay away from Marseilles and Aix-en-Provence. I knew that what those areas held for me would be certain death if I exposed myself to the dangers. I headed east, then north of Aix-en-Provence and continued to work my way to the border separating the "free zone" from the occupied north.

My companion left me to head in a different direction as I caught rides with local farmers carrying their produce to market. I rode either alongside the farmer as he held the reins to guide the horse on its familiar route, or I hid, stuffed between bags of potatoes or whatever produce was being carried. I was terrified of the *gendarme* patrolling on their bikes, and also Petain's militia was a constant threat.

When I reached the border, I soon realized that the security system made penetration far more difficult than the first time I crossed accompanied by the adonis who had been prostituting himself with the Judge in Riom. Although I found a slender opening when the sentries were separated from their guard dogs, he had not made it across. This time I discovered fortification that made the passage far more perilous.

I traveled west for nearly 75 miles before finding an opening. A local farmer directed me to a creek running through his fields that held ideal crossing if breached at night.

When I finally crossed, I was very close to my grandparents. I went eagerly to the farm seeking my family. The welcome was accompanied by tears of joy as I found them living in much the same way they had always lived. Their profound relief — disbelief at my being alive — produced an outpouring of emotions. I spent several days with them eating the wonderful food that I remembered well and had been starved for, for what seemed a lifetime.

It is impossible to find the words to adequately express the depth of my feelings in returning safely to the place where I spent the first years of my life and many happy, tranquil periods as I grew to manhood. The absolute contrast of the security and safety of my cocoon to what I had experienced in the past several years was similar to a diabolically orchestrated nightmare. We spoke of family. They had little news to report as communication with other parts of the country did not exist. They were totally isolated. They had not heard if my uncles, who were still serving in the military, had survived. Months and years went by with no knowledge of what had happened to loved ones.

I left my grandparents' farm to continue the journey toward Paris. Not knowing if my parents were still in Brittany or even still alive, I wanted to visit Le Vesinet. I contacted relatives in Paris who told me that Mother and Father returned occasionally to Le Vesinet to help Mr. Oliveaux manage the meat market. I was making contact and I was closing on my target.

I remembered well the changing expressions of shock, disbelief, and joy on Mother's face when I returned from the exodus years before. She had firmly believed that I was one of the many victims of the marauding Germans as I joined thousands of fleeing French citizens. I had been absent for months. This absence had been of longer duration with periods of imprisonment that had reduced my strong adult physique down to death-threatening skeletal proportions.

While I had regained some strength and muscle after the incarceration in Aix-en-Provence, I was still a shadow of the son she knew. The scars from all the horror endured could not be hidden from a mother's searching, innate awareness. I was not at all the son who left Fegreac to save himself and his parents from torture at the hands of the Gestapo.

Mother was in the market when I entered — so completely unexpected — and I will always remember her reaction. She first looked at me, blinked her eyes, and looked again as if to clear her blurred vision. She reached out to hold on to the counter in near collapse, blessed herself, and thanked God audibly for the scene before her. We held each other tightly as the tears flowed. I was more stoic. Father had taught me that men do not cry, but I was filled to overflowing with gratitude; her tears touched me and I cried.

I did not see Father until later that day. His reaction was predictably without much emotion, but he was obviously deeply touched by my presence and asked many questions to fully understand what had filled the many months of flight. He was horrified by my tale.

Being home and being safe were dichotomous illusions. I could not stay for long. The Germans were actively engaged in the continuing purge of Communists and Jews and arresting young people not in their labor force. I had to move about the area with extreme caution. I visited with Paul and Maguy. I met with Simone, but our time together, renewing our physical and emotional commitment, was too brief. We knew it would not last.

I was more deeply aware of the various reactions to the state of affairs experienced on all levels of society. Paul was embittered by the annihilation of the defending French military as well as by the German occupation, but expressed abhorrence for what he recognized as a great disparity in having been pressed into the battle by his own government. He carried hatred and resentment for Pierre Laval and other members of the French Government whom he had trusted and whom he felt had so tragically betrayed their fellow countrymen.

13

THE FREE FRENCH
Les Forces Libres

Mother and Father, while making occasional visits to Le Vesinet, still lived in the large stone house on the hill in Fegreac set serenely in the lush landscape seemingly untouched by war. The false tranquility would soon alter dramatically as the skies filled with Allied bombers flying overhead at 30,000 feet on their missions to bomb St. Nazaire. I left Fegreac after living in the Rennes forest for two years, then spent another year successfully skirting the Germans, in and out of jails in the south of France and in Spain. My return to Brittany was met by the daily noise and sightings of the bombers which produced dramatic repercussions on the German occupation. My direct involvement in the battle was about to begin.

The Germans had occupied St. Nazaire, using the critically strategic port as a submarine base to build and maintain the U-boats that were such a menace to British shipping. It was a prime target of the Allied Forces but was impenetrable in its densely fortified concrete bunkers which staunchly suffered the bombing raids.

The Germans were mobilizing their forces in lieu of an imminent invasion. They were unsure of where it would come, but braced for whatever the Allies planned in their war-game. With the urgency for massive defense measures being taken, the danger to me of being picked up decreased. One day I watched from the house as an enormous movement of German troops approached with an artillery unit, an 88mm gun pulled by a team of eight huge horses as well as other similar armaments. The German officers came to the house to request the use of Father's barn. Obviously Father could not turn them away. They settled into our home for an indeterminate occupation. They aimed the 88mm gun at the road heading north. This activity was extremely upsetting to Father. He had spent eight years in the artillery in World War I and knew full well that whenever a gun is set "on placement" something significant was indicated, and he felt the house was now going to be lost, a direct offensive target for the Allies.

There were two noncommissioned officers who moved into the house. We could not bar them from setting up a temporary post on our property. We had no choice. The local officials, pro-German Frenchmen, made it eminently clear that this was the law of war, and we were to furnish shelter to any occupying German troops. Fortunately, the officers were polite and did not request that we move out. While the artillery troop had their specific digging-in to perform preparing for battle, they did not question my presence. They were setting up a defensive position to counter the massive onslaught of Allied paratroopers expected soon.

We witnessed another defensive operation. On the plain below our property, hundreds of French people began setting telephone poles in place. Thousands of the poles approximately 50 feet apart were set to block what would have been an ideal landing area for the parachutists and also the gliders that the Allied Forces used to penetrate the coastal areas as well as inland targets.

The commanding officer of the 300 man unit complemented by ten guns and approximately 150 horses, sat every evening after dinner to discuss the War with Father. I was fascinated as I watched and listened to these encounters. The conversation was in German and while the attitude and demeanor of the two men was quite friendly, the points of view were obviously completely opposite. The noncom, who seemed very well-educated and polite, held firmly to the premise that the War would be won by Germany. Father, who listened to the BBC everyday, countered the officer's dogmatic opinion. Father expressed knowledgeably that the odds against Germany were great with the enormous economic power of the American-backed Allied Forces and the resiliency of Brittany. Not only had the Germans never succeeded in invading Britton, the German forces under Rommel had taken a tremendous beating in Africa. The dialogues were unique, and I could not imagine them occurring in Paris or for that matter, anywhere else in France.

It was a most extraordinary and privileged situation that held my rapt attention, but at the same time it was frightening to think that we were now a target. Father's opinions and his predictions had been right on the money up until now. I could again realize fully that his fears were well-founded with our home and property overrun with German militia. The house with thick walls and huge basement made an ideal bunker, but one bomb could easily destroy everything we had. Our safe haven away from the heat of the German concentration in Paris was no longer safe. We were suddenly right in the center of the proposed battlefield with the large unit of manpower, their horses, vehicles, and weapons, dug in. The cannons were set in the hillside around the house and completely camouflaged with nets and foliage. From all appearances the enemy planned to stay for a lengthy occupation.

As the days passed, a part of their routine became fascinating to me. Nearly everyday punished German soldiers were taken by the *feld webel* (noncom officers) to a ten-acre field owned by my parents and surrounded by very thick hedgerow. Intrigued by the hoarse German commands and the screams, I decided (against Father's strict orders) to take a peek at what was occurring through the dense cover of hedgerows. I crawled through the heavy growth and watched with horror the cruelty of the Prussian noncom to young German artillery men. While standing at attention each man received a blistering single hit across his face with a heavy rawhide horsewhip. As the disciplinary measures continued, the men were ordered to jump and then fast-crawl carrying their heavy rifles tucked tightly inside their elbows, rolling over in the mud. Each turn was sanctioned by vicious kicks to the ribs by the giant *feld webel*. The intense brutality lasted nearly two hours in unrelenting physical abuse.

I only watched the torture on one occasion. If found witnessing the process, I would have been shot. Father knew well what their disciplinary measures were and told me, "Look, these are their soldiers, their type of discipline, and they certainly don't want a young Frenchman observing. If you are a witness and if you are caught, you will be killed; but you will be tortured before they do away with you."

I did mention to Mother that I saw the disciplinary measures. She was horrified by my disclosure and that I took the chance against Father's strict and dire warning. Poor Mother was having to bear much anguish because of my unbridled fearlessness. The gravity of Father's fears was again confirmed when two blue-eyed German soldiers committed suicide and were buried in the local Catholic cemetery. Father knew the facts behind the tragedy as did I.

As the bombers continued blanketing the sky day and night, some were shot down. We never had a plane downed closer than ten miles from the house, but heard the sounds of fire and hits that sent them crashing in the distance. It was at that time that the special German force following the path of the downed plane quickly moved in to recover the pilot to gain a prisoner and valuable information.

Another strange sighting occurred as the Allied planes flew over. Silver foil was dropped to counter enemy radar with the result the landscape, the apple orchard, hills and valleys surrounding the farm glistened with slivers of silver.

In June, 1944, D-Day, the expected invasion did materialize as Allied troops invaded northern France. It took three weeks for the invaders to secure the beachhead. With Allied Forces penetrating Brittany, we saw from our house hundreds upon hundreds of retreating Germans, many wounded, suddenly transformed from arrogant occupiers to a beaten force of humanity. In the midst of the retreating Germans was a large contingent of White Russian troops on horseback, Cossacks mounted on small horses wearing the furry hats of the Russian cavalry and carrying daggers. There were many waves of enemy soldiers that passed through Fegreac as we watched and waited, expecting each day to be invaded or shelled.

After the beachhead was secured in Normandy, 150 miles distant from our home, reconnaissance from the Third American Army was sent in and the German artillery removed from their entrenched positions in and around Fegreac and headed south. We were not sorry to see them go.

A substantial battle took place just three miles from our property in an apple orchard. The battle lasted about three hours with American forces in jeeps, half-tracks, and armored vehicles entering the fray. The Americans had not anticipated the strength of the German force and after fighting for three hours, retreated toward Normandy, leaving some of their men dead in the orchard. The following day I rode my bike to the location of the battle. There were French *gendarmes* roaming through the battlefield. There were bodies of young American soldiers, so still, so utterly sad to observe, along with the German casualties. Soon American jeeps with Red Cross insignia arrived to recover their fallen. There were some German snipers in the woods firing on the Americans. More firing continued before the medics could successfully retrieve two of their dead. They placed the bodies of the fallen soldiers in a jeep to be removed from the scene. They stopped at my parents' home, and I saw close-up the bodies, young men dirty with heavy beards and haggard expressions, frozen and motionless, unreal, unnatural, a grim spectacle etched in my mind. We placed flowers on the bodies before the jeeps left Fegreac.

The Germans established a line of defense five miles south of Fegreac near a river with swamps on either side. The Germans occupied one side of the river. The other side was held by the French Resistance, the Communists who wore red arm-bands. Both sides were armed and attempted to control the bridgehead. There were skirmishes with losses on both sides. As the signs of direct involvement continued all around, I felt the need to actively involve myself. With fighting on our doorstep and many different factions meeting in armed conflict so perilously close to home, I knew the time had come when I would become a part of the battle. I wanted my role to support the Free French forces, not an unallied splinter group, but a substantial patriotic organized power to counter the enemy of our nation and of all Europe. I wanted to join the Allies in what seemed the strongest and most effectual force to sweep the Nazi stronghold out of power and out of existence.

I said goodbye to my parents and to Simone again. It was becoming routine, this severing of ties to leave under the continuous threat of permanent loss. Possibly they were reconciled to my absence and knew that at 21, I had to serve regardless of the consequences. I left by bicycle heading west toward Normandy. The going was immediately complicated by retreating German military convoys that completely packed the roads away from Normandy. I was one person on a bike stemming the great tide of retreating soldiers and disabled military vehicles left smoldering.

There were 88mm guns, ack-ack and other armored carriers that had been hit by the British and American Air Forces. It took a day and a half before I reached the Norman Flan where German troops were dug in.

The Germans were in a strong offensive position holding their line against the invading Allied Forces as I crossed through their camp. I was fortunate that they did not target me. I attempted to stay clear of the enormous militia with machine-gun-armed infantry by the thousands, panzers, grenadiers, and tanks. I was getting an instant indoctrination into German methodology as I passed by tanks so well-camouflaged that even within 15 feet it was difficult to recognize the hulking machines completely covered with heavily-leafed tree branches. I saw a lot of disabled equipment and tragically for as far as the eye could see, the desecration of land pockmarked from weeks of shelling. I was appalled and sickened to see the small villages that had fallen to the holocaust of fire with buildings reduced to rubble-covered foundations, trees blackened, and bodies everywhere, all victims of a place and time of insanity.

There were areas from 300 yards to ten miles of no-man's land to maneuver as I sought side roads to take me away from the crush of warring humanity and suffering in search of the Allied Forces. French villagers were my informants of the changing position of the front line. Many of the inhabitants, innocent frightened victims, buried themselves in the dark recesses of their basements that held huge barrels of cider. The massed barrels formed a natural shelter from the brutal invasion and destruction of their homes.

I met an American mounted cavalry unit — a reconnaissance spearhead unit — light armored vehicles with thick tires supporting .30 and .50 calibre machine guns. I flagged them down. In halting English I communicated and showed them my papers, proof that I had graduated from the Preparation Militaire School in Rueil barracks. I was then directed to the *Bataillon de Renfort,* which was a part of the Second Armored Division comprised of about 10,000 Frenchmen and several thousand armored vehicles. I knew immediately that I was in the French section without a word uttered. The French refused to wear the combat helmets of the Allied Forces. They preferred to wear the *kepi,* which was worn by all noncommissioned officers and officers of higher rank. The soldiers wore caps of different colors to indicate the different branches of service. The Navy was represented and in charge of the destroyer tanks. The infantry soldiers were wearing the small white hats with red pom-poms atop, all of which looked absolutely ridiculous. The officers had their navy blue or pale blue *kepi,* which struck me as being totally out of place as well.

I spoke to some noncoms. I was interrogated thoroughly by the commanding officers. They were very nervous about spies entering the units. As I was approved for possible inclusion, the officers recognized the schooling in Rueil, and some had even attended the same military training school. One noncom remembered me as being a fellow student, and with that recognition I was received into the division. Very little time elapsed before I was issued a uniform, assigned to a pup tent with two other guys, and quickly indoctrinated with knowledge of the weapons I would be assigned to use. These weapons were completely different from the weaponry I had trained on years earlier, relics from World War I.

In the boot-camp atmosphere, I was instructed in the care and handling of the Colt .45, and the 30 and 15mm machine guns as well as the U.S. 30mm carbine and the bazooka. I was most impressed with the machine gun and learned quickly how to clean and take it apart. Our days were comprised of ten hours of learning to be a combat-ready soldier. We were taught procedures for defensive maneuvering, which instantly served us well when the Germans strafed our position.

I was reminded of my first strafing episode while attempting to transfer some valuable papers out of Le Vesinet years before. I felt the fear and saw the panic of fleeing Frenchmen and realized how deadly the low flying bombers could be. The RAF also flew over Normandy, filling the sky with many dog fights. The constant bombardment of shells from navy guns and ground weapons exploding in an unceasing rain of terror was background to our preparation for deployment, to prepare us for war — but nothing could do that.

My first assignment came much sooner than the estimated month of training. As a member of the *Bataillon de Renfort,* we were standing by to be a reservoir to fill the gaps created by loss of troops already in the field. Six days into training, I was singled out along with another trainee named Stunner, whom I had met years before in Rennes. We apparently had demonstrated certain abilities which elevated our position and combat readiness. Stunner spoke German fluently and had a very refined appearance. He also maintained an equally defined determination to kill Germans. We left to begin active duty. I was imbued with a great deal of enthusiasm as we joined the Second Armored Division which was catching hell on the battlefield.

My enthusiasm was based on finally being in a position to help rid my country of the many evil forces that were in authority, forces that had paralyzed the country in fear. But I entered the service with mixed emotions. I had experienced the German persona under many different circumstances. I had witnessed benevolence and good manners in giving up a seat on a crowded train. I had witnessed courtesy and politeness as they came into the shop in Le Vesinet as customers. I had witnessed the random questioning of citizens, then watched as seemingly innocent people were pushed into vehicles to be taken away from loved ones for no apparent reason except religious or ideological differences. I had heard Father speak so openly against Hitler and heard him participate in sane and calm discussions predicting the defeat of the Germans with the officer who resided in our home. I was impressed by our house guest who seemed so well-educated, who expressed his love for France, and who seemed to trust us enough that when he retired for the night, his P-38 pistol and holster were slung openly over the bannister outside his bedroom. I realized that many Germans were cultured, intelligent, and even compassionate. But I knew that cruel discipline and torture were innately part of their military posture.

I was going to fight alongside my fellow countrymen and the Allied Forces, most of whom expressed absolute abhorrence for Hitler and his racist policies. They hated all Germans claiming, in some instances, that the whole German race was "Vermin that had to be eradicated from the face of the earth."

I knew that many Germans possessed the fear, emotions, and desires that I felt. I knew, too, that some in the German ranks were totally opposed to the War. But each of us had a job to do and in so doing, my country was pummeled as the warring factions moved through Brittany leaving gruesome remains of humans, animals, villages, and foliage that had once held life and great beauty. The carnage, the holocaust was everywhere.

As a part of the unit, I wore a helmet and was happy to have the better protection as the skies filled with a rain of shells night and day. I saw quickly that the pride my fellow soldiers displayed in their determination to wear the *kepi* resulted in very dramatic consequences. The German snipers easily picked out the French officers so clearly marked by their headgear. I was proud to be part of the French unit, where as my first duty I was assigned to a half-track, an open-top flatbed vehicle armed with .50 calibre machine gun. I was moved from one unit to another as the casualties mounted. I was assigned to liaison duty driving either a jeep or a motorcycle between headquarters. Sniper bullets whizzed by as I crouched low over the grips of the motorcycle with no protection.

The half-track was not such a solitary duty. It carried 15 soldiers along with the gun. I was the driver. I had received wonderful tutelage in driving skills by Father at an early age and was proficient at the duty.

The new assignment was to a regiment led by General Jacques LeClerc whose real name was Philippe du Hodecloque. He was a nobleman who, at the time he joined deGaulle in Africa, changed his name to protect his family. He carried the prestigious title of *Maréchal du Tchad*. As a member of the regiment, I wore the insignia (which I still have in my possession) showing the head of a camel on a bronze background.

General LeClerc had gained great honor for his successful campaigns in the Chad region of West Africa where a very small convoy of various armored vehicles led by LeClerc crossed the dessert and overran the Italian outposts. Italy fought on the side of the Germans and was in control of the whole region. LeClerc performed his mission with one-tenth the manpower of the Italians and returned home a hero. He was trained in England with the remaining members of the convoy and became the leader of the Second Armored Division. As a member of nobility and an outstanding officer, he was so completely different from any other officer, his character and appearance totally unique on the battlefield. He always carried a cane — never a weapon — and wore the light blue *kepi* of the French cavalry. He chose his officers well. They were brilliant and tough bulldogs.

My commanding officer in the field was Lt. D'Jambekoff, a handsome, elegant white Russian who wore a peasant-type blouse and carried two guns in a similar posture to Patton. He was about 50 years old with green eyes and a small mustache — he resembled Clark Gable. D'Jambekoff demonstrated a fearlessness and a hatred for all Germans and was not in favor of taking prisoners. I witnessed many incidents while moving on villages where we would engage the enemy as we approached in a surrounding, synchronized assault to flush them out. The defenders would fight from the houses, the church, and any hiding place until their backs were to the wall and they could hide no more. As they came forth with arms extended over heads in obvious resignation and surrender to end the onslaught, I saw too many beaten soldiers cut down in a bloodbath of infamy as machine guns riddled their defenseless bodies. The brutality of war was profoundly eroding my enthusiasm as I watched in every direction, every encounter, the tragedy that is armed combat between humans. We continued our relentless search-and-destroy missions and lost many men and vehicles as we inflicted similar heavy losses on the enemy.

Normandy

We moved through the village of Ste. Mère Église, located near the first landing sight of the Allied Invasion Forces. The losses had been tremendous with smoldering tanks, bodies folded in two hanging out of turrets, hands dangling as if disconnected. American parachutists had been dropped in back of the German line, and many of them had been killed. There were bodies hanging in trees where the chutes had become tangled. A chute covered the village church steeple with an American paratrooper hanging, lifeless, from the escarpment. A startling sight was of members of the British force, women in uniform, climbing poles to cut off the equipment carried by the victims. Their job was to recover the new equipment to be shipped back to England.

As we continued to advance, the battles were like a see-saw, moving back and forth as the Allied Forces took the offensive and then suddenly retreated to defend a German reenforced position of strength to recapture an area, a village, or a bridge to hold until a counter force would move in to take over in unrelenting battle.

The fighting initially was contained in a very small portion of Normandy. The weather was horrendous with the worst storms seen in years. It seemed like the heavens were aiding and abetting the earthly storm of annihilation, as rutted, washed-out lanes stalled the heavy vehicles and bogged down the procession to provide sitting-duck-targets for enemy fire.

When I was relieved as driver and moved to gunner position on the half-track, I became responsible for the operation of the .50 calibre heavy machine gun. There was little protection to the gunner as the upper half of my body was exposed and vulnerable.

In addition to the inherent danger of the open vehicle, there was the added danger from the physical aspects of the countryside of Normandy referred to as the *bocage*. The farmland was divided into thousands of small plots edged by hedgerows six or seven feet high and ten or 12 feet deep. The hedgerows provided a natural shield for the Germans and created severe logistical problems that impeded our progress. The conditions were impossible.

The Americans addressed the problem by designing, on the spot, a mechanism to cut through the dense hedgerows. A huge metal spade was crafted, weighing about a ton and a half. Mounted on a 35-ton Sherman tank, the blade fashioned with a pointed leading edge cut through the hedgerow like a spoon moving through butter. The innovative design was a monumental breakthrough for our forces. We were able to move more swiftly in pursuit of the German army.

The French Second Armored Division had been fighting since mid-June; the Third Army would not become operational until August, and Patton was an unknown entity before he became commander of the Third American Army.

Patton had achieved great success in Sicily and entered France from England. When he landed, he began his tour of duty traveling through the area to visit all units under his command. The Third Army was huge; and he made it his duty to know where the units were located and how they were occupied in routing the Germans. I saw him from time to time and always knew when the official cars appeared that Patton had arrived to question his officers.

One day he questioned a group of us, "What are you doing here? Where are the enemies?" He had an interpreter and when I told him that the way was not clear ahead because of snipers, he shrugged and commanded his driver to move out as they took off with great dispatch. Called "Blood and Guts," Patton was very visible and I saw him often. He was not a damned bit intimidated by any battle scene and was often right in the middle of the action.

When we received orders to take Alençon, our attempted assault could not break through the lines. An American unit fighting alongside had trouble getting through as well. Our tanks and the 35-ton Sherman tanks used by the Americans were no match for the German tanks. Finally support for our effort came in Allied air power with carpetbagging attacks that unceasingly pulverized the land and enemy position, which opened the way for our assault unit and others to break through.

As we worked our way into Alençon, we saw burning tanks and charred bodies hanging from opened turrets cut down in their escape, cooked in their protective vehicles. Germans were lying everywhere in grotesque, unnatural poses stopped suddenly in the horror of war, never to move again. Hundreds of German horses were more tragic, lying with legs stiffened — faces with expressions that belied any pain or knowledge of the madness being enacted. It was later estimated that three divisions of about 45,000 Germans were annihilated around Alençon.

This was real war and very far from any conception that I could possibly imagine. I remembered Father's words: "War is hell. It's unbelievable — it cannot be described — you have to live through it or die in it. I was lucky." Everyday saw buddies carted away on stretchers. I could do nothing to change the horror, to alleviate the suffering and loss. I could only press on to purge the enemy until the violence ceased.

I realized that my experiences in the bloody slaughterhouse first as a youngster, then while hiding from the Germans and the Resistance forces near Fegreac, had in a way prepared me or at least inured me to a degree to what I witnessed on the battlefield. But this was utterly horrible. Humans, as well as animals, were slaughtered on a monumental scale.

I drove a Sherman tank one day while a young, commanding officer stood next to me with the upper portion of his body outside the tank as he scanned the horizon with field glasses. I sat below at the controls. There was no shooting; all seemed quiet and calm as we parked in the middle of a field of gently waving wheat catching the soft breezes as the sun glistened on slender shafts. Suddenly, with no warning, the young officer's body silently fell in a clumped mass to the bottom of the tank. I looked, startled, as his eyes widened and his mouth drooped; his body lay motionless at my feet. I was stunned and puzzled by his bazaar behavior. I called to a buddy and with his help looked for the cause of the officer's collapse. We found no sign of a wound until we looked at the back of his head. There was a huge gash where a bullet had exited the back of his neck, the flesh ripped apart. We examined him further. A sniper's bullet had caught him under the chin. The entry hole was small and clean and did not bleed for minutes. I thought at first that he had suffered a heart attack. He had not been in the field one day. He arrived from England the day before and had not fired a single shot. His war had lasted less than 48 hours.

Our food was Army K-rations that came in tins. My favorite was the pudding for which I gratefully traded my cigarettes. I also drank the whiskey when it was passed around in the evening. Whiskey did not appear every evening, but when it was offered, it indicated a tough pending battle. I appreciated the elevation of spirits and then the numbness induced by the liquid spirits to relieve the daily suffering.

With all the suffering, it would have helped to have had the luxury of mail service. No mail and no clean clothing. There was no such thing as a shower or a hot tub bath. I wore the same uniform and underwear every day for weeks. We were issued a dress uniform that stayed in my duffel bag stowed in a truck, damp from the moist, lousy weather that only cleared intermittently. The rain created many hazards but was welcomed to freshen dirty, unshaven faces and hands encrusted with grime, soot, and oil as we slogged through areas where smoldering ruins thickened the atmosphere with acrid smoke and blocked our path. We physically removed bodies and disabled vehicles to clear the way. As we moved and labored, in spite of Allied supremacy in the air, German bombers broke through and threatened our position. There was so little time for rest and no safe place as we moved sluggishly through the battlefield.

The Second Armored Division was a mixture of anything you could call French with diverse ethnicity abounding. The infantry was comprised of tough North Africans, a few Negroes from French colonies, and many Spanish Communists who hated the Germans for putting Franco in power. The Spanish soldiers were bloodthirsty, capable of brutal atrocities. Patton highly respected the predominantly European French Armored Division. Having great élan among its forces, men from so many regions fought together tenaciously. Its troops also came from the French Underground; Frenchmen who had lived in exile for years as refugees were trained to return to fight on home soil, absolutely focused and determined in their resolve. Some members of the Underground had been out of the country for several years and their loved ones thought they were dead. I witnessed reunions as the expatriates passed through their villages totally unexpected by family and joyously received, to rapidly leave again as we moved on in the unrelenting battle — the quest to return our country to freedom.

With much tragedy, pain, and suffering everywhere, relieved briefly by the joy of a homecoming, everyday held intense drama. I witnessed a mass hanging. We passed through a village and were stopped in our tracks by the sight of a flatbed truck holding five American soldiers with ropes tied around their necks. A chaplain read from a Bible. Suddenly, the truck pulled away to leave the men dangling to die as the nooses tightened. The ropes, tied to a beam, held the bodies, soon limp and motionless. My English was not good, but I managed to communicate with officers who informed me the men were put to death for entering the village and raping women. There had been witnesses to the crime and the victims, bruised and battered, had taken the description of the truck carrying the rapists. The crime was heinous and its penalty death by hanging, performed in front of the townspeople to demonstrate the Allied commitment to protect citizens from crimes enacted even by the Allied Forces. It was just another numbing reality of the brutality that filled each day as we continued our march.

In August, a breakthrough of monumental proportion occurred when Rennes fell to the Americans. The Germans lost their stronghold in Brittany. My unit joined the fray near Avranches as one of many Allied Forces units pouring down from Normandy to form an advancing thrust eastward into the heart of the country. The pounding in its wake, artillery a constant companion of the armor and infantry, kept the Germans in retreat. We witnessed the German Army crumble. There was much death and devastation left from Patton's "Blood and Guts" approach to the unceasing bombardment. I firmly believe Patton's ruthlessness, his cavalier attitude, only further accelerated the carnage and even overlooked some of the atrocities. He was a great general and I'm certain he was what was needed in order to win the War, but his unwavering, relentless vision created the tremendous number of casualties. In three weeks of battle, 11,000 men in the Allied Forces were lost. The massive plundering created many blockades. We could not move until bulldozers were brought to clear a path through the bodies of men, horses, burned-out vehicles, and armament that glutted the roads and countryside.

When we did flush out a pocket of Germans, sometimes there were hundreds at one time coming out from hiding, with white banners to signal surrender. We were ordered to take their rifles. Mostly we didn't bother with the rifles but instead sought souvenirs. Walther P-38 sidearms were coveted mementoes. I was particularly fascinated by the daggers that the German officers carried. Some of the daggers were presentation weapons commemorating special honors, handsomely crafted with steel engraved blades made in the Solingen foundries. Our commanding officer reprimanded us for not following the order to disarm the enemy soldiers. We usually took the bolts out of the rifles and threw them away, making them inoperable. But it was the holstered pistols that were coveted and the daggers that found their way into our duffel bags. The booty became substantial enough that it had to be put in separate bags, often ultimately stolen by our very own drivers. I managed to keep a number of the daggers that I maintain in my collection of memorabilia to this day, constant reminders of the horror, but also handsome examples of craftsmanship by the artisans of Solingen.

In moments of reflection or in the heat of battle, I often felt we were mere puppets worked by the aspirations of our commanders, men of great ego and determination of purpose whose strengths and weaknesses clashed. General LeClerc was determined to take his army to Paris in honor of de Gaulle. General Patton's purpose was to rid France and all of Europe of Nazi tyranny, but he wanted LeClerc to fully realize who was in command of the Third Army.

The Germans became trapped in a pocket, a small portion of Normandy, as Allied Forces swept down the coast toward Bordeaux. The Third Army continued to hurl its strength into the center of France. The retreating German bastards were in a vice with Allied Forces converging on the heart of France narrowing the gap, the only means of retreat left to the enemy. Word of the rout and evidence of the great German Army disintegrating sent tremors through Paris. In the meantime, I learned after the War, Eisenhower opposed taking Paris. The plan was to bypass the city as the Allied Forces did not have enough supplies to care for the three million inhabitants struggling to survive after years of starvation — the result of strict rationing and occupation.

The Resistance movement, the Communist Parisian Underground, was bolstered by information of the success of the Allied Forces and by what they witnessed in the city as the Germans braced for invasion. At the same time, the Free French anxiously awaited the opportunity to liberate their city and their country. They were actively engaged in preparation, armed to do combat against the Nazi oppressors. As the Allies closed on Paris, all hell broke loose with the Communists taking strong measures of defiance against the fleeing Germans. De Gaulle flew to London to petition Eisenhower. His request was for General LeClerc's Second Armored Division to enter Paris before any other divisions.

The casualties and devastation in Normandy had been great. The French citizens were in no mood to celebrate the rout; but as soon as we broke through Avranches and headed toward Paris, a wonderful change in atmosphere became apparent. A complete transformation took place. No longer was our progress impeded by the carnage of war, but in every village throngs of French men, women, and children who had witnessed the retreating Germans ran to bring us wine and flowers and jumped on the tanks and half-tracks. They surrounded us with not only their physical beings, but also a spirited, celebratory outpouring of emotions unlike anything I had ever witnessed. The dawn had broken; the savior had arrived. The dark and ominous pall that had blanketed the entire country for years was beginning to lift.

We were, blessedly, seeing villages that had not been destroyed as we moved away from Normandy, where villages were still intact. It was unbelievable to see the unbridled joy, to feel a sense of normalcy, and to experience the hope that maybe the War was truly going to end. Possibly it had ended. But our joy and our hopes were dashed by the blasting of 88mm guns and tiger tanks as the Germans strongly defended a perimeter line on the outskirts of Paris. It was a rude, cruel awakening that took us instantly and menacingly back to the nightmare of the holocaust. We suffered many losses breaking through the lines into the city.

It was vital for de Gaulle to establish the fact that LeClerc and the Second Armored Division be first to enter Paris, to secure a political hedge in a city racked by turmoil with many different factions seeking to take command in the wake of the fleeing Germans. The greatest fear for de Gaulle was a Communist take-over.

There were mine fields and artillery barrages to avoid. In the city, the Germans manned tanks along the Champs-Élysées and in the Place de la Concorde; they maintained a stronghold in barracks very near the Eiffel Tower.

We entered the city on August 23, 1944, through the gates of the Port d'Orléans, and worked our way to the Île-de-la-Cité in the heart of the city where we joined the Fighting Free patriots. As we entered, there were skirmishes and sniper fire accompanied by cheers and spontaneous demonstrations by celebrants in lieu of a liberation party. The Americans followed and encountered German resistance to be flushed out near Notre-Dame and the Louvre. The German retreat met assault by the Underground forces, the American Armored Divisions and the Free French while, at the very same time, de Gaulle was organizing a liberation parade. We were in the city for nearly two days when we received an order to move to Nanterre on the west side of Paris. We were ordered to clean up the vehicles for a parade of strength and support to be led by de Gaulle.

It was beyond belief that a parade could actually be in the planning stages in a city under siege, but what did I know? We continued to experience sniper fire as we moved through the convulsed city.

We settled in a fine neighborhood under a tree in Nanterre to clean the half-track. We had run out of water. I went to the door of a magnificent mansion to request water for the men. The door opened to reveal a stunningly beautiful lady about 30 years old. She invited me into the entry. I was filthy from months of battle with no chance to wash myself except for the rain and an occasional rinsing in a river or stream. My cloths were grimy, and I must have been a frightening apparition as I stood looking around in utter amazement at the beautiful home, waiting for the lady to bring the water. There was an air of elegance in the surroundings that I had not felt or seen in a long time.

Apparently there was something about me that appealed to the lady. She asked if I would like to return to the house after delivering the water to the men and dine with her. I saw no reason to decline the extraordinary invitation with the half-track parked within sight of the house. I could return to it on a minute's notice. The men were very capable of cleaning the vehicle without me. I accepted her invitation, took the water to the eagerly waiting men, and informed them of my intention to spend several hours in the house. They were madder than hell that I was going to be inside while they remained outside to sit by the vehicle all night.

I took off my dirty clothes and enjoyed the hot shower that was offered. It was the first shower in months. It all seemed like a wonderful dream, and I hoped that I would not awaken. The beautiful lady was alone in the house. Her husband was obviously a man of means and politically influential. There was no sign whatsoever of any sort of deprivation suffered during the Occupation. When I emerged from the shower, clean clothes were offered, and we talked, then dined on the most wonderful pâté and gourmet foods, champagne and wine, and even butter, while the rest of Paris was feeding on rats after the dogs and cats had all been eaten.

Following dinner, I returned to the half-track to get cigarettes to give the kind lady. My buddies had a difficult time dealing with my good fortune. I told them that she wasn't interested in entertaining the whole Second Armored Division, but that I sure as hell wasn't going to deny myself the privileged and beautiful opportunity.

I returned to the house, and we talked more of the situation in Paris. I asked of her husband. Her replies indicated the marriage was less than satisfactory, but that he was a very important government official. I could feel the frustration as she spoke of their relationship. She asked if I would like to enjoy a hot bubble bath. As the evening progressed, I knew that I had left hell and arrived in heaven as I looked upon my lovely companion, elegant with high cheekbones and gorgeous hair typical of someone from the northeast of France.

After the bath, she changed into a revealing negligee, and we went to her bedroom. It was beyond imagining the many different sensations I felt as I slipped beneath the luxurious linen, wrapped in her embrace, bodies indulging every sensual yearning so long suppressed. It was like exploding cannon fire, but we were so far away from the battlefield in a safe and secure place. We were in another world. We enjoyed one another for several hours. I knew that it could not last forever. I returned to the half-track and back to reality to spend what little remained of the night. I didn't want to leave my beautiful bed mate, but feeling satiated, I knew that duty called.

The following day, August 26, General de Gaulle, Savior of France, entered the city to the accompaniment of the "Marseillaise." We wore our dress uniforms for the occasion and proceeded according to assigned routes toward the Champs-Élysées, the main display avenue in the center of Paris. D'Jambekoff rode, standing in a half-track at the head of our company, while General LeClerc led the entire division in an open common car in clear view of the thousands of exuberant French citizens lining the parade route. Charles de Gaulle, looking taller than ever, stood to salute his officers, some of whom wore fresh bandages from recent wounds. De Gaulle was surrounded by his London staff officers and *aides-de-camp* in addition to high-ranking Parisian city officials who were ready to move into key positions in the "liberated city." The parade and the cheering and singing was accompanied by sniper fire. Even German bombs accentuated the procession of 15,000 men and 5,000 vehicles filling the wide boulevard in the greatest military procession in the history of the country. Behind the Second Armored Division came the American troops, which must

After the Liberation. I'm standing second from right. We were mimicking LeClerc.

have been a source of great annoyance to LeClerc who wanted nothing to detract from the honor, glory, and moment orchestrated to elevate de Gaulle and only de Gaulle.

I was able to contact relatives. I had a cousin in the city. The phone service had been reinstated and I talked to my parents. They had not heard from me as I battled across western France. It was imperative that I assure them of my survival, of all that I had experienced and the loss that surrounded me. My poor mother could never adjust to what I was putting her through. I imagine the only comfort she felt was in sharing the very same fears and doubts with so many others.

I had left Le Vesinet and Fegreac for long periods of time because of the extreme danger. When I left on my bicycle to join the French and Allied Forces, soon followed by reports of heavy Allied casualties, their concern must have been horrendous. I was in the heat of battle witnessing loss, destruction, and carnage; every incident was like a scene in hell. It was nearly impossible to react to everything that happened. But I knew through all the suffering and pain that Mother's thoughts were constant and prayerful, and I knew that she and I were sustained to a degree by the constancy of their existence. While my parents had to continue living in fear that I would not survive, I, too, realized that at every turn my life could end. But at least in Paris there was a sense that maybe we saw the decline of German domination. I had no idea of what was ahead.

After the parade we were dispatched to the Bois de Boulogne, a huge park within the city limits, where we camped for a week. Pup tents were set for a period of rest and recovery which was welcome but illusive because many women anxious and willing to help us celebrate the liberation of Paris visited our tents. Then during the night, the husbands and lovers came to inquire if we had seen their errant women. The women did provide more than sexual diversion. They mobbed our handsome Lt. d'Jambekoff, who went off on leave for several days and left one of my buddies, Didier, in charge of his jeep.

Didier was quite an extraordinary character. Small of stature, he had been shot in Normandy but was treated and rejoined our unit as we made our way into Paris. One night as we sat around a campfire discussing what we had done in private life before the War broke out, Didier startled me when he openly admitted he was a "thief." I found his statement incredulous and asked him to repeat.

"I'm a thief!"

I replied, "You must have done something besides stealing from people."

He answered, "No, I was born in poverty. My father was an alcoholic and he beat me. My mother taught me how to steal."

I said, again with disbelief in my voice, "You did that . . . and then joined . . . volunteered for the duration of the War? Usually people like you . . . never volunteer."

"Well," he answered, "I only volunteered to get rich."

I looked at the small man sitting next to me and searched his face to discover his reason for entertaining us while we sat around the fire in the middle of a war where getting rich was the farthest thought from my mind. I was absolutely stunned by Didier's admission.

He went on, "Well, every time one of these guys got knocked off . . . in Normandy . . . I stole his rings."

I asked, "You got a lot of rings?"

"Yeah, didn't I ever show them to you?"

With that he pulled out a bagfull of rings, gold cigarette lighters, and gold-plated cigarette holders. I was naïve as hell, thinking I was surrounded by men gung-ho and loaded with patriotic fervor. Not so Didier. He was a thief and saw the War as the best venue to ply his trade with money, jewelry, and anything he could swipe off the fallen soldiers. He ignored the guns when he encountered a wounded or dead soldier or those who surrendered. He went first for the money, a ring or other jewelry, and then looked further for any other small items that were saleable.

Didier's occupation made him particularly crafty on the battlefield. He managed to stay out of danger except for the wound in Normandy. He survived many treacherous and life-threatening encounters along the way to fill his pockets with bounty as he moved through France and into Germany. He served me well in Paris.

Under the pretense of road testing the Lieutenant's jeep after changing the oil and servicing the vehicle, Didier invited Stunner and me to accompany him. We took off for Le Vesinet only 40 minutes from our bivouac in the park. We carried our weapons as if in a war zone. There was so much happening all around us that was dangerous, particularly for the collaborators who were picked up by the Communist underground. They wanted to purge the traitorous French who had committed themselves to the German cause or who were thought to be sympathizers of the Occupation. There were reprisals that involved many innocent people as chaos continued to overwhelm the city.

It was shocking to visit in the shops in Le Vesinet. My young friends were gone leaving the owners, friends of the family, all thinner versions of their former selves. I learned that food rationing had been severe. Sugar was just one item that was impossible to find. German-produced saccharine had replaced sugar, the ultimate cause of cancer, as a lingering remnant of the War.

I asked about Paul le Royer, who had disappeared. Prior to the Liberation, Paul performed with a circus located inside the city, the Amar Circus. We drove to the location. Most of the performers and animals were still present, but operating as if in shock in the atmosphere of mistrust and upheaval that gripped the city. The performers were not able to tell me much of Paul except he had been shot days before. I was stunned. My informant went on to explain that Paul was sitting in the bleachers one morning watching an animal trainer work his act when shots rang out hitting Paul in the thigh. The bullets went through his leg. He was taken to a hospital. No one could tell me which hospital.

I asked about Maguy and was told that she had been seized by the Underground and taken away. We were very near a complex called Drancy used as a concentration center by the Germans to house political prisoners, slave laborers, and people to be screened to determine whether they were to be released or sent to camps outside the city for lengthy incarceration, torture, and almost certain death. As soon as the Liberation took place, the French Resistance took over the building, liberated the prisoners, and immediately began using the huge complex for their own purposes.

We went to Drancy in full combat gear in Lt. d'Jambekoff's jeep, which added a certain legitimacy to our appearance. I carried a Colt .45 and a Thompson submachine gun. Stunner and Didier carried army carbines and sidearms. We pulled up in front of the 30-story building controlled by French Communists wearing the signatory arm-band of the FFI, French Forces of the Interior. Most of the control people were in their mid-forties and had been allied with the Germans before the Liberation. They were the most dangerous and powerful group in Paris at the time, and it was for that reason de Gaulle stipulated the Second Armored Division move into the city before the FFI gained political power.

We bluffed our way into the complex and soon saw the horrors of what the FFI was capable of perpetrating on their fellow countrymen. In a huge center yard, men and women were packed together, some standing, some sitting on the ground. There were corpses intermingled with the living dead in the terrible scene. The basement and first floor areas housed the bad guys, mostly former members of the French German Legion.

The Germans had organized sympathizer groups all over the country. The groups were issued flags, sworn in as official members, and fought alongside the Germans in the battlefields. Also incarcerated were members of the security force, the Gestapo.

As we looked around in search of Maguy, we saw victims who had been shot, some were still living, some had been beaten and tortured, some murdered, lying motionless with frozen expressions, eyes opened, blood staining their clothing. As my eyes searched through the agonizing, pathetic crush of humanity, which was like an insane asylum, I realized that I had joined forces with a system to eradicate the Germans only to witness terrible atrocities that my countrymen perpetrated on fellow humans, more cruel and more utterly horrible than anything I had witnessed on the battlefield. One man's body was particularly gruesome with holes where his eyes had been, perhaps cut from their sockets. It was awful beyond belief and in this hell-hole I was seeking Maguy. My God! How could this be happening? I was sickened and repulsed.

Suddenly, my eyes focused on a familiar face across the human morass. It was the commanding officer who had been in charge of the camp outside Marseilles where I had been injured by the flying axe handle and treated in the infirmary by the officer's nurse-girlfriend. He had looked upon my presence and the treatment required with such hatred. I felt he had been the one to give the order to have me picked up when I escaped, which led to the stable jail in Aix-en-Provence, where I had given up any chance or even desire to live. He did not recognize me as I crossed the room stepping over and around pathetic bodies. I explained to him that I recognized him even if he did not have any memory of me and pointed to a guard standing close by. I indicated that with very little prodding I could have him tortured and put to death, but changed my feelings.

"I'm not going to report you . . . but it's strange that I find myself here and find you in a worse situation than I was in Aix-en-Provence."

We left the officer never to know what fate he met and moved on through the building to find Maguy. On the second floor there were rooms, some of which opened onto the yard below. In one room was a very prominent person, who the guards directed us to — Sacha Guitry, the famous artist, writer, playwright, and producer detained as a collaborator. I was not familiar with his political stance, but he did prosper abundantly during the Occupation and was just one of many prominent personalities picked up to be put on trial. I requested the favor of the opportunity to talk to Guitry. The guard advised me to talk fast because, "Guitry may well be shot in a couple of days."

I countered his comment, "You cannot shoot that man without a trial!"

"Oh, there will be a trial, but he will be shot."

The great artist, an elegant man in his sixties, had an aristocratic profile similar to Barrymore. We found him unshaven and sitting on a straw mattress when we entered his room. I asked Didier and Stunner to watch at the door to secure our safety. One look at us, carrying weapons, and Guitry turned pale. Our uniforms did not particularly align us with the Free French, and we had decided before entering to trust no one and be prepared to shoot. I'm certain the prisoner felt we had arrived to take him before the firing squad. I introduced myself to allay his fears, as a friend and also an appreciative audience well-acquainted with his success and talents in so many areas of the arts. I asked him, "What do you think is going to happen to you, Sir?"

"I do not know except I see a lot of people being killed here without trial and I have a problem . . . I cannot even go to my balcony . . ."

I noticed there were several rooms with balconies overlooking the crowded courtyard.

He went on, "If I go to the balcony, I will face that huge square filled with people who were on the streets last week admiring my work . . . and when I go there they clap their hands . . . they demonstrate their respect and admiration . . . obviously this is no good for me at this time . . . so I stay sitting on this bed waiting . . . waiting . . . and when I saw you coming I thought this would be the end . . . and . . ." his voice broke as he finished his thought.

I said, "Sir, it is a great honor to meet you . . . I wish that I could do something for you, but I do not have that power . . . but I will talk to some of the people running this camp on my way out." He arose from the bed, took my hand and kissed it. I was deeply moved as I turned and left the genius fearing he would be executed within days.

We moved to other camps and jails in search of Maguy. We finally found her in a converted school on the east side of the city in an area called St. Mande. The school was being supervised by members of the Resistance, dressed in street clothes and berets and wearing the tri-colored arm bands. D'Jambekoff's jeep with official code markings again was a tremendous asset in our ability to gain entry. We informed the officials we were investigators for the intelligence service of the Second Division. The prisoners, all women, had been beaten; most had blackened eyes and bruises and some had shaved heads. Many were naked. I spotted Maguy across the room. She was dressed; her head was shaved. I went to her. She looked in my direction but through me, as if I did not exist. There was no recognition in the vacant stare. She pulled back as I approached, weathered and unshaven, combat helmet and uniform, grenades in place and carrying the machine-gun. She looked pale and frightened like a trapped animal. I spoke her name, "Maguy? Maguy, *ce moi*, Robert; don't panic."

Her eyes opened wide as she looked into my face, "God, thank God, thank God."

I wanted to take her in my arms, to hold her, to console her, to let her feel the love and caring that I felt for her, for her pathetic condition, but it was not the time nor the place. I said, "I'm going to play a part and I want you to do just as I tell you."

She barely spoke, "*Oui, oui.*"

I stood back and pronounced with authority, "You are Madame le Royer?"

"*Oui.*"

"We have instructions to take you to headquarters. You are to be interrogated by the armed service. Will you please take your belongings and come with us."

"I don't have any belongings."

I stood on one side of Maguy and Stunner stood on the other while Didier led the way. We were intercepted once, but I informed the official that we had instructions to pick up Madame le Royer to take her to headquarters for questioning. The official asked my name which I avoided divulging, but I did indicate that we would return Madame le Royer after interrogating her. We walked to the jeep and took off. Our next stop was Le Vesinet where Maguy would stay underground with friends. I was relieved to know that she was safe — alive — that I had been able to save her from further torture, rape, or death. We returned to our division and returned d'Jambekoff's jeep, a vital asset in helping secure someone very important to me in a city in tumult. The blood continued to flow.

The Germans took a stand within the Le Bourget Airport. They tried to cover their massive exodus. A young lieutenant from our division was dispatched to the airport by jeep. He arrived to see the white flag of the German occupation and then was immediately cut down, riddled with sniper bullets in front of the flag. Hundreds of German prisoners sat, massed together, in an area of the airport held captive by FFI members. In retaliation for the murder of the young officer, the prisoners were all massacred on the spot by their captors. The German military in turn opened fire on the FFI guards. My unit was assigned the following day to go to the airport. When we arrived, we saw the remnants of the bloodbath, hundreds of bodies lying where they had been sitting or standing the day before. German prisoners of war were slowly removing the bodies from the grim scene, another in a never-ending panorama of carnage.

That night we settled in to occupy the airport and for the first time saw the V-1 rocket that added a new dimension, a ghastly addition, to the German arsenal of destruction. It was nearly midnight, a clear night with stars filling the darkness as the scream, then flash of light split the dark silence like an enormous blowtorch aimed at us. Fortunately, it missed the mark landing two miles west of our position in a tremendous explosion. We were shaken by the drama and vivid indication of the capabilities possessed by the enemy just east of Paris — in the path that would soon be ours.

14

CHASING THE GERMANS
La Poursuite des Allemands

Our assigned route took us east through many small villages. We continued to see the most disturbing sights: victims of the punishment meted by members of the FFI, men and women who were thought to be enemies. The women were beaten and their heads shaven, and men were similarly beaten and tortured — even murdered. It was our job to intervene. I now was in the ironic position of having to point my weapon at my fellow countrymen, which was a vile and accursed order but absolutely necessary to protect other French victims from brutality. In Troyes, members of the FFI visited our unit and brought us wine one evening. When they left they carried off many of our individual weapons. The town was soon surrounded by our company, and an order issued by our command to the citizens demanded the weapons be returned in 24 hours under immediate threat of martial law. If any persons were caught carrying a weapon or concealing one in their quarters, they would be shot. After the incident fraternization with the Force of Resistance was totally suspect.

We headed next to Chaumont to set a trap for the Germans escaping from the south. The First Army, under the command of General Jean de Lattre de Tassigny, had established a beachhead in Marseilles. The Allied Forces pushed the Germans north. We were hidden in foxholes and our vehicles buried, in command of the highway that was a natural route for the retreating Germans. Our orders were to lay low and wait, let the spearhead pass through; and then, when the full mass of the convoy arrived, open fire. It was a nerve-racking wait made more harrowing by a different enemy. New recruits had joined our unit in Paris, young men who had not experienced the battlefield and were damned nervous. We waited for a couple of weeks. The woods surrounding our emplacement were filled with wild boar. The watch in pitch darkness and severe cold in the unknown forest was a trial compounded by the raging groups of 200-pound vicious boar. They startled the young sentries who created danger and fear by indiscriminately firing their weapons which resulted not only in pig, but human losses as well. The young, trigger-happy recruits could not tell the difference between Germans creeping through the dark, ominous woods or the equally menacing wild pigs.

We were more than anxious to move on when orders came moving us to Vittel to again sit and wait. There was a noncom officer, who had served with LeClerc since the beginning of the War. He was about 35 years old and had a drinking problem — he drank a lot of vodka plus anything else he could get his hands on. We all would have indulged more under the circumstances if it had been available. The weather was brutally cold, and if there was time to sleep, it was often out in the elements or in a barn devastated by shelling or fire. If the shelter was a barn or a bombed-out farmhouse, the officers always took the portion that provided the most protection. The conditions were so harsh that drinking tended to inure the senses. But the *L'Adjudant* was obviously sharply aware of pending danger and confided in me, "I have a bad feeling about today."

I responded, "Well, you would probably have a better feeling if you wouldn't drink so damn much."

He was not the only officer who drank heavily. Lt. d'Jambekoff also drank from early in the day, everyday, in the company of his sergeants. The young officer went on to describe a premonition. He said he felt that something was going to happen, something different, and not good for him.

As soon as we began moving through the woods, we encountered a sniper, as well as artillery fire. I was no more than 300 yards away when I saw the officer fall, shot in the chest. A soldier next to him tried to pick up the fallen man, but he let out a yell and dropped as well. Another soldier, witnessing the event, began to crawl through the underbrush to where the sniper was hiding high in the branches of a tree. I watched the drama unfold as a shot from the man's Colt .45 knocked the sniper from the tree. I vividly recalled the verbalized feeling of peril so quickly and assuredly confirmed. It would recur as we continued to move on.

Stunner, my friend and confidant, comrade in arms who had fought closely alongside me in every battle from Normandy through Paris, had been reassigned. I missed him and I thought of his parting words that he too felt a premonition of death.

I had met Albert in Rennes when I was on the run hiding in the forest near Fegreac. It was a complete surprise to meet him again as a fellow member of the *Batallion de Renfort,* to train in the boot camp in Normandy, and then be pulled out at the same time to serve together in the Second Armored Division under d'Jambekoff and General LeClerc. We had been through so much in the past months; It was a most incredible sharing of battle and survival, witnessing many fellow soldiers who did not survive the carnage who accompanied us on the journey from Normandy into Paris. Albert, exceptional in many ways, was well-educated, a fine strong athlete as well as a sensitive gentleman in an infantry filled with tough, gutsy guys who, for the most part, were not well-educated or culturally attuned to the many common interests that connected us.

My background was quite removed and apart from so many of the men I found myself with, in such intimate daily activities. Albert was a very special friend, a brother, someone who understood me well, and I understood and loved him.

The weather had been gloomy and wet as late summer turned to fall. Winter arrived with ice, snow, and freezing temperatures in an already uninhabitable atmosphere of death, suffering, and plunder.

In a sense, Paris had been like the eye of a hurricane, the calm before the other side of the storm. It held a certain premature optimism as we paraded down the Champs-Élysées. However, we were quickly shaken from any such luxury by the German bombs dropping on the city celebrating "liberation." And then more upheaval followed.

Albert was assigned to join a command company where his fluency in German could be used to interrogate prisoners. His last comment to me was that, like me, he "volunteered for the duration of a fighting war." He did not like the idea of moving papers while we were exposed to death. But he also confided he had a premonition of impending death and would not fight the transfer. I hated like hell to see him move on.

As we moved closer to the German border, the fighting continued to be fierce. It was cold and had rained for days. There was a break in the weather one afternoon as we moved through the Ardennes. Lt. Couteau ordered me, "Robert, take three men and a half-track and follow that road to the first left. Then go on another 200 yards and you will see Capt. Boussion. He is having a war council with some of his officers."

We took off down the road in the half-track, turned left, then continued on until we arrived at the designated location where four jeeps were parked. I reported to the group of noncom officers and Capt. Boussion. For days we had advanced through the forest without sleep; we were all exhausted. Capt. Boussion and his men poured over maps as he directed me to take my position at the .50 calibre machine gun to guard the area while the officers planned strategy.

I had the feeling the idiots had gotten us lost in the forest as they pointed to the maps and debated our next move. I took my position, my finger on the trigger, aware that there were Germans all around us in the woods. There was a bullet in the chamber and the safety was off as was standard procedure in the field. I was prepared to shoot to kill at first sight of the enemy.

As the officers continued to map and discuss strategy, a warm ray of sunlight broke through the clouds and filtered through the trees. Exhausted, with the rare and welcome warmth of the sun, I must have dozed for a fraction of a second. I was brought instantly to attention by the explosion as I accidentally pulled the trigger. The shot caused all the officers to hit the ground. Capt. Boussion, navy *kepi* askew, turned to look at me. He had turned pale and I could tell from his expression as he glared at me that he was livid. He lifted himself from the ground and slowly, menacingly, approached, ignoring my apologies as his hateful words and pronouncements of my ineptness filled the air.

When he ran out of appropriate vile expletives, he said, "Listen, I'll tell you something, I haven't killed any Germans lately, but I'm going to kill a Frenchman!"

With that he pulled his Colt, cocked it, and pointed it at me. He took a bead as I stood, shocked and shaking, thinking, the son of a bitch is gonna kill me! Meanwhile, some of the noncoms raised themselves from the dirt and rushed to restrain the Captain. He angrily ordered me to report to my commanding officer to be punished. His officers later reported his behavior and, instead of me being reprimanded, it was Capt. Boussion who received a strong reprimand for being out of order.

A few days following the incident as we advanced through the forest, I saw Capt. Boussion riding in a jeep on my left flank. Suddenly he fell, shot between the eyes by a sniper's bullet. The driver turned the jeep around to rescue the Captain and rush him to the command area to receive medical attention. He was dead on arrival. I could not fault the man. We were all under extreme pressure and my accidental firing days before obviously frightened him into the crazed retaliation. His fears were well-founded and a bullet had found its mark.

Part of our division had been assigned the job to cross the Moselle River after a wet, sleepless night filled with constant artillery fire. As a grey dawn broke, we were pounded by 88mm shells. General LeClerc, with cane, *kepi*, and aristocratic profile, watched along with his *aide-de-camp*, driver and officers all saluting him — I couldn't help but think that he appeared to be "on the way to the Forum" in his imperious attitude. During the night our troops had built a pontoon bridge, but had not escaped enemy fire — the losses were heavy. Corpses, rigid testimony to the grim reality, lay wherever they had been pulled from the water. Many bodies had been carried down stream by the swiftly moving current.

As soon as we crossed to the other side, sniper fire and artillery increased. We moved through a clearing as incoming shells fell on all sides. Fortunately, we did not suffer any casualties during the first encounter.

We entered the forest with the objective to take Manonvilliers, a village located on the edge of the river La Vezouz. As we moved through the heavy timber on a slippery, muddy, rutted road, we began to see the effects of our own artillery — German soldiers hanging high in the trees, bodies limp like disarticulated puppets. There were fresh tracks from German tiger tanks. Through the trees we could see German tanks moving from place to place. We were closing on the enemy, and I thought of my good friend and fellow warrior, Albert, whom I missed greatly.

There was a pause in the battle. Some of our guys found eggs. Soon an omelette was prepared as 12 of us waited in great anticipation for the gastronomic delight and diversion from the monotony of rations. Suddenly, a barrage of 88mm canon fire hit our position. Everyone dove for cover. The omelette, which was coveted more than anything at the moment, was lost in the scramble for shelter.

Advancing through the forest was hell. There were many hazardous areas like quicksand. The Germans dug slanted holes where they backed their tanks with 88mm guns to cover our offensive. The guns were completely camouflaged with freshly cut greenery. In no time, we had five or six lead vehicles burning and blocking the clay road. There was no place to turn with rain-filled ditches on either side.

The infantry, assigned to cover our flanks and reconnoiter, had been left behind in the mire. Lt. Couteau, an inspiring young officer, lay in a prone position with his *kepi* slightly ajar when he signalled me to crawl next to him. He asked for volunteers for liaison duty, and I had answered his call. He told me he picked me to be *homme de liaison* or liaison man. Radio contact had been lost, and I was to carry verbal messages back and forth to the company commander two kilometers to the rear.

I took an army carbine as my weapon. As I began the new duty, I ran about 50 feet before German fire hit so close that I dove behind a tree. My experience in the woods reminded me to hit the ground behind the largest tree in the vicinity. I waited, then ran another 50 yards, and hit the mud behind another tree until the sniper fire ceased for reloading. Then I sprang again seeking another tree, all the time looking out as well for the personnel mines. It didn't take long before I was discovered — the bullets came closer with targeted accuracy. One tracer caught me and left a flaming hole in my sleeve. I changed my tactics and distances and began to crawl through the underbrush, zigzaggging to strategically located trees. I managed to carry information on the location of the platoon to the company commander and orders to the platoon back from the commander as I traveled back and forth.

Once I landed in a water-filled ditch beside the clay road where a tank battle was taking place almost at point-blank range. As I crouched, stunned, in the freezing water, enormous tree limbs and leaves fell on me as they were blown from the trees. Chest deep in the icy, muddy water, I held my weapon above water level and my head below bank level. Suddenly something hit me. One of the two fragmentation grenades hooked to my belt had been struck and torn off my equipment. Fortunately, it did not explode.

At first, I thought I had been hit by shrapnel. I looked up into the dense foliage and caught the tiny glint of bright metal. The Germans wore combat boots studded with steel nails. Just on a hunch, I fired a whole clip from my carbine in a vertical spray into the foliage. Nothing happened for a few seconds. Then a body tumbled down the bank and rolled into the water two feet in front of me. It was a very young German radio operator. He had lost his helmet, his blond hair was muddy and his blue eyes pleaded for mercy. "Comrade" was his last word before he fell forward spewing blood onto my uniform. I was horrified and yet could not move until I felt the way clear.

I wanted badly to take his submachine gun as a souvenir but felt it would be cumbersome. I was sickened by the encounter — knowing I had ended the life of the young man — knowing fully that it could just as well be me lying face down in the bloody water. I crawled out of the ditch and rejoined Lt. Couteau, who by this time had lost his *kepi*.

Later that day we finally reached Manonvilliers in time to see German light-armored vehicles moving by at full speed on a paved road. All our guns fired on them with no more success than the Germans had shooting at me all day. Within minutes of our arrival, a tremendous artillery barrage was directed at us. I somersaulted from the half-track into the thickest part of a large cow manure pile at the side of the road.

After 15 minutes, the shelling subsided and everyone emerged from their hiding places. One of my buddies ran to me yelling excitedly, "Robert . . . in the ditch next to the road . . . under a big tree. Stunner is wounded!"

I ran as fast as my legs could manage in the direction that he pointed and found, between two wounded soldiers, my closest battlefield friend and compatriot, blue eyes and mouth wide open, his uniform lacerated by shrapnel. His premonition had been correct, and I was absolutely devastated. I looked at his face. The grotesque look of anguish was frozen, never to change again. I would never hear his hopes and dreams. He was a young, talented,

I'm standing on the right of a burned-out U.S. armored vehicle.

educated man who was my closest friend in war. I stood, staring, and I cried at the horror of it. Tears wet my cheeks. I didn't care or even think about what Father had said, "Men don't cry!" I cried for Albert and for all that was happening in a world gone mad. I could not afford the luxury to stop and think, to feel the pain or self-pity at the loss.

I moved into the next assignment with a heaviness of grief that would remain for a long time. We moved on to another village five miles from Manonvilliers. The roads were clear with forest on one side and a valley on the other. A small village that fit snugly into a hill in the distance was our next target. As we approached the final twist in the road, we came upon five of our own tanks that had been destroyed the day before. The bodies of our men were encased in the disabled, smoldering tanks, ovens that sealed a horrible death. We could go no further on the road but had to take to the woods on foot.

The Germans dug a series of trenches on both sides of the road. When we began crawling through the woods and came upon the first trenches, we found them filled with bodies of dead Germans. Our tank command had been successful in silencing the enemy-filled trenches before they in turn were destroyed.

We had a couple of hours to relax before moving on to the village. I found a piece of cardboard and made a sketch of the scene with trenches containing dead Germans holding their long-handled grenades which looked like giant potato-mashers.

Another vivid recollection from that day reminded me of something that Father told me about his war experiences. He said that if you were at a particular angle from the flight of a bullet, you could actually see the shell moving. I found that quite unbelievable at the time and doubted his veracity. But now I was in a trench and crawling over German corpses trying to get close to the enemy to reconnoiter or take some prisoners. I stuck my head up to look over the four-foot parapet and, sure enough, from a gun fired at about 1000 meters away, I actually saw the bullet in flight. It appeared like a bee coming straight at me for a fraction of a second. The shot missed me by inches.

The next day I again experienced sniper fire when I felt a heavy impact on my combat boot. I pulled the right boot off, revealing two severely damaged toes from a bullet that had smashed through the leather. I could not walk nor put the boot back on. I was loaded into a jeep along with other wounded soldiers and a few corpses. I don't know how the driver maneuvered the jeep so heavily laden with bodies, but we were delivered to a field hospital set in a huge tent in the middle of woods.

As we pulled into the clearing, a group of Germans ran toward the jeep. I cried out, "Jesus Christ, the Germans have taken over! We're dead for certain this time!" I was too quickly reconciled to my fate. Finally, I realized the Germans were prisoners of war doing their duty to empty the vehicles as each arrived. I was taken by stretcher into the open-ended tent where there were six other wounded soldiers waiting treatment while five or six surgeries were being performed.

As I waited, lying patiently and in far better shape than some around me, I surveyed the activity in the sheltered field hospital. There were women busily cutting pieces of cloth to wrap open wounds, and some assisted with the surgery. Off to one side were garbage cans with arms and legs sticking out, limbs amputated and dumped in the trash. It was a ghastly sight — a human slaughterhouse. I waited, wondering if my foot would end up in the garbage.

The large toe and second toe had been shattered. The doctors did little at the field hospital. They cleaned the wound and wrapped it in a dressing. I was then transported to a hospital in Reims where I was given penicillin. That was a first for me. The injury required surgery which created a great deal of pain. The doctors attempted to save the big toe by splinting the bones, but I lost all feeling in the toe. The small toe could not be saved. I was again bandaged and ordered moved to Paris to the military hospital Le Val de Grâce via a hospital transport train marked with red crosses.

There were thousands of wounded aboard, each car stank with a strong, decadent odor from festering wounds. Gruesome sights and sounds filled the train as it moved slowly toward its destination. There were soldiers who had sustained wounds weeks earlier who died en route, and their bodies were moved to an empty car in the rear. Next to me was a dark-skinned fellow from Morocco who had sustained a ghastly wound to his midsection. His guts were in a plastic bag attached to the front of him.

With bridges destroyed and replaced by temporary spans, the passage was slow and agonizing. About two hours out of Reims, we were strafed by the *Luftwaffe*. The train was halted for six hours while antiaircraft guns were attached to the front and rear of the train. The Allied Forces had moved out of France to strategic areas east, leaving behind many Germans who welcomed the opportunity to engage any and all targets, even those displaying crosses. As the trip continued, nurses came through the train administering pain-killing drugs to lessen the anguish. For some, the pain ended more quickly. For others, there was promise for recuperation and a return to battle. For me, there would be a respite, a time to reflect on what had happened before, the death of Stunner, and so much more.

Le Val de Grâce in the center of Paris had been in existence for many years serving the needs of the military in wartime. Everything was antiseptic and spartan with white iron beds filled with war casualties. I had a second operation. To save the toe, my foot was cut to the center and a cast put on to hold the injured big toe in place. The pain from a wound to the foot or hand is far greater than a wound to a fleshy muscular part of the body. The many nerve endings and small bones created many more complications, but I managed to be up and hobbling around on crutches several days after surgery.

One day the patients and staff were informed that "a very important commander is expected." We were given less than an hour to straighten our beds, if able, and to tidy the area. I was back in bed, when General LeClerc appeared, elegant in beige *kepi*, his buckskin gloves carrying the malachite cane. His attending staff officers also wore the kepi and carried similar canes.

During my recuperation, I was given leave for a visit to Fegreac. I remember the visit as being marked by a blanketing snowstorm. Getting around on the healing foot was not easy. It was good to see my parents, and I spent precious hours with Simone. She was more beautiful than ever, and so much had happened since our last time together. With families still politically worlds apart, our meetings required the utmost discretion. Simone was absolutely paranoid about her father learning of my presence. We met twice to make love. It was so wonderful to hold her, feel her next to me. It was an emotional time, a needful time, and the softness of her body pressed close to mine helped fill the emptiness I felt in Stunner's death and in all the lives I saw ended in battle. It was but a brief interlude of intense beauty in a world of ugliness and loss.

I had written to Stunner's wife when I knew that I would be in Fegreac. She was living in Rennes at the time, and I knew that she had been informed of Stunner's death within days of the tragedy; but I knew as well that she would not know the details. I felt compelled to go to her and offer whatever solace I could to the young widow.

I visited her apartment and found her composed, but I knew she had been crying for days. She did not cry in my presence and that helped me get through the visit. I told her that Albert had been transferred to the intelligence unit two days before his death. I also told her that when I reached him, I knew that the end had been quick; he did not suffer long. I did not tell her that I took him into my arms hoping that life existed and could be sustained. I am certain when I left the modest apartment in Rennes she knew that I loved Stunner and cared for him in a very special way, and that his loss would stay with me for all the days of my life. I would battle on for Stunner and for France and for Robert.

I returned to the hospital for a final checkup and release. My foot still bothered me. The doctors determined that I required more time for the wound to fully heal. It was still oozing fluid which required a daily change of dressing. That was easy enough in the hospital, but the doctors knew that would not be done on the battlefield where infection and frostbite would lead to amputation.

I grew more impatient each day as trucks left the confines with patients who had been declared fit enough to rejoin their units. I continued to bombard the dispatcher with requests for dismissal until one day he said, "Well, if you want to get your ass busted again, it's fine with me. I could keep you here another month, but if that's what you want to do, go ahead. It's your ass."

Ordinarily the trucks transporting the recuperated soldiers back into infantry were closed. On the day of my release, the truck was an open flatbed with side panels that did nothing to protect against the elements. The weather was freezing as we left Paris under threatening grey skies which soon became white with snow. I was one of 25 men packed closely with only a piece of canvas to pull over our bodies. The snow fell heavily making the drive hazardous. We were soon lost from our convoy and the highway. Body heat was not adequate.

We finally implored our driver, warm in the heated cab, to pull over at a farmhouse where we were given a brief respite from the misery. Hot soup and hot coffee were provided and even hot water to soak frozen feet and hands. But the journey had to continue, and we left to again huddle close in the back of the flatbed for the duration of the trip. It meant another night and day of freezing, bumpy, brutal, desperate circumstances to finally gain access to our individual units.

There had been other dropping-off areas. I was dropped, along with a buddy, at the side of the road where an MP pulled out a map and directed us to where our Armored Division was located. The MP realized we were not armed and called for weapons to safeguard our passage. Needless to say, there was no limousine service available for the trip of about 20 miles.

Our unit had been assigned to take Strasbourg during the time that I had been in the hospital. I missed that action. The unit moved on to the Black Forest. If we continued for 20 miles to a stream, crossed the icy water, and continued another six miles, we would be home.

We decided to hitchhike, but the snow stopped all traffic. We began walking but that was going to be impossible particularly for me. My sore foot was numb and ached. We needed some sort of conveyance. I spotted a farm in the distance. We approached not knowing if a sniper or German occupants were inside with guns aimed at us.

The farm appeared abandoned. We spotted a motorcycle

outside and went to the door. Inside we found an old lady hiding, trembling. There were two teenaged girls hiding in the cellar. We liberated the bike. It did not have much gas, but we soon came to a small village with a service station and a long line of Germans holding cans to collect their gas ration.

At first we decided to get in line and wait our turn. Then I realized that we were fighting against these people. We held the upper hand and could go to the front of the line to demand the gas. That was a highly unpopular stance. We moved to the front, and I confronted the stern-faced attendant, "Listen . . . I want the gas now!"

My request was completely ignored by the man who kept serving his countrymen, who were looking at me. I became incensed by his attitude and the obvious hate that everyone in line seemed to convey at my spoken demand, which exposed us as French intruders. I felt that the man would serve everyone ahead of us and perhaps run out of the precious fuel before our turn. I looked beyond the attendant to a large glass sign that held the name of the gas, took aim and shot the glass out. The explosion caught everyone's attention. The attendant, startled, turned angrily as I again raised the gun and shot at the sign a second time. I yelled, "I want the gas NOW!" We were served with dispatch and took off down the highway.

I soon spotted a house located across a creek running parallel to the highway. There were two vehicles in an open garage. We drove up, again not knowing if there would be armed German SS troops or Gestapo within, guns trained on our arrival. We heard nothing and saw nothing before rapping on the door. We broke into the house and found an occupant, a dignified, pretty lady in her forties who looked upon us with much disdain as though we were the vilest vermin. I asked her if she had the key to the Mercedes. She said she did not. I said we could start the car without the key, but it would be damaging and we preferred to have the key. I explained the car would be returned. It was obvious she was uncooperative so we searched the house.

We found a man hiding in the cellar. I presumed him to be the husband and held the gun on him, requesting the key. He looked at us with hatred in his eyes and said he didn't have the key, his wife did. I explained to him that we had already been rebuffed by the lady and were losing patience.

"We are running out of time. We don't want to harm you, but we already talked to your wife and she said she didn't have a key. We're not going to stand around here. We're going to use the Mercedes, and we want the key NOW!"

He snarled, "You are not going to get the key."

I angrily demanded, "Well, then you will come with us and we are going to shoot your wife in front of you." I was bluffing, but I did spray the wall with my .45 before the key materialized.

We jumped into the Mercedes, a magnificent automobile, and took off over the bridge onto the highway toward the Black Forest. We pulled right up to the area where our unit was bivouacked. Lt. d'Jambekoff's attention was quickly aroused by our arrival. He issued his customary welcome.

"You son of a bitch! Where have you been all along and where did you steal this thing?" He pointed to the car as I told him the story followed by his rejoinder, "Well, will you please get your ass next to your half-track and leave the car with me. I will keep an eye on IT!" That was the end of our Mercedes. It was back to the half-track and the unit.

One night soon after our return, to warm ourselves, we lit a fire against regulations. We were freezing. We dug a hole in the ground and poured gasoline in to ignite some wood and whatever we could find to burn. Suddenly, a shot rang out, and Lt. d'Jambekoff went down clutching his leg.

"Jesus Christ, a sniper got him!" I exclaimed.

It turned out that someone had put refuse in the pit containing misspent ammo and a bullet went off hitting our brave leader in the calf of the leg. He had fought gallantly through Normandy into Paris, then into Germany, escaping enemy fire only to be wounded by a stray bullet from a warming fire. He refused to leave camp for medical attention, preferring to be patched up by the medics, and continued to perform his duties using his trusty cane. He was truly one of LeClerc's tough bulldogs.

Munich was our next assignment. The Americans had entered the city to face a strong German resistance. When we arrived, the city was still burning from thousands of phosphorous bombs which left the city smoldering in a thick acrid smoke. Civilians had been driven into the cellars and were still in hiding.

We were told to separate and search for any German soldiers left behind. In my search, I found a very beautiful German girl, about 25 years old, hiding in the cellar, and we began to communicate. I wanted to put her at ease. She spoke French very well, and we shared similar emotional responses to the horror of what put us in this place together at a time when dreams and hopes were being dashed. We decided that our situation was perilous and our chances for survival were not good, that we should grasp the moment and find whatever pleasure we could in the limited time we had. We were just two young people. She was not my enemy nor was I her enemy. We were both victims in a diabolical plot against humanity with needless pain and destruction leveled at so much that we cherished. There was a bed in one of the rooms in the cellar where we made love while Munich smoldered around us.

I left Munich with thoughts of the girl and many unanswered questions. Would I ever see her again? Would she survive? Would I survive? Would the fighting, the warring ever cease?

Our next job was to head southeast to take Berchtesgaden. It was late April and the weather began to improve. The Royal Air Force had preceded us with massive bombing of the area surrounding the heavily fortified mountain retreat. We encountered sniper fire as we approached the hallowed sanctuary so revered by Hitler as his mountain getaway. It was also the repository of many treasures stolen from culturally rich European collections. The area was densely forested in all directions which provided good shelter for the SS troops that were Hitler's elite corps. They were the bastards who perpetrated such vile and brutal atrocities wherever they invaded. They were trained to fight tenaciously to the end.

As we approached the mountain complex, one of our men discovered a hole in the midst of the rubble leading into a huge cave. It in turn, tunneled into passages leading to a winery beneath the huge bombed-out retreat. The Fuehrer's house contained many rooms and chambers filled with booty liberated from the cultural centers of Europe. The winery was stocked with hundreds upon hundreds of bottles of the finest liquors, brandies, and wine. Within four hours of the discovery, nearly 2,000 men were quite drunk. If the Germans had emerged from the forest, they could have easily mowed down our forces. But the drunken revelry was not detected or disturbed by the enemy.

We were at Berchtesgaden in May when VE Day was declared to jubilant cheers throughout western Europe and wherever the Germans had been in control. I did not witness the delirium that existed in Paris and the small villages throughout the country celebrating freedom and liberation from the vile oppressors as we fought against the German SS troops in the forest. The sniper fire continued after VE Day as the War for us was waged at a high pitch for weeks after the end had been officially declared. We heard the news that the Germans had surrendered, but that word made no impression on the hated elite troops trained never to give up but to fight on, whatever the circumstances.

We remained in the forest for weeks before heading back to Paris. The return trip was made easy by the use of the autobahns. I enjoyed the smooth and wide highway system in Germany. It was such a pleasure after the muck and rutted cross-country travel. As students in France, we received propaganda that France had the finest road system in the entire world. What a farce! Our roads were no better than those in Belgium and were far inferior to the German system. The only time we had to return to battlefield conditions was when a viaduct or overhead bridge had been bombed and a detour was designated. The return trip was swift, smooth, and peaceful.

Once back in Paris I was able to contact relatives. I visited Le Vesinet; my parents were in Brittany at the time. My division was moved to a position outside the city. VE Day was weeks old but the celebrations continued all over France with dances, parties, drinking, and joviality unmatched in the history of the war-torn country, a country emerging from more than five years of brutal occupation that touched every individual and left lifelong scars.

The *gendarme* was unable to cope with the massive celebrations where people of differing political philosophies congregated and became drunk and disorderly. What began as a friendly celebration often deteriorated into fighting and disorder.

I received the assignment to patrol one of the parties being held in a school building. Six men were ordered to serve under my authority. I carried a Colt .45; my retinue was armed with Army carbines. We were the MPs for the civilian gathering. From the start we were insulted while the revelers were sober — easy enough to ignore. But I could see that the volatile situation could deteriorate quickly if we didn't maintain a strong posture and demand compliance. The Communists in the group were calling us Nazis just to get our attention. I told my men to remain cool and under no circumstance were they to use their weapons. I was the only one authorized to use force if warranted.

The dancing began and the drinking continued. I had posted a man at each of the six exits. One approached me, his face awash in blood. He was nearly in shock; I was stunned by the severity of the injury. He said one of the revelers had broken a bottle of wine and buried the broken bottle in his face. I asked who assaulted him. He could not see through the blood, so I took him to the wash room. Upon returning, he pointed out his assailant, as civilian volunteers approached to offer assistance. I assigned my men and the volunteers to guard the doors and sent one of my men to capture the attacker, who by this time was trying desperately to escape from the building. He became frantic as he tried to break through to each of the guarded exit doors.

Suddenly I saw him running to my door, and I braced myself, with a carbine in back, ready to swing. As he came through the door, I swung the carbine and hit him in the head, knocking him off his feet. That's when the fun began. The crowd turned hostile. Bottles flew through the air at my entourage gathered at the exit door.

We grabbed the attacker and retreated outside to get to our jeeps. The vehicles were gone. We struggled to a small café where I phoned company headquarters to alert them of the incident and our need of transportation away from an angry crowd. Exiting the café we were met by nearly 500 hostile people ready to tear into us.

I gave the order, "Stand by to open fire . . . load your weapons . . . shoot right above their heads!" The report from the semi-automatic weapons immediately scattered the crowd. Five vehicles showed up and we, along with the bottle-wielding celebrant, departed quickly for headquarters.

Meanwhile, the Communist-controlled press learned of the incident, and the headline in the leftist paper the following day read: "LECLERC TROOPS OUR CURRENT NAZIS."

In the following days, spurious articles were written demanding an investigation. I was summoned to division headquarters to answer questions and to write a lengthy report. I was removed from the unit to another unit pending my "court martial."

Many witnesses were questioned during a thorough investigation and I was exonerated, not court-martialed. Ultimately, I was congratulated on my prudent handling of the incident and even promised an elevated rank.

On July 25, 1945, I was made Corporal. I received the honor and the rank with ambivalence. I was gratified by the recognition, but had no interest or intention of staying in service. The War was over. I had not joined the army to make it my career. I joined at a time when the German Occupation had disrupted every semblance of normalcy in the life of my country, and I had been on the run for years and could run no longer. I simply took a stand. I had no thoughts whatever of being a military man. I felt it was with the military, the Free French, that I could best effectuate my goal which became my commitment; but I did not care to continue serving my country in military service. My officers began to apply pressure. They were most flattering and encouraging in attempting to persuade me to consider signing on for a longer term. I was given a pass to visit my family which would provide time to make a decision.

My parents had survived the War well. They were in a far better situation than if they had remained in Le Vesinet. Because of the farms all around, once the fighting moved to the east, living conditions in Brittany normalized to a degree with access to meat, butter, and other foods scarce in Paris and wherever German concentration was heavy. Uncle Gauthier was still helping Father run the farm. Father's delivery route kept him occupied, and the apple orchard continued to put out a good yield. The immediate grounds showed evidence of previous German emplacements. The farm had not sustained any damage, and the house itself, massive with slate roof over wood beams, had survived the War but had developed problems of another major concern.

One day Father showed me what he had discovered, which would ultimately necessitate selling the farm. He took me into the enormous attic supported by handcrafted 400-year-old wood beams. He whispered, "Don't make a sound . . . don't talk . . . just listen." We stood quietly and soon heard the hum of insidious industry. Father pointed to small mounds of fine sawdust. Termites were busy eating the wood beams, and the cost to replace the roof was prohibitive.

German POWs helped with the badger hunt.

Father had acquired a thoroughbred horse, a filly, that he enjoyed riding. It was a reminder of his days in the horse-drawn cavalry. He also kept a watchful eye on the market in Le Vesinet. He was continuously active and productive in many diverse ventures. He could not tolerate idleness.

The small villages were being rebuilt with the help of German laborers housed in a camp within view of the farm. There were 200 prisoners of war detained in the camp, and they would remain in the area for years. They provided help on the farms. The Mayor, Mr. DuDresnay, was still in charge of the local government in Fegreac and treated me, in uniform and elevated to corporal, with greater respect. He had been staunchly pro-German — one of many sympathizers who must have feared for his life when the purges to eradicate the collaborators began. I felt his neck was saved because he was a member of local nobility in addition to the esteem in which the farmers held him. Also the church, which he strongly supported, was influential in exerting pressures to secure his safety after overlooking many atrocities during the Occupation.

My parents had kept some of my hunting dogs, and I enjoyed going into the forest after badgers and foxes. I have a photograph of a German prisoner helping me drive the dogs through the woods to ferret out game. And I met with Simone. She was employed by the Resistance, the organization fully and loyally supported by her father that actively engaged in exposing collaborators and any Frenchmen who were stigmatized by their loyalties to France and France alone, and did not espouse Communist doctrine. Our clandestine meetings, of necessity, were discrete. I loved her deeply.

When I returned to Paris to rejoin my unit, we were sent to the Pyrenees in the south of France. We were billeted in homes near a small town called Pissos. My quarters was a small castle. When we became occupied in daily drills, target practice and maneuvers, we used pup tents in the field. The combat had ended leaving us time to enjoy the countryside and the warm weather.

One day I met a very beautiful young girl who was spending the summer with her family in a cottage in the pines. The wealthy family came from Bordeaux, an hour's drive from Pissos. Anette DuBonette was a well-educated brunette and an amorous young lady. Several days after we met, she joined me in my tent, and we made love. I saw her frequently after that to indulge our romantic dalliance.

Anette and her parents took the relationship more seriously than I and invited me to accompany them, when I had leave, to their home in the city. They obviously were people of means as members of Bordeaux nobility. Their home was most impressive and Mr. DuBonette's business, wholesale fancy food distribution, apparently prospered well. My future 'mother-in-law' was a good-looking, aggressive lady who was the driving force in the family. My future 'father-in-law,' more subdued, always seemed to have his head in the newspaper quietly puffing on his pipe. They apparently viewed me as their future son-in-law and spoke of traveling to the north to meet my family. I did not share the commitment, but Madame DuBonette had her own ideas. She was the director of the whole production.

The training continued in the mountains for months as did my romance. From the beginning, rumors abounded to justify our occupation with deGaulle as our leader. The most apparent reason for our assignment was as a possible invasion force to invade

Spain which, under Franco, had sided with the Germans during the War. We were strategically situated on one side of the mountain range with a strong and well-armed Spanish Army on the other.

When the order came to move out, it was not into Spain but back to Paris. I said goodbye to Anette not knowing if I would see her again, but caring deeply for her. The army was jerking me around, and I was becoming less enamored with military life. My goal had been accomplished.

The French Army was actively involved in a conflict in Indochina where unrest required reinforcements be sent to the colony in the Far East. The pressures on me intensified. The army was playing a game of semantics holding up to me and all the other volunteers who had joined to fight in Europe, that there was still a war going on involving France and our commitment and our duty was to fight that war as well. I did not feel that I was still under army jurisdiction.

D'Jambekoff, elevated to Captain, was one of many officers who wooed me. He invited me out to drink on several occasions and after several vodkas would say, "Listen, we are going together over there ... I don't want to stay in France — it's all torn up ... Communists everywhere ... it's going to be politically insane ... you can make a career ... you are a natural born leader ... you don't know what you are doing if you don't join up."

He was intent on convincing me as he continued, "LeClerc is already serving out there. We were a great team fighting the German bastards ... how can you not continue to serve under such a great commander?"

It was thought at the time that the war in Indochina would be of short duration. Little did anyone know how complex the situation and how a deteriorating alignment over a period of many years would end with France withdrawing to leave the United States embroiled in what became the most controversial and unpopular war ever fought by the U.S. forces — Vietnam.

All I knew at the time was that Robert Baudy knew very well that he did not want to have anything to do with a war in the jungles. I was sick of the military and wanted to become a civilian. I stood firm in my resolve. I got the hell out.

15

FREEDOM
La Liberté

I left Paris for Fegreac with a brief visit to Paul's compound. The consummate trainer was actively engaged in his work and had a new girlfriend — a stunning brunette. Maguy was out of the picture. Paul had moved from Le Vesinet to a townhouse in St. Mande. There were new acts being developed with bears, leopards, some dogs, monkeys, and ponies. Paul asked if I would be interested in working for him. I was undecided.

My return to Fegreac did not hold any career plans. My parents welcomed me. It was good to be home, to be free and to be close to Simone. My first civilian position came through Mayor DuDresnay. The job was as a courier but with the added qualifications of having an art background.

A referendum had been passed by the farmers before the War. The government plan called the *Remembrement* was created to consolidate the land holdings in all of Normandy. The *Bocage,* which historically had been divided into many thousands of small plots, was separated by hedgerows and passed down in families from generation to generation. The plan called for repartition where many parcels would be exchanged for a single parcel of equivalent acreage. In order to fulfill the tenets, a dossier had to be prepared for each farmer's holdings. It was my job to bicycle to the farms around Fegreac to do an evaluation. I took pictures and drew topographical delineations. I cycled over 100 miles per day in what began as a well-received labor.

However, on one of my excursions I was met by a drunken,

irate farmer who threatened to throw me off his property. I felt no guilt. I received threatening and even violent reactions to my arrival as the plan began to take affect. Farmers were given land far inferior to what they originally owned. The majority of the peasants in Brittany were uneducated, tough, hard-working landowners who felt the government was cheating them. They took their frustration at the injustice out on me. I went to Mayor DuDresnay and told him that his job was not a job. I was not armed to protect myself and felt he should get the marines in to do the work. I quit and learned later that the Mayor eventually had to resort to bringing troops in to enact the highly unpopular government-sponsored program.

Father heard of a job with a printing company in Morlaix, two hours from Fegreac. The job description required an artist to design wine bottle labels. My training at the art school, Nicole Estienne, had prepared me for the position. I applied and was accepted. Mother accompanied me to Morlaix where we found a large ground floor apartment to rent. I became a resident of the city.

There were 50 lithographic machines in the old building which housed the printing company. A glass-enclosed, soundproof cubicle in the center surrounded the artist. My drawing board in the center of the cubicle isolated me from the noise of the printing activity although I could see all that was in the works in the on-going production of labels. I created the original art from which color separations were made. The designs were then put on blocks of stone for the final printing process. I enjoyed the meticulous detail required, which I performed with much expertise and to the total satisfaction of my employer, but I hated being in the fish-bowl. I felt trapped. After living outdoors for years, to be incarcerated for hours every day behind the drawing board was stifling.

I did manage to find a diversion in Morlaix. There was an outdoor market set up on Mondays where merchants from the surrounding area displayed and sold their goods. In one of the stalls I spotted a gorgeous, green-eyed Irish brunette from Bretagne named Odette. She sold lace. When I first saw her, she wore a lace hat which typified the costume of the region. I was intrigued by her beauty and her innocence when I introduced myself.

After several conversations, I invited her to join me for dinner. She accepted. Knowing that Odette would be in the city on

Monday enhanced to some degree my industry in Morlaix, but it was not enough to make a career of the position. I made several trips with Odette to the fishing village of Le Guilvinec, her home on the coast. I met her family and enjoyed the welcome that was forthcoming; but I also recognized that Odette, a virgin, was strictly raised and closely supervised by parents who followed to the letter the strictures of the Church. I knew that I had to step cautiously with the innocent beauty.

Our romance remained platonic until one evening when we had dinner. We enjoyed a bottle of wine and were caught up in the charm of the intimate restaurant, putting us both in a romantic mood. Odette asked if I would take her to bed. I did not dissuade her. I could not take her to my apartment nor could I take her to a place where she would be recognized. It was vital that her honor be protected. We booked a hotel room.

I recognized that Odette was becoming seriously involved with me, but I had been with experienced women and was not anxious to be her teacher. I was completely fascinated by her innocent charm and her beauty and cannot deny that I found her desirable. When I held her and entered her for the first time, I think her innocence had not prepared her for the act. We continued to make love all night that first night together. I did not see her again for several days, but when we met, we again made love.

When I left the job in Morlaix, I promised Odette to return for visits. She traveled to visit me in Fegreac, and we enjoyed trips to Paris. She became a very passionate lover, but I was not willing to make a commitment. I enjoyed my freedom and had no intention of marrying. When I was in Fegreac, I enjoyed being with Simone. I would have married Simone if the obstacles were not so profoundly overwhelming.

My return to Fegreac as a corporal, touted as a war hero by the locals, gained attention and notoriety that only served to deepen the bitterness that Simone's father felt for me and for my family. She worked as secretary to a leader of the Resistance, the group that resented my position as well as my political preference. One day when I was at the farm, plainclothesmen came to the house to question me. I was not available to see them. They were members of the Resistance occupied in interrogating citizens whose crime was their loyalty to France and opposition to the leftist powers in government. They knew my parents were in opposition to their ideology and were intent on letting us fully realize their strong-arm capabilities. It was one of many incidents that clouded my relationship with the love of my life.

As I look back, I realize that Simone was the woman I loved more than any other — she was the only one for me. But to protect our parents from the pain and embarrassment and even danger that our union represented, it was imperative that our romantic interludes be indulged surreptitiously.

At a time when two women were emotionally and physically involved with me, Anette, and her domineering mother and docile father came from Bordeaux to visit. They came to discuss "our" future plans. They slept in bedrooms on the second floor of the farm with balconies that looked over the valley for miles, affording a view of the charming village. They stayed for several days and my parents were the ideal host and hostess, offering the comforts of our home to the Spanish Inquisition. Mother was a wonderful cook and prepared sumptuous meals for the DuBonettes.

While "our parents" discussed "their children," I invited Anette to accompany me on a visit to the orchard. It was a lovely warm afternoon, and we wandered along hand in hand until we found a secluded spot far from the house. We embraced and then made love in the shade of an apple tree. All was quite wonderful until Uncle Gauthier came upon us. He was shocked by his discovery. Anette and I were embarrassed and I implored him to keep our activity secret. Uncle could not keep quiet about the interrupted amorous interlude. I'm certain he hadn't seen anything quite so provocative happen in the orchard. He shared the secret with his wife, who in turn leaked the information to my parents. Father came to me outraged with questions of my sanity in performing such a gross impropriety. He asked, "How could you put the young lady and her family in such embarrassment?"

I could not feel as strongly as my father, nor was I bearing any guilt. The young lady was a willing, wonderful, and beautiful partner, and we enjoyed one another enormously. At 22 years of age, I could not fully appreciate the depth of Father's anger, concern, or embarrassment with an activity that seemed so perfectly natural and beautiful. I was caught participating in an activity which held so much unrivaled pleasure, and I was involved with consenting young ladies who seemed to feel exactly as I felt. I harbored no guilt or remorse. And, after all, I was indulging a passion that had been predicted and diagnosed by a therapist friend of Mother's years before who said that I loved beautiful women and would probably go through my entire life admiring and desiring the company of them. I was not only fulfilling the therapist's analytical diagnosis but was having one hell of a wonderful time.

The reason for the visit by the DuBonette family was to arrange a date for the marriage of Anette and Robert. My parents prevailed upon me to visit with them

With Mr. Oliveaux.

in Bordeaux in the Landes Region of southwest France. The air, as I recall, was redolent of pine, thyme, and rosemary, and held a freshness that was so completely different from the north of France.

Immediately upon arrival, I detected an edge to our relationship. Madam DuBonette was particularly haughty. I questioned Anette who admitted that her mother had become aware of the promiscuity of our relationship and was hurt and violated by our indiscretion. I quickly realized that the affair could not go on. I was not going to place myself in the position of having a domineering mother-in-law running my life. Madam DuBonette ran the family business and she also ran her family, her husband, and Anette. But she sure as hell wasn't going to run me. She eventually arranged for the marriage of her daughter to a wealthy, local young man who more suitably fit the desired role.

I returned to Fegreac and questioning by Father, "What are you going to do next?" He offered me the meat market in Le Vesinet. He explained that Mr. Oliveaux had managed the business very well, and it was a highly prosperous business which held security, stature, and permanence. He knew that I could take over with few problems having garnered enough experience working with him before the War. He would give Mr. Oliveaux three months notice and a fair severance, and I would be put totally in charge. My reply was not well received. I was not interested in the business; I wanted to do something in the animal training business. Father became enraged and went into a tirade. I left to visit Paul.

Paul had sold his home in Le Vesinet for a substantial sum and bought the townhouse in St. Mande next to the Bois de Vinsennes, a beautiful historical park in the center of Paris that surrounded one of the oldest castles dating from the French dynasty. The castle was ultimately used as a dungeon during the Revolution. There was a yard behind the townhouse surrounded by adjoining buildings and separated by a high wall providing the privacy Paul required to train animals. The yard was approximately 150 by 200 feet. He indicated to me that he separated himself from Le Vesinet and from Maguy when he realized she was involved with German officers during the Occupation.

Paul had signed a contract with the Amar Circus to go on tour in North Africa to Algeria and Morocco. He would be gone for a year. He would leave dogs, a horse, and some ponies at the compound in St. Mande. Paul also was committed to promoting a book for children *Mitchi L'Ourson* — little bear cub. He had many irons in the fire and a wonderful career while I was floundering, in neutral. But all would soon change.

Brittany has always been like a separate country. Its language, culture, historical roots, and ideology differed from the rest of France. Breton was the spoken language, quite different from the French language in its unique dialect. The Bretons coveted their isolationist posture and government, creating many problems during the course of history for the Romans and every ruling empire down through the ages. They even revolted against the Napoleonic empire. Father was raised in Brittany but did not speak the language. He knew well all the characteristics of the predominantly Communist culture, and soon I was to become involved with a Breton in a relationship that I never intended.

I went to visit Odette, and she told me she was pregnant. The news dropped like a bombshell shaking my world. My initial reaction was complete and utter shock. My mind raced to seek escape or denial. I felt a vice closing down around me. I was trapped — frantic. I felt duty-bound to marry her unless . . .

abortion . . . never . . . her background . . . her parents . . . the Church . . . it could not be a consideration. Abortion and marriage — two inviolable precepts. I had to marry her.

Odette informed me that her parents knew of her condition. I did not want to share the news with my parents, whom I knew would be extremely disappointed in me. They were exasperated with my indecisiveness in not taking the job running the market and vacillating on a commitment to any permanent position. But I knew that Odette's parents would be the informants if I was not. I went to my parents. Father exploded in a raving harangue that questioned the depths of my intelligence and ended in the final analysis accepting the fact that I would have to marry the girl, but he asked, "How will you support her?"

There were many unanswered questions but not a lot of time to formulate answers. We moved into wedding preparation with the families meeting to discuss the alliance. We had to keep the pregnancy secret. Odette's mother and father arrived in Fegreac, her mother dressed in the folk *coiffe* (lace headpiece). Madame and Monsieur Toularastel were welcomed by my parents, and the plans for the nuptials discussed and agreed upon. The occasion called for me to have a suit made for the formal affair, totally out of character for Robert Baudy. I have never liked wearing a suit and tie, but protocol was important even if I felt like a trapped animal.

16

MARRIAGE TO ODETTE — PERIOD OF THE CARROTS
Le Mariage, Odette, et les Carottes

*W*e were married in Guilvinec. The Mayor officiated at the civil ceremony in City Hall attended by our parents and other close relatives. The Politics of Breton is neither left or right but nearly 100-percent Communist. The Mayor, a staunch Communist, stood in formal sash to perform his duties in recognizing our marriage. In my mind, and I'm certain in the minds and hearts of my parents, he looked much like the devil placing his seal on the nuptials. After the civil portion, we moved on to the church where the Priest, also a Communist, performed the religious ceremony. All during the symbolic litany, I could feel the noose tightening around my neck.

Odette was a very beautiful bride and a passionate lover, and we were committing ourselves to an irrevocable contract. I was certainly not at all aware of its depth, nor was I willing to completely fulfill my side of the agreement. I was going through the ritual of a serious performance, and I intended to perform as well as I could. My vows held such promise of piety and faithfulness. How could Robert Baudy perform all that was included in the vows? How could Robert Baudy change his life so completely? My heart was not in it.

Many of the townspeople witnessed the church wedding in the little town of Guilvinec by the ocean. It was a bright day in contrast to all the grey, misty days that preceded and followed it. But the brightness did not lessen my ambivalence. The heavy seas breaking along the craggy French coastline echoed my emotions.

We did not make love on our first night as man and wife in the Toularastel home. I was too upset for that. We went away for a brief honeymoon and then to Fegreac where we stayed at my parents' farm for a couple of weeks. My father again offered me the business in Le Vesinet, but I was determined that I did not want a career in the meat business.

We visited Paris one evening to attend a show at the Olympia Theater. The star of the show, Yves Montand, was involved with Edith Piaf at that time. Paul was also performing, and we had the opportunity to discus my future with Paul. He spoke again of the North African tour and asked if I would stay in the townhouse and care for the animals left in his absence, which would be for a year. It seemed like an offer that I could not refuse. I would have a fine place to stay with Odette, and I would be working with animals, an ideal solution. I agreed to his offer and we moved into the townhouse in St. Mande.

I refer to this period in my life as the "period of the carrots." Food was still scarce in Paris. Carrots were the only commodity that was plentiful and affordable. We gratefully accepted packages every two weeks from Odette's family and from my parents. They knew too well how we were struggling. When I look back, I realize that our parents must have been worried sick over our marriage. I was not involved in a remunerative labor while my wife was fully involved in a labor that would produce another dependent on what was a meager subsistence at best. The family largess of butter and sausages broke the monotony of the fried, boiled, or raw carrots.

In addition to caring for the animals, Paul left me to fulfill his contract on the book *Mitchi L'Ourson,* about the little teddy bear. Paul had signed a contract for a substantial sum of money, and he stressed that it was important to fulfill all of the contractual requirements and agreements which consisted first and foremost of producing a bear cub. I was to receive 30 percent of Paul's commission for the promotion of the book. It was vital that we succeed.

Mr. Houlet owned a large pet shop in the center of the city. He was to deliver the bear cub to me. A month before we were

On our wedding Odette became Mrs. Robert Baudy.

scheduled to show the cub in the first promotional setting, Mr. Houlet notified me that he could not find a bear cub. I was more than disappointed with his news. I was frantic. I felt responsible and informed Mr. Houlet that if he didn't come up with a cub, Paul would be sued for breach of contract. Mr. Houlet helped me in what became a desperate search for a proper cub for our performance. We attended every circus within a 100-mile radius of Paris. Finally a week before our debut at the Printemps Store (the equivalent of Macy's in New York City), we found a bear.

Our find was disappointing, but we had no choice. "Tommy" was performing with a small circus owned and operated by a band of Gypsies. I arranged to rent the bear, a black Himalayan about four years old and weighing 250 pounds, hardly the cute, cuddly, brown teddy bear described in the book to be sold in the book department of the prestigious store. But we had to go with Tommy. I had a notarized statement from Mr. Houlet that the promised teddy bear was not available. The arrangement was to have Tommy delivered to the compound and picked up after the show. Tommy was delivered, a mature black bear with a white crest on his chest, and I began working with him a week before the show. He behaved well as long as I kept plying him with sugar during his training. I saw no problem with the bear except he was not small nor was he cute.

On B-Day a truck arrived to pick up Tommy in a heavy traveling cage with iron bars, the whole load weighing nearly 800 pounds. When we arrived at Printemps, the caged animal was moved into a back room behind the book department. The press and special invited guests were seated as the director of the *Printemps* magazine nervously prepared for the special event. Everyone awaited the grand entrance of little Mitchi. The staging consisted of a cave entrance which opened to a small stage surrounded by the nicely dressed audience. Odette also attended. My job was to lead Mitchi down the corridor and out the cave to the seated crowd.

When I received the signal that the cameras were rolling, the footlights turned on, I began to lead Tommy by a rope leash down the passage. I detected the bear was upset. Bears make a muffled gurgling sound when they are not happy, and Tommy demonstrated very strongly that he was not happy with the arrangement. I didn't know what to do except to hold on to him. When we exited onto the lighted stage, his nervous gurgling increased. I attempted to hold his attention by commanding him to stand on his hind legs. With that Tommy bolted and took off into the crowd. The rope burned a cut in my hand as Tommy burst through the press and the invited guests and quickly disappeared from sight. I called to Odette to bring more sugar.

The director, realizing the gravity of the situation, escaped to a cubicle made of lightweight boards — display pieces. I yelled instructions to the security guards to clear the floor as people ran in all directions in search of a safe place. Bedlam prevailed. I hardly knew where to go or where to look with people diving under counters, but soon the situation seemed to settle and the area became quiet. Tommy was nowhere in sight. I saw the director move to the side of his cubicle, raise his head to gain a view of the department, and his sudden shock at being nose to nose with the bear. The man screamed and fell back in sheer fright as I rapidly moved to put the leash on Tommy. I quickly led him out of the department and secured him in his cage. We were relieved to get him back to the compound.

The bear was on lease. I had prearranged for the circus

owners to pick up the bear when I had performed the promotional show. When I went to arrange for Tommy's return, the owner of the circus was not on the premises. I returned on two occasions but was unable to make contact with the Gypsy owner. Finally I talked to one of the animal grooms.

"What's the matter with you guys? The bear is yours. I'm not going to be stuck with the bear."

Paul had built a substantial cage for bears at the compound, and Tommy seemed content to stay. But I didn't want the added work, responsibility, or cost of caring for the large animal — one more mouth to feed. I was really upset as I talked to the groom who tried to ignore me. He was busy cleaning up after some elephants. Finally he turned and said, "Oh, Tommy! Well, I'll tell you, Mr. Baudy, I don't think we want Tommy back."

I answered, "Well, you are not the boss. Obviously, I would be talking to your boss, but he isn't here today."

The groom continued, "Well, he may be my boss, but I'm the one that got chewed up by that bear!"

"You got chewed up? When I leased the bear, they told me that was the tamest bear on earth."

The groom looked at me. "Ha! That's the meanest son of a bitch . . ."

As he spoke, my mind raced to the scene at Printemps, and I nearly had a heart attack visualizing the "meanest son of a bitch" black bear loose aggressively exploring the departments of the exclusive store. I was stuck with the son of a bitch. I tried to contact Paul but was unable to reach him.

Soon after the incident I answered the door of the townhouse to a most impressive sight — a man nearly seven feet tall with curly red hair combed straight up in a most peculiar fashion that added inches to his already enormous height. I was stunned but also fascinated by his appearance as he introduced himself as Simon, The Wild Man Of The Ardennes. He said that he was a very close friend of Paul's. He owned six bears of his own and was an authority on bears. I felt that I had before me a most peculiar gentleman. I saw behind him, parked in front of the townhouse, a luxurious truck with a painted sign which gave a certain credibility.

I invited him inside. Lunch was ready; Odette was serving carrots fried in butter. A bottle of wine was opened, and we shared the gourmet repast with our visitor. He proclaimed that Tommy was a good bear. Meanwhile, Tommy was sleeping peacefully in his cage across the room. I knew better from my experience at the department store, the groom's opinion, and the fact that the Gypsy circus did not want him back. I continued to listen to the "Wildman" as he explained that I simply lacked experience where bears were concerned. As we enjoyed the wine, I listened patiently.

When I explained the situation at Printemps, he explained, "It's a question of expertise. When you go with a bear, you pretend you're a piece of wood — you must imagine that you are not a human being, you're something dead. When the bear comes to you and carefully sniffs, and inspects you — now keep in mind you don't even want to think about the bear — you are convinced that you are made of wood. If you do that about four or five times . . . most of the time you would only have to do that one time . . . you sit in there and let the bear inspect you. They are very intelligent and will not attack something that they do not feel threatened by."

I continued to listen to his speech. I respected what he said, realizing that I could learn from someone who obviously knows better than I from experience. He pulled out some pictures of himself working with bears, and I was completely convinced that he was an expert.

He said, "Let me demonstrate to you." He walked to the padlocked cage. Tommy continued to sleep on the cement floor in the corner of the large cage oblivious to the attention in his behalf. The "Wildman" requested that we unlock the door. I asked Odette to open a second bottle of wine instead and asked the man to sit down.

"You know this is Paul's home, and I am just working for him," I said." I don't want anything to happen . . ."

He interrupted, "Paul is an intimate friend of mine, and I want to help you with the bear." He again insisted that he demonstrate his technique.

"I don't want any help because I'm not going to use the damned bear any more."

He insisted, "Listen, you got a good bear there," and with that he stood up and asked for the key. I motioned to Odette to bring the key, which he used to open the door, and then entered the cage. Odette and I sat outside to watch the performance. The large red-headed man was obviously at ease as he sat on the stool in the center of the cage and became motionless, rather like a piece of wood. Soon Tommy began to waken. Himalayan bears have poor vision but a keen sense of smell and hearing. Tommy must have detected a presence in his cage as he moved, then yawned, and slowly stood up on four legs. He lumbered over to the Wildman waiting to be examined.

The bear made a gurgling noise in his throat as he first smelled the man's boot. Then his nose went to the man's kneecap as he continued to make noises. He moved around the man and smelled his rear end. By this time Tommy stood on his hind legs and smelled the Wildman's shoulder and then his face. The man remained absolutely motionless. Tommy next moved his nose down the man's body to again sniff his boot.

Suddenly, Tommy imbedded his teeth in the man's thigh. The stunned "piece of wood" let out a loud and frightened gasp. I yelled to Odette to get me an iron bar. I was not properly prepared for what was taking place in the cage. I fully trusted the man's experience to produce positive results. I grabbed the bar and entered the cage where our bear expert was down on the cement after the stool collapsed under him when Tommy savagely tore at his leg. I hit Tommy in the head with a massive blow and he fell, stunned, to the floor. The man quickly dragged himself to his feet and out of the cage. I locked the door behind and looked at the tall, red-headed bear expert who had escaped death but was bleeding profusely; his boots were soaked with blood.

I asked him to remove his trousers. He hesitated, embarrassed, not wanting to take his pants down in front of Odette. I said, "Listen, Mr. Simon, you have no idea how bad the wound is. You may be bleeding to death. Look at the amount of blood you are loosing! Drop your pants!

He let his pants drop to the floor revealing filthy legs with crud encrusted everywhere. It looked as if he hadn't seen a bar of soap in months. There were three large chunks of bloody flesh hanging from his thigh. I asked Odette to get the alcohol and apologized to the man before administering the painful application. He turned white and was close to passing out as Odette worked to put the pieces of flesh back into the open wounds. We bandaged the Wildman's leg and cleaned up some lacerations on the other leg, then opened another bottle of wine to dull some of the pain. We helped him to his truck, and suggested he drive to a hospital, but he insisted that was for sissies and he was heading back to the Ardennes.

As a postscript to Simon, the man did survive the horrible mauling by Tommy and all future animal encounters, but was electrocuted eight years later while rewiring a bear cage on a rainy day. I eventually found someone to take Tommy. I gave him away with an honest warning of his transgressions although he never gave me a bad time. I always told Tommy, "I am NOT a piece of wood!"

My salary from Paul was minimal. He could not afford to pay me what a married couple required to sustain themselves. I needed to seek another source of income. We were struggling to survive — Odette was getting larger by the day when Father came to visit.

He arrived unannounced to witness the situation, and I knew was horrified by what he found. He came laden with food. Odette prepared a wonderful meal that we enjoyed in the large formal dining room of the townhouse.

Father explained pleadingly, "Robert, the purpose of my trip . . . I had to come to Paris on business . . . but more than that I wanted to talk to you. This is ridiculous the way you are living from day to day . . . you have no future. You have a good education; you are talented; you are good-looking . . . you are wasting your life. You are probably going to be killed in this business."

He continued, "You survived the War only to get killed by a damned bear. I spent all that money and all that time on your education . . . and your mother is absolutely devastated . . . and now you are going to have a baby . . . I beg you to take over the meat business."

I spent the whole afternoon listening to him. He told me so much that I had heard before, but now under far different circumstances with an expectant wife and a baby about to enter the picture. It was a very difficult decision, but I turned him down again. Odette, too, implored me to consider taking the offer. She could envision all the benefits, but she knew as well that she had married a man who was determined to find his way unaided — to do what he enjoyed. I knew that the meat business was not for me.

I did not make my parents or Odette happy. Father left totally frustrated and extremely disappointed. I knew he could handle my refusal, he was tough; but I was disturbed by the fact that I was causing Mother so much anguish.

I knew that I had to make a positive move to create an income. I painted a large sign 8 feet by 16 with a masterful rendering of the head of a vicious German Shepherd. In bold type I printed "HAVE YOUR DOG TRAINED BY ROBERT" along with a phone number. I placed the sign on the main street, a legal form of advertising in those days.

Soon my first customer called and then others. Many business people and private property owners had dogs to be trained as guard dogs, a very costly and time-consuming occupation. Before long I had five dogs at the compound to be trained, which required hours and hours of repetitive commands and actions done with each dog all day long. I sent off to Brittany for a young man who had worked with me years before with my hunting dogs. The fellow was not well-educated, but he came to St. Mande to be my first employee. I demonstrated to the red-headed fellow just how to work the dogs. I demonstrated the very same moves and verbal commands to direct each dog. I was surprised and disappointed to witness that while the dogs received my commands and responded by performing well for me, they did not respond to his directives — given in the same tone and with the same motions.

I was being educated in the nuances of animal training. Training is not a science but an art. There is an innate sense and transferable communication between trainer and animal that not everyone possesses. Apparently, I was imbued with the certain something that the animals sensed and to which I received obedience and respect.

There was a café five blocks from the townhouse. The owner brought his mongrel shepherd to me and explained, "I think this dog has the potential to be a good watchdog. I've been broken into three times and I need to have him trained to guard my place better." He agreed to pay what I requested, a third down with the remainder to be paid at the completion of and satisfaction with the training.

The man left the dog and I immediately prepared for the training process. The first step was to chain the dog outside to a doghouse with no food for a couple of days so that the animal would lose his excess body fat and develop a voracious appetite. When the dog was given his first meal, a helper dressed in special padded protective covering, approached the dog to take the food away. Obviously after two days the dog was covetous of his first meal and attacked the interloper. The helper again passed by the dog closely, and the aggressive dog went for him.

After days of training, when I felt the dog was properly programmed, the owner came with friends to witness the dog's behavior. I asked one of the gentleman's friends to put on the protective covering and walk to the dog. We watched as the dog tried to attack on command. When the owner was satisfied, I turned the dog back to him and received my pay in full. He was given explicit directions on handling the animal.

I had a phone call from the café owner three days later. His establishment had again been broken into and the dog did not respond. The man initiated a lawsuit against me to get his money back. He hadn't followed the directions. He let his friends interact with the dog on a friendly basis. I had instructed him emphatically that once a dog is trained to be an attack dog, the animal is no longer a pet; it is a weapon and must be treated accordingly.

Training guard dogs was tough and not so lucrative. I went in the dog-selling business but in a modest way. Dogs were scarce since the War, but I was able to secure some mongrels that I advertised for sale. One couple came 300 miles to purchase a beagle-type dog. They liked the dog, paid for it, and left to take the dog to their home. The dog, miraculously, returned to the townhouse two weeks later. The homesick dog found its way all the way back to St. Mande. I sold the same dog three different times.

The back yard of the townhouse was large enough to accommodate about a dozen dogs. However, the barking created an unpopular noise level that drew frequent complaints from the neighbors. I had to develop another means of income.

At that time I had an interesting visitor. There was a prominent dog dealer in Paris who had a shop on the Champs Élysées, as well as shops in other locations scattered throughout the city. I'm certain his business could not have been lucrative.

Paul had spoken to the man before leaving for North Africa about some greyhounds the man had ordered for a special client.

Odette, a valuable partner at the le Royer compound.

There were ten of the lean racing dogs to be used in a fashion show. The gimmick was for the models to walk the runway with an elegant dog on leash in a parade of chic clothing and sleek dogs. Paul asked the shop owner what he planned to do with the dogs when the show was over.

"I don't know," the man told Paul. "Greyhounds are raised and trained to run after a rabbit and after killing the rabbits, they run like hell after the electrical rabbit at the track. They don't make good pets; they want to kill any small animals they see."

The shop owner arrived at the townhouse asking for Paul. I told him Paul was away and asked, "May I help you?"

He asked if I would be willing to board the greyhounds for him for which he was willing to pay a good fee.

"Look," I said, "I already have ten dogs I'm working with, and I don't know about taking care of more at this time."

His proposal sounded reasonable. "Listen, I only want to leave the dogs for a month or six weeks, and I will pay you in advance."

The offer was too good to refuse. I accepted the dogs and the money. It didn't take long for me to realize that the man had no intention of returning for the greyhounds. I was stuck with them.

After several days I began to think of a possible act using the dogs. I would attempt to train the greyhounds. I put up a ring about 30 feet in diameter behind the townhouse and then began the training process for a circus act where the dogs would perform like horses in a ring. I leashed each dog and worked each individually having it run at a controlled pace around and around the ring first in one direction and then on command, reverse the direction. The effect that I wanted is known in the circus as the "horse drill" where the horses move in a precise, synchronized line performing tricks on command as they move back and forth.

When the time passed for the dogs to be picked up by the dealer, I realized he wasn't coming. The man did not answer my calls nor did he come forward with any more boarding fees. I decided the dogs were mine, and continued to work everyday with the greyhounds. They began to respond in a positive manner to the training as my enthusiasm carried me through each day. As the weeks passed, the dogs demonstrated the very real possibility of a viable act.

There were a few monkeys at the compound and, as an addition to the dog training, I began to train the monkeys. I taught the dogs to pull a small stagecoach, a replica of one from the American West with a monkey inside the coach, a monkey driving the coach, and four monkeys each riding on a dog behind. In four months of daily training, I had an act that was ready to go somewhere. I had the feeling for the first time in my life that I had finally discovered a way to make an independent living in a profession of my own choosing — working and performing with animals.

Odette shared my enthusiasm and worked hard alongside helping to care for the animals and preparing food to sustain us all. During the months of daily work with the greyhounds and monkeys, I was also working with some young bears. The activity at the compound was brisk. There were visits from Paul's friends, mostly other animal trainers who did not know that Paul was on tour.

One day a man came to the door accompanied by a little boy. The short man, in baggy pants and a brightly colored plaid jacket, was about 50 to 55 years old. He spoke with a gravelly voice as he introduced himself as "Mr. Arnauzzi." The little boy, Arnauzzi's son, had a sweet angelic countenance and walked with a limp.

The minute the man pronounced his name, I recalled Paul's

description when we spoke of circus dog trainers: "You know of all the 25 or 30 dog trainers in all of France, or even all of Europe, the best is this damned drunk, Arnauzzi. The man is an alcoholic but he's the best. I don't know how he does it, but he's the greatest."

It was soon apparent that the great Arnauzzi wanted to tap Paul for a loan. He told a sad tale. Recently his wife of many years, who had been the mainstay of the family, passed away. She was a palm reader; he, a circus acrobat. He had been forced to quit his act due to an injury and had begun working with small dogs. Mr. Arnauzzi was on the skids. I looked down at the boy, so quiet and polite, his sweet, expressive face appealing, his lameness evoking pity. But I also realized that his father was the man who Paul described as a "damned drunk" and I could not give him a handout. I didn't have any money to give. I told him that I was too busy to talk to him at the moment and asked him to return the following day.

When the man and his son returned, Odette prepared a meal for the guests and we talked. I showed Mr. Arnauzzi around the compound and discussed the dog training that I had been performing. He said attack dogs were not his cup of tea, but he was interested in the greyhound training. He explained that he was best known for his work with small dogs, including "dogs in the hand," a delicate trick where a small dog balances on one leg on the man's palm, then on his forehead and finally on the tip of a finger. It was an extremely difficult performance requiring great patience and skill. The act demanded not only specialized training, but the trainer had to be a juggler as well. The little dog, swung into the air by the trainer holding the hind legs, landed with one front paw balancing first on the palm of the hand, and then was swung again to land on the forehead, and so on. The tossing and catching of the small animal done with utmost dexterity required many hours of intense training.

Mr. Arnauzzi proposed that I acquire the dogs. He would do the training, and we'd split any profits 50-50. I knew too much about the man's drinking problems to invest any money in his scheme, but I did have the facility in which to do the work. The top floor of the town house had been converted into a rehearsal room 35 feet by 45 feet with a solid wood floor and bars on the windows where

Arnauzzi working the little dogs.

Paul worked with leopards, bears and ponies in privacy. I told Mr. Arnauzzi that dogs were very difficult to find in Paris except for attack dogs.

"They ate all the cats and dogs during the War."

"I can find some dogs, don't worry!" he boasted.

I was very firm with him. "We have to have an understanding. I don't care what you do after hours, but you cannot drink here. At lunch you may have a glass of wine, but I can't have you drinking during working hours."

During the next week, I managed to collect a few black and white fox terriers, mongrels, but I could find no other dogs. One day Arnauzzi came in with a cute little dog, well-groomed, and obviously well-cared for. I asked where he got the dog knowing that he didn't have any money. He did not answer my query. A few more days passed, and he again came in with a beautiful little poodle dog, very well-groomed, and I again asked where he got the dog. He was evasive in his reply. As the days passed, several more dogs were introduced into the compound by the little magician who was not having any difficulty producing wonderful dogs.

"You must tell me where you are finding these dogs."

He answered in his gravelly voice, "Oh, I knew a lady who liked me and she told me she was getting tired of her pet . . ."

The little boy came in with a wicker basket containing a beautiful fox terrier about two or three years old wearing a fancy collar and an expensive lead that had been cut. I stared at Arnauzzi who stood looking down, a cigarette dangling from his mouth.

"Listen, don't tell me that people are giving you all these dogs. They are expensive dogs and I noticed this little dog has a cut lead."

He became defensive. "What do you expect? I don't have any money and those people have plenty of money."

"Are you telling me that you are going out and stealing dogs?"

"Oh, no, we are not stealing dogs."

I went to the little boy to avoid further confrontation with Arnauzzi to get the facts. He was candid. As he looked up at me, so innocently, he said, "We look for an old lady who has a little dog. I run into her while Father comes from behind and quickly cuts the lead. While I apologize to the lady for hitting her, he takes off. It all happens so quickly that the lady cannot react soon enough, and I leave her screaming about the dog. He's gone by that time."

I was horrified to think that in Paul's compound I sheltered stolen, precious property and was in business with a thief. I placed ads in the newspaper and did manage to return some of the dogs. The owners offered substantial rewards, money they insisted be accepted. I felt guilty as hell in what had developed into an illicit enterprise. I had not stolen the dogs and did not want to implicate Paul in Arnauzzi's heist. We were unable to locate the owners of a couple of the dogs. They became Arnauzzi's pupils.

I was in cahoots with a Gypsy. I had observed Gypsies all my life. The first recollection was when I was three, watching a Gypsy with a bear on a leash perform in a village close to my grandparents' farm.

When I was six years old, I saw the first cat-and-rat act performed by a group of Gypsies who had set up a temporary staging with a wire strung from one pedestal to another. A fat house cat sat on one pedestal with a rat seated on the far pedestal. At a command from the Gypsy, the animals stood and began walking toward each other, balancing on the wire as they held on with their back paws. When they met in the middle, the cat carefully stepped over the rat and proceeded to walk along the wire to the opposite pedestal where he sat. The rat continued on to the opposite pedestal to sit. I was fascinated by the animals' clever performance, not appreciating fully that the simple maneuver required hours and hours of diligent training and utmost patience.

Gypsy bands roved the countryside in their colorful horse-drawn wagons always with trained goats, bears, or monkeys in tow. They worked the animals on a leash or even off the leash directly in front of and close to the spectators who came to be entertained. If they were lucky, the audience would throw money into a hat or onto the ground. There was either a trained monkey to catch the money or a young, appealing child. The dark-skinned vagabonds, referred to as *manouche* in France, spoke a language of their own and traced their ancestry to Northwest India.

Arnauzzi was not a pure Gypsy but had been raised and trained by Gypsies. He possessed all the innate characteristics, many of which produced suspicion and even contempt. As a rule, Gypsies lived and performed outside legal boundaries, roaming throughout the country, never settling in one place.

Most of the circus acts involving animals also involved Gypsies, who were among the most talented trainers. As I watched Arnauzzi work the little dogs, I realized the dedication that was inherent and the results that were its reward. While I knew that Arnauzzi was not above stealing a valued pet, he also possessed much talent and tenacity. I learned a great deal to incorporate into my training of the greyhounds. In that sense it was a privilege to work with the man in spite of the many derogatory epithets describing the accursed "Gypsies."

I had been accustomed to watching Paul work, and while there were similarities, there was also diverse approaches. Paul was an artist and a consummate showman, but he also enjoyed his leisure. He always took time off, turning the training over to an assistant. Not so Arnauzzi, who worked nonstop all day for weeks until he was satisfied with the results. In no time the little man in the baggy pants had a finished act ready to stand the "test of fire" in the public arena.

When the long-awaited day arrived, his lame son and I helped Arnauzzi load four wicker baskets of different sizes, one to fit each of his little dogs, and some other props into a cab for the ride to the outskirts of the city. We stopped near a flea market where the pedestrian traffic was brisk. He set up a small fold-up bench and then opened the wicker baskets. The little dogs immediately jumped out and ran to their spots on the bench. He set up hurdles for the dogs to jump over. The show was ready to commence. I was along to help and to observe all that was involved in the "test of fire." Complications unique to a live performance were always a possibility during the first performance. The animals might break away and escape which wouldn't happen in an unobserved rehearsal where there were no distractions or possible escape.

Arnauzzi had trained his son well as his partner. When people began to congregate around the little dogs seated on the bench, Arnauzzi started his speech, rehearsed and convincing, even heartrending, evoking sympathy as he told of the sadness he and his son suffered as they looked upon his wife, the mother of his lame son, lying paralyzed in a hospital bed with no money to pay her costly medical bills. This had forced the fine trainer to resort to begging on the street. He had told me a different story when he first came to the townhouse. I listened to him so convincingly reveal his anguished plea to a wet-eyed audience, I wondered if his wife really was dead. The man was a hell of an actor.

Dog in hand.

There wasn't a dry eye in the audience as he began to put the little dogs through their routines. His costume was a clean outfit with large patches covering holes in the worn fabric of his baggy pants and multicolored jacket. His son stood nearby, looking pitiful in long, baggy pants with patches of different colors. Arnauzzi, having captured the rapt attention of the audience, signaled to the first dog. The dog, wearing a little hat and a little skirt, jumped from the bench and walked on its hind legs around the hurdle and then returned to the bench.

Dog #2 then came off the bench, jumped over the hurdle, and returned to its seat. Then the next dog went under the hurdle, followed by the last dog walking to the hurdle and knocking it down with his front paw to the gleeful delight of the spectators. Arnauzzi then went into the balancing routine with a small dog balanced on one paw on his hand, then his forehead, and finally on the tip of his finger. All went smoothly without missing a beat followed by the hoped-for applause and tossing of money.

Suddenly, one of the little dogs took off. Arnauzzi had prepared me for the possibility. It was the boy's job to chase after the dog while I stood guard with Arnauzzi over the remaining dogs, not only to watch for the cops, but also to pick up the money. When the boy returned with the dog, the animal was welcomed back with no reprimand. That was a key feature and a very important lesson for me. The reprimand was absolutely necessary but never administered at the scene of the performance. That would come later in the training ring where the dog would be encouraged to break away again and then be reprimanded sternly. It made sense that if reprimanded at the performance where the dogs were rewarded, it would not only stigmatize the performance, but also confuse the animal.

After several days of going out on location, we ran into the problem of the city cops patrolling their beat on foot. They made us move on for begging and showing animals in public without a permit, which was in violation of the law. When our legitimacy was questioned the first time, I showed my military papers certifying I served in the prestigious Second Armored Division — *liberators of Paris*. I pleaded that I had just been demobilized from the army and had no income and my partner, Mr. Arnauzzi, had a crippled wife who desperately needed care.

The first cop who closed us down said to me, "Look, Mr. Baudy, I'm not going to arrest you, or impound your dogs, but will you please get your ass off my beat!"

"Okay, thank you, sir."

And with that Arnauzzi whistled to the dogs sitting obediently on their bench. They jumped into their baskets and away we went to a subway to take us a couple of miles to another location to set up another show. We performed five shows a day if we weren't hassled or delayed by the cops. But we soon ran out of ideal locations. Obviously the chosen spot was important. We couldn't drum up enough business in the poor sections of the city but had to go where we thought we could make the most money quickly before being busted.

One day we did get busted. A cop who had told us to move on previously found us infringing on his territory for the second time. He called the paddy wagon. I felt shabby about the whole damned business and knew that if Father witnessed the company I was keeping and the performance, his worst predictions for my chosen lifestyle would be confirmed. When the wagon arrived, they loaded the dogs in their baskets aboard and then Arnauzzi was pushed into the back along with his son and me to be taken to be booked.

When I stood before the judge, I recognized the man as having served in the Second Armored in another unit. Our paths had crossed as we fought together against the Nazis. He was a kindred spirit. He took me aside and said, "Robert, listen, I'm going to turn you loose, but please, I beg you, don't come back in my court."

The experience of working with Arnauzzi had many facets — some smooth, but most not so smooth. I hated that the dogs were stolen, I was embarrassed about the arrest, and I was also embarrassed about taking money that was tossed at us. His planned performance was definitely overplayed in extending far beyond the little dogs obediently going through their routines. He gave some coins to the first onlookers and cued them to toss the coins onto the ground when he gave the signal. He used the audience as shills and instructed the boy to wait until there were many coins thrown and accumulated before picking them up. He was to wait until there was the equivalent of five dollars. That was a lot of coins.

As the boy began gathering the money, Arnauzzi addressed the audience to thank them for their generous support in his sorrowful plight as his eyes moved in every direction watching for the cops. When the payoff was substantial, it took a long time to gather the coins. Often while the boy worked feverishly, Arnauzzi watched for the cops and secured the dogs from running off and said to me, "Robert, you better help pick up the money."

I hated the request and the occupation, but knew that I was only temporarily involved and kneeled down to help the boy. Father's opinions went through my mind — derogatory remarks about the Gypsy beggars and thieves, and now I was akin to the thievery. I had become a beggar, and it was damned humiliating. However, I must admit that after gathering my first handful of coins and returning to St. Mande to split the take, I found the money to be quite satisfying.

Food had become more plentiful in the city, but our limited budget forced us to continue dining on carrots as our mainstay. With Arnauzzi's bounty we were able to indulge in an occasional steak plus fruit and other vegetables — even butter. I continued to work the greyhounds everyday knowing that soon my own act would be ready.

17

CIRCUS FAME AND A BABY BOY
L'Etoile du Cirque et Papa

After months of training, the greyhound act was nearly ready for its debut before a live audience. I had to find the audience. It was time to visit the "mud" show.

The Cirque Fanny was an old family-operated circus in existence for years in Paris — it's still operating today. It had become an institution, and every Parisian youngster was traditionally taken to the small circus when it played in town squares all over the city. The family circus was accompanied by a small group of musicians consisting of an accordion player, a trombonist, and a drummer. I decided to talk to Madame Fanny, owner, operator, and choreographer of the circus.

A fat woman of 70, she made certain that each location of the show as it moved from place to place was situated within a short walk of a café to indulge her wine as she sat on a barstool and supervised the installation and performances. Madame Fanny liked her glass of Chablis; and when I went to talk to her, I found her in the café. I introduced myself as being a good friend and employee of Paul le Royer, whom she knew very well. I told her of the greyhound act and she replied in husky voice, "Well, if you have worked for Paul, you must be pretty good, so I'll give you a break. You can start right away."

The time had come to test and demonstrate the thoroughness of months of training. Now I had the problem of moving the dogs, the ring, and props to the Cirque Fanny. Arnauzzi's little dogs in their wicker baskets had been easy to transport. The greyhounds were not. A neighbor of Paul's offered the use of his truck. I built wooden crates to hold the dogs, the monkeys, and the stagecoach, and other props in addition to the small ring. After setting the ring in place at the Cirque, I worked the dogs with some of the circus workers as my audience. As predicted, most of the dogs took off. Madame Fanny's workers helped recover them. After several days the dogs adjusted to the ring and to the audience, and the act went smoother with each performance. It was well-received right from the start. I knew I had found a career.

Soon after my debut, Odette went into labor. It was April, 1947. She had become enormous with child and knew that her time had come. I called the hospital. They did not have an *ambulance* to pick her up. I called a cab and took her to the hospital. With so many obligations at the compound, I could not remain with Odette, who proved to be a brave trooper. I received the call several hours later informing that a healthy, beautiful boy had been born. The message also assured that Odette was fine and sleeping after her ordeal. I went to the hospital the following morning to meet my son, Gerard Robert Baudy, and to see Odette.

The new mother was feeling sore and sleepy, but very relieved. I was proud to be a father, but with so much work facing me every hour of every day I could not indulge in the luxury of dwelling on my new status. I returned to the townhouse to pass the news along to relatives. I barely had the privilege to sit and think about a son since there was more work for me with Odette absent.

The usual hospital stay for childbirth was at least a week or two, but Odette came back to the townhouse after three days. Her mother came to help and stayed for three weeks. My parents came to visit but stayed for only a few days. I think the lack of communication between the two grandmothers was not conducive to their remaining in the townhouse together for an extended length of time. During the following weeks, other relatives and friends came to meet little Gerard. It was a hectic time. I was engaged in performing with the Cirque and also caring for Paul's animals and monitoring Arnauzzi.

I had been with the circus several weeks when an agent, Monsieur Marouani, came to see Madame Fanny about some horses and caught my act. He approached me. The man was a well-known agent whose office was on the Champs Élyseées employing five or six subagents. He was encouraging.

"I think that you have the material and potential to have a first-class act, but you have to smooth some things."

He was extremely flattering and also generous with his criticism. He continued, "You've got to change your costume."

I thought I was quite elegant in dark suit, white shirt, and white tie. He went on to describe what he envisioned.

"First of all, you must have three sets of different costumes for different types of audiences. When you have a premier, there will be lots of wealthy people in the audience, and you will need tails. Instead of black, you should wear an electric blue . . . something with class and color, and you must make certain they are well-tailored to fit properly. You should wear patent-leather shoes, the buggy whip should be nickel and chrome-plated, and you should be wearing a showy ring."

He was full of all kinds of advice as he continued, "I think you should call your act Baudy's Greyhounds — The Aristocracy of Breed and Training."

All of what he described sounded wonderful to me and also very expensive. But I felt extremely fortunate to have his professional expertise and keen interest in guiding me. When he offered me a contract, I knew that a momentous opportunity had presented itself. My hours of labor were finally rewarded.

Odette was an adept seamstress and she began to work on my new wardrobe to achieve the image that Marouani described. The agent also recommended that I have a sporty outfit similar to the "riding to the hounds" red coat with black velvet trim and patent-leather riding boots. The boots were highly specialized. The only company making boots after the Occupation was in the custom-made business. The footwear company broke their policy of demanding payment in full when the order was placed and accepted my deposit. I had the boots in five weeks. By the time the boots were ready, I was making money with the greyhounds and gaining stature through newspaper reviews.

During the hectic pace of maintaining the compound, establishing a circus career, training the greyhounds and monkeys where Odette was vitally important and involved, baby Gerard added other time-consuming demands. He was a good baby and slept in a bassinet on the second floor of the townhouse.

The weather was warm and the windows were open letting in many flies, at least more than usual, attracted by odors from the animals. A fine lace veil made by Odette's mother was used to cover the bassinet to keep the flies off the sleeping infant. We were busy downstairs when Odette decided to leave her sewing to check on the baby who seemed "too quiet." I heard a scream from the bedroom and rushed to find Odette looking into the bassinet. Gerard had become entangled in the thin veil that had tightened around his neck and body as he struggled to escape. He was blue.

I reached for the little guy, freed him of the veil, turned him upside down, and slapped his back firmly a couple of times. In a few minutes, he began to breath normally. We were badly shaken by the incident — we had come too close to losing our baby.

A tough decision was made. It would be in his best interest if he went to stay with his grandparents. The activity at the townhouse was impossibly hectic with Arnauzzi still working the dogs. I still trained the greyhounds daily. In addition to the performance at the Cirque, there were the guard dogs, bears, and ponies that required daily care and attention. Odette was an extremely valuable helpmate with many chores to accomplish in addition to caring for a new baby. It was impossible. But it was similar in a way to what my parents faced when I was an infant — attempting to run a hotel and restaurant. Being raised in the ancient monastery by loving grandparents had been a positive, healthy experience.

We had very little choice. We packed Gerard's belongings and took him to stay in Fegreac with my parents. Leaving Gerard was not difficult for me. Odette was devastated by the separation but fully realized with a burgeoning career there was no alternative. There was no time to dwell for long on the absence of her baby. We knew his care would be attentive and indulgent, freeing Odette to devote her full attention to a career that was taking off quickly and assuredly.

The Cirque Fanny was open daily with a small stage at the entrance. The small band, each member in uniform, played as the bearded lady and other performers made cameo appearances and the ponies were lined up smartly. It was a very popular entertainment and a wonderful launching pad for my act. All but two of the greyhounds bolted during the first performance as they got their "feet wet," but with diligent training and exposure they adjusted

Herman became one of the stars of the greyhound act.

after several days.

I learned so much from watching and working with Arnauzzi. A vital lesson was that dogs are far more difficult to handle in an act as opposed to other animals. Monkeys, for example, are simple. The monkey is perfectly trained after a few demonstrations and performances of a particular routine. The monkey becomes almost robot-like and will repeat every learned behavior pattern over again and again without constant reinforcement. The dogs, once they realize that they will not be punished in front of the audience, lose the sharpness of their training.

After the six-minute show was complete and the public gone, I had to take the dogs back in the ring and work them for another two hours. That daily routine was the only way the quality of the act could be maintained. It required much discipline and time. Initially, I took the dogs back and forth from the townhouse to the circus the first two weeks, but then I built an enclosure out of snow fencing material so the dogs could remain at the circus with a groom to tend them.

The Cirque played at the Portes de Paris, the main gates dating from the 14th century that led into the big city. As a matter of fact in 1925, they referred to the *Fortifs*, the doors between the main gates in the enormous 30-foot-high wall surrounding Paris. Each entrance name designated the location, and at those gates the Circus was set up, either inside or outside the city limits. But the location was carefully selected to be close to heavy traffic and always a café to indulge Madame Fanny's daily ration of white wine.

Gravelly voiced Madame Fanny informed me that she had been in the circus business for 65 years and had never signed a contract with any performer. She said that she was well-known and good to her word, she paid well, and that was all that was necessary. However, if I wanted to sign a contract with her, she would make an exception in my case. I was flattered. She paid me promptly and while the fee was not great, it was the most money I had ever been paid for performing my own act. More important than the monetary reward was the exposure. She gave me the opportunity to "finish" my act before a large audience. When I felt fully prepared and Marouani felt the act was polished, he arranged for my first contract with the Circus Medrano.

Marouani was the exclusive agent for the Medrano, the prestigious circus dating back to its namesake, the famous clown Medrano, who performed during the Napoleonic Era to great acclaim in a traveling show. His success led the family to build the Medrano in Pigalle, the red-light district of Paris.

The Medrano was a perfect jewel of a building designed and

CIRCUS FAME AND A BABY BOY

Buster Keaton began his career as an acrobat.

built specifically for circus performances. All of the seats were lined in red velvet surrounding a 13 meter ring with a dome-shaped roof. It was an ideal setting for the many fine acts that performed over the years in the fabled showplace. The arena was attached by a corridor to a huge stable about 75 feet distant housing the animals — the cats, horses, dogs, monkeys, bears, and other larger animals, elephants etc. There were nicely appointed dressing rooms for each of the performers. It was not easy to get a booking at the Medrano. Each booking was a four-week engagement. Marouani was the contact that made it happen.

The circus business had not been good since the end of the War, so a headliner was booked to stimulate attendance. Buster Keaton, the American star of the silent movie era, was the headliner during my four-week engagement. I felt extremely fortunate to be included in such good company. The audience drawn to see Keaton was classy with some very fine-looking members of Paris society. Not only was I in good company, but I was paid four times what I earned with the Cirque Fanny.

The newspapers were well-represented for Keaton's performance, and the reviews were unanimous in reporting that the overall performances, even Keaton's, were disappointing. But, "there was one outstanding act and that was the Greyhounds of Mr. Baudy." We were launched! When we saw the reviews, both Odette and I were exultant. There was good cause for celebration and even tears of joy. After a long period of hard work and deprivation, the light shown brightly.

As the weeks passed, the raves were coming my way, and the house was filled by people who wanted to see Buster Keaton but also wanted to see Baudy's Greyhounds. Keaton's performance consisted of a parody of a duel with the band leader. His script was not clever; and while I could see the greatness of the artist in the man as he went through his routine, it took more than a duel to make the French audience react. Baudy's Greyhounds became the stars of the show. One day I chatted with Keaton. He was obviously impressed with our success and was telling me how his career had begun as a clown and an acrobat. He must have been in his late sixties as he stood talking and then, suddenly, did a standing somersault. I was astounded by the dexterity of the amazing little man closing on his 70th year. His career was coming to an end; mine was just beginning.

It soon became apparent from all the attention I received that Odette had a jealous nature. I hadn't detected it prior to the adulation attained through the extraordinary publicity. She seemed almost paranoid. The attention from the ladies was embarrassing, but I must admit that I enjoyed every bit of it. Odette did not. She was a wonderful, hardworking helpmate, and we were a damned good team; but I loved beautiful women and could not resist temptation. I had known some very beautiful and fascinating ladies and I think I always resented having to marry Odette. I felt I was pressured into the relationship and resented her hold on me. I was beginning to think that the marriage might not hold together, particularly with the circumstances of newfound fame and all the attending adulation.

I had traveled to see my parents in Fegreac during the time that Odette was pregnant. She remained in St. Mande to care for the compound. My visits home were brief, but I always managed to see

Simone. She also visited Paris occasionally as part of her job as secretary to the influential official with the Communist Political Organization. Her boss, a married man who was also in love with her, was a tyrant and had told her that if he ever caught her in bed with me, I would be murdered. When she came to Paris, we met at Montparnasse and went to a secluded place to make love. She had been devastated by my marriage to Odette but realized that I could never marry her. The violent opposition to the relationship made marriage impossible. Our love, however, was deep and abiding, and no one, no circumstance, could prevent us from renewing and expressing that love whenever we had the opportunity.

There was another woman in Paris who had been my lover prior to marrying Odette. She was Paul's mistress after Maguy had been dismissed for being involved with the German officers. Paul had never married, but he always managed to have gorgeous women around him. His new partner was a brunette who performed along with Paul and went on tour with him to North Africa. She became pregnant and returned to Paris to have her baby. Odette knew the lady, but she did not know of my involvement. We saw very little of her after her return from North Africa. I was too busy to indulge any romantic dalliance except for Simone. We had vowed to be lovers for as long as there was life in either of us. That was a vow that I fully intended keeping.

Arnauzzi was creating problems. He continued doing the street shows with his son as his assistant, but through Marouani I was able to get some solid contract work in night clubs for him for which I stipulated a 50-50 cut. He balked at the financial arrangement claiming that I was no longer a part of his act and 50 percent commission was exorbitant.

"Listen, I got the contract for you; you didn't get the contract. They didn't want to book you. They think that you are a great trainer, but you're not a showman and the little boy is lame." I pointed out other things. "The props are not what they should be; they should be chrome-plated instead of made out of wood. If you don't feel comfortable with the arrangement, we'll work out something else."

One thing that triggered the need for a tough arrangement was knowledge that Arnauzzi was cheating on our initial agreement of an equal split of the profits as long as he used the townhouse facilities.

Odette had a cousin living in Paris who was employed as a city cop. It was still illegal to show the animals on the street without a permit, and I knew pretty well what the take was in the various locations where the little man in baggy pants showed the little dogs. Odette's cousin, dressed in plain-clothes, followed Arnauzzi; he even counted the money that was being made. When the Gypsy came to settle with me, he was lying, holding back, claiming that he was giving me my 50 percent when really he was taking 75 and even 90 percent of the take. There were even occasions when he came in late at night and told me he hadn't worked the act that day. Then I got the report from my spy that the man had gone from one performance to another and another before the day was over.

I could not abide his lying, nor could I be with him to keep him honest. I finally approached him with an offer to buy me out. I told him what I thought was a fair price of my cost in having him use the facilities. He agreed to the arrangement and left with the understanding he would make payments routinely to me until he paid me off in full. Arnauzzi did not have the capacity to be legitimate and I knew better. I knew he wouldn't honor the agreement, but I had to sever the relationship. Police officers came to me from time to time asking if I would be responsible for some illegal activity attributed to Arnauzzi, but I refused to go to his aid. I never got another dime from Arnauzzi.

My contract with Marouani was an exclusive agreement which included any and all engagements in Europe effective for several years. I do not recall the exact terms. Marouani was running a very large and prestigious agency with the leading theatrical performers of the day as clients. I was in the company of movie, theater, and nightclub stars. A novice at such arrangements, I was flattered to be represented by the elite organization.

When the four-weeks engagement at the Circus Medrano was fulfilled, I went on to perform with the Amar Circus which had several different traveling shows. I was also booked into nightclubs in and around Paris. The reviews continued to rave about "Baudy's Greyhounds" and my clipping album was filling up. The money was good and the activity hectic as I worked each day to keep the animals at their peak — that alone was demanding. Odette was totally involved in helping me. There was much to do caring for the animals at the compound every day, keeping my costumes in order, and helping to supervise the ongoing responsibilities to Paul when we left the compound. The work was unceasing.

When there was a brief pause between commitments, we visited Fegreac to see my parents and Gerard, who seemed to be prospering in their care. Father remained staunch in distrusting the ethics or permanency of such employment even after scrutinizing my contract and seeing the clippings giving credence to my success. As far as he was concerned, I could be making more money in the meat business in a secure and dignified occupation. Mother expressed a strong desire to attend a performance, but Father wouldn't hear of it. They never came to see the act. Father, tough, granite-headed Breton, could not admit that he had a son in show business. Admittedly my life would have been vastly different had I accepted his offer and settled in Le Vesinet with Odette and Gerard. Possibly my marriage to Odette would have been more stable. But I had chosen my path and I was caught up in the excitement, the audience's acceptance of me, and my performance. It was thoroughly compelling, not only challenging but stimulating, and completely fulfilling in every aspect.

I suffered some guilt where Odette was concerned. I was not totally honest with her; but we were a team, and she seemed a very willing and eager partner. We had been through a difficult year and were starting to reap some rewards. She was a beautiful lady and I was proud of her and of the attention she, too, received from the people with whom we began associating as we continued to tour and play different venues.

There was an incident that spoke eloquently of how jealous Odette became with the attention I received and as a reaction to her suspicions that I was involved with other women. She knew too well that I was passionate with others. We were playing the Medrano at the time. We had finished the performance for the evening and had gone across the boulevard to the *Brasserie* in Pigalle for a snack. Odette told me that she was tired — she was going back to the hotel. I said that I had work to do at the circus and would join her later. I did return to the arena and I did work with the animals. There was a problem in the performance that I needed to work out. It took longer than I anticipated and I returned to the hotel very late.

When I opened the door to our room, I saw the bed was empty — Odette was not where I expected to find her. I entered the room and was totally startled to see Odette coming at me from behind the door with hands slashing through the air. Her nails caught my face as she yelled accusatory, unflattering expletives. I managed to grasp her hands in mine as I attempted to soothe her, telling her that I did nothing of what she insinuated but worked with the dogs later than anticipated. I should not have been so surprised by the assault. I was guilty on other occasions of her accusations, but I was innocent as hell of any wrongdoing that particular evening. It was one of many incidents that demonstrated her frustration and jealousy. But it, like others, passed, seemingly forgotten as she became involved in the activity of the following day.

Our relationship began to take on more of a business partnership than a marriage although we did continue to share some passionate lovemaking from time to time. There was so much that she did for the performance and I loved her in a special way, but I loved another woman more and other women as well. Mother's analyst friend years before had been correct. I would never outgrow my desire for beautiful women.

Paul fulfilled his contract in North Africa and returned to France. My career was launched, and it was time to move on. My contract called for us to leave the city, so we turned the townhouse in St. Mande over to Paul. The Era of the Carrots was behind us.

18

EARLY TOUR ENGAGEMENTS
Le Début sur la Route

*I*n October, 1947, we were booked for four weeks into Bordeaux with the Amar Circus. We packed the dogs, monkeys, and props for the trip south by train. The advance publicity in newspaper articles, ads and billboards proclaiming our imminent arrival notified the inhabitants of the city. Madame du Bonette prepared well for our arrival. She put Anette under house arrest for the duration of our stay. Anette tried to contact me and I wanted to see her, but that was completely impossible. When she was not at home with guards around the clock, she had someone with her at all times. Her mother attempted to maintain a chastity belt around her daughter who had not been chaste for some time.

During the engagement there was another circus performing across the street from the Amar featuring a Czechoslovakian trainer, who showed eight Russian brown bears. If I remember correctly, the name of the other circus was Pinder. There were nearly ten circus organizations operating in Europe at that time, and the Pinder was one of the leading companies.

The helpers working in the circus after the War were primarily German prisoners of war. For years the French Government, for political reasons, held hostage many German prisoners to perform all sorts of labor. They seemed determined to keep the prisoners longer than the French soldiers were kept in Germany to get even for the atrocities committed during the Occupation. There was such a revulsion to what the Germans perpetrated. Many of the German prisoners were decent, compassionate humans suffering at the hands of their captors — a policy that I strongly felt was undeserved.

The workers in the Pinder Circus were strong men in their mid-forties, very capable but obviously not overly loyal or supportive of their captors, and particularly nonsupportive during life-threatening situations. They had survived the War, and I'm certain, hoped to survive the incarceration to return to Germany.

One day I exited the ring having completed a performance, and was hot, sweaty, and tired from the workout. One of my men came running toward me.

"Robert, across the street — the bear man is being attacked!"

I dropped my buggy whip and ran like hell out of the Amar tent to the street and then crossed to the Pinder Circus. The panicked spectators poured out of the circus blocking my passage. I frantically searched for a way to get into the arena. Dressed elegantly in tails, I found an opening to crawl underneath the canvas to gain entry. In the middle of the performance cage, I saw the trainer, dressed in costume with high boots, lying face down in the sawdust, holding desperately to two heavy pedestals as a huge brown bear was pawing, mauling, and attempting to turn the man over. Every bear man knows that the bear will go for the victim's abdomen, the softest tissue, for the intestines which hold the tastiest portion of a human. The man screamed for help as the Germans looked on from outside the cage. The other bears, foaming at the mouth, ran around the steel arena.

I attempted to get some of the Germans to help me in the rescue, but it was obvious they were not going to risk their lives to save the life of one of their oppressors. I grabbed a heavy iron pipe and an iron stake and went to the double safety doors of the cage. I positioned one of the Germans at the outer door and one at the inner door.

"I'm going to go in there and I'm going to hit the bear to kill. I'm going to drag the man through the door. You men grab the guy by anything you can — a hand, a boot, anything — and you drag him out of the cage while I'm fighting the bears."

I got close to the inner door as people were still pushing, shoving, and screaming to exit. Mayhem accompanied the bears' screaming and pacing as the brass band played loudly. Bears make a high-pitched scream when they are disturbed and charging, a sound that is hair-raising and frightening.

The atmosphere was completely chaotic as I entered the cage and began to hit the attacking bear. The iron pipe just bounced off the huge bear with no apparent affect except to further anger and excite him. One of the other bears took a swipe at me ripping off a large piece of fabric from my tails. I realized that I was not going to be successful with the rescue.

I quickly exited the cage and then, looking around, saw some long pieces of pipe, one slightly bent at one end. I picked up the bent pipe and stuck the end in a crevice of the stage to bend it to form a hook. I ordered eight men to grab hold of the long pipe which we snaked into the cage close to the trainer who by this time was being attacked by three bears. One bear had him by the inside of the thigh, another had hold of his right boot and the third bear, unable to flip the man over, was chewing on the victim's side. I don't know where he found the strength to hold himself so firmly belly-down, but he grabbed hold of the pipe and we pulled him out of the tearing, bloody clutches of the bears, sliding his ravaged body to the inner door.

As the men slashed pipes at the angry bears, we pulled his body out of the cage. The bears became frenzied and began to climb up the sides of the open-topped cage. The Germans, aware that their lives were now imperiled, aggressively hammered at the sides of the cage to keep the bears contained. The police finally arrived and drew their guns to shoot the bears. I took command of the situation from the start and begged them not to shoot. The damage had been done and the trainer saved from further mauling. Animal trainers who work with dangerous animals fully realize the potential danger. They will concede to kill the animal at the point of attack if a life is threatened; but once the threat passes, the animal is too precious to be killed. The time to shoot the bears had passed. The police yielded to my impassioned plea.

The circus owner arrived as the trainer was being moved to a chair, weak, and bleeding profusely but miraculously still conscious. I could see in his eyes that death was not far. We waited for an ambulance. The circus owner disappeared to make a phone call. He called the media and soon there was a stampede of photographers and reporters to give the whole scenario their full-blown, reportorial attention and to take pictures of the dying man and the caged bears. It disgusted me that the circus owner had so little compassion for the victim, preferring to direct the whole media performance of vultures attempting to grab every gory detail to publicize a tragic performance. I exploded violently against the owner in a rail that expressed my vilest feelings for his absolute lack of compassion for the dying trainer. The ambulance arrived too late; the trainer died within minutes after the shameless publicity session was over.

The episode brought to memory a similar incident years before which held tragedy and death in the ring. I was working with Paul at the time who was performing a bear act for the Medrano Circus. Gina Manes was the famous headliner. Gina, a very beautiful and talented silent screen star, was 60 at the time but still possessed great charm and appeal to a most appreciative audience. Mr. Medrano was away on business in the States and had turned the direction of the Circus over to his sister-in-law, whose name I don't recall.

The lady had been in the boutique business and knew nothing about running a circus. She was distracted by an involved love affair with the ringmaster, a member of the famous Trubka family. She was also married to a diminutive, impeccably dressed, pious man who was obviously bored with his job of ticket-taker and also totally dominated by his wife. The husband began to spend his time during the shows in the attic of the building, field glasses in hand, watching the female ushers, hustlers who performed sexual favors in the dark recesses of the building. It was quite a comedy to observe the many unplanned, unrehearsed sideshows.

To stimulate business, Gina was booked and outfitted in a sexy animal trainer costume of white leather with shimmering rhinestones. The lady manager also hired a tiger act from the Pinder Circus. The Pinder had winter quarters two hours south of Paris. The contract required Gina to spend four weeks prior to her debut learning to perform with the tigers at the winter quarters.

Gina Manes became a pupil of Mr. Spessardy, the trainer of the tiger act as well as part owner of the Pinder. His cat act was smooth and gentle with no contact made with the tigers. There were two male bengals in the act known to have bad tempers. A whip was used to direct the tigers, but under no circumstances was it to touch either of the cats. I was with Paul at the premier of Gina's performance. She was scheduled to perform after the 15-minute intermission during which the center ring cage was prepared for the featured headliner. When the spotlight went on, it focused on the blue backdrop curtain behind the cage concealing shoots leading to the menagerie 75 to 100 feet away.

Gina came through the curtain to the enthusiastic applause of an adoring public. She was absolutely stunning, elegant in a sexy costume holding the heavy whip, then proceeded to move the leather whip in a circular motion as the crowd gave her a standing ovation. She entered the cage and gave the command to have the tigers released. The spotlight followed each tiger dramatically as they came through the shoot one by one and moved to their respective stools. The lady then circled the whip above their heads to begin the act. Not having the experience of years of handling the whip, she must have touched one of the male bengals as she directed the whip over his head.

Before anyone could react, the tiger was in midair and never touched the ground until it landed on Gina. The audience gasped as if on cue and began to leave their seats. The tiger dragged Gina around the cage holding her firmly by the breast. A second tiger attacked her leg as the audience continued rushing, screaming toward the exit in what became pandemonium. The police arrived armed with .22s and began to shoot at the tigers.

Paul and I held on to his bear, which reacted to the agitated situation. We were helpless as we watched the nightmare unfold. We were aware of further potential danger with bullets going into the cocoa matting, hitting the concrete, and ricocheting into the audience. None of the tigers were hit as they moved quickly and wildly inside the cage. In the meantime there were firemen standing by who turned their powerful hoses toward the tigers and successfully knocked off the attacking tigers. But as soon as one was forced away, another tiger pounced on Gina's body as yet another powerful stream of water was directed toward the brutal mauling.

Finally Mr. Spessardy arrived, went into the cage, and backed the tigers off. Helpers rescued the bloody screen star who was taken by ambulance to the hospital. After numerous surgeries, she finally died. The whole tragic scenario made a strong impression on a young, aspiring animal trainer.

With each dramatic and life-threatening encounter witnessed,

I was being educated to the inherent dangers in dealing with wild animals. The potential was always present for lethal injury and extreme precautions were absolutely essential. There was much to draw upon as I became more involved in my own animal performances. I felt privileged to have witnessed much that did sustain me over the years and to have met the many talented, inspirational individuals who were the leaders in their field.

One prominent man was Alfred Court. Paul introduced me to Mr. Court when we went to his winter quarters outside Paris. Court, from a wealthy family, chose to follow a different path in life. He had the option to become a multimillionaire and run the large family corporate holdings, including the *Savon L'Abeille*. He was fascinated with the circus at an early age and ultimately bought his own, which he named the Zoo Circus.

Beginning as an acrobat, he was a powerful man who worked with a partner in an act where Court took the man by one hand, lifted him above his head, and held him, miraculously, balancing the full weight of the man with only one hand.

The animal acts hired to appear in his circus intrigued Court, who was also called upon to fill in when his lion trainer got drunk. Alfred stood in without the privilege of any prior training or rehearsal. He had observed the performance many times and worked the act flawlessly.

From that precipitous occasion, he had one passion: to become the best wild animal trainer in the world. He possessed the financial means to make his dream reality, and I must say that he was very successful in dealing with all animals, none of which were declawed or defanged. His animals came from the jungle: mature bears, leopards, jaguars, pumas, lions, and tigers. Over the course of his career, Alfred Court trained many hundreds of animals and many books have been written about the man who became a personal friend. He lived to be in his late nineties.

I was becoming indoctrinated in the nuances of my own performance and with the many individuals involved in the circus business as we toured from city to city, country to country. There was much that was compelling and fascinating, but there was also a definite seamy side to the business. The Amar Circus was owned by an Arab family consisting of three brothers who operated two separate circuses. In Bordeaux I worked under Sherif Amar, whose reputa-

Alfred Court, trainer extraordinaire.

tion for honesty was questionable. However, my contract was in good order and stamped by the French Labor Department.

Near completion of the four-week engagement and closing on payday, I heard news of an incident in which a dog had been killed outside the circus. I paid little heed to the report until Mr. Amar accused me of neglect for letting one of the greyhounds loose as the killer. He explained the circus was being sued for a large sum of money and the potential loss, which he would suffer in high court fees, would be deducted from my pay. I told him that what he was proposing was not only illegal, but it was impossible for my dogs to have committed the crime.

I was furious with the accusation and the thought of losing a month's pay after fulfilling my obligation. My act required many hours of work to prepare and the performances had gained rave reviews. I went to the local Labor Department and presented my case, using my military credentials to lend credence to my position as an honorable man being taken advantage of by a thief. It was amazing how quickly justice was enacted by the authorities, closing the whole company down within two hours of my plea. The police arrived and every group was restrained from leaving. Obviously, Mr. Amar did not fully realize the power I possessed. He was forced to back down. In a couple of days, he came to me, paid me in full, and the restraining orders were lifted.

But I knew that I was still in danger of having the money recollected by his goons. The man surprised me. He came to me, laughing and in good humor, slapped me on the back, and said that he had no idea what influence I possessed. He even apologized for the incident and promised to book me again, which he did attempt on several occasions, but I turned him down.

Amar's accusation was preposterous. I kept the dogs secure in a pen while not performing. I also kept them leashed whenever they were exercised. After spending thousands of hours training the animals, they had become precious to me and a vital part of the business at hand. To jeopardize them in any way would be insane, not to mention very costly. There was at least a year of training invested in each animal, and it was imperative to maintain utmost security and care.

However, there is an aspect to animal training not generally known by the public, particularly where large animals are concerned; lions, bears, elephants, etc. There is so much labor involved in the training and so many hours spent in intimate proximity that the labor, burden of care, and attending danger actually produces ambivalence. At the same time the trainer fully realizes that each animal's care and safety demands extraordinary measures. I am not saying that all trainers feel an emotional detachment from their animals, but it is quite prevalent.

It was a tough, demanding, dangerous business that I chose as my career. And free time between engagements, when we could break away for brief respites, was spent visiting Fegreac to reacquaint ourselves with family and baby Gerard, who was not a baby any longer. He was thriving in the care of his grandparents which made our absence more bearable. My parents, particularly Mother, adored and doted on the boy.

The next contract arranged by Marouani was for a 12-month period in Spain working for Sr. Carcelle. I signed a double contract, one for the greyhounds and monkeys and a separate agreement to supervise the 15 men in charge of the menagerie the elephants, camels, bears, horses, and chimps. The contract also allowed for more pay if I introduced other animal acts. It held incentive money available and while I had a great deal of responsibility and was making excellent money, I began to search for additional acts. I broke in a chimpanzee act. The chimps were not easy to work. They had been imported from the jungle and were mature at six years of age. They were also dangerous, attempting to attack everyone who came close and had to be restrained.

Sr. Carcelle, a close friend of President Franco, was about 60 years of age, very distinguished, and obviously very powerful. He was also well-educated and a ruthless businessman. Sr. Carcelle dressed quite elegantly, wore gold-rimmed glasses and sported a most impressive diamond ring.

The star performers of his show were three clowns, the *Hermanos* (Brothers) Moreno, who had been incarcerated during the Spanish Civil War as political opponents to the government. They had established careers before being jailed, and Sr. Carcelle used his influence to bail them out with the proviso they sign a ten-year contract with his circus at a minimal wage. This was highly unfair and an indication of the way the man operated.

He also had under contract a Gypsy family named Dolas. The matriarchal group was led by a dark-skinned old lady who wore gold rings and chains; all the family was similarly adorned in gold. There were four brothers. The oldest, a strikingly handsome man, worked a lion act, a fighting act with lions charging around the ring after Dola who moved just fast enough to escape being mauled to death Clyde-Beatty style. It was strictly a growling demonstration with the Spanish audience clinging to the edge of their seats. There was little training involved, but a good deal of showmanship.

The three other brothers were Sr. Carcelle's enforcers. Carcelle had his strong-arm men, and I wouldn't put murder past them. I was in bed with a damned tough bunch of cutthroats in a country less than friendly. I found the Spanish landscape breathtakingly beautiful, but the people distrustful of all foreigners. There were German, Italian, and French performers in the show, giving it a distinctly international flavor, but also placing an aura of discomfort among the participants.

Sr. Carcelle had two units traveling through Spain at the same time. The way he operated was to have one crew install a wood and canvas structure to house the show, a sturdy construction that included dressing rooms. When the installation was complete, we moved in to fulfill the performances. While we were thusly engaged, the construction crew moved ahead to the next town, village, or city to install another housing to await the next show. In this manner there was very little time between appearances.

On one move we actually transported the animals by boat. The next location, near the coast, provided an adventure more harrowing than facing a ferocious animal in the arena. The performers not involved with an animal act rode by train. Odette went by rail while I accompanied the menagerie. We were under way, loaded aboard a large fishing boat, when a violent storm materialized. The heavy seas pounding the boat pushed it from side to side, and the large pens containing the animals began to shift like loose cannons. We were too far offshore to make landfall, being swept further away from safe harbor. It was impossible to tie down or secure the heavy crates as they continued to crash into the sides of the boat and into each other.

The animals, first sickened by the upheaval, became crazed by the unceasing turbulence. I wondered how long the boat would stay together and afloat. The visibility was reduced by fog, and the captain became disoriented. The camels and bears emitted shrieks of desperation, and the elephants were completely wild. It was a nightmare.

One of the camels went into the water. There was no way to save the animal. Most of the crew and passengers were seasick, and the deck was slick with salt spray and vomit. I stayed busy attempting to secure the sliding cages as the boat pitched violently. We tossed for 24 hours before a small fishing boat located our position. The captain of the boat boarded as we began taking water and then quickly left to seek help at the nearest port. Several boats came to the rescue to transfer the animals and humans ashore.

When we finally reached land, I was completely whipped from the pounding, relentless seas, the horror of the bellowing animals, and the absolute fear permeating the entire nightmare that none of us would survive. I never had such a strong feeling of death, not even while I battled the Germans with artillery fire on every side. Whatever fame I had achieved would go into the record books without further embellishment. My thoughts had been dour and scattered as I worked feverishly all night and the following day to preserve life — mine and the animals.

The animals took days to fully recuperate; it took me just as long. But we did survive and we went into the season fulfilling the contract, also embittering some of the other members of the circus. There was great resentment building. Sr. Carcelle had many differing financial arrangements. He had two contracts with me and a possible third, which paid quite handsomely. The Gypsy family was making only half of what I made.

It was company policy that no one be privy to the contractual agreements of others, and I told Odette to keep her mouth shut and not divulge what I was being paid. There was a French couple performing a bicycle act. We talked to them and knew they were well-paid, but the actual amount was not discussed. However, it became common knowledge that the Spanish performers were being paid poorly and the Gypsy enforcers even less. Our popularity among our compatriots was not enhanced by the situation, and there were indications that the intense bitterness could evoke violence against us or our animals. We had to be on guard.

In our traveling retinue was a comedy act that held a good deal of subtle humor. The act, French adagio dancers, comprised a handsome couple beautifully dressed, gliding arm and arm romantically to a waltz or similarly graceful dance rhythm. Suddenly a little dog came from the side of the arena and grabbed at the man's pant leg. The startled, serious dancer first tried to shake the dog loose without breaking stride as if nothing was occurring to prevent the continuance of the dance. The tenacious little dog refused to be ignored as it held onto the trouser leg, chewing the fabric. It became difficult to continue dancing with the feisty dog holding fast. The man's attempt to remain dignified only created more hysterics from the delighted audience.

As the man kept kicking his leg, the dog's grip became more determined and soon the pants were tattered and all dignity dissolved. Obviously, the trained dog was the most important part of the act. The dancers were not animal trainers, but they had the animal well-trained by a top French dog trainer in Paris.

One day the dog became violently ill, and the couple frantically called me for help. We had all dined out on Spanish *paella* the night before and had brought back leftovers as a special treat for their star performer. The native dish consists of clams, scallops and rice and quite often contained small broken pieces of shell. My suspicion was either foul play or food-induced illness. I advised against going to a Spanish vet, feeling that the animal doctors in Spain would be fully involved in patching up stuck horses eviscerated in the bullring and not so well-versed in more delicate practice. I suggested that a medical doctor would be preferable. When we located a doctor, the dog's stomach was pumped and then on my strong recommendation, an x-ray was ordered. It was not such a simple procedure, but the picture of the dog's abdomen was taken and developed for everyone to see.

As we looked down at the x-ray, we all noticed a straight foreign-looking object across the abdomen of the 25-pound male fox terrier. I knew what I was looking at, but everyone was talking at the same time, registering horror at what they guessed to be a large piece of shell inside the dog. The doctor suggested immediate removal of the object which could be the cause of the dog's malaise. I was horrified at the thought of an operation. I attempted to convey my opinion to the highly charged and excited group.

When I had their attention, I explained that a dog has a bone in its penis and what they thought had to come out was a natural and coveted part of the little dog. The doctor, who had done all his training with humans, and the dancers, who certainly didn't know about dogs' penises, began to laugh as the little dog opened his eyes to look around. The dog never thanked me officially, but I felt I had been an important advocate when the little guy and his desperate owners needed me. Not only did I save him from a life-altering surgery, I left the doctor's office with the knowledge that it was prudent never to take any animal to a Spanish M. D.

To break some of the tension from the jealousy and also avail ourselves of Spanish culture, we used time between appearances to attend the *corridas* — the bullfights. The national pastime of Spain had been witnessed in the south of France years before and did not favorably impress me. French *corridas* did not kill bulls or cows for very practical reasons; the fevered beef was not considered proper or safe for French cuisine. The animals used in France were inferior to the Spanish bulls, wildly elegant animals raised under semiwild conditions in huge *ganaderias* and strictly selected for conformation, speed, and meanness. The proud, fierce beasts were the living evolution of the extinct, prehistoric wild *aurochs*. I was particularly taken with the bulging, lean muscles, perfect horns, and silky black coats of the *toros* that were in such strong contrast to the domestic cattle. They almost appeared like a different species.

The ritual and pageantry of the spectacle was also unique and quite enthralling. While the sad termination of the bull was almost physically painful to me, I enjoyed attending the *novilladas*. The one we attended in Madrid was particularly edifying. *Novilladas* are the testing fights where promising, very young, and often handsome *toreadors* and *matadors* are given their first opportunity to be in the ring with top, selected *toros* instead of the smaller, inferior beasts from their native villages.

The tension before the release of the first bull, with one of the young novices waiting, filled the arena. Thousands of onlookers remained perfectly quiet, hushed, knowing fully that the novice was in extreme danger; the bull's survival favored. The first-time situation, the young bullfighter exposed to the big city crowd, the fine *toros,* and being watched by family and friends held much danger. The novice also took extreme chances to graduate instantly to the fame, big money, and national acclaim warranted by the significant accomplishment. Quite often terrible injuries and death took place. Death In The Sun — the tragic death suffered as thousands watched, screaming in shock and compassion while the raging bull savored his extra minutes of admiration before being put to death. As I watched the style of the proud *matadors*, I prepared myself for some of the same precise motions that I would later incorporate in my tiger-and-lion acts.

Other memorable performances took place when we were showing in Seville. We attended a fair where I particularly enjoyed the exquisite poise of male and female riders wearing traditional black hats as they rode the supremely elegant Andalusian horses. It was a feast for eyes and mind to carry with me and relive many times when the performance was completed, so majestic in its beauty. At the same fair were the *flamenco* dancers reflecting 800 years of moslem domination of Spain. They took me back to the French version associated so well with my first lover, La Esmeralda, ten years earlier. As I watched the dance, I was instantly transposed to the cottage where the first introduction to sex had so thoroughly fulfilled and satiated a young, adept student.

In spite of our attempts to find escape in the spectacle of the bullring and in other uniquely Spanish diversions, the suspicion and tension continued to build between the different factions in the circus. One evening Odette accompanied me as we left the dressing room. From the shadows came three of the Dola Gypsies. Two grabbed me by the arms as the other punched me in the face. I fought as Odette screamed. Her outburst gained the attention of the Morenos who came to my rescue. The assailants fled.

The enemy was becoming bold and violent. It was most disturbing, and from that moment I knew that there was danger outside the arena as well.

On another occasion I helped load the animals from the showplace to a conveyance to carry them to the railroad station. We had been paid that afternoon, and I had many *pesetas* in my wallet. It was 3:00 in the morning as we drove the truck filled with animals. I was seated on the right-hand side of the cab. The truck stopped on a narrow street when out of the shadows three guys ran directly to the cab. They were not the least bit interested in the animal cargo. They stabbed the driver and then came around the cab after me. As I jumped out, I grabbed the oak-and-steel elephant hook, used to maneuver the large mammals. I swung the sturdy weapon in a massive thrust that caught the first guy in the chest. He fell away. Another assailant caught me in the chest with a stiletto. Fortunately, the knife hit my stuffed wallet, thick with passport and Spanish currency. The blade cut through the fabric of my jacket, and into the wallet, through the papers, money, and leather about an inch into my chest.

It was a hit-and-run operation; our attackers left quickly fearing the tough Spanish police. We made it to the railroad station and sought medical attention for the driver who had been severely injured. He survived as did I, but the thugs intended to kill both of us. There was never any doubt in my mind that the attack was organized by the Dolas since no other circus trucks or artists from the show experienced any such threats or attacks.

Marouani had committed us to one hell of a deal. The tension did not abate as I continued to work the greyhounds and also the chimps. I was inspired by memories of Paul's chimp act produced years before at his compound in Le Vesinet. When I felt confident in the finished product, I began to show the chimps and the audience reception was gratifying — they loved it!

When Carcelle joined up, I cornered him and asked why he wasn't paying me the extra money promised for a new act. He said, "Well, I'm not satisfied with the act." I was damned angry.

"The public is, and there is nothing in our contract that is very specific about the act. It just says as soon as the act is performing, and they are performing; they ride their bicycles. I have the chimps seated, dressed up dining. They ring the bell and another chimp comes to serve them. Everybody loves it."

Sr. Carcelle continued to resist my request. I was beginning to wonder as the tour was winding to an end if I would be paid and, if paid, if I would be successful in getting the money out of the country. With Carcelle's political influence, all my doubts were valid. A month before the end of the contract, I cornered him alone and expressed dissatisfaction.

"I am not too happy with the arrangement."

He countered, "Well, Mr. Baudy, I'm not too happy either. I'm sorry but I don't know what I can do."

I answered, "You are a businessman, and obviously a very successful businessman, and you know the act of performing is tough. I have introduced these different acts . . ."

I had put together a horse act working with a group of six Norwegian ponies in addition to the chimps and the greyhounds and monkeys. I was averaging three hours sleep per night, and this was one period of time in my life when I did not find the time for sex. I was so exhausted that I could barely stand up and when prone I needed sleep. That was an indication of how hard I was working and damned if I didn't feel deserving of my pay. I hated that I had to fight for what I earned.

I talked to Odette repeating to her what Carcelle had told me.

"You know, if you are not happy, I have the power . . . you may go, but you may not go back to France." I was shocked.

"What do you mean by that?"

"Well," he said, "You know I've seen acts like this . . . they were not happy and I was not happy . . . but instead of going back to Belgium they stayed here for three years."

"What did they do for three years?"

"They performed in my circus."

I was furious and also frantic with thoughts of the lengthy tour and difficult, consuming labor performed for naught, the physical abuse at the hands of his thugs, and the possibility of becoming a prisoner of the ruthless entrepreneur. In relating the conversation to Odette, I realized more fully what was transpiring, what the possibilities were, and I began to formulate my own plan.

Two weeks before the contract expired, I took all the cash we had saved to a place where they sold gold, and I purchased coins and ingots. Spanish currency was not convertible in Europe once taken out of Spain. I knew firearms very well. We visited Toledo, a city where the artisans specialize in the manufacture of fine metal art objects and guns. I ordered a custom-designed, beautifully scroll-engraved, double-barrelled 16-gauge shotgun that would appreciate in value if I could remove it from Spain.

The time came for us to load the animals and board the train to France. It was a most welcome but a highly nervous day. I was anxious to put the year behind.

I knew we would be stopped at the border and searched extensively. I had purchased a large quantity of rice. We had been cooking rice and mule or donkey meat daily for the dogs. There was no such thing as prepared dog food in Spain at that time. The dogs seemed to thrive on the less expensive beef and rice. Since rice was not available in France, transporting a large quantity would not arouse suspicion. I had three boxes manufactured of light wood, each to contain over 300 pounds of rice. In one box I put the dismantled gun carefully wrapped in thick oil paper to prevent pitting and rusting. I didn't mention any of the preparation to Odette.

I also found a way to hide the gold. When the train arrived at the border, the Spanish customs officers boarded and proceeded to conduct a comprehensive search of our possessions. They asked that every piece of luggage be opened. I saw Odette's face go ashen as she visualized the pay for twelve months of labor confiscated. She had accompanied me when I bought the gold and felt certain it would be detected. She began to cry.

"Listen," I told her, "I had a sneaky feeling about this border crossing and whatever happens, don't get hysterical. Just stay cool."

"What did you do about the gold?"

My rejoinder quieted her. "We'll talk about it later . . . don't worry."

The agents requested we pull out every shoe and every article of clothing while they detained the train for three hours. They checked other passengers' luggage in a cursory manner. I knew Carcelle was responsible for our detailed search. The agents were disappointed, and I hoped Carcelle suffered the same emotion.

When we were finally released to cross the border, the French customs found the shotgun. The agent threatened to arrest me on the spot for the "serious offence." I pulled my military papers and pleaded my case justifying the method as securing a year's pay from a country whose currency was worthless. The agent took pity.

"Since you are a veteran of the Second Armored Division, I am going to give you a letter to take to the Customs Department in Paris. If you offer to pay the taxes on the gun, you may have a chance to keep it."

We were grateful to be back in France, alive and free. Odette felt safe in asking where the gold was hidden. I took her to the vehicle carrying the dogs and monkeys and showed her what I had done. I had purchased 30 pounds of bananas before we left Spain and pushed the gold coins through the skin on the hidden under side of the fruit. The skin sealed itself. I also had custom collars made for the greyhounds designed like sleeves or a money belt. I rubbed the leather to make them appear worn. The dogs, some of them very aggressive with strangers, each carried two pounds of gold ingots around their necks. Obviously, the agents were not enthused about searching the animals too closely.

Working for Marouani established early recognition.

Our first stop was Fegreac. I gave the gold to Father for taking care of Gerard. I bailed the gun out of customs after paying the tax and gave it to him. The first thing he did was sell the damned gun. My father did not want anything, even a handsome piece of art, associated with my career. I could not satisfy him or gain his recognition as long as I remained in show business. His attitude only deepened my resolve to build on the success I was achieving. He was a tough man and I, too, was becoming tough.

19

EUROPEAN ACCLAIM
Le Succès en Europe

*B*eing home in France was cause for celebration. There was much to celebrate. A successful career was uppermost. We were not to be home for long before our next tour commenced. Every moment with Gerard was important. I wanted him to know me as Father although the time spent with him was too short. We all dined out in fine restaurants and went to a show in Rennes.

One day I was in the kitchen with Gerard and Mother. There was a wooden spiral staircase going from the kitchen up to the first floor. I held Gerard in my arms, dancing with him. He was two years old at the time, just a little guy who seemed to enjoy the dance as I tossed him laughing and twirling in a wonderful, joyous romp. Not realizing how close I was to the staircase, I swung the boy playfully away from me. As I did, his head caught the wooden stair and the solid impact stopped the motion of his body. I caught him firmly, drawing him to me, stunned. His head went back and he screamed. Mother gasped. The boy stiffened in my arms and went limp. I put him down on a settee. A large bump quickly formed on the back of his skull, and we put cold compresses to the injury. I was in a state of shock; it was such a stupid, innocent accident. We were having a wonderful time when it all ended so suddenly.

The doctor was called from Redon. After attending the boy, he assured me that he thought Gerard would be fine. I was relieved with his assessment and encouraged when the little guy finally got up and moved around. But as I watched him, I felt that his reflexes were not sharp. He was not himself as he played and interacted with me and with each of us. I never expressed the fear that I have carried for years, ever since that horrible accident, that perhaps it was the beginning of the problems which surfaced later in the boy's life. I never verbalized this fear to either Mother, Father, or Odette. It was too painful and useless to discuss. I knew the blow had been severe enough to cause serious, life-threatening damage, but I could never talk of it or think that I had done something which might possibly plague him with such serious repercussions. With each passing day, he seemed to improve.

Soon after the accident we left Fegreac. Marouani committed us to a full schedule of contracts all over Europe. There was too little time to spend with family. Our first engagement was at the Medrano, which ordinarily would be for four weeks. After the month when all acts changed, the billboard read "Mr. Baudy and his greyhounds held over by popular demand."

Marouani had us booked into many one-day gala performances. The national lottery was held two or three times a year, staging an impressive production to attract a wider audience to participate. The salary for the single event was five times what I was paid for a day's work at a circus performance, but the single show required more work to organize.

The galas were performed under such totally different circumstances and in so many varied facilities, where the stages were high, the lighting was different from the circus, and the personnel were neither animal trainers nor circus people. The animals did not adjust well to the elevated stages or all the many differences, which created anxiety. It required two to three days of work in order to ease them into the new surroundings, only to be worked in one show and then moved on to another, requiring all the adaptation to be repeated.

We moved from France to the Ancienne Belgique nightclub in Antwerp. The dressing room was in the basement under the club in a dark, musty old building. In order to reach the stage, I had to pass through a narrow tunnel under the stage used by all the performers. There was barely enough room for a single body to pass through at one time.

During my engagement there was another act, performed by a man over seven feet tall in special lift shoes performing his interpretation of Frankenstein. He was a masterful actor who spent over two hours each day having his make-up applied. He brought out in me something which I had no idea existed. I did not think I had any sort of phobia, but I must admit that every time I walked through the tunnel, I felt shivers of fear — real fear — when I saw the ghastly apparition with bolts coming from his head and blood dripping from a distorted mouth, and livid, brutally scarred, green face. The man was a fright in ordinary lighting, but in the eerie, blackened tunnel I had no sense that he was a fake. As we passed closely, the man gave me a silent, friendly smile bearing oversized stainless steel teeth and unfortunately exhaled a foul breath that perfectly matched his impersonation. I was very happy to complete my contract and leave the Ancienne Belgique and the "friendly" hideous monster.

A far more pleasant sight in Antwerp was the impressive zoo. It was amazing to me that so many animals had survived the War and were so well kept. The Belgians must have hidden their animals. During the War, most zoos lost their stock due to lack of help, supplies, food, money, and often destruction by Allied bombing. The Antwerp zoo contained many rare species which provided a stimulating educational display to enhance the hours spent in leisure enjoying and studying the animals.

As the tour progressed, I tried to investigate each city and country during my free time to broaden my knowledge of the uniqueness of each culture. When we played in Holland, I was quite fascinated by the red light district. The prostitutes were framed in windows effectively designed and lit to show their wares. I had no idea the Dutch people were so liberal. The presentation made by each of the ladies was like a framed masterpiece of lighting and design, art if you will, in prostitution, like I had never seen before or since. They did not get my patronage.

We were on the move constantly doing cities in the Netherlands before moving to England. Booked into about a dozen theatres, we played the Leicester Theater, one of a large chain of similar venues dotting the British Isles. Included in the show were vaudeville acts. England at that time did not appeal to me as the country recuperated from years of war. The food situation was quite appalling, unimaginative, and not well-prepared. I also found the cities depressing as we passed through the many outskirts of somber, endless identical brick row houses under cold, grey misting skies that chilled the body and spirit. The rural areas in contrast were quite lovely with many superb, well-kept medieval castles set in lush countryside as well as manicured suburbs. Another negative feature of the British tour was the strictly enforced animal quarantine. They had to be housed and maintained in the dressing room, which was a tough regimen for me and for them. However, the money was good, and we were hailed as the "outstanding novelty act from France — Baudy's Greyhounds. "

One night in Leicester I realized I had not done something with the animals that required attention immediately. It was 3:00 o'clock in the morning when I left the hotel by cab to return to the theater. I went into the large dressing room where the dogs were kenneled. The room was cramped with dogs, luggage, and our traveling paraphernalia. I discovered quite by surprise two gentlemen, nicely dressed, going through our belongings. Startled by their presence and thinking them to be thieves, I approached on the offensive. They quickly presented their badges identifying them as members of the British Secret Service.

"Why are you here?" I asked. "Am I suspected of hiding something?"

Initially they did not reply, were evasive, then apologetic, and even embarrassed in being caught red-handed in the clandestine search. I'm certain their supervisor was less than impressed with their fruitless and clumsy mini-Watergate activity. When I mentioned the incident the following day to the theater manager, he was unaware of their intrusion and was most apologetic but not overly surprised. He explained there were rumors of Nazi saboteurs everywhere and that Russia was actively introducing agents into England. I don't know if the British Government was in touch with the Vichy Government, which in turn may have transferred records revealing my imprisonment in Aix-en-Provence. The episode would always remain a mystery.

We left England to return to France and another engagement at the Medrano. We spent two days in Fegreac visiting my parents and Gerard. I had expressed to Father that I did not want him to be as tough with my son as he had been with me. I did not approve of strict physical punishment being administered. I must have made an impression. Both Mother and Father seemed to enjoy having Gerard with them. Odette and I felt fortunate knowing that he was far better cared for in Fegreac than he would have been on tour. I witnessed performing families, little children being raised in the tough circus environment, and felt compassion for the innocent victims. While the young were well-attended by their hard-working parents, school-aged kids did not receive the best education and exposure. I knew that the atmosphere was not what I wanted for Gerard.

It was increasingly difficult to keep in touch with all the family. If there was a birth, a marriage, or a death which coincided with a lull between engagements, we could break away. On those occasions, we joined the family gatherings at the farm in Nièvre for the traditional two days of feasting that accompanied such events. It was an opportunity to compare life experiences and mine were stranger than fiction.

On one such occasion I learned the full story of Uncle Louis, who had finally returned from Germany after the War. He survived although the family had given him up for dead years before. Taken prisoner, he had been put to work on a farm. He worked so well that he was put in charge of running the farm and even elevated to the role of stand-in for the farmer as surrogate husband. The German husband was off fighting as a member of Hitler's army and Uncle Louis filled all the gaps.

When he told me the story, we laughed heartily of the "hardships" of war. When he returned to Nièvre, he told his wife about the relationship. She was understanding and even acquiesced realizing he had been in exile for years. She even overlooked his return trips to Germany to visit his "German wife."

Returning to my grandparents' farm was always a wonderful reunion. The ancient thick-walled stone monastery, always cool in spite of the temperature outside, had provided so many wonderful memories of my early years. The gardens were redolent in varieties of flowers and savory homegrown vegetables and fruits. My favorite fruits were the enormous gooseberries as well as the white and black plums, the sweet fruit on which I regularly gorged myself in spite of the guaranteed diarrhea that always followed. The fruit attracted many bees as well which did not hamper me. I was willing to be stung to satiate a greedy appetite.

The rolling countryside lush with foliage and the gently flowing River Allier created a serene atmosphere for our gatherings to relax and renew. It was refreshing to return to the place of my formative years where I idled the hours watching and interacting with the animals and joining my uncles, nieces, and nephews for swimming, fishing, and hunting excursions. Visits also renewed for me so much that was meaningful in my life. I developed and deepened my knowledge of the natural order of life's intermingling relationships, both the human and animal kind. It was more than a return to a 500-year-old monastery. It was a return to a decades-old tradition of living rooted in hard work and simple pleasures unmolested by modern conveniences or the stress-induced pace of an industrialized society bursting from the bondage of war and occupation. Life there was unchanging, and in a way I cherished the simplicity.

I valued the saneness of it as I found myself on a hectic carousel, whirling along with Odette from one engagement to another, feverishly building on the fame and fortune coming my way. Some relatives acknowledged the fame and seemed genuinely impressed; some came to watch the performance and were exultant in their praise. But Father remained staunch in his view that I had made the wrong decision. He would not concede even with all the acclaim that there might be something worthy in what I had chosen, what occupied my life and my very being. I was engaged in what would be a lifelong endeavor, to understand and work creatively with wild animals. There was no way that he would ever understand that compulsion, at least not while I was in show business.

In 1949, I signed a contract for the summer to perform in the prestigious Schumann Cirkus in Copenhagen. The Schumann family, the Royal Equestrian Dynasty of the world, had produced the internationally acclaimed shows for over a hundred years. 1949 marked their 101st Season in Copenhagen. The solid structure that housed the Schumann was an absolute jewel of a facility, originally designed exclusively for equestrian and circus shows that attracted Danish nobility. The royal blue-velvet-decorated ring was precisely 15 meters in diameter. The public seats and background curtain were also deep blue and gold velvet. The animals were kept in the huge basement where over 300 large animals could be accommodated. The Schumann was located directly across from the famous Tivoli Gardens, a wonderful combination of beautiful gardens and a variety of

The ultimate European venue.

rides. My favorite was an ancient but spotless merry-go-round featuring hand-carved wooden mounts that stimulated artistic sensibilities.

The circus directors included the venerable Ernest and Oscar Schumann. At the opening of the show, the two aristocrats made an appearance dressed elegantly in tux with tails. Their pres-

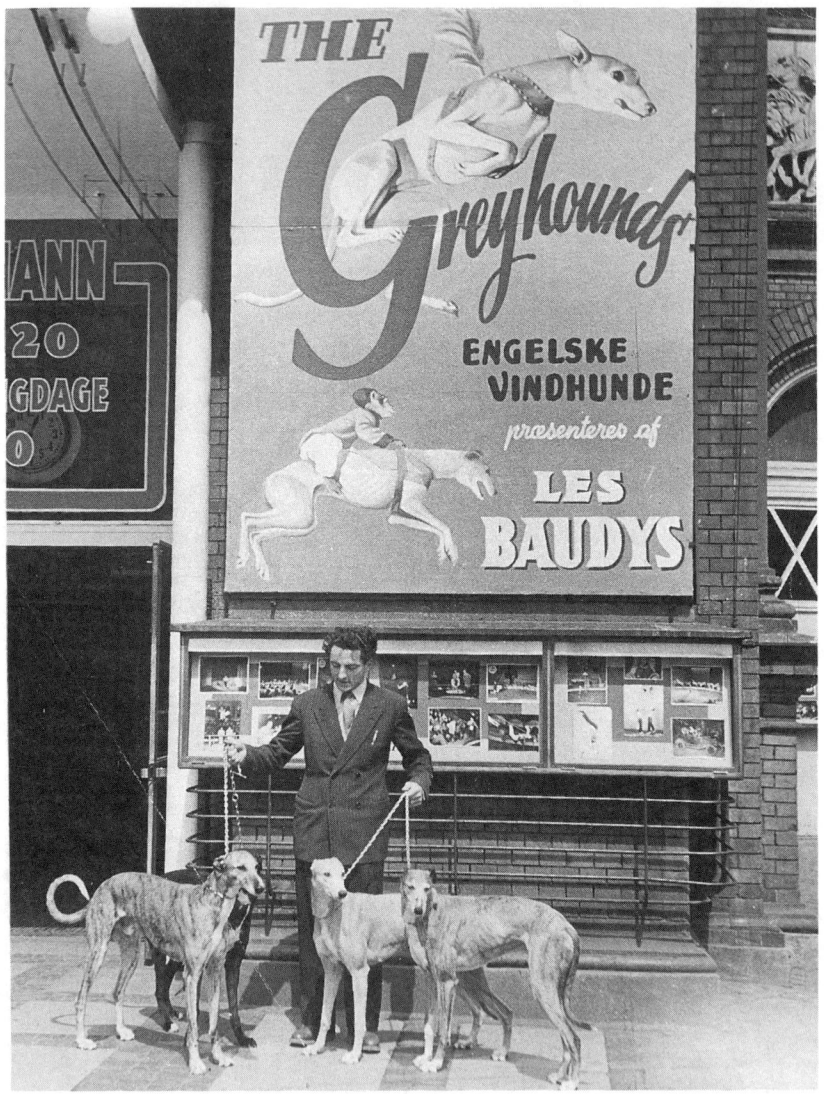

Top billing at the Schumann gained an American agent's attention.

ence was always cause for a standing ovation. The show itself consisted of 15 acts, three of which were advertised in giant, hand-painted billboards at the main entrance. Upon arrival I was surprised, delighted, and flattered to see that "The Greyhounds and Monkeys of Robert Baudy" were among the three headline acts.

Our radio and media reviews from France, Portugal, Spain, and Belgium had obviously preceded us to Denmark.

From the very first time that I stepped onto the hallowed ground, I was enormously impressed by what the Schumanns so magnificently performed. I already had a solid foundation in circus horse training, but I was completely unprepared for the exhibition and rehearsal of horses conducted by the two heirs of the dynasty, Albert and Max. Albert, tall, blond, and blue-eyed, was the complete opposite of Max, who had dark hair and dark eyes. They did have in common extreme handsomeness and unbelievable mastery of horses.

The French have a long history of expertise in fine horse training, and through Father and Paul, I was well-acquainted with procedures and terminology such as *passage, piaffer, rassembler, pirouette, balancer, cabrer*, etc. But watching the results of six generations of master horse trainers was pure ecstasy for me. I was so deeply impressed as I watched the performance that I ached to have Father and Paul present to share in the grandeur and excitement of the execution. The scheduled acts in the program were dramatic and performed with such precision with Albert mounted on a silky black stallion dressed in the gaudy French *spahi* officer's uniform with gold and baby blue *kepi*, the very same headgear that cost quite a few officers' lives in Normandy. Without any coercion, Albert would put ten Arabian stallions, mounted by realistic, turbaned, life-size dummies, through precision drills. I never tired of watching the men and horses perform and was particularly intrigued early in the morning, in the quietness of the dimly lighted arena, as Albert and Max rehearsed the different groups of horses for the next season.

A striking performance featured 20 white horses, naked, without bridle or harness. Max, from the center, mounted on a black stallion would cue the whole group of horses to circle around him first at full gallop as a loose, beautiful wild herd. The flowing manes and tails were a spectacle of strength and beauty that was dramatic and absolutely breathtaking. Then, speaking in a low but commanding voice, he signaled the group to gallop single file, then by twos, then fours and finally by tens with Albert in the center of a perfectly straight line of 20 horses. The finale was Albert suddenly calling the group to him, rearing his mount, and ordering the other horses to raise up on hind legs simultaneously. The elegant, dynamic maneuver of power, control, and precision was unlike anything I had ever seen before or since.

After the Schumanns practiced their horses in the morning, the ring was made available to other animal trainers. Since there was only one ring and few hours available between the horse session and the matinee show-time, all the trainers fought for rehearsal privileges. However, the Schumanns always made certain that "Mr. Baudy" had first access to the ring following their routines.

Their instruction created jealousy from the bear and elephant trainers. The elephant act consisted of one giant, male Indian elephant sporting enormous tusks. The animal was the property of an Austrian circus and handled by its owner, Mr. Reberning. Between shows the magnificent mammal was chained in the basement. Mr. Reberning warned me that the bull was dangerous. He did not have to tell me. Each time I went to tend the dogs, housed 100 feet from the elephant, the huge trunk suddenly reached for me.

Toward the end of the season, while I was busy near the dogs and close to a huge, concrete supporting column, a large projectile hit the column, ripping a ten-pound chunk loose that hit me in the back. I stiffened at impact, then turned to see what was assailing me. The frustrated elephant had picked up a heavy iron bar and propelled it with enough force and precision to decapitate me if it had been six inches closer. I had watched the bull perform many times from ringside within easy reach if he wanted to assault me, but during his performance he was under Mr. Reberning's absolute control.

The finale of the act was a wonderful display of the huge beast snatching from the audience a startled midget in black face wearing a grass skirt. The elephant then ran around the ring with the supposedly terrified midget, held by a custom-designed belt, and hoisted high in the air as the elephant reared on its hind legs. The termination of the act was dramatic with the diminutive clown in such stark contrast to the huge elephant. The applause was thunderous and always begged an encore. About 15 years ago, I read with regret that the magnificent creature, the only adult performing male elephant in Europe, had gone on a rampage in a German city and had to be destroyed by the police to avoid human casualties.

Often while performing, I noticed some of the Schumanns

watching my act. I questioned Oscar who gave me an explanation for their special interest. Many years previously, one of the elder Schumanns had tried to duplicate their horse routine with a large group of greyhounds similar to mine. While they did succeed in training the dogs in the practice ring, they could never get the animals to stay in the show ring. The dogs escaped in typical greyhound fashion — 40 miles an hour in every direction. I received a great deal of pleasure realizing that I accomplished a dog performance that the horse "masters" had found impossible.

As I practiced in the late morning, I noticed an audience of one. In the fourth row sat a beautiful, statuesque blond, young lady who returned several times to watch my rehearsal. Finally she introduced herself. She was Danish but spoke some French. She stated that she was fascinated by my technique of gently but firmly training the dogs. She invited me to join her for lunch in a restaurant in Tivoli Gardens and then after several other meetings, she invited me to her apartment in downtown Copenhagen. She was a leading fashion model in Denmark, well-paid and living in a handsomely appointed apartment. I was intrigued not only by her beauty, but by the passion she shared for animals. Our conversations primarily involved animals.

Circumstances often create crime, and our love for animals and our conversations drew us into an intimate relationship. Odette became aware of the involvement, but said nothing of it to me. Instead, she became extremely demanding of me in bed, and I must admit that leaving Copenhagen when the contract was fulfilled perhaps saved my sanity. Satisfying Odette and sharing lovely romantic interludes with the blond model in addition to daily rehearsals and performances left me in an extremely weakened condition. I needed badly to return to France for a rest.

Before we left Copenhagen, I was contacted by a Mr. LaTour. The elderly gentleman from New York represented the Hamid-Morton Circus as a scout seeking European performers to sign for an American tour, which would include circus, TV, carnival, and many other show-business arenas. I was flattered by the offer and challenged by what I envisioned in taking the greyhounds and monkeys to the states. I signed the contract calling for a 25-week minimum guaranteed schedule to begin in January, 1951, and paying three times the normal European fee.

There were many European performances to fulfill my commitment to Marouani before leaving for the States, and on several occasions the beauty from Denmark showed up at a club in Paris or at a circus or wherever I was performing. She had the financial means to follow the act from city to city. She was obviously fascinated by the animals, and we indulged in many conversations in addition to enjoying some wonderful sex.

I began to formulate the idea of including her in my performing retinue. She spoke several languages and seemed an ideal employee to work an animal act if I trained other performing animals. My plans began to expand to include the additional rolling stock and props necessary to show several different acts. I discussed the possibility with Odette, who did not express any objection to the arrangement. However, my relationship with the blond came to an abrupt end. We were in Paris at the time, and I invited her to join me for dinner to discuss my proposal for her inclusion.

As I explained my plans she interrupted, "Robert, there is something that I must tell you."

We had been talking in some detail about the particular act that I felt would best suit her talents and interests when she stopped me.

"Look, I'm going to put my head back."

She raised her face and pointed for me to look inside her nose. I could see clearly and horribly that the septum was eaten away. In my naïveté I exclaimed, "My God, you have a cancer!"

"No," she said, "Drugs!"

She was perfectly candid in her confession to the addiction — emotional as she explained how much she wanted to work with me, to be with me — but also knew that if I took the time and went through the labor of breaking an act for her, she could not be counted on to be available. Her addiction was life-threatening, and I was completely stunned. It was the end of a beautiful relationship.

The idea of introducing more acts into the show was not new. I had kept some bears at Paul's compound, but did not work with them primarily because there became a plethora of bear acts after the War and I didn't need to add to the glut. Many German circus performers were protected and given special civilian status due to Hitler's and Goering's affinity for the circus. Some Germans fled in all directions through countries such as Switzerland, entering as

Germans and leaving dutifully laundered as Austrians or Lithuanians. Some of the acts being performed were mediocre, but I chose to work with other animals.

It was at this point, when my career was blossoming, that Paul le Royer disappointed me. Paul had been such an inspiration ever since I was a small boy. As I grew up I held him in awe as an idol, a mentor, and someone I respected greatly.

Paul trained many different animals and was a fine mentor.

He had also provided a place to live for a struggling, newly married couple and a place to break in what became a successful act on the European continent.

I was absolutely stunned and disappointed when Paul approached and asked if I didn't feel obligated to him for achieving the increasing fame as the greyhound and monkey act continued to garner rave reviews. He even requested a commission based on his influence. I was hurt by Paul's financial claim and had no compunction in turning him down. I admired the man tremendously, but when I took Odette to live at the compound in St. Mande, it was to help Paul as well. He left for a year of touring in North Africa, which stretched into a longer period, and he desperately needed someone to stay at the complex to care for his animals and property. Because I did not collect much for our services, I felt his request was totally unjustified. I did not feel indebted to the man for enabling a career, but instead felt hurt and disillusionment when my refusal breached our friendship.

Marouani booked us for a five-month engagement in Blackpool, a seaside city on the west coast of England. It was a lengthy booking that would serve to prepare us for the longer contract with Hamid to follow in the States. The housing at Blackpool was a huge tower connected to a system of buildings which included a permanent circus similar to the Medrano or Schumann. The circus building was attached to a zoo operating at that time but has since closed down. The environs were a very popular resort area for the English people to spend summer vacations by the sea. The weather always seemed to be windy, rainy, and cold; I never went for a swim. I could not understand the attraction to the grey, drear, seaside, but there were large and enthusiastic audiences to fill the shows — perhaps because the weather was so bleak. The contract was an extremely well-paying one.

The Tower Circus, the equivalent of Atlantic City's Steel Pier, was a British institution operated by a very distinguished lady named Mrs. Williams, who was in her sixties. She also had a lovely young daughter named Pat, who was her mother's assistant. The show included performers with whom I had previously shared billings many times. The Tower boasted the finest group of talent in one circus that I ever had the privilege of performing with in a single engagement.

Pierre Alizes was one of the entourage. Pierre performed a wonderful flying act. We had worked together at the Schumann as well as other major shows. Gilbert Houcke of the Houcke dynasty of circus performers was showing tigers. His brother, Maurice, was presenting 12 beautiful Freisans horses from the famous Knie Circus. Nadea Houcke, their beautiful sister, was not performing her riding act at Blackpool, but I did meet her at other European shows. The French Houcke family, going back to the 1800s as circus performers, escaped France in the thirties to become Swedish citizens. By allying themselves with the neutral country, they did not perform military duty during the War. The Houckes were consummate showmen with a great deal of charisma.

Also in the Tower show was the handsome Australian family booked as the Seven Ashtons. The members, all blond and blue-eyed, were dynamic young athletes loaded with good looks and talent. Their performance, a Risley act, was a spectacular routine using one or two of the smaller members as props. The other members of the family, using specially designed stools for support, used their feet to propel the lighter members into the air in a juggling exhibition that required utmost dexterity and precision as the double somersaults and other tricky maneuvers were executed. The Ashtons first appeared in flashy gold and red costumes wearing capes similar to the Spanish matadors and accompanied by lively upbeat music well-synchronized to the six-minute routine that was absolutely breathtaking and always received by a cheering, enthusiastic audience.

The overall quality of the English show was superb. The food was not superb, and our lodging was a simple trailer located out in the country away from the circus. We had Sundays off and I often used the free day to join Pierre Alizes for a day of salmon fishing. The English countryside was quite beautiful which served to enhance the pleasure of the outdoor adventures. I also hunted with Pierre's partner in the flying act, Jacques. Jacques was a handsome adonis married to a very pretty, jealous brunette named Maryse. With so many good-looking, talented athletes involved in one arena, the interrelationships of the lengthy engagement became volatile.

Jacques became involved with the young Ashton girl, who was an absolute knockout. I knew of the affair and felt it held promise of serious repercussions. Gilbert Houcke became involved with a member of an influential British family, a dalliance which could also create far-reaching problems.

Gilbert, in a Tarzan outfit to work his tiger act, attracted a great deal of feminine attention. I was quietly observing the intrigue around me, but was innocent of any involvement. I worked the dogs early in the mornings while Odette remained in bed until noon, then performed at show times, and spent my free time in healthy, outdoor sporting adventures.

One morning I noticed Pat Williams watching me put the dogs through their routines. We talked briefly. She returned the following morning, and the next, and again the morning after that. This time she asked if I would accompany her to visit the family country home.

I enjoyed the beauty of a ride through the countryside in spite of the consistently foul weather, and I was flattered by the lovely young lady's seemingly innocent invitation. I felt no harm in accepting an automobile ride. But Pat had other ideas. She was extremely aggressive, and I did not resist her advances when we found ourselves alone in the country house. We made love the first time and returned to the house whenever we could discretely leave Blackpool to enjoy rapturous clandestine hours together. She became an ardent lover, and we met occasionally early in the morning when we were alone in the Tower. Pat even visited the trailer to share a meal with Odette and me. Odette was hardly naïve and soon realized that I was involved with the young lady, but my jealous wife's reaction surprised and baffled me. We did not discuss the situation; but I knew that she knew, and yet she continued to tolerate Pat's visits. In the meantime, the intrigue and emotional attachments were deepening.

The Ringmaster for the circus was a man named Delbosq. He was in charge of the circus performances working under Mrs. Williams. Pat told me that she had an affair with the handsome 40-year-old Delbosq. When she confessed to her relationship, I realized why he was so hard on me, giving me hell for the most trivial details, and even fabricating complaints. The man was obviously jealous as hell and after my hide.

He warned me about not maintaining the dogs properly — I kept the dogs immaculately, but it was tough under the strict quarantine laws. When I signed the contract, I knew the British law required the dogs be housed in the basement with little opportunity for exercise. I hated the conditions because it was an extreme hardship on the dogs and spoke to Delbosq about some sort of arrangement for exercising the animals. He was friendly and eager to accommodate my request at that time.

A street separated the circus from the beach. I asked for special permission to walk the dogs during the five-month engagement, which was absolutely essential. He suggested that if I wanted to take the chance, I should walk the dogs late at night when there were no witnesses to the illegal activity, but covered himself saying, "Mr. Baudy, this is a conversation that never took place." I agreed with him, feeling the incarceration of the dogs excessively cruel and was prepared to shoulder the consequences if caught. There was a car at our disposal for running errands, and often in the middle of the night I drove from the trailer to the circus to walk the dogs, one at a time on the beach. I was not getting much sleep.

One day Delbosq said, "I want to have a talk with you."

"Fine, let's have a talk."

"I know that you are having an affair with Pat."

I tried to act surprised. "Well, I don't know that, but if you know that . . . you obviously have some information . . ."

He bristled at my response. "Let's not try to fool each other. I know what's going on."

"Well, on the basis of the information that you have and in view of the fact that you wanted to have a talk with me . . . what is the bottom line?"

He heatedly replied, "Stop!"

"You mean that I should stop talking to the girl?"

"Oh no, you don't have to stop talking to the girl, but you better stop the rest, because things are going to happen very quickly. I'm warning you . . ."

The romance with Pat was risky, foolish, and should not have happened. But it was a fact not to be denied and knowledge of it was no longer secret.

Soon after the conversation with Delbosq, I was walking one of the dogs late one night when I noticed in the distance another person, something I had not seen previously. I had always managed to walk the dogs in complete anonymity. On two subsequent occasions my clandestine walks were again observed which distressed me, but I was powerless to prevent the intrusion.

Then, one day, I was requested to make an appearance before Mrs. Williams. She was in the presence of her personal secretary, a good-looking silver-haired man in his sixties. She came to the point quickly and directly.

"Mr. Baudy, I do understand that something is taking place between my daughter and you." My English was not good, and I used its lack as my excuse for not understanding what the lady was proposing, but she continued. "This is something that cannot be tolerated." I began denying some of what she was accusing when her secretary opened a side door to an adjoining office and ushered in two security agents. The men read a report exposing my pattern of behavior which included visits to the family home with Pat. I was shocked.

"What's next?"

"What's next?" my accuser repeated. "You are leaving England."

My English suddenly improved. "But we have a contract and as far as my contract is concerned, those allegations have nothing to do with the contract. The British have always been known to respect a contract . . ."

She stared at me icily. "But you have broken the contract."

"How did I do that?"

"Because, from this date," she pointed to the date on the report, "to this date, and even early this morning at 3:30 a.m., you took the greyhounds on leash on the sidewalk, and this is where the quarantine law comes into effect." At that point, the quarantine officers entered from another room. Her case was sealed. The officers recited what the law directed: my arrest and confiscation and destruction of the dogs. My hands were tied.

I had talked previously to a friendly British vet who offered to be an expert witness in my behalf if I needed him. He was horrified by the potential loss of animals for any infringement of the law. I felt that even if I fought the case, the danger of the animals being put to death was great. I decided to accept the offer made, to be paid for the period of time that I had performed, and be released from the remainder of the contract if I would leave the country with the dogs immediately.

Within a matter of hours the animals were packed. We were put aboard a truck bound for the railroad station, accompanied all the way to Le Havre by British agents. The agents sat behind us on the train and on the boat crossing the Channel. They spoke French, but did not communicate much during transit.

I was in immediate contact with Marouani who arranged commitments to fill the Blackpool cancellation. We played at Medrano, and in galas and some club engagements until the time for the trip across the ocean. It was time to fulfill our American contract.

We headed first to Fegreac. I wanted my parents and Gerard to see the dogs and to share in the excitement of the pending voyage and all that it held. The local press covered our visit with five articles written and published including photographs. The articles described the international exposure enhanced by proposed performances in the States, in Canada, and on television. It was an exciting and very special time together. We left the dogs in Fegreac for a couple of days in the care of Uncle Gauthier. Mother, Father, and Gerard accompanied us to Guilvinec to visit Odette's family. We were scheduled to be away for a year. The 25 weeks of actual commitments would be extended by travel between bookings.

Our departure date arrived full of varying emotions. Excitement prevailed, but leaving Gerard was hard. We knew he would be well cared for, and I promised Father that I would send money to cover any expenses for the boy. We loaded the dogs and our trunks on a train for Le Havre to board the cruise ship *deGrasse*, nearly too exhilarated to fully realize what we were leaving behind and the potential problems that would evolve.

20

AMERICAN TOUR BEGINS
Le Début en l'Amérique

*W*e sailed out of Le Havre on a sea journey for which I felt a great deal of ambivalence — apprehension for the length of time proposed for the confinement, but anticipation of promised opportunities at journey's end. The ship, the *S/S De Grasse*, a luxurious ocean liner, was over 500 feet in length. Our cabin was handsomely appointed. With pristine service and gourmet food the passage promised a wonderful holiday atmosphere.

Within days we were in a violent storm which reminded me of a similar sea adventure. I did not think I would survive the first calamity, and I certainly never wanted to repeat the nightmare. I found myself regrettably under the same dire conditions with absolutely no control over what was happening to me or to the animals. The huge ship was violently tossed about just as the small fishing boat off the Spanish coast the year before. The dogs were contained in individual kennels on the top deck. I had to tie myself to a stanchion to keep from being slammed into the sides of the holding area as the thunderous seas churned below. The dogs were violently ill.

The Captain ordered me not to go on the upper deck, but I explained that the animals were my livelihood and I felt compelled to ride out the storm with them in spite of the peril. He told me he was not responsible for my safety.

The temperature was below zero as we rode the seas, whipped to frenzied turbulence by 70-mile-an-hour winds with stronger gusts. It was another nightmare from which we might never awaken, and I

AMERICAN TOUR BEGINS

Shipboard command performance before the seas turned rough.

thought many times during the passage that death would be less painful.

The scheduled seven-day journey extended to 14 days, five of those spent going in circles. We arrived in New York to freezing temperatures, high winds, and grey skies. The dogs were seriously dehydrated, and I was so ill I could barely walk. It was hardly a grand entrance.

People from Hamid's organization met the ship and took us to a hotel on the west side of Manhattan, a depressing accommodation called the Belvedere located across from Madison Square Garden. The animals were taken on to Trenton to be housed at an old fair grounds owned by George Hamid. I checked into a hospital where I was diagnosed with a kidney infection and double pneumonia. I spent several days in the hospital while Odette worried about the animals and me, struggling to communicate in a foreign country so far from home. What a hell of an ordeal.

When I was released from the hospital, I began a daily trek to Trenton in spite of four feet of snow which turned to grey slush, creating hazardous driving conditions. There were so-called grooms at Hamid's complex in Trenton to care for the animals, winos who knew nothing about the care and feeding of the dogs and monkeys. I was not comfortable with the set-up, but saw no alternative for the time being.

There were other animals housed in the facility which became our base of operation. There were elephants maintained in a filthy barn by the "animal crew," a sickly family group. The son was a handsome boy, tall and blue eyed, but emaciated; the father was a heavy smoker with little flesh on his bony frame, and the daughter was pathetic. My original reaction was confirmed when I witnessed the health department employees arriving. Hamid's crew all suffered from TB.

It was one hell of a situation. I was caught in a bind, under contract, and feeling the pressure to gain success in a country so totally foreign in every way. I said to Odette, "This is going to be a long 25 weeks of hell, and then we're going back to Europe." Little did I know at the time what life in America held for Robert Baudy.

Mr. LaTour, a subagent for George Hamid when he found me in Copenhagen, signed me to the contract. Hamid was involved in many show business venues and provided 30 percent of the acts that performed on the *Ed Sullivan Show* at that time. It was with the promise of TV exposure and other enticements that I signed on for the American tour. Admittedly, I was a neophyte to so much that was different in the American experience, but I knew the television appearance would further my career toward achieving international recognition. American fame was the dream of almost every European performer. Hamid also hired acts for state fairs across the country in addition to Circus-theme TV shows and cabaret and night club appearances. I had to focus on the positive aspects of the commitment and suffer the inextricably allied negatives .

It took two weeks to recuperate from the ocean crossing, my malaise, and my disappointment with the crude hotel accommodations in Manhattan and the squalid animal housing in Trenton. It was a time to adjust and soon it became time to leave the Northeast for the first live performance in the States at a Shrine Circus in Memphis, Tennessee.

We welcomed the diversion as an escape from the crude quarters in spite of the fact that our traveling companions cramped into the rolling stock were Hamid's unhealthy, unsavory crew. While the animals were carried in the rear of the semitrailer rig, Odette and I shared the cab with an unbathed, cigar-chewing driver who filled the air with unpleasant intermingling odors. As we drove south, I began to fully appreciate the vastness of the country. It made the European countries pall in size. It took two days of all-day driving to reach our first destination; I was unprepared for the amount of miles traveled. We also witnessed a rather dramatic change in climate. There was so much to learn and much to appreciate in the changing scenery.

In Memphis, the Baudy Greyhounds was only one of five acts being performed at the indoor Shrine Circus. I was accustomed to performing under the same tent or in the same housing with other acts, but never in conjunction with so many performing at the same time. I found it distracting and totally unsatisfactory. I was the focal point in the European arena but not in Memphis, despite being center ring. I felt the audience was cheated; there was no way they could focus on any one act. It was another disillusioning factor uniquely part of the American tour. While the money was more than twice what I had been paid in Europe, I appreciated the qualities involved in the foreign tour where the performers were treated with more respect. I felt from the very start that the American tour did not suit Robert Baudy.

We worked a couple of shows on the return trip to the Northeast. The animals were returned to their housing in Trenton, and I was taken to New York City to be introduced to the producers of the Sullivan Show. The time had come for our first appearance on national television. I had to make arrangements for the animals to be housed near the theater.

The performance was to be rehearsed requiring that we be in the theater at 9:00 each morning for five days prior to the actual show. I had no idea how precise the demands of the television production were, nor any concept of the time and detail devoted to each and every element of the production. The music was coordinated with each motion, and marks were placed on the stage to indicate my position and the position of the dogs as we moved through the routines to properly synchronize the music and to achieve the optimum camera angles. Every act on the *Ed Sullivan Show* had its own musical accompaniment. It was a wonderful education, but a hell of a labor.

We worked some days from 9:00 in the morning until late at night. We rehearsed, then we rehearsed again, and then we rehearsed some more. Dealing with people is one thing, but involving the animals adds a certain unpredictability that could put the whole performance out of sync where timing was of the essence. There was no such thing as color television then, and the lighting was tricky with various shadows to be eliminated. I rehearsed with and without the animals. The dogs tired and became nervous. There were rehearsals where all the other performers attended, and the whole show was put through the paces. Some rehearsals I worked alone and then with the dogs in a grueling effort to achieve a five- or six-minute spot that was finally performed in front of a studio audience of about 300.

When I signed the contract with Hamid, I thought the money almost scandalous for a single performance. I soon realized, in the heat of the preliminary work, that every dollar was earned and justified. If anything, it made Hamid a thief and me a fool. The time and effort did pay off, however. The performance went beautifully. We received rave reviews and were promised return engagements on the popular Sunday night television show. Soon other TV offers came my way.

Another facet of the American tour made quite an impression. I was being educated in the American labor movement. When the dogs and monkeys were brought from Trenton to Manhattan, I drove the truck carrying animals, props, and some handlers to unload the cages and equipment. I soon learned the labor law prevented my handlers from touching the animals once they were on the premises of the television studio. I was upset by this completely unheard of arrangement, but I soon found that I had absolutely no say in the procedure. The unions were all-powerful. Even the props were to be handled by union members *only*. The animals did not react well to strangers moving them. The greyhounds were high-strung dogs that had to adjust to much that was foreign to them.

In signing the contract, I had agreed to a weekly salary based

AMERICAN TOUR BEGINS

on the 25 weeks guaranteed. Those weeks of work translated into over 40 weeks including travel time, that would ultimately extend the tour through the year. My salary was a pittance compared to the many thousands that CBS paid Hamid for the greyhound act. George pocketed the difference. Granted there were engagements that paid far less, but I felt outraged at a contract that was highly favorable to Hamid and slighted Baudy. I was determined to rectify the arrangement.

Odette with Chief Poking Fire and friends.

We traveled all over the North American Continent. We went into Quebec and played some Canadian fairs that took us as far north as Rivière-du-Loup, "the Wolf River." On the Saint Lawrence Seaway, Rivière was the northern-most spot accessible by road at that time. The scenery was spectacular.

There was a huge Indian reservation in the area, and I spent free time visiting and observing the Indians. I was fascinated by their culture and hunting methods. They were extremely good shots as evidenced by stacks and stacks of bear hides; each bear was felled by a single bullet through the head. The Indians lacked power in their 22-guage shotguns and did not enjoy the luxury of unlimited ammunition. Every shot counted. I spent many hours watching the natives skin the animals, stretching the hides, and performing the tanning process. Their primitive methods were very effective. I bought hides and managed to barter and communicate quite well in spite of the language barrier. They spoke a mixture of old French and a unique dialect difficult to decipher, but I managed well enough. I enjoyed the experience and likened it to what I had read years before — The Lewis and Clarke Expedition describing the Canadian *Coureurs des Bois* (woodmen).

After most lengthy tours, we always returned to Trenton which, as we continued traveling to other parts of the country, did not compare well. Winter at Hamid's fairgrounds was dreary and depressing. From my observation of the conditions and the treatment of the elephants by Hamid's crew, the grossly inadequate facility was an excellent example to inspire the animal protection people to seek litigation to protect animals' rights. The handlers living in an old barn on the grounds were no more than resident guards. I could never figure why Hamid kept the elephants, never shown or used for any purpose as long as I was on the premises, but housed along with the crew in less than sanitary quarters. It was despicable and in sharp contrast to the way the man lived.

One day while sharing friendly conversation, George revealed to me that he came from extreme poverty. He was raised in the circus and performed as an acrobat. He told me he had vivid memories of sleeping under the Atlantic City Steel Pier while performing with his family years before. I was performing at the popular attraction in New Jersey at the time. George was quite proud of the fact that after humble beginnings, he ultimately bought the pier and also became recipient of the Horatio Alger Award. I'm certain the honor bestowed was worthy and he knew firsthand much pain and suffering in his life, but I experienced the financial ruthlessness of the man; and it was more than disillusioning.

With plans to eventually escape the snare, I began to search for kennels in the area for Great Danes. I had visualized an act using the large dogs to appear like lions. I wanted at least eight to ten dogs and looked for the toughest and the best of breed in two-year-old animals. I scoured kennels in New Jersey, Pennsylvania, and New York State. I was completely ignorant of the attending problems that came with the huge animals sired by different breeders.

As I began the training process, I worked with powerful grooms using heavy ropes to guide the dogs. It was impossible to physically restrain them myself, and the instant discipline was broken, they went for each others' throats. It was a demanding, treacherous act to break involving tedious, dangerous labor to achieve success with the 200-pound dogs.

There was another problem associated with one of the dogs.

In my initial search, I was put in touch with a leading breeder whose kennels were on a large and impressive estate in New York. The lady had been married to a prominent motion picture studio head. She told me she was divorced and lived alone except for her dogs. I had been told previously by an informant that a good and reliable source divulged a scandalous tidbit concerning the lady and "Samson," her favorite pet. She was reputed to be involved in a sexual affair with the animal. A very wealthy woman, if outward appearances were an indication, she raised outstanding stock. The lady, in her mid-forties, slightly plump but very attractive, showed me her dogs. I saw three that were for sale and would suit my needs for the act, but they were not the beige color that I sought. She kept all the animals in kennels except one — her favorite, Samson. He lived in the house and was a gorgeous specimen. His conformation and coloring were just what I wanted. I had been forced to purchase some brindles, but I preferred the beige-coated animal. I saw that Samson followed the lady like a shadow, very protective of his mistress. He growled when I stood too close. I told her I would buy the three dogs that were for sale if I could buy Samson as well. She nearly cried.

"Oh, Mr. Baudy, I cannot sell Samson . . . he is my companion . . . he is my friend. We have a very special relationship and I would be lost without him."

"I thought you told me that Samson was not so great in shows, and I thought you raised only show dogs!"

"No," she continued, "but he is a very special dog and my constant companion, and I couldn't think of letting him go."

"Well, in that case . . . Samson is the dog I want. This dog looks like a lion . . . he's big . . . he's absolutely perfect for the act. But I really cannot deal with you if you will not sell him. If you change your mind, and I hope that you will, contact me." I went away on a continuing search for other breeders and did find dogs that were suitable, but none as fine as Samson.

Two weeks passed and I received a call from the lady requesting that I meet her for lunch. When I arrived at the appointed place, she told me that she had a change of heart, and decided I could purchase Samson if I bought the three other dogs. I was extremely pleased to get the handsome animal.

Samson was an extremely intelligent dog, very powerful and

very sexy. I quickly learned that I had not fully realized the ramifications of Samson being sexually involved with the lady. He was obviously accustomed to having relations routinely. Whenever any of my female helpers were working around the dogs, if Samson was loose, he always attempted to mount her. That was a shock to the unsuspecting victim every time it occurred. We had our hands full with Samson.

Suddenly the situation with Hamid changed dramatically. Our contract called for all transportation and travel arrangements be furnished by the Hamid Organization for the duration of the winter season. After the winter tour, I would be on my own to purchase rolling stock and to get the greyhounds, monkeys, and their props, plus my handlers and Odette from one engagement to another unaided by Hamid. I was approached by many agents as I worked the various bookings that Hamid committed us to as we toured the entire country. Hamid made the contracts and set the rates, but we were on our own to fulfill them and to find adequate housing along the way.

It was puzzling to me how quickly Mr. Hamid arranged for me to go to the GMC dealer in Trenton to pick up a truck and trailer. The ground work had been planned in advance. It seemed to me, in retrospect, that this was a lucrative gimmick Hamid used to entice performers to sign contracts. He made it appear to the foreign performers he engaged that all arrangements were made. The innocents, who had no concept of the enormous size of the country and of the wear and tear on the rolling stock, were sucked into a situation that became extremely complex and costly to maintain. I knew from the amount of driving involved that I had to have new and mechanically sound equipment, anything less would be costly in breakdowns and possible no-shows. It was imperative that we have equipment that served us well and equally important that I was knowledgeable in working on engines, able to repair flat tires, and perform the myriad of details that totally filled every hour of every day as we crisscrossed the country in a caravan of animals and circus performers.

Fortunately, Odette had learned to drive the family vehicle in Fegreac after we married. However, driving through the countryside in Brittany was quite different from driving through Detroit or Chicago traffic searching for the next location on our schedule.

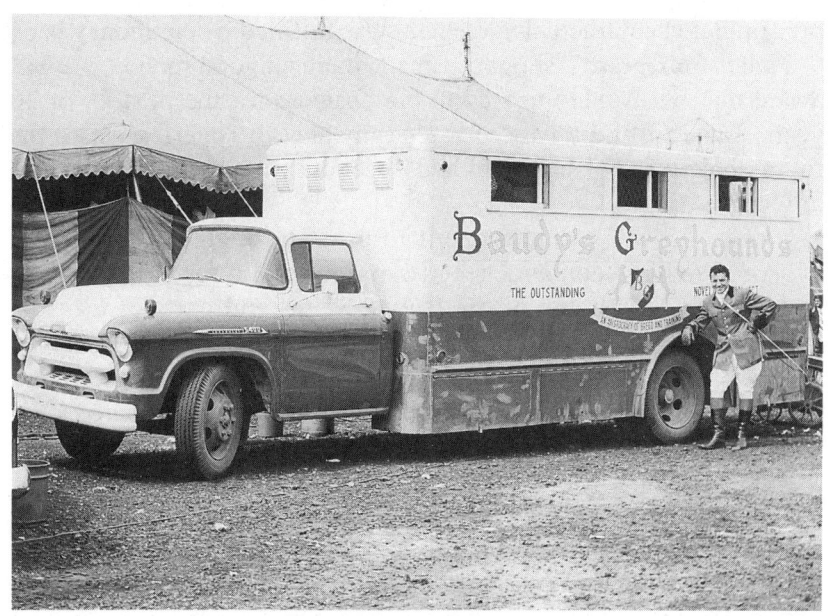

My first self-owned rig.

It was a labor involving a great deal of stress. During the winter we struggled through snow storms, and once when we were in Canada for a winter engagement, we awoke to find the landscape blanketed and the vehicles buried under five feet of snow. We had to drive in the worst conditions averaging 100,000 miles that first year. Often an engagement required driving straight through taking two nights and a day. Some days we covered 700 miles with few interstate highways. Odette and my handlers helped drive the rolling stock. There were also the added problems of keeping the animals warm and protected from the elements. It became a brutal, physically exhausting occupation moving in and out of motels, cities, and towns dotting the landscape in addition to rehearsing the animals and putting on actual shows. The behind-the-scenes labor was all-consuming. When we returned to Trenton, there was no vacation or even relaxation. I concentrated on working the Great Danes.

Hamid had me signed to an iron-clad contract. I worked without the privilege of a green card, having come to the States under a limited visa arranged by his organization, which would expire after my stipulated contractual agreement was fulfilled. I sent money back to Father for Gerard's support. I made damned good money but was aware that if I wanted to stay in the business for the next 20 or 30 years, I had to find a way to extend my stay in America where the future looked promising, but I had to get out from under the clutches of George Hamid.

The 25-week commitment took us through the Christmas Season. We had been under the Hamid umbrella for nearly a year, and we had seen much of the United States and parts of Canada. We had performed on the *Ed Sullivan Show* and other TV shows. We had played Las Vegas, all the big cities in the country, small towns, fairgrounds, with circuses, and in clubs all across the continent. We had been transported by Hamid's semitrailers and traveled with his employees, who were a motley group of winos for the most part. Then we were cut loose to fend for ourselves. We stayed in many motels and hotels and dined in restaurants of every description from elegant to awful. We had experienced every kind of weather and every kind of hazardous driving condition imaginable and had to perform some masterful mechanical work on vehicles to keep the stock and our reputation rolling. We lost some greyhounds to illness and accident and had to replace and retrain.

When there was time, I continued to work the Great Danes, which was a tough job that held much danger and great challenge. The year had produced some wonderful reviews to further enhance my reputation, but served as well to deepen my resentment toward the grip that Hamid held over every aspect of our lives. There was no such thing as a day off. Odette and I labored together but it was tough and demeaning. She found solace in a constant flow of letters to and from her family. We called France often to keep in touch and to keep track of Gerard's accomplishments. Photographs were exchanged which only served to deepen the separation. I must say that Odette was damned stoic under the brutal circumstances of our Gypsy lifestyle so far removed from family and our son. But she received plaudits, and she enjoyed the attention from her own fans, of which there were many.

Show business is a tough and fickle business. It does have redeeming features, but the price paid is dear. When the audience is on holiday sharing a special occasion with loved ones, when Christmas comes or Thanksgiving or any other major religious observance is celebrated, the performers are occupied in their labor. There was no such thing as a holiday for us. And Christmas, 1951, found us booked into Radio City Music Hall to fulfill the final, lengthy commitment to George Hamid. We were booked for four weeks to appear in the special Holiday Show. It was to be an exciting and exultant way to end the year and our contract with Hamid.

The stage at the Music Hall was the largest I had ever seen or worked. The whole facility was well-equipped to stage an absolutely magnificent production. The world-famous theater, regarded as the epitome of American show business achievement, the pinnacle, would also serve to introduce us to some fascinating people and to justify a determined effort to remain in the States to build on our success.

Consoling a member of the troupe.

The gentleman producing the shows at the music hall, Mr. Leo Leonidoff, was a small man of great genius who could speak five languages fluently including French. He knew all about my act and wanted the dogs and the monkeys specifically for the Holiday Spectacular. The entertainment was geared toward the family audience. At that time the Christmas Show at the Music Hall was a must-see seasonal event for most every family in and around Manhattan as well as from the neighboring states and other parts of the country. Leonidoff, a man in his fifties, communicated well with me, and we formed a great mutual admiration. He was a bright, intuitive fellow and held the respect of every employee at the Music Hall in addition to every performer who worked the hallowed theater.

The Christmas Show included a live recreation of the Nativity with camels, donkeys, and even an angel flying through the air propelled by invisible cable. It was truly a masterful production of much genius, spectacular in color and grandeur that seemed larger than life. I was extremely honored to be a part of it.

Mr. Leonidoff called me by my first name, "Robert, let me tell you something. We have a large number of dressing rooms . . . and I've already got your number."

"You have that?"

"I'm going to give you a beautiful dressing room with bath, shower, and the only room in the theater with a couch."

I laughed, "What's the idea? I never take a nap during the day."

"No, but as you will see, the chorus girls are very attractive, and there are 50 of them. The point is that you will be part of a production number. I know that between shows you will want to rest and you might just want to have room for company."

The engagement called for four shows per day, a tiring, grueling, engagement. Sure enough, Odette would sometimes return to our hotel leaving me at the theater to work with the dogs, or rehearse, or to prepare for the following show. Then I would return to the dressing room, and it was ideal for entertaining visitors.

The chorus girls were everything Leonidoff had described: absolutely gorgeous, long-legged showgirls. I was perfectly happy to have them come to my dressing room to talk and even stretch out between shows. It was a stimulating engagement, and I met some exciting women at the music hall.

Terry Barton was from the Midwest, a staunch Catholic who seemed to enjoy sharing serious theological discussions. I knew the beautiful lady was a virgin and I had no intention of violating her physically, but I did point out some hypocrisy in the Church which she had never dared question through a dogmatic upbringing. I may have influenced a broadened perspective in the naïve and sheltered innocent. Our special interludes in the quiet of the dressing room held serious, mind-bending philosophical discussions.

Another girl came into my life at that time. Virginia deBoner was a friend of one of the girls in the chorus. Virginia was a dancer

Whether on the Ed Sullivan Show or at the Music Hall or the many other venues, the Greyhounds and monkeys were a hit.

with the June Taylor Dancers appearing at the Roxy, and we had an immediate attraction for one another. She was a beautiful free spirit. We became intimate and I enjoyed her visits to the dressing room enormously. We had a wonderful rapport and some beautiful sex. When she left me, I knew she had other men and she knew I had other women. There were no strings attached to the open relationship.

When we left the Music Hall, we returned to Trenton and, for me, the labor of working the Great Danes. It was a long, involved process using my handlers to control the large dogs. Each time I returned to the training, it was like starting from the beginning. I had not been able to devote undivided attention to the new act due to recent arrivals, four imported wild-caught leopards, a black and three spotted, from India. I planned to work the cats into an uncaged leopard act, which would be unique, having never been done before in America. I had so many plans and so much work to accomplish and a wife who was more a business partner than a lover. Our relationship had changed and I could feel the discontent, but I also felt that other problems had to be addressed. Uppermost in my mind was to rid myself of the Hamid Organization.

Mr. Leo Grund was a subagent for George Hamid. He was one of many agents who presented various proposals as my fame grew. I received advice from many sources and also became wiser in my own right. George had signed me to a contract that was lucrative for George Hamid, but not lucrative for Robert Baudy. When I made the decision to stay on in the States for more than the 25 weeks, I was naïve in thinking that when my contract was fulfilled, I would automatically be a free agent. Not so. Hamid had other ideas. I was offered contracts by some of the largest agents in the country, and I asked George to release me. He was candid.

"Well, Mr. Baudy, you cannot work for anybody else."

I was shocked by his refusal. "This is the country of the free, and you are telling me I cannot work for anybody else!"

"You came with a temporary immigration visa and you are going to stay with me. This is what I want you to do, because I think that is what would be good for you and for me. I would advise you strongly to listen to a man of experience. You do *want* to stay with the Hamid Organization for at least three years."

I told him I was not going to do that. One heated word led to another and an exchange that ended in his threat, "I could create some serious problems for you!"

I had contacted French expatriates when we first arrived in Manhattan. I was anxious for a touch of home and sought French-speaking people in the city. Odette and I became friendly with a couple who owned a café. Through business connections they knew George Hamid's reputation and had warned me early on that while considered a very successful businessman, he was also reputed to be absolutely ruthless. I learned firsthand, but was powerless to affect a change while under contract.

As part of the tour, we had gone to Canada a number of

times. Some of the engagements were in Quebec where French is spoken, but a form foreign to me. The French I learned as a child had been constantly rejuvenated by foreign colloquialisms, unlike the Old World language spoken in Quebec. I did manage to communicate and was informed that if I were to leave the United States and not return to France, I could go to Canada. I could apply for a green card by presenting my military papers verifying the tour of duty under Patton as a member of the Second Armored Division. I would then be granted a green card gaining free agent status, which would obviate any previous contractual agreements.

We packed the animals and moved to Canada. I acquired a lawyer, who began the tedious process of separating us from George Hamid. It took months to accomplish our goal, with Hamid a very powerful entity.

One of the hurdles was to pass an extensive health examination. I was in excellent health when I went to be checked by a doctor with the U.S. Health Administration. The young doctor was obviously influenced by Hamid. George had threatened that there was no way I was going to outsmart him or the American system. He had far-reaching connections to block any and all entry attempts. I became engaged in a battle for my freedom and was as determined to win as George was determined to prevail. The young doctor ordered chest x-rays. He brought the developed x-ray to me and said, "Mr. Baudy, I have bad news for you. You are a sick man." I was stunned by his evaluation feeling in peak health.

"I am?"

"Yes, let me show you."

One thing that struck me as I sat in his office was that every x-ray on his desk seemed to have a patient's name printed on the surface. The one offered as mine had no name. He took a pencil to pinpoint a very small, light spot and explained.

"We do have a problem here. We have some kind of tumor. Are you coughing a lot? Do you have a fever?"

I was impatient and angered by the prognosis.

"No, never . . . oh, I had been very sick when I came to America a year ago, but that's been a long time and I'm feeling fine."

"Well, I cannot help it, but I can't give you a recommendation to be admitted as a citizen of the United States until we do have some subsequent appointment to keep track of this thing."

I asked him what I had to do next.

"The problem is that I don't think on the basis of my recommendation that you will get the green card."

I had not reckoned with Hamid's far-reaching influence, but I knew damned well that I was healthy as a bull. I was also suspicious of the unlabeled x-ray. I left frustrated, not knowing what course of action to take, but wanting badly to get the card. I returned for four examinations, every one administered by the same young doctor, who initially turned down my application and continued to find me in "ill health." I kept seeking justice and finally had a physical exam by a different doctor, who found me in fine health. I qualified for the green card.

21

NEW TOUR AND FREEDOM
Les Nouvelles Libertés

As a free agent, free of George Hamid, I determined that I would never again become committed to a binding contract nor one that I did not fully understand. I would govern the guiding elements of each and every contractual agreement henceforth. I would find work through many different booking agents as a single, independent performer.

I had witnessed what occurred to performers who were flattered and courted, as I was, by an offer to sign with a prestigious company, be it Ringling, some other famous circus or agent, or any of the large touring companies. The contract ordinarily was for two or three years, and during that time you are a slave to the company, owning nothing of your own, not even your soul. The company owns you, your animals, your whip, your boots, and even, possibly, your wife. I felt very comfortable owning my own custom-built and designed trucks and operating as a free agent, utilizing the expertise of many agents to arrange individual contracts. Never again would I be married to a George Hamid.

We were obviously not welcome at the Hamid animal compound in Trenton. That was not unexpected or even disappointing; other arrangements had to be made. We had become acquainted with Frank and Betty Minor, who operated Woodborn Farm, a horse farm in Bucks County owned by a wealthy family named Swan. I arranged through Frank to lease some empty stalls which became my winter quarters. Odette and I rented an apartment in Trenton to use when not touring.

Settled into new quarters with contracts to fulfill, I was eager to begin the new tour. There were two bookings during this period that were amusing. One was to perform the greyhounds and monkeys at a winter rodeo in New York City. The star of this particular engagement was the handsome, popular Hollywood cowboy, Buster Crabbe, who had the dubious distinction of being one of the first actors to portray Tarzan in the movies. The show was held inside a large armory; the concrete floor was covered with a heavy layer of clay and dirt topped with sawdust. When the typical calf-roping, bronco-busting, and bull-riding was over, the audience eagerly awaited the grand entrance of the famous star. The lights were killed to produce near total darkness. A single floodlight focused on Crabbe, following him into the arena as he came at full gallop mounted on a white stallion. Dressed elegantly in white-fringed buckskin and a white Stetson, even his six-shooters were silver and ivory, the saddle and bridle flashed chrome and rhinestone; the entire outfit was dazzling. I watched from the sidelines. Crabbe performed the finale of each show by rearing his horse and saluting the crowd as he raised his white hat. There was not much depth to the actual performance, but the crowd seemed very impressed with the modest trick-riding act and the dramatic close.

On the last night of the week-long engagement, I watched again as the "white knight" rode gallantly into the arena on a surface which had become, after many consecutive performances of many animals, a mixture of manure and urine-soaked mud. I had the impression from the instant Crabbe entered that he was either under the influence of extreme fatigue or alcohol. He was not quite so gallant or in command of his performance. When he signaled his horse to rear, he slid down the back of the mount and settled clumsily into the muck. The stunned cowboy, fallen from his glorious pedestal, was booed by the audience who reacted unsympathetically to the fallen idol (who was not nearly so white or dazzling). His horse proceeded to gallop out of the arena.

In the cowboy mode, I played another circus with Mr. Chuck Connors of TV's *Rifleman* fame. I had performed in many venues along with Hollywood stars who were the headliners, and I became acquainted with many of them. Some were friendlier than others; some were prima donnas who didn't acknowledge anyone. Connors had a reputation for being distant, and I wondered

Daily work with the greyhounds was needed to keep the performance sharp.

as I watched him perform what the great attraction was. His whole act centered around the twirling of his custom-made rifle. I was apparently not alone in feeling that the man was actually perpetrating a fraud on an unsuspecting public. One day the security people and even the police were brought in to search for Connors' "missing rifle," so vital to his performance. Whoever secreted the gun did a thorough job, and Connors had to go "on" without his trusted prop. His final performance was sad to watch.

It was obvious there was little room for pretense in an arena of hardworking performers who spent long, hard hours perfecting acts requiring skill and talent. An actor or performer who foists an inferior act and then maintains an attitude of superiority was more than an insult. He or she was fair game for some character-building abuse. I saw two cowboy idols temporarily fall from their lofty pedestals and I must admit amusement at the sight.

As more bookings materialized, we mapped out our planned journey to cross the country again, this time totally on our own. It was winter and the weather was bleak. There were few interstates; the turnpike from New York did not cross the state line. We fought our way through snow storms on icy or rain-drenched single lane roads. The conditions were brutal for the drivers and the vehicles, and the toll was showing on Odette. As we continued tramping across country from city to city, I was aware of her increasing abhorrence to the demands and stress. The American lifestyle contrasted drastically to life in Europe. The hardships created by thousands of miles traveled and the seamy individuals involved in the business accentuated the differences in the many fine people we met along the way. Many openly told us that Odette was too good to continue living this way. She spoke English with a heavy accent, which seemed to charm the men and even the ladies. There were producers, agents, members of our audiences, and Shriners and their wives who became friends and invited us into their homes.

One agent told me candidly, "Robert, we're not booking you for your animals. We're booking you for your wife's legs."

I knew Odette enjoyed the accolades, the friendships, and hospitality. I tried to encourage her and was gratified to see her positive response, but the disparity between the adulation and refinement of other lifestyles stood in stark contrast to the tawdriness of our vagabond existence which only served to deepen her discontent. She was emotionally distancing herself from me in her frustration as she continued to listen to the many voices around her. Well-to-do professional people who invited us into their homes provided wonderful diversion from the tour, but also a glaring comparison to our lives, rootless and lacking in the refinement she craved. I am sure that in her search for solace she believed that as long as she remained married to Robert Baudy, her life would become a continued routine of motel rooms, animal cages, circus riffraff and a tough Gypsy existence. My behavior was not always conducive to easing the burdens. There were times when things went wrong and the pressures came crashing down, and I went into tirades. Finally, I knew that she could not tolerate our life on tour — that we would eventually go our separate ways.

As far as I knew, she did not have any extramarital affairs. However, she was well-attuned to my infatuations and indiscretions which fulfilled me and were so indelibly a part of my existence. In a way, I thrived on every element of the tough life. I was often exhausted from the demands, but I was at the same time stimulated by the interaction of the many animal acts in the works. I was stimulated by the people I met, particularly the beautiful women. My adrenaline flowed as I labored and loved through every challenge and escaped life-threatening encounters. I knew well that I could never live a sedentary existence where animals and beautiful women were not major players. I could not settle into a home in Bucks County or anywhere else. The nature of the business kept me constantly involved and that is what I needed and wanted.

In the early spring we had returned to Bucks County when Mother came to visit. She had never experienced such a trip beginning with the long flight across the ocean and finally seeing her son perform professionally. We headed toward an engagement in the Midwest. Mother accompanied us on tour. I was very proud to have her join us, and she seemed elated to watch the act and the audience reception, which had been denied her in Europe. Our caravan of trucks, trailer, and shiny new Oldsmobile was traveling through Texas when the timing gear went out on one of the trucks. We were in the middle of nowhere. We had the shelter of the trailer which provided our accommodation for the night. The darkness and remoteness was further embellished by frightening howls of coyotes, absolutely petrifying Mother and impressing her with a dramatic experience of the American West. I'm sure she expected an Indian massacre to follow.

The following day I drove to the nearest town 60 miles away from our temporary lodging. I felt fortunate to locate a mechanic who could repair the timing gear, but he did not have the part which I found after an additional 100-mile drive. The entire day was spent securing the precious part. The desert wild flowers and cactus fascinated our visitor, but the monotony of the same scene for two days followed by the noisy coyotes punctuating the darkness did not

The Great Danes performed some amazing feats and were good pupils.

enhance the trip west. The passage, likened to a western wagon train, held so much that was foreign, but it gave Mother a view of what we experienced when tramping across the huge country. I'm certain the account carried back to France, while colorful, did nothing to ameliorate Father's image of my chosen career. During Mother's visit, Odette was attentive and seemed to enjoy her presence and conversation of home and family, but it did not allay her feelings of growing enmity for our life together.

During this unsettled period with Odette's emotional outbursts, there was so much to occupy me, so many demands. In addition to working the greyhounds and monkeys, I continued at every opportunity to train the Great Danes. When I began the search for the massive dogs, I initially sought ten, knowing that out of the ten I would ultimately eliminate two. There was much to learn about the large show animals that I purchased. As a common denominator, I knew that you can take a tough animal down, but you cannot take a shy animal and bring him up to the level necessary to tolerate the nuances of the performance. The noises, lighting, and audience interaction affect a gun-shy animal. While it was possible to train such an animal, it required more time and effort. The fact that "show" calibre dogs, which I sought for their wonderful conformation, were developed for their looks rather than intelligence, created a greater challenge than I anticipated. A dog bred for intelligence, such as a German shepherd to be a guard dog or a herder, or a French poodle naturally endowed with genius, is far easier to train. With inbreeding and line breeding to produce a show dog, the result is often a good-looking idiot, and that is what I acquired. It required five times the amount of work to produce the results that I demanded of myself and of my animals in all the acts I performed. I also knew that natural attrition would occur. I began the preliminary planning stages of the act soon after we arrived in the States knowing well that I had a couple of years or more of work ahead. Soon after breaking away from Hamid, I began concentrating all my free time on the Great Danes.

I envisioned the performance as a comedy act, one with the animals charging from behind the curtain wearing huge papier-mâché lion heads. They actually looked like lions when they first appeared. The act was to parody a Clyde Beatty fighting act. I cracked the whip and treated the dogs just like a ferocious pride of lions. I am jumping ahead of the story, but when I finally had the act completely perfected and showed it at the Palace Theatre on Broadway, the audience in the front rows actually left their seats when the dogs charged onto the stage. The animals moved aggressively like untamed attacking lions. With the large heads and no cage to contain or protect them from going into the audience, the spectators reacted to their initial shocked instinct and moved quickly to escape the charging beasts. When they looked again and realized that they were watching a stage full of large costumed dogs, they settled back to enjoy the unusual performance. The dogs instantly responded to my commands and very obediently went through their routines, some getting up and walking on their hind legs, which was a dramatic and totally unexpected move for the enormous animals. Two of the dogs sat on pedestals holding a rope, taut, as a monkey dressed in a ballet tutu and leotard, holding an umbrella, walked the tightrope. It became a very popular act in spite of the tough training and the problems encountered behind the scenes.

For the two years that I showed the greyhounds and mon-

Great Danes and some great dames helped put on a unique act.

keys, I also worked the Great Danes and continued working the greyhounds as we did lose dogs from time to time due to accidents or illness. I had to replace dogs, retrain and constantly work the new additions into the act in an ongoing labor to maintain discipline and quality of performance in the original dogs.

When I introduced the Great Danes to the public, I learned that I could not book both dog acts into one engagement except on rare occasions. My acts were very expensive to book. I was being paid about five times what other dog acts were paid at that time. While the two acts were entirely different, most houses adhered to budgets that did not allow for the cost of both. It became necessary to hire someone to perform the Great Danes, which seemed like the ideal arrangement, but not so easy to do. The dogs, accustomed to me as trainer, did not get out of control even as they left the stage to return to their kennels, but when someone else was working them, they sensed the difference and took advantage. When commanded "GO," their signal to run from the stage to their kennels, they began to attack each other. Breaking up Great Danes tearing at each other's throats is quite different from breaking up poodles or terriers. Some of my hired people were badly hurt in the process. I continued searching for someone who could handle

NEW TOUR AND FREEDOM

the large, unruly beasts.

In addition to the dog acts, I worked the leopards. The amount of time between an act's conception and its finalization is at least two years or maybe three. The preliminary stages begin in the mind and then delineations are put on paper with every detail visualized, planned, changed, and rehearsed for months before the animals are physically introduced. I had little time to devote to the leopard act, but my creative processes were continually at work with the anticipation of hiring other people to help perform and handle the animals. While many of my ideas were original, I was influenced greatly by mentors Paul le Royer and Alfred Court. Not only was I duplicating many of their training methods, but Paul always had wonderful-looking ladies in his entourage. I seemed never to be without ladies, and I might as well put them to good, productive labor.

Odette and I had been involved with John Cuneo on many occasions as we played dates across the country. John was, and to this day is, a wealthy impresario who wanted to be an animal trainer. He owned many animals and had many employees under contract, working out of a most impressive winter quarters in Libertyville, Illinois. He had indicated more than a cursory interest in Odette, but I was too busy to pay attention to the evolving relationship. When Odette informed me that she was leaving to perform an act for John Cuneo, I was absolutely stunned. She declared that she could no longer tolerate the lifestyle we shared. She accused me of many infidelities and enumerated the horrors of life on tour; she was fed up with the on-going struggle. I could see that in going on her own she was jumping from a tough situation into a tougher situation. I'm certain Cuneo promised her the world, and he could afford to give it to her. I could not fault her for leaving. She had been a magnificent trooper for seven years, all of them filled with unrelenting work and hardship with not much pleasure for her. I never attempted to be faithful, and it was one hell of a life for Odette, actually a culture shock for the Breton. I could not nor would I ever protest her leaving. She deserved a better life, and I hoped she would find it with Cuneo.

Never once did I feel I had to justify my behavior to anyone. I was a serious and dedicated professional animal trainer. I worked hard and long hours developing and perfecting many acts. I spent most days either physically working or mentally designing and imagining, putting ideas together that would enhance and build upon what was already being performed or could be included in the act in future. There were no holidays, no vacations, and very little rest. When I went to sleep, many nights were filled with vivid nightmares depicting the horrors of the battlefields in France and Germany. When I was with a beautiful lady or a fascinating individual, I found escape and relished the pleasure of it. I badly needed the brief periods of diversion and relief from a demanding and dangerous preoccupation. The women whom I loved helped to keep me in balance. They provided an outlet and a gentleness so necessary in an occupation that was rigid, structured, and tough. I am not so sure that there is a woman alive who could stay the course with Robert Baudy. Many women wanted to share the hours and the days of my life, but I never met one who could withstand the rigors that I absolutely thrived on. There was no way that I could provide the proper lifestyle for Odette. Cuneo may have promised to provide it. He put her in touch with a leading attorney out of Chicago named Kalcheim. I was unprepared for the battle. I was almost too busy to react to the legal ramifications of divorce.

There was a great deal of bitterness on Odette's part. She was hurt badly by the very act of divorce, so alien to her wedding vows as a devout Catholic. The whole process was abhorrent and against what she believed. Cuneo's lawyer set the terms, most of which I agreed to. We established joint custody of Gerard, with me assuming the cost of his education. I sent money to my parents to care for the boy and that would not stop. There was no physical property to fight over. I owned the rolling stock, which did not interest Odette in the least; she wanted no part of it. I had two bank accounts, one in Chicago and one in New York. One contained $18,000 - $20,000 and the other $5,000. I thought they were secret, but Kalcheim found both and froze my financial assets. I was angered by the search and seizure, but it did not hamper me. I was paid in cash at most bookings. Since I was not always able to get to a bank or to take the time to send a deposit, I carried a large amount of money in the trunk of the car in a bank pouch. In spite of the danger of carrying so much money, it enabled me to keep touring with no disruption in schedule.

I was upset by the allegations that surfaced and by the hold that Kalcheim had, but objectively I have to admit that Odette had performed loyally and with a determined effort to maintain the marriage. The business of touring the country with no real roots, thrown together with similarly unsettled individuals who chose show business as their career, and all of the many attending temptations did not produce enough stability to hold a relationship together. This was especially true if the relationship was not founded and supported on a foundation of commitment and total devotion by both partners. And I was admittedly less than totally devoted. I was perhaps more devoted to the animals, at least they seemed to take priority.

Gerard with his maternal grandmother grew up without us.

Cuneo had been after Odette during the preceding year. I was too busy to take notice or to take his intercession seriously. He had offered to include her in a stage bear act being performed by his leading bear man, Paul Lemery. Cuneo felt that Odette's beauty would enhance the act. At the time I thought he may have had other ideas using the bear act as a ploy to woo her. But very soon after she left, she was actually showing with Lemery and his "bears on leash" under the auspices of John Cuneo. A network of communication exists among circus people. Through the channels I heard that Odette was not doing well in the act and Cuneo was dissatisfied. He had hired her for her good looks in the hope that her appeal alone would carry the act, but the bears were not fully trained and did not cooperate. Odette was frightened by the large, dangerous animals, and I heard later that shortly after Odette left the act, one of the bears killed Lemery as he tried to muzzle the animal. Paul died in the ambulance on his way to the hospital — his gut torn apart.

Odette returned to France by ship. I would not have been surprised if she remained on the continent. She missed, like so many other expatriates, not only family, but French customs. I knew many French citizens who gave up golden opportunities and success in America to return to their native country to live in humble retirement, enjoying the crepes, cognac, and two-hour lunches of fine food. The hectic pace on tour and the fast food did nothing to inure or enhance the American experience. However, after two months visiting family and friends, one month spent in Fegreac with Mother, Father, and Gerard, she purchased with her own money a trained dove act from a friend of mine whom I had worked with in Spain. She returned to the States prepared to do a nightclub act with the backing of John Cuneo.

I was in contact with my parents, who remained neutral through the divorce proceedings. I'm certain Odette painted an unhappy and unflattering, maybe too honest, picture of our life together on tour. I was not present to defend myself from any allegations. My father said he did not think the marriage would last from its very inception due to the circumstances of the forced alliance. He knew me well, and while he had been absolutely dogmatic in his opinion that I had no other course but to marry the pregnant girl, he felt the union was doomed from the start.

When Odette left, I realized I needed a beautiful lady to help with the animals and learn to work one of the acts. I had remained in contact with Terry Barton, who lived at home with her family in New Jersey. We had met two years before during the Christmas Show at Radio City Music Hall and had shared many memorable conversations concerning our feelings about Catholicism. Terry had been raised in a strict Catholic family and had remained chaste in spite of the many temptations directed at the gorgeous, leggy, showgirl. I was fascinated by not only her extreme beauty, but also stimulated by our theological discourses. She seemed similarly fascinated by me. Since my days at St. Nicolas and even

Odette wanted an act of her own.

before, I had questioned the tenets of my inherited religion. As I matured and traveled, I observed so much that I found hypocritical, excessive, and even cruel in the Church; I became more pragmatic. Our talks seemed to expand her thinking to question some of the dogmatism.

Terry was a serious and dedicated entertainer, anxious to elevate herself from the chorus line to a solo performance. I offered her part-time work with the incentive of eventually performing one of the acts. I even had thoughts of marrying the girl, but I was still reeling from Odette's accusations and adjusting to being on my own with no strings, no boundaries. She accepted my offer and we worked together when I was at the compound in Bucks County. She also continued her dancing engagements at the music hall. I was extremely attracted to the virgin and wanted to make love, but I honored her deep convictions with utmost respect. We continued to enjoy the time spent together and did manage to maintain a platonic relationship.

I was booked into an engagement in Albuquerque. I had been paid cash for a previous booking and was carrying about $20,000 in the trunk of my car. Having the cash had sustained me after the break-up with Odette, but on this occasion it nearly cost my life. I was driving a 98 Olds at the time, a new car in a model that never failed me. I always bought a new car every year, and while I occasionally bought other brands, the Olds was by far the most dependable. On the trip across the Arizona desert, the car had a flat tire. My semi equipment and the animals had preceded me to Albuquerque. I was 30 miles out of the city accompanied by an employee whom I never trusted. I don't recall the circumstances as to why he was with me, unless he had been delayed, arriving too late to ride in the semi. In any case, I had to get the spare out of the trunk, and the man helped to lift it after I had moved suitcases and other items. The money pouch was obvious, but I was focused on the task at hand. I became busily engaged in positioning the jack to lift the car. The sun at my back cast my shadow and the shadow of the man standing behind. I observed his shadow moving and saw it reach for something in the trunk. I realized that he was raising an implement over his head. With lightening speed I grabbed for his ankle and yanked it toward me; he fell backwards. When I raised up and turned, I saw that he had the tire iron in his grip. I landed on top of him, instantly administering a karate chop to his neck with such force that blood began to flow from his mouth. I got a gun out of the car, which was standard equipment, and I put it in my belt after directing the son of a bitch to a spot where I could finish the job with one eye on him. When the tire was replaced, I took off leaving the thief in the hot desert. Just another misadventure in the life of Robert Baudy.

The incident in the desert was an excellent example of the diverse retinue of helpers in my employ. When Odette was with me, I could turn to her with a problem. She was there and was concerned and helpful, a good sounding board. Loyal employees were few, and permanency and continuity rare in a business that seemed to attract vagabonds and unsavory characters. I even hired felons from time to time. Occasionally, I was tipped by friendly local deputy sheriffs of a fairly reliable delinquent being released from jail. On what I judged to be good and honest information, I took the chance and appeared at the time of release to offer employment to a designated detainee, knowing he was out of work and out of money. I managed to hire men who worked quite well for me.

In my constant search for good help, I approached Charlotte Walch to join my entourage. I knew Joe Walch and I knew of the tragedy that took his life, leaving Charlotte alone to work the dangerous bear act for Cuneo. Whenever I saw her perform, I always made a point of asking her to join me. When she finally made the decision to accept my offer, a new chapter began in my life and in hers.

22

CHARLOTTE

Charlotte was born in Georgia in 1928 to a mother who was part Creek Indian on her mother's side, and a father, George Hensler, of German-Dutch descent. George was a dairy farmer who quit the milk business and went into construction, which did not prove profitable. He moved his family to Alabama where Charlotte remained until she was 17 years old. She then joined the Hamid-Morton Circus as a web girl entitled "Peaches." She was one of 15 girls dressed in dazzling, sexy, sequinned costumes holding onto ropes that hung around the center ring suspended from above and swung by men standing below. After her initial introduction into the circus arena, she moved on to a female flying act. Charlotte was a handsome woman with high cheek bones, dark complexion, and a beautiful athletic body molded by the labor of the circus. She was a stunning Yvonne DeCarlo look-alike who got us a ringside table at the Copacabana when we went to see Frank Sinatra perform. But that and other perks came later.

Her circus background brought to my employ a seasoned American-born performer who possessed more than good looks and talent. She had some vitally important experience with the American tour enabling her to work well with the stage-hands, all union employees. She approached these men with flirtatious ways and was able to accomplish much to smooth any inconveniences or complications in setting up for a performance.

She had learned to drive when she was 12 and handled the large rigs like a pro. She was also able to handle the mechanics and performed repairs on the rolling stock. If we arrived at a location where water or an electrical hook-up was necessary, she knew exactly what to do. And her varied experience with animal training was unique in preparing her to handle my acts as well. She was a multifaceted, talented individual who had lost a husband and was attempting to support two small children by performing a highly dangerous bear act.

Charlotte married Joe Walch in 1946 when Joe was working for Alfred Court. Alfred Court brought all of his animals to America when he realized the Germans under Hitler were going to invade and plunder neighboring countries. During the War years, Court was the headliner for the Ringling Brothers Barnum and Bailey Circus furnishing the three cage acts of the giant show. Court had three large steel arenas filled with different animals. A lion, tiger, leopards, bears, and dogs all in one cage performed in what was a most difficult act to integrate. It was difficult enough to work an act with one species, but Court mixed his animals. Their performances were spectacular, unusual, and dangerous.

He also had many people in his employ, including members of the Trubka Family and Joe Walch, who was his number one animal man. After the War, Alfred Court returned to France with plenty of cash, but he didn't get to keep it for long. He was home in his magnificent mansion with his wife when members of the French Mafia invaded the premises and held the Courts at gunpoint demanding the money. They beat Alfred, who never gave in to their violent demands, then tied up his wife, and began to burn the soles of her feet. She talked and they fled with the cash. The story ends with the crooks being captured several years later; the money was never retrieved.

When the world-famous trainer left the States to return to France, he sold his animal acts to various performers and companies. The tiger act went to the Benson Wild Animal Farm in New Hampshire, where Joe and Charlotte worked the act and remained there for several years. Joe was injured badly when he attempted to break up a fight between a lion and a tiger. He'd had stomach surgery prior to the brutal encounter between the cats, and in the melee, his stitches broke open requiring further surgery and a period of recuperation. In 1950, they went to Florida. Charlotte then went to work for Dick Clemens, who had a ferocious lion act which she learned to perform. After Joe's recuperation, he went to work for Clyde Beatty to break 22 lions. The Beatty Circus was based in California at that time where Charlotte joined Joe and learned to handle an act in which a tiger rode on the back of an elephant. Barbette was her instructor.

Barbette, famous throughout the Circus World, was an extremely talented and well-educated multilingual homosexual who at one time worked a single-trap act dressed as a woman. He achieved fame as a performer before taking a fall that inflicted severe injuries and left him with a dramatic limp. He then became the number one choreographer for Ringling Brothers, training many women to perform various acts. It was quite an experience to watch Barbette work with a group of pupils, all ladies, sharing many of his traits, or I should say, it was difficult to distinguish the man from the ladies. Even his teaching performance, which was worthy of an audience, totally captivated me whenever I had the privilege to watch.

It was during this period that John Cuneo entered the picture. John was a well-to-do impresario interested in every phase of the circus, particularly animal acts. He had the financial means to indulge himself. He was and still is today the exception to the rule, a successful "animal junky." He did it all with a great deal of tenacity. He is still involved in the business with two elephant acts, three tiger acts, and a bear act on the road at the present time. He hired circus people along with their animals to copy their acts, and then he bought animals and hired people to train and perform them. Cuneo had many different bears at his compound, the Hawthorne-Melody Farms, in Libertyville. He hired Joe to work a unique act with 15 bears representing the 12 different bear species, all working peacefully in one cage. He owned a Kodiak bear, a brown bear, a black, a polar, a Himalayan, and so on. Such an act had never been performed before. It was damned tough, suicidal work. Only Joe Walch could put together and perfect such an act. Charlotte helped him with the bears when she wasn't busy tending their twin daughters.

Joe, short but sturdy, was of Austrian descent with a limited education, but great talent with animals. He was also a heavy drinker. It required months of work to bring the bear act to perfection, but when he felt the show was ready for the public arena, he loaded Charlotte and the girls (two years old at the time), and the bears into a semitrailer for a nighttime run to their first engagement. Joe parked the rig on top of a hill on a two-lane highway in Illinois, while he crossed the road to purchase cigarettes.

When he started back to the trailer, a drunk driver came over the hill and hit Joe, sending his body flying high into the air. He never knew what hit him. Joe was killed instantly as the driver of the vehicle sped away from the accident scene leaving Charlotte and her girls in the cab of the semi. The 15 bears, instinctively aware their master had been killed, screamed and reacted to the fatality from inside the trailer. Charlotte attempted to revive Joe as he lay broken and bloody in the middle of the highway, then waited for hours before the horrible scene was cleared. An autopsy revealed that every bone in his body was broken in the hit-and-run. She was a gutsy lady who took control of her life and also resolved to fulfill the contract with Cuneo by performing the bear act.

The first time I met Charlotte was at Cuneo's place in Libertyville. She was rehearsing the bears in what I found to be a fascinating display. As I watched, I recognized that one of the bears was getting very agitated. Cuneo was present at the time plus six men standing outside the cage. A Himalayan was getting nervous and out of control. As I watched, the bear got off his designated stool and swiped the air in a half-attack toward Charlotte. She commanded the animal to do a roll-over. The bear had other ideas.

I said to Cuneo, "John, to be on the safe side, why don't you put a long rope on that bear so that some men on the outside could restrain him before he attacks Charlotte."

Cuneo replied in a whine. "Now, don't tell me that that tough woman is going to be scared of a little tiny bear!"

"John, let's not joke about this. They have a vicious bite, and they always go for the stomach. They eviscerate people."

Within minutes the bear charged Charlotte, and all hell broke loose as the bears began to move from their set positions. The attacking bear pinned Charlotte on the ground, his teeth between her legs going for her female organs. Cuneo screamed as the helpers ran around the outside of the cage. I ran into the cage and picked up a steel stool, using it as a shield to ward off the attacking bear. Some of the men came in to help Charlotte escape. She could barely walk and was bleeding heavily. She went to her trailer located within 50 yards of the ring. I didn't think I'd see Charlotte for a long time. I suggested to Cuneo that he call a doctor because bears are dirty animals and their claws and mouths could induce infection. I felt that unless she had professional attention, she stood a good chance of getting gangrene. About 20 minutes later, a very pale Charlotte reappeared in a change of clothes, bruised, bandaged, and limping, but she reentered the cage with the bears. This time a rope tethered the Himalayan as Charlotte, in obvious pain, continued to complete the rehearsal. She knew what all animal trainers know to be absolutely imperative: Never leave the training of an animal with the animal having the upper hand. No matter how small the success or accomplishment of the trainer, it is vital that the trainer be in command. And Charlotte was most definitely in command. I could hardly believe the courage of the woman who seemed fearless and extraordinary.

Charlotte was committed to a long-term contract with Cuneo which took her cross-country to many venues where I occasionally played, and we always talked. I was playing a Shrine Circus in St. Louis where I once again met the courageous lady. She told me she was recuperating from a fall. The finish of the bear act involved a rather complicated maneuver using a contraption that came down from the rafters, a sturdy steel ring about seven feet in diameter with three mouth pieces attached, designed to swivel and support the weight of the bears with a similar mouthpiece in the center to hold Charlotte. The ring was pulled to the top of the building as Charlotte and the bears held on by their teeth, swinging and turning above the arena containing the remaining 12 bears. The bears on the ground began to fight with each other, which upset her helpers engaged in supervising the pulling mechanism on the cable powered by a small tractor. The driver jerked the vehicle to a stop and possibly did not set the proper gears to maintain the cable, which crashed down on the bears. She could have been killed in the accident, but her fall was cushioned by the battling bears below, and miraculously she did not sustain any injuries. She reestablished order using experience, speed, and strong commands to break up the bears. However, a similar fall took place later when she again performed the finale. The cable broke, sending the 1,200 pounds of rigging, bears, and trainer crashing to the bottom of the arena, missing the other bears as a cushion. She sustained some fractures, but the bears were not injured. She told me it took months to fully recuperate, but she was again showing the dangerous act.

I watched her perform on another occasion when the bears began to threaten her during a performance. There were two bodyguards outside the cage armed with shotguns loaded with rock salt. Coming from the European training school, I was not prepared to see such tactics; but when the bears attacked her, the men opened fire. The pellets stung the bears and were effective in repelling them. The shooting was definitely not make-believe, but a real life-and-death situation, the constant in such a performance. The audience may have been deceived by what they thought to be dramatics to enhance a performance, but I knew better. I spoke to Charlotte after the show.

"Charlotte, you're going to get crippled or killed if you continue doing this act."

"Yes, you may be right," she replied, "but I need the money. I'm broke, I've got no insurance, and I've got two kids."

"I've made offers to you before to come work for me," I said. "Why don't you reconsider?"

I knew she was a hard worker and had been experienced enough in working with animals to be a major asset. But she told me that after watching Joe work the bears, she felt she could handle the act on her own. She also felt obligated to fulfill the contract for John Cuneo. It was also an opportunity to have an act of her own. She indicated that John had suggested more than a business relationship. At one time he mentioned marriage to Charlotte.

I was still working on the cat act. To work the cats on leash rather than in a cage required infinite patience. The leopards were not bottle-raised. They were jungle-born, but young enough at eight months to learn what I needed to teach them to perfect the new act. The training session for cats of that age lasted three or four minutes to be repeated over and over again as many times during the day as my heavy schedule would allow. In between chores or shows, I returned to the trailer and took one leopard out at a time to leash-break the animal. The training was demanding because I could not use any sort of restraining mechanism that

Charlote was well-accustomed to working with animals.

would traumatize the cats. I kept them calm by using food as a reward, tidbits instead of meals, during the day every time I took them out. I also exposed them systematically to the lights, music, and to people in order to introduce them to all elements of a live performance. I was seeking another black leopard and put out some feelers.

I was performing with the greyhounds and monkeys in New Mexico when I had a call from Charlotte stating that she wanted to come work for me. This came as a total surprise. I had not heard from her in some time, but I was extremely gratified to have her accept my employment offer knowing she would be a wonderful help with the animals and employees. We agreed to meet at my next engagement, a fair in Illinois.

On the stipulated day, I was busy setting up equipment. The weather was foul with grey skies still dripping rain, the ground was full of many large puddles. Charlotte pulled her station wagon onto the grounds and drove to where I was working. She had the twins with her, not yet three years old and dressed in spiffy little dresses and patent-leather shoes, designed I'm sure to make a good impression on "Mr. Baudy."

The black leopard came from the Lincoln Park Zoo.

Charlotte left the girls, Leida and Linda, with me while she used the bathroom. I stood awkwardly attempting to talk with the angelic darlings when suddenly one began to walk into a large puddle. I tried to coax her away from the ankle-deep water praising her pretty shoes.

"What a shame to get them wet and ruin them."

My plea fell on deaf ears. The girl preferred to defy me as she continued to walk through the puddle swishing the water, all the time watching for my reaction. I knew from that moment that I was in trouble.

Charlotte came to New Jersey with the girls. I had purchased a Vagabond camping trailer designed with a steel frame, reputedly the best vehicle of its kind at that time. It would house Charlotte and the twins. She came with knowledge and experience of the tour and began immediately to take care of the animals and learned to perform with the Great Danes. I knew from watching her that she would be magnificent with the large dogs as they performed their lion impersonation. She was also good with the heavy whip that snapped through the air as she commanded the large dogs through their various routines. She had all the showmanship necessary to put on a beautiful production. The Great Dane act finished with Charlotte commanding all of them to stand on their hind legs. I had been told that the conformation of the animal — large head and upper body heavily out-proportioning the rear quarters — made such a move impossible. I not only achieved the finale, but Charlotte was able to continue right in my steps. She was an artist and I knew from the outset we would be a great team as we began to sign contracts to take us cross-country.

Gerard, a sweet little boy, with Cousin Claire.

An early assignment took her to Chicago. I was a member of the American Association of Zoo Parks and Aquariums and received the monthly surplus list of animals available at the 300 zoos in the United States. It listed two black leopards at the Lincoln Park Zoo in Chicago. I had met Marlin Perkins previously when I played the "Windy City," I contacted him and arranged for Charlotte to fly there to examine the two partially bottle-raised leopards. I planned to use the black leopard in a performance leaping into my extended arms. I preferred the black cat, credited with a reputation among leopards and panthers of having a bad disposition, to heighten the drama and suspense of the move as the animal flew through the air for my jugular vein. Charlotte's assignment was to select the calmer of the two cats. She arrived in Chicago and spent hours watching the young cats in their playtime, then made the decision. The zoo crated the leopard and they flew back to Trenton.

I had not been to France since the winter of 1949. I had missed seeing Gerard grow into the handsome little boy I found when I returned for a two-week visit. My family had moved. When Aunt Clementine died, she left some of her properties to Father. She had owned, in addition to the farms and large home near Fegreac, a townhouse in Rennes. The move to Rennes placed them closer to a good

I carried the photograph of Gerard in cowboy gear.

Catholic school for Gerard, a library for Father who was an inveterate reader, and also simplified their lifestyle. They eventually liquidated the property in Fegreac including the land near the forest where I spent so many eventful years before the War.

We spent hours conversing, and they seemed very keen to hear of all the adventures of my American experience. Gerard, while very quiet, was well-behaved and attentive listening to all that I shared. I missed the beautiful apple orchards where I had spent many hours eating the fruit, watching the wild rabbits, and the birds and other creatures that so abundantly inhabited the serene and lush countryside of Fegreac. I missed the horse pasture and the sight of Father's favorite mounts. Also, without fully realizing at the time, I had missed the formative years of my son's growth. But it was a special time to share and to enjoy one another.

We left Rennes for a visit with relatives in Paris and then went south to Nièvre to visit the old monastery of my childhood and to see my grandparents, uncles, cousins, nieces, and nephews. Grandfather had retired years before from his farm labor and worked on a maintenance crew in Nevers. He had become senile, and it was sad to witness his decline, but he seemed quite happy in his oblivion.

One day during our visit, I was driving back to the farm when I spotted Grandfather working alone with a shovel in hand, clearing some debris from the roadway. I stopped and hailed him — he was cordial, but obviously did not recognize me. He called me *bon Monsieur* — good sir — a term little used in this day and possessing the height of respect for a gentleman. I asked if he wanted a ride home. He declined the offer and kept working. As I pulled away, I was saddened in a way, but realized that in his mid-eighties he was physically able to work and seemed happiest when productive.

When my tales were told and I had indulged in the good food and good wine that always accompanied any visit home, we returned to Rennes and I saw Simone. It had been too long since our last meeting. There was so much to talk about and so much to share. We made love and talked and made love again. She had married an executive with an American company, the sole distributor for their products in western France. He was well-paid, and they enjoyed an active social life and an elevated standard of living. She expressed her love for me, and I told her that I would never feel for anyone the depth of love I felt for her. I sustained that emotion through all the years that we were not together. I held her in my thoughts and in my heart after we parted. I returned to Paris for the flight to the States.

Grandmother and Grandfather still resided in the monastery near Nevers.

When I bought the trailer for Charlotte and the girls, I also purchased an enclosed truck to carry the Great Danes. Charlotte drove a Dodge station wagon, so I hired a helper to drive the wagon while Charlotte drove the truck pulling the trailer. Our tour was about to commence. She sent the girls to stay with her parents in Center Hill, Florida.

One of our first bookings was an engagement in the Midwest to show the greyhounds. Charlotte was with me to help with my act and to continue working the Great Danes. Cuneo arrived totally unannounced. I found him in one of my trailers talking to Charlotte. He was attempting to persuade her to return to him, saying that she still had a contract to fulfill. I was due to put on a performance, but waited patiently outside the trailer. As time passed, I became angry at the delay and entered the trailer to tell

John that he was holding up my performance, which I did not appreciate. He was also invading my privacy in my trailer and detaining Charlotte. I informed him that I did not intend to be late for the show. I was damned angry with the man who seemed completely oblivious to the great dangers that Charlotte faced in continuing to perform the bear act. I was also angered by past memories of Cuneo's role in my divorce from Odette. It was he who had put her in touch with the hotshot Chicago attorney who represented her. I had to restrain myself from getting physical with the man. I wanted to throw him out bodily.

Cuneo left and we went on with the show. We went on with many shows. We were booked solid into contracts that called for me to show the greyhounds and in rare instances, for both dog acts to be performed at the same engagement. Charlotte had her own bookings with the Great Danes for which she loaded the truck and trailer and with her helper went off to fulfill a contract. We were in touch by phone when not together. The Great Dane act was tough, and there were problems for the lady to handle, but she managed and she persevered. She drew significant reviews in her own right as she artistically handled the dogs on stage. It was as they were leaving the stage or the arena to return to their kennels when fights broke out and serious problems occurred. I had created a monster in the act with the large dogs, but she pressed on and continued to be well-received by audiences across the country unaware of what went on behind the final curtain.

I was playing a club in the Midwest when I had an interesting visitor. Nadia Houcke came to see the show and came backstage. It was like reunion in Vienna or some other faraway place that brought back many memories of the European Tour. We embraced like long-lost lovers although I had never been intimate with the elegant lady who I had seen last at Blackpool. Her brothers performed along with me in what had turned into a three-ring sex ménage for which I was sent packing back to France. Nadia did not perform at Blackpool on that occasion, but I had seen her perform many times in Europe as she went through the elegant motions of the high school horse routine as a part of the Houcke Dynasty of circus performers. I was attracted to her in Europe, and I was very excited to have her visit me in the States. She was booked into another show at the time, but we had time between

The Shriners were always anxious to have me pose with their children.

shows to share dinner and conversation. It was *deja vu*. I thoroughly enjoyed sharing hours comparing notes on the European tour experiences and even laughing about the great contrast in the staid, elegant European circus dynasties as compared to the American circus comprised of such a diverse retinue of performers.

We wondered how Nadia's father would react to such an arena where so many acts were performed at once. The old boy would be quite lost. He was the ultimate, elegant French *boulevardier* in a handsome well-tailored suit holding a fresh rose in his boutonniere, hat and tie in place, and gloved hands carrying a cane. He was a dapper gentleman of the old school and a marvelous horseman, well-respected as leader of the very talented Houcke Family.

After several intimate dinners, Nadia shared in the nostalgia and also felt a release from the restrictions accompanying performances with the family on home turf. We made love one evening after dinner, and we continued to see one another for the duration of the engagement which lasted three weeks. It was a beautiful interlude before we went our separate ways. But that is so much of what life on tour holds. The meetings, the time together, and then the partings. It was not an avocation designed for permanency or stability. But I thrived on every day and took each one just as it came by reacting and performing in whatever way seemed appropriate.

News from France affirmed the need to live each day as it came. Grandfather had died in Nevers leaving Grandmother alone in the old monastery. Life seemed ever more precious.

Virginia deBoner came into my life from time to time. As our paths crossed on tour, we enjoyed many shared hours comparing our experiences and making love. I had met her when I played the Music Hall in New York. I became friendly with Virginia's family and happily accepted invitations to visit their Bronx home for homemade ravioli and great red wine. I even had thoughts of marriage to the beautiful show-girl with the most beautiful legs, but that did not materialize and yet our relationship was open and honest, with no strings. We met, we loved, and we went away knowing that we would meet again. One time I was playing Las Vegas while Virginia was dancing in Lake Tahoe in a show where Rock Hudson was the headliner.

When we met she told me, "Man, what a hunk of a man! I'm going to try to make him."

"That would be quite a coup because he makes a lot of money. Who knows, maybe in a year or two, you will be inviting me to your mansion on the West Coast." We joked about that. Two months later we met, and she told me about her strange encounter with Rock.

"Robert, I never saw a son-of-a-gun like that. He brought me flowers every day. I made advances to him. I received him in my dressing room in my negligee and did everything I could to turn him on. He's so nice and so polite, but I wonder if he has any sexual organs!"

When the winter season ended, there had been many TV shows as well as club dates and circus performances and every sort of venue to show the greyhounds and the monkeys and for

Charlotte, the Great Danes. I diligently worked the cats between shows. It was good to work our way back to Woodborn Farm where our summer schedule allowed for Charlotte's girls to visit, where we could enjoy the luxury of time spent in the Northeast. There were some bookings that were filled out of the quarters in Bucks County. There was more time to concentrate on the cats, but little time off — always much work to perform.

Terry had been working for me part-time whenever I returned to New Jersey. She was dancing at the Music Hall and in other club dates. I invited her to join me for dinner at a fine restaurant in Trenton. We met at the appointed time and enjoyed a wonderful dinner, some wine accompanied by romantic music in the charming intimate surroundings of the secluded rendezvous indulging in stimulating conversation which continued as we walked to my car. Once inside the safety of the car, we embraced. I was feeling the wine and feeling very much in love with the lady in my arms. I held her, kissed her, and began to caress her body.

Terry had never made love before that evening, and when our bodies touched, she became alive. We could not contain the physical yearnings, and I took her for the first time. She did not resist. She was even aggressive in her arousal. When I released her, she began sobbing, and I again took her in my arms. But she withdrew and continued to sob. In her mind she had committed the ultimate sin, had participated fully and gloriously, and was now reacting predictably to her shame. I have never had a lady react in such a way, and I didn't know what to do or where to turn.

I drove to the farm to ask Charlotte's advice. Terry remained in the car still sobbing. I went to Charlotte's trailer and explained Terry's emotional trauma and the reason for it. Charlotte told me to return to Terry, to be gentle and understanding, then drive her home. Charlotte comforted me further by stating that Terry would survive the incident. She was so right. Terry and I made love many times after the first night that opened such a flood of emotions.

She continued to work with me and with the animals at the compound, and we made love many times that summer in Bucks County. She was a passionate lover. I had thoughts of marrying her, but with the demands of work and the freedom from any legal commitment, it didn't make sense at the time. I was wary of repeating what I had experienced with Odette. There were few women who could withstand the rigors of life on tour with Robert in a marriage. With Charlotte working for me, showing the Great Danes and being my sounding board plus the many beautiful women who drifted in and out of my life, it didn't seem honest or fair to all the parties concerned to commit to a permanent involvement. I was meeting so many women who were focused and intent on making it big, just waiting to be "discovered," to be propelled to stardom and a Hollywood contract. They were not willing or desirous to be committed to any alliance that would hamper their mercurial rise.

There were TV shows and club dates in Manhattan. We spent many free evenings doing the high spots of the nightclub circuit and socialized with other show business entertainers at places like Jilly's. I had become a familiar face to the TV audiences and when I drove along the streets of the city in my convertible, people called to me; some pulled up alongside and engaged me in conversation. To be recognized was compelling and seductive. I was asked to sign autographs, which was a unique difference from the lack of adulation on the European Tour where the star performers, while elevated to lofty positions, were allowed their privacy. We found ourselves caught up in a whirl of glamour mingling with many famous people. We also met mobsters and city girls, the handsomely supported girlfriends of the gang members, businessmen, and political figures of the day. We frequented the so-called "in spots" along with a diverse group of characters who hung on and hung out. Charlotte seemed content with her lot. She had an act gaining rave reviews; and when she was off the road, she had friends with whom she spent time. She remained a hardworking and willing helpmate.

We had been working the acts separately and together for nearly two years when I took another trip to France. I had mailed clippings from newspapers around the country, detailing the reception and some of my more prestigious involvements with prominent people, to bolster my fan club at home — my family. Even Father was seemingly impressed. Before the winter season began, I drove my new, powder blue Oldsmobile with white trim to the docks on the Hudson River to have it loaded for the ocean crossing. I was prepared to make the Grand Tour, and I intended to do it in style.

I flew into Paris and spent several days in the city before venturing to Le Havre to pick up the automobile. While in Paris I

Clementine's house in Rennes was more than my parents needed.

met a very beautiful lady who impressed me with not only her stunning good looks, but also her elegant couture, large diamonds and clever, charming repartee. She was most appealing and after some conversation, I invited her to dine with me at La Tour D'Argent — then and still to this day a most exclusive restaurant.

Over a romantic and enjoyable dinner, the beauty informed that she was married to a wealthy man, but was very unhappy in the marriage. I listened to her lament but could not stay with her. I had a car to pick up and a tour to make, but I did promise Rachelle that I would return in a couple of weeks and would meet with her again. I picked up the car from the dock at Le Havre and drove to Rennes. The reception I received en route by natives who had perhaps never before seen a recent American luxury automobile was quite extraordinary. I arrived in Rennes and received a full-blown welcome that was more directed to the impressive automobile than to its driver. My parents had sold the townhouse and were residing with Gerard in an apartment more suitably located to schools, shopping, and Mother's hospital, where she was a devoted volunteer. I parked the car on the street in front of the apartment building.

Late one night after I'd been in Rennes for several days, I looked down at the car and saw a crowd standing around the vehicle and someone under the car. I thought it curious, but did not investigate. As I drove in Rennes I created a bit of a sensation, and had become accustomed to the curiosity. We left the following day on the tour. My father was amazed and impressed with the smoothness of the ride and the quietness of the engine. We had the Riviera as our destination as we drove first through Brittany and then into Paris to visit relatives. We went on to Nevers to visit Grandmother still living in the old monastery. We were touching many bases, and everyone was quite in awe of the car and of the apparent success that I had achieved in the States. My cousins, nephews, nieces, uncles, and aunts still living in the provinces were far removed from the bustle of the city as well as from the fast pace and dynamics of the show business career I had chosen.

As we continued, we drove the Esterel, the snaking, mountainous road. The air was filled with the aromas of lavender and thyme along our twisting passageway into Nice. As I began to negotiate the sharp turns, I suddenly felt a looseness in the steering mechanism making the final leg of the trip extremely hazardous. When we arrived in Nice, I found a GMC dealer with an authorized and knowledgeable mechanic to work on the car. An investigation revealed what the curiosity-seekers in Rennes were actually doing to the undercarriage. They had loosened the bolts in the front end and had deeply scratched into the metal the words "Yankee go home." It was a miracle we survived the trip south.

Following the grand tour, I met Simone. The time spent with her was too brief. She told me of her social obligations, her family, and her husband's display of jealousy which made our meeting more perilous, but we shared a beautiful intimacy before I left Rennes. I deposited the car in Le Havre to be shipped home, and returned to Paris for my flight.

I spent three days with Rachelle who told me that she also went by the name Rosina. She joined me for dinner and the theatre the first evening, then for some lovemaking in my hotel suite in a completely pleasure-filled interlude. She was a wonderful conversationalist in addition to being a wonderful bed mate and a gorgeous woman.

She shocked me totally the last night. She informed me that she was not married, had never been married, but was in fact a highly paid, selective prostitute with a list of clients that included some very well-established gentlemen in the world of business and even top law enforcement officials in the government. She was protected by her pimp, a tough man who was a member of the French Underworld.

When I registered disbelief, she said, "Well, maybe you will believe this." She drew a card out of her purse, which had to be presented each week to the board of health in order to maintain her status. It confirmed her occupation.

Stunned by the revelation, I said, "My God, we have been together for three days and nights and when I leave you, you must go home. What do you say to your old man?"

"Well, I tell him that there is no business."

"What would happen if he finds out that you have been with me?" I asked.

"If he finds out I'm going to be beaten badly."

I continued questioning her as she revealed the dangers involved in what I thought to be an occupation hardly befitting the elegant lady. I tried to convince her that she possessed the potential to do so much better. She did not try to defend her position but did promise to visit me in the States some day.

"Robert, I am going to join you in America."

"Please do," I answered, "but give me a week's notice."

23

MANHATTAN

My return was met with many obligations, much work to perform, and a new season of touring about to begin. I had the leopards growing into a workable act and the greyhounds to sharpen for the new season. Charlotte was working daily with the Great Danes. Samson was our oversexed problem child, but Charlotte managed him well and commanded respect and discipline from the animal. He did like girls better than boys.

We left the compound to begin the trek across country, shuttling animals and the small retinue of workers. There were many performance dates and many stops along the way. It becomes a blur of TV performances, Shrine Circus arenas, and large city stage shows with mostly indoor venues filling the winter schedule. Charlotte and I knew each other's schedule, which occasionally placed us quite close, and we met to compare notes and react to any problems that existed on either tour. There were engagements when we both appeared with the two acts. I continued to work with the leopards in addition to the greyhounds and monkeys. It was a tough, demanding schedule with little time off between engagements.

After the winter tour, there was a break at Woodborn Farm and then the summer tour commenced. The majority of bookings were outdoor fairs. Many outdoor events had a western theme and were orchestrated by a top Chicago agency owned by Sam Levy. The Levy organization furnished talent for all the state fairs west of the Mississippi, and nearly always featured a popular Holly-

The leopard act attracted some interesting fans.

wood motion-picture or TV star as the headliner performing as a singer or in a cameo role designed to attract a large audience.

I was playing at a western fair in Billings, Montana, with Amanda Blake of *Gunsmoke* fame as the featured attraction. I watched Amanda perform and was quite taken with the beautiful lady who was quite inaccessible between shows, surrounded by an agent and entourage protecting and catering to her. I began to notice that I received an inordinate amount of attention from the lady as I worked the cats. I was flattered by her attentiveness. As usual, I was keeping late hours, never retiring before 1:00 a.m., but I was always up and in the ring rehearsing by 7:30 each morning. I was alone with the animals at that time except for a few workers cleaning after the night before or preparing for the next show time.

One morning a limousine pulled up and Amanda exited. She came into the arena to watch as I went through the routines with the leopards. She sat quietly on the sidelines. I didn't speak to her the first day or the second; but when she returned the third morning, I told her I enjoyed watching her performance at the fair. We talked about the cats. It was immediately evident she had the "animal virus." She was a consummate animal lover and explained that she had a house full of pet cats, impossible to train. She was absolutely fascinated watching me perform and amazed that I could train the leopards to react not only to audible cues, but even subtle motions of my body. She inquired if I possessed mystical powers. I found the lady to be most attractive and was more than happy to have her watch as I demonstrated the unrelenting, patient training process that went into working the cats.

I also invited her to have dinner with me. It was, as usual, difficult to include after-hours activity into already full schedules, particularly with Amanda being followed and watched by her retinue of protectors, but she did manage to join me for dinner. We enjoyed the private meeting and made another date. When we again met at the stipulated place, we took a cab to a remote restaurant, then went to a hotel where we shared the first of many fulfilling sexual encounters. It was the beginning of a long and well-guarded relationship. Amanda had a reputation to maintain, and the press watched every move. We were careful to keep our meetings strictly private. For several years whenever our schedules permitted, we met and shared many hours of stimulating conversation and lovemaking.

As a postscript, Amanda Blake, after her retirement from show business, gathered a fine collection of cats, ultimately becoming one of the few people to breed cheetahs successfully. She also raised other animals on a large ranch in the Southwest and was spotlighted as an active advocate and supporter of animal rights' organizations. She introduced me to her last husband, ex-movie star John Gilbert, a strikingly handsome man famous during the silent movie era. He was a fine specimen even in his eighties, married to an elegant, articulate lady with whom I shared a love affair.

After the wonderful week in Billings, I moved on to Boise, Idaho. One afternoon I was paged to answer a long-distance call from Manhattan. Charlotte telephoned from time to time, and I had Amanda on my mind. I also received other calls as I traveled from one engagement to another. I was caught off guard by the voice at the other end. It was Rachelle.

"Robert, you remember when I saw you last in Paris? I said that I was going to come to see you in America and you invited me to come?"

I answered with obvious surprise in my question, "Where are you?"

Her reply was in French. "I'm in New York at the Belvedere Hotel!"

I asked her when she had arrived.

"Last night, and I hate this town . . . it's dirty . . . it's cold . . . they don't speak French . . . and I'm so lonely."

"What do you want me to do?"

"Well, I do expect you to come and get me."

I was stunned. "Well, I cannot do that. I'm in Boise, Idaho!"

"So what? Come and get me!" was her demand.

I just shook my head and then continued, "Do you realize where Boise, Idaho, is?"

"Well, it must be some town down the road."

"Yes, some town 3,000 miles from New York, about 4,800 kilometers."

"What?" she exclaimed loudly.

I repeated the kilometers which seemed finally to impress her.

Her silence was eloquent and then she cried, "You must be bull-shitting me!" I knew she was dejected, even devastated as she continued in French to lament her grievous situation.

I told her to stay where she was. I would try to work something out.

A fellow worked for me, an excellent driver, who looked like an ex-Mafia member who'd been run over by a truck, his face scarred and pockmarked, never broken by a smile. His thin lips gave the cold appearance of a killer. But he was a fine chauffeur. I said to him, "Look, I have a dear friend who is staying in Manhattan at the Belvedere Hotel. I want you to take my Oldsmobile and make a beeline for Manhattan, pick up the lady and make a beeline back — nonstop. Here is 300 bucks." I looked the guy in the eyes and added with obvious resolve, "If you fool with her, she'll tell me and I'll kill you."

"Yes, sir!" was his only reply.

Six days later my man returned with Rachelle in the Olds.

The car pulled into the fairgrounds, and she exited the automobile totally transformed from the lady I had met in Paris. She did not look like the glamorous sophisticate. She was disheveled, her clothes wrinkled, dark rings under her eyes red from little sleep and her jet black hair was a mess, (She did have the most beautiful hair of any woman I ever knew). She fell into my arms crying.

"This is America? America is so much of nothing. I had to go through the desert for days, and it was horrible."

I calmed her and arranged for her to stay in a nice motel where she took her meals and watched television, although she understood very little of what she heard. In a few days she was back to her gorgeous self, and she enjoyed seeing my performance in Boise and even asked to accompany me on tour through the West and Midwest. She even helped with the packing and unpacking, which was totally out of character for the fancy lady from Paris. She enjoyed the scenery of the West, but she disliked the American cuisine, which she labeled primitive. When the season ended, she said, "Robert, I'll be frank with you. First of all, this is a rough life; the climate and the distances are killers, and the food is terrible. What would make me happy is to stay in New York. I would be happy to go out from time to time and to do the only thing that I know very well."

"Well," I said, "If that would make you happy, maybe I can arrange that."

When we returned to the East Coast, I leased an apartment in Manhattan. I found a nice place in the east 50s in a brand new skyscraper and furnished it handsomely. I spent $5,000 dollars on a beautiful aquarium filled with tropical fish from all over the world. I set Rachelle up in a comfortable accommodation in the cosmopolitan surroundings which suited her. Whenever I was off the road, I left the animals with Charlotte at the compound, and settled into the Manhattan apartment to sit back and enjoy the tropical fish and the beauty from Paris, who had learned how big America is via a unique guided tour.

I was in the apartment one day when I received a call from Leo Grund excited about a prospective offer and asking if I could be available the following day for an important interview with a New York VIP. Leo was noticeably reticent to divulge many details of the planned meeting, which in itself was unusual behavior from the man who was my agent from time to time and also a good friend. Leo convinced me it was a wonderful opportunity. I agreed to go to the interview.

The following day precisely at the appointed time, I arrived at Leo's office where he stressed to me that the meeting could result in a very lucrative deal for me and for him, but he again denied me the identity of the principal. Soon a liveried, tall, about six-foot-eight, chauffeur materialized at his 22nd floor office in Rockefeller Center and escorted me to a long, black, luxurious limousine double-parked in front of the building. In a matter of several minutes, we reached our destination, the Chrysler Building, and again the driver double-parked in view of a tough "Irish" cop, who ignored us. The chauffeur accompanied me into a private mahogany wood-paneled elevator that whisked us rapidly up a number of floors where my escort led me through three separate offices until we finally reached the VIP's door. Bronze letters were my initial introduction to Walter Chrysler, Jr.

The man, in his fifties, good-looking and smiling as he sat behind a handsome French Empire desk, invited me to be seated and excused the chauffeur. The impressive executive lost little time explaining the reason for the meeting. He was the financial backer of several Broadway shows and looking for a character to play the part of a French lover, who would be one of the leads in one particular show. I must interject that he had apparently done his homework and had more inside information on Robert Baudy than I cared for him to know, but in honesty I felt that I could probably do a pretty decent job in the role of French lover without acting.

Mr. Chrysler explained that he was a friend of Leo Grund, who had recommended me, and then he pulled from a drawer a thick stack of black-and-white, eight-by-ten photos of me, most were close-ups. He went on to say that fame and money would be coming my way in far greater quantities than I could ever imagine if I gave up the animals and accepted his offer. It rang a familiar tune that I had heard many times before from Father.

He continued his proposal by offering to house the animals, at his expense, at the Trenton Fairground. He said rehearsals would begin immediately, and I would begin receiving pay during the rehearsals. As he continued to impress me, he stood up and walked to my side of the desk and sat in a chair next to mine.

Before I knew what happened, he took my hands in his, well-manicured long fingers, massaging and caressing my hands, as he pressed closer to me, a passionate look searching my face.

He was perspiring and his smiling lips began to tremble. I pulled my hands from his, gained my voice, and told him that I would have to think about the offer. I rose from the chair and backed away from the desk as I told him I would make a decision and be in contact through Leo. He beat me to the door and stood in my path. But he could see that I was determined to exit, and I'm sure he knew that I had already made my decision. The chauffeur awaited, led me to the elevator, and we reached the street quickly. Before I entered the limousine, I looked up at the gigantic building with the glittering cathedral top soaring to the sky. It had been an interesting encounter.

Leo was disappointed with the outcome of my meeting with Mr. Chrysler. Perhaps he knew what had occurred, but I didn't mention the physical advances. I told Leo it was foolish to even consider placing the animals in a holding situation after the many thousands of hours invested in them to accommodate a show that may or may not be successful. Leo accepted my decision.

It was time to get back to business. There was always training to perform with dogs, monkeys, and leopards. Fortunately, Charlotte was there to help. I valued her work ethic, her ability, and her professionalism. We were not romantically involved, and I was determined to keep our relationship platonic, business only, so that there were no emotional ties to further complicate the ongoing busy schedules that we each maintained. When we returned to New Jersey, I escaped to the Manhattan apartment. Charlotte enjoyed the city as well and shared visits there with friends she met through business.

There were many hang-outs. Toots Shor's was one. Popular with Jackie Gleason and other show business luminaries, it was always a colorful "habitue." Another "in-spot" was Jilly's, on the west side of the city, owned and operated by a man of the same name, who was one of Frank Sinatra's best buddies and his body guard. The bar is still operating at this time. When Jilly died a few years ago, Sinatra was reported by the media to be inconsolable.

One evening I needed to contact Charlotte on an important business matter, and I learned through inquiry that she had gone by cab to Jilly's with a friend, a prostitute involved with the mob. I went to Jilly's and approached the bartender who knew me well. He was an enforcer for the Mafia, an ex-pugilist complete with broken nose, a rough character who looked the part. When I asked for Charlotte, he told me that I was foolish to let any woman get to me and not to worry about her. He refused to give me any information about either Charlotte or her companion.

I was upset by his cover-up and insisted that he tell me her whereabouts, but I continued to get nowhere with him. When I think back on the episode, I know damned well that I was flirting with disaster by asserting myself in such a hotbed of mob activity where any outburst or demand, or even a threatening look could offend and incite foul play. I could easily have ended up on a concrete slab with my bullet-ridden body encased and dumped into the Hudson River. I was out of control, but fortunately the bartender was a good guy and let me off the hook. I wasn't much of a threat actually, and he knew it. He was in a good mood that night, but I didn't like Charlotte spending her time in the company of mobsters and yet had no say as to how she spent her time when she was not working.

I was booked on many TV shows and other shows in the metropolitan area. I took my meals out and dined frequently at the Steak de Paris Restaurant on 49th Street. I was friendly with the owners who introduced me to another regular customer, a beautiful girl from Quebec who spoke French.

Paulette and I dined often in the restaurant and became confidants. I liked the girl and listened to her tales of the city. I did not know that she was a prostitute until she felt she knew me well enough to confide the fact. After she told me about her occupation, she absolutely fractured me with the details of her experiences. Her previous evening rivaled any soap opera episode, except Paulette's story was true. We also enjoyed the same culinary offerings, lapin sauté chasseur (rabbit cooked in wine), our favorite. It was cooked for us by Edmond, the owner, who always sat with us to enjoy the conversation and our obvious delight in eating his culinary masterpiece, which was not on the menu but prepared especially for us.

Paulette's occupation was not a secret to others. She talked openly about her pimp. She apparently had the toughest "old man" of any prostitute in Manhattan. Her boastful talk was designed to keep other pimps from moving in. One day Paulette invited me to go to her apartment. Her invitation was as one friend to another. Sex was not contemplated by either of us. Our relationship was primarily based on our shared dinners and conversation relating to my show business adventures and her evening intrigues. Besides I was well-cared for in that department by Rachelle and was even dubious about consenting to go to her place. I hesitated but she prevailed. I was wary of being accosted by her "tough pimp" and expressed my feelings.

"I don't think he's going to be tough with you. I talked to him about you and you are welcome."

We went to her apartment and settled down on the living room sofa to have a drink. I heard stirrings from an adjoining room, which I assumed was a bedroom where her "old man" awaited her. She said, "I'm going to show you what my tough man looks like." With that she cracked the door, and I looked in to see an elderly woman of about 70 sitting in the bedroom. Paulette introduced me to her mom who was watching TV. We indulged in friendly conversation as I relaxed and enjoyed the company and the evening conversing in French. I was totally surprised to discover that Paulette did not have a man protecting her. Her secret was absolutely inviolable and she made me swear to tell the world how impressed I was by her "tough man."

One day I went to the Steak de Paris and the bartender asked, "My God, did you hear what happened to Paulette?"

"No, what happened?"

"A black mob kidnapped her."

"They did what? What happened to her, where is she?" I was shocked.

"They picked her up from in front of a bar on Third Avenue and threw her in their Cadillac. She's gone."

I went to her apartment and found her mother crying. She said that Paulette had been gone for two days and she feared for her life. I felt pity for the mother and daughter, whom I considered friends, obviously friends in grave danger. I knew the life of a prostitute was a tough, dangerous existence that Paulette performed to help support her mother. I felt absolutely compelled to save the woman's life if there was any way that I could find her.

I knew many people in the city in those days. I dined in the popular eateries and drank in the "in" bars, so I began to comb the different establishments inquiring about her. I finally found someone who knew where she was being held. I also learned more gory details than I ever wanted to know about the life of a prostitute and why they have strong-arm men to protect them. If they are very good looking and very popular, it is common for gangs to abduct them, drug them, and become their enforcers. That is exactly what had happened to Paulette. She was held in an apartment heavily guarded by her abductors. It was going to take invasion tactics to release her.

I gathered five tough, French dock workers who were not a bit intimidated by the dangers I described in what I proposed as an act of mercy to save a beautiful lady's life. They were incensed by her plight and joined *en masse* as we piled into two cars and drove to Harlem to the apartment. My tough compatriots fought the mob members as we crashed through the door where Paulette was shackled to an iron bed. We freed Paulette and returned her to her apartment and a relieved mom. They moved out the following day. I never saw her again, but I did see firsthand the extreme dangers involved in the seamy side of life in the "Big Apple."

I mention this misadventure without boasting nor was there any disposition of valor or pride in the tactics required. It was simply a circumstance which I exposed myself to, a part of the all-encompassing retinue of show business performers and the subcultures that surrounded and permeated so many facets of the business. We were individuals attempting to fulfill a life-dream in an arena filled with highly-charged action and danger, good looking athletes and performers placed in a unique occupation. We became a family of kindred souls.

We were a large, albeit diverse, family as we networked across country from town to town, city to city, and from one arena to the next. We played to the same audiences and performed our acts with strength, honesty, and solidity that often belied that which existed behind the scenes. While there was glitter and projected refinement in the arena, there was much sadness and tragedy when the curtain came down. But I had chosen my path and chose to participate fully and actively in whatever circumstances presented themselves. I never hesitated to get involved if I thought a positive action was warranted.

When Paulette, whom I considered a friend, was in trouble, it seemed perfectly natural to go to her aid. I knew from witnessing firsthand Rachelle's ambivalence with her chosen occupation that it was a slow but certain insidious degradation, a trap. But in the reality of not having a strong "pimp," she became enslaved by a bunch of nihilistic hoodlums who would drug her and break her spirit and make her their own.

It was a subculture within a subculture that filled the streets and the spaces of a tempestuous over-crowded city that held many excesses: a city of passion and hatred, a city of elegance and squalor, a city with riches in art, culture, and education and also much illiteracy and depravity, a city filled with intermingling humanity and base emotions. My whole life had been filled with action and danger, and I understood base emotions well as I dealt everyday in training dangerous animals with potential death a threatening constant. I did not flinch at such an assignment nor shirk from the danger involved in facing down Paulette's kidnappers. I took on every challenge as my sustenance, the charge of my lifework. And I did not look back often.

My view of Rachelle changed dramatically after Paulette's release. Rachelle had been staying in the apartment for well over a year when she was busted by an undercover agent with the vice squad. The man was an agent working for the City of New York, who showed Rachelle his badge after he tried to engage her. She refused his offer, but was not able to refuse the consequences. She was taken into custody and booked, treatment so foreign to her where French rules protected her profession as long as she was registered and reported to the Health Department routinely.

Mutual friends contacted me, and I immediately went to her aid. I knew people who knew the ropes better than I. I was put in touch with a lady lawyer whose specialty was to represent prostitutes. She was passionately devoted to helping women and hated the pimps who degraded and enslaved them. With the lawyer's help, I was able to bond Rachelle out of jail and took her to the apartment.

She was horrified by the whole experience. I was horrified as well, and it brought into focus so much of what had been my personal experience in associations outside the performing arena — associations that needed to be changed. The attorney educated me to the fact that I could be implicated for trying to play the

Good Samaritan and could spend ten years in jail. I told Rachelle that I had provided a place for her to live and had been tolerant of her lifestyle and even unobtrusive. I had given her free rein and tried to be a friend and supportive of her wants and desires, but I had contracts signed two years hence, and I would not jeopardize those agreements or my reputation. I could not afford exposure or media involvement implicating me even if found innocent. Rachelle was obviously extremely upset as she listened to my explanation. I knew she loved me and I loved her in a special way, but I did not love her enough nor did she love me enough to effect a change. I told her I had to let her go. She had to leave.

Soon after the emotional encounter, I arrived at the apartment and knew that Rachelle was gone. There was evidence of a hasty retreat. She left behind her mink coat, her diamonds, and other possessions indicating a serious and hurried departure. There was no explanation and no more Rachelle. I soon gave up the Manhattan apartment and for a long time feared the worst for her. I thought she had been kidnapped although it was a puzzle to me why the expensive coat and jewelry were left behind.

As a postscript to the story about Rachelle, I was in Paris three years later and had spent an evening at the Moulin Rouge in Pigalle seeing Paul le Royer. After the show I was seated in front of the famous old Red Mill when a new cab pulled up along with many other vehicles. I was absolutely flabbergasted to see what looked like Rachelle's twin driving the cab. I did a double-take and realized it was Rachelle. I called to her but we could not speak for long as she had to move in the flow of heavy traffic. However, I did arrange to meet her for dinner. When we met she explained that a change in French law promoted by a female deputy in the austere deGaulle Government named Marthe Richard had passed legislation making the oldest profession in the world illegal, creating a minirevolution in France. A friendly vice squad supervisor immediately advised Rachelle to purchase a cab and operate from her home on wheels. She said business was quite good.

24

GREAT DANES
Dressage de Danois

Charlotte worked the Great Danes for nearly four years. The act never held the danger of the bear act that she worked for Cuneo. The dogs behaved well for her during the actual performance where she held the large animals in perfect control. It was as they left the stage on the signal "GO" and headed to their kennels when fights broke out and injuries were inflicted on one another as well as the handlers. Separating four and sometimes six 250-pound vicious Great Danes was, ironically, almost as dangerous as working a real fighting lion act. I chose the dogs for their dispositions, their spirit, but the large dogs originally bred and trained for war to be attack dogs, were unrelenting in the heat of battle, similar in nature to the pit bull. As time went on the incidents of injury became more frequent.

Samson continued to be the most powerful and the biggest troublemaker. When Charlotte worked the animals in training, she snapped the whip to break up any altercations. Samson immediately sided with Charlotte and viciously attacked the other dogs. He also went after Terry one day when she was picking up something on the ground in the training compound. The dog, obviously obsessed, could not resist temptation. He mounted her, penis erect, vigorously attempting rape. It was nearly impossible to break the grip held on stunned Terry, who firmly fought the powerful animal with determined strength and persuasion, but he was equally determined, having become accustomed to sex with his former owner. I'm sure Samson was frustrated by the coitus interruptus.

The large dogs could be vicious backstage which belied their performance.

Charlotte's helper on the road with the dogs was an alcoholic. On one occasion the man got into the fray attempting to separate the dogs after a performance and was severely bitten on the arm. He was rushed to a hospital where surgery was performed to save the arm. After several days I had a call from the doctor asking permission to amputate the limb. Apparently the surgery had been successful, but the man's blood from years of alcohol abuse did not facilitate healing. The doctor explained he could not find any relative to ask permission to remove the limb, and the patient was emotionally in no condition to make a determination. I told the doctor under no circumstance was he to amputate. The arm was saved, but the recovery period was lengthy and the unfortunate incident became another strike against the dogs' questionable record.

Some of my booking agents complained about the danger. Once the Great Danes performed on a TV show sponsored by Sealtest Ice Cream in Philadelphia. It was a children's circus theme show. Charlotte put the dogs through the performance with no problems, but they got into a ferocious battle after the show. When she reported the incident, I decided I could no longer afford to keep working the act, whether by me, Charlotte, or anyone else. It had become a liability.

The decision made, word spread through the network, and I began to receive offers from animal trainers interested in purchasing the dogs and the act. I was offered substantial money, but I had to live with myself. I knew the dogs would continue to vent their frustration on each other and there would always be major problems breaking up inevitable battles. The dogs were so programmed they could never become pets. They had to be destroyed and that decision was painful, but absolutely necessary. I had invested thousands of hours, actually years, in training and working the Great Danes.

In retrospect, I learned a lesson that it was a mistake to raise and train an animal for a single purpose which obviated any and all other possibilities. But that is exactly what I had done and I had to be honest with myself. I had created the dangerous act, and I had to put it to rest; there was no alternative. Both Charlotte and I were devastated to see the large dogs go. They had filled many labor-intensive hours and had provided pleasure to audiences across the country, who applauded the majestic animals as they so handsomely performed their routines. I felt a piece of me wrenched apart with the Great Danes no longer a part of our daily lives.

However, the nature of the business provided constant and immediate demands which prevented dwelling for long on any emotionally compelling happenstance. Whether the emotion was exhilaration with a performance well received by an appreciative audience, the gratification of a prestigious booking, the tragedy of seeing a fellow performer injured or killed, an animal suffering illness or death, or a wonderfully fulfilling romantic interlude, the origin of the emotion or the depth of response did not matter. There was always something equally compelling to capture one's attention, to respond and react, to train or perform — the compulsion, the need to move on. And there was always the challenge of transporting animals and people safely across the continent on a tour so very different from the European tour, where the distances were far less between engagements. We moved at a fast pace and had more than a tiger by the tail.

With the Great Danes no longer part of the repertoire, Charlotte became my driver of the semitrailer rig to transport the greyhounds, monkeys, and leopards from one show to the next. I had a specially designed rig built in Jacksonville at a cost of

$33,000, the equivalent of about $150,000 today.

There were times when Charlotte would precede me to an engagement. When I caught up, I slept in the forward compartment of the trailer or took a motel or hotel accommodation. I did this for several years before I ever shared her bed. Charlotte was not promiscuous. She was dedicated to performing her work in a strictly professional manner and was also dedicated to her daughters whose care and education held a high priority. She visited the girls in Florida as often as our busy schedules permitted, whether on tour or back in Bucks County at the winter quarters. But our contracts and commitments kept us on the road much of the year. There were times we were stranded on the road due to weather conditions or mechanical breakdowns. We had refrained from becoming sexually involved by mutual agreement, but circumstances made our continued abstention impossible.

We were in Chicago when I booked a room in a fine hotel. We had shared so much over the past several years, and it seemed quite ridiculous to book two rooms. Our working together and practically living together produced vibes of another sort. We shared more than the room that night in Chicago, an intimacy that was fulfilling and one that produced an entirely new and wonderful aura to what had been a strictly working relationship. I had so much respect for Charlotte. She certainly knew my pattern and past history of promiscuity, but she respected my talents as a trainer and soon she found me to be a passionate lover as well. Our feelings for one another were immediately enhanced by the emotional and physical joining which carried over into the show arena. We became a cohesive, intimate partnership with so much in common to share, enjoy, and suffer together.

The uncaged leopard act had been in the works for several years and had been well received. I knew it would become a fine act, one ideal for small stages and club dates where the dog acts were too unwieldy. With the cats I had the flexibility to play in the large arenas as well as nightclubs. That expanded my horizons tremendously and also produced a great deal of revenue.

The practice of using the family name for an act or acts had been established years before in the European Circus. All of my acts were entitled "The (Animals) of Robert Baudy." However, with Charlotte no longer performing the dog act, I decided to call

There were many performers sharing the arena.

the leopard act "Charlotte Walch — Uncaged Leopards." I was still working the greyhounds although I did perform the leopard act with Charlotte. When I was booked to perform with the greyhounds in conflict with the leopard act, Charlotte performed solo.

On one such occasion, I was performing at a fair in Northern New York State while Charlotte was working in Kansas City. She had completed the engagement and had time off before her next booking. Without my knowledge she went to a clinic in Kansas City to have an abortion. I knew nothing of the pregnancy. We had discussed often the absolute necessity to maintain a childless relationship, knowing fully that we could not continue our careers with children involved. It was an impossible life for children.

As she later explained to me, she felt ill soon after the procedure, climbed into the rig and drove nonstop through the night to be with me in upstate New York, arriving totally unexpected at the fairgrounds. I don't know how she physically accomplished the trip. I took one look at her and exclaimed, "My God, what happened to you? I must get you to a doctor immediately!"

She was green, her pallor the color of a dead person. She explained the procedure in the clinic in Kansas City. I located a doctor through one of the local Shriners, who had arranged for my engagement at the fairgrounds. After an initial examination the doctor came to me.

"Mr. Baudy, you're going to lose this lady!"

"What's the matter?"

"She has a blood infection — gangrene. We've got to take her in right now or she will die."

Charlotte was taken to the hospital where it was discovered that a second fetus had died within the uterus. Miraculously, the doctor saved Charlotte's life and prescribed medication which she took for months during a long, slow recovery. She had fought excruciating pain and weakness caused by the loss of blood and the onset of infection following the first abortion. Somehow she had survived the drive through the night handling the semirig in her determination to be with me. She continued to amaze me with her courage.

25

FLORIDA

I had investigated central Florida in 1953 when I played a performance at the fair grounds in Tampa. I had also taken the opportunity while in Tampa to visit special friends, the Zachinnis, a close-knit Italian family, who performed the number one cannon act in the country at that time. Eddie and Josephine had raised well-disciplined, intelligent children, who participated in the act with Egli, the beautiful daughter, fired from the silver cannon to climax every show. Egli, in a white leather formfitting costume, was sensational as her slender body hurtled through the air, arms extended, to form a graceful glider caught by the waiting net and then catapulted back onto her feet to turn and bow as she received the thunderous applause of an enthusiastic audience.

Eddie and Josephine were multilingual, fluent in Italian, French, and Spanish. The first time I worked a show along with the family, Odette and I were delighted to converse in our native language. The family was not typical of most circus people for many different reasons. When we left our French acquaintances in Manhattan, life on the road was barren of any reminder of home. The Zachinnis became like family when our paths crossed as we toured the North American continent. When we were booked together, we always took a close accommodation to enjoy the camaraderie outside the arena, to interact with the family members who seemed so normal and sane in a business that was neither normal nor sane. It was certainly a lifestyle that made any semblance of continuity rare and precious.

In Florida we spent more time with the twins.

    In 1953 I traveled alone to Tampa and took the opportunity to spend time with the family and to drive through the center portion of the state to research the possibility of eventually settling somewhere in the South. I was greatly impressed with the natural beauty of the land. Lush farmland and oak hammocks abounded in a warm climate that seemed ideal for housing and maintaining animals in an open, shady, year-round environment. An important plus factor was a short, but definite winter season with freezing conditions, absolutely essential in triggering estrus (cycling) in northern species, such as Siberian lynx, snow and Amur leopards, Siberian tigers, etc., which I planned to acquire later. Without the cold temperatures there would be no cycling and no breeding. All of the positive attributes were here. When Charlotte sent the twins to stay with her parents in Center Hill and began to travel to Florida to visit, I accompanied her from time to time. On each trip I continued to search the area for the ideal setting for permanent quarters.

    When the decision was made to give up the northern quarters at Woodborn Farm knowing that we could effectively work out of Florida, Charlotte found an old barn on a piece of property in Webster, seven miles from Center Hill. We rented the huge, tin-roofed barn and settled the animals into what had been used as a packing house for produce. It contained two large fans, one at each end of the building, to keep the air circulating and cool. I was limited as to improvements which could be made to property owned by the city of Webster. As a footnote, the barn is still owned by the city and operated as a flea market, open every Monday and drawing over 40,000 people during the winter season.

We spent two seasons at the quarters in Webster working shows that took us cross-country and into the Northeast. The greyhounds and leopards were featured attractions on TV shows, in circus arenas, nightclubs, Radio City Music Hall and the Palace Theater, as well as many other entertainment opportunities. The Florida location provided a testing ground over a period of time that proved to be ideal while I continued to search the area for permanent quarters.

During this time, I learned about Odette's career through the "Jungle Telegraph," a network that kept information flowing through circus and allied entertainment fields. From what I heard, I imagined that she was not happy with her career. I felt compassion for the lady, who had been my wife and mother of our son, attempting to make her way in a tough field of endeavor so far from her homeland. But I was too busy working the animal acts with Charlotte and other business ventures to dwell for long on our broken marriage and the past bitterness. My mind was focused on the present and on a new act working with tigers.

I had already done the preliminary planning of how the act would appear, how many animals, the precise amount of time that each routine would last, etc. There was an established six-minute minimum for an act up to a maximum of 17 minutes. The blueprint had been formed a long time before I began to look at animals to purchase. I had even decided on the types of props to be designed and fabricated; among which a globe would be part of the performance, and it would take time to build it according to my precise specifications. In the meantime, I had temporary props in the working stage to practice with in the initial rigors of training.

There was a myriad of details to work out as I planned the entire act down to the color of the spotlights and the costuming in what would be a totally different offering to catch the imagination of agents and producers. I hoped it would result in substantial monetary reward for me. There had never been a tiger act performed other than the typical Clyde Beatty bravura performance, where the animals charged around the cage threatening the trainer. At that time Ringling Brothers and Barnum and Bailey had the only group of tigers on the road, presented by a trainer named Mr. Trevor Bale, who performed as a permanent part of the large circus. There was little competition for a uniquely conceived, independent act.

I visualized that the tigers would be transported in individual cages, wheeled to the large arena, then released and entering one animal at a time after the houselights were killed, a yellow flood focused as each animal moved separately to the dramatic beat of jungle music. The cats would move slowly, stealthily to designated pedestals, the lighting and music designed to entrance the audience. Roars would purposely be elicited from the beasts as they obediently followed my commands through one routine and then another.

Mother with Gerard.

One planned routine called for the animals to form a pyramid using two tigers on their hind legs standing on low stools as the base reaching to two tigers standing on higher pedestals on their hind legs reaching two more tigers, their bodies crisscrossed to form a symmetrical peak ten feet in the air. The training for such a routine would take months of daily work and much discipline for me as trainer and the animals as my students.

Another planned highlight of the act was to direct one of the tigers to walk 38 feet backwards, on its hind legs, roaring with each step. I would continue to command and control the animal, snapping a whip to accompany its threatening behavior, with each step. I had in mind finishing the performance with one tiger left in the ring after the others were contained in their rolling cages backstage. My menacing protagonist, after being directed to a pedestal, would stand dramatically in the spotlight snarling and roaring. Watched by the tiger, I would circle the whip above my head in a slow twirling motion, then, instantly, cracking the whip and releasing it up into the air as signal for the animal to leap 12 feet from the pedestal directly toward me as I immediately went into a kneeling position on the arena floor, the tiger landing just inches from me.

I envisioned drawing a dagger from my belt and holding the blade at the throat of the roaring animal, he placing his head ever closer to my face, giving me a kiss and me giving him a kiss. Then I would stand and make a pass at the huge beast with a wooden pointer, toreador style, and leap onto his back to ride him out of the ring and spotlight to the thunderous applause and standing ovation of an excited audience.

With all the preplanning, I was determined to produce a performance totally unique from the sedate exhibition of seat-warmers which produces a boring act. I didn't want to portray the noisy, graceless Beatty style with gun and chair, the usual props. It was my intent from inception, through meticulous training, to keep the tiger's instinctive reaction intact, to roar fiercely at scheduled and timely intervals. I wanted to establish the appearance of a cage full of extremely dangerous animals with me orchestrating every motion, every dramatic reaction. I knew it would be sensational.

All of the performance was planned in my head and then on paper with every detail specified, imagined, and visualized before I bought my first tiger. I was determined to use the difficult snap and toss of the whip to heighten the drama. That very important detail brought to mind many memories over the years of watching Paul first, then learning to use the whip, the vital tool of every animal trainer. It had fascinated me as a youngster in Le Vesinet at Paul's compound and then at St. Mande, his mastery so effective with every animal he trained. I eagerly practiced by the hour the simple *coup droit* motion, sending the whip out in front with a single crack. As I practiced, I succeeded one in three attempts, but I was determined and spent hours working the snake-like leather until trial and failure became success and confidence.

Paul's lessons were invaluable as I began to work with the greyhounds. As time passed, I watched Alfred Court and his protégé, Joe Walch, who so brilliantly used two whips at the same

It would take time before my dreams for a tiger act looked like this.

time, one in each hand. Joe had sustained an injury forcing him to become ambidextrous. He was one of very few performers capable of such a feat.

As I became proficient, I sought to enhance my knowledge through literature regarding the historical origins of the whip. Predating Roman times, the whip was first used to domesticate animals. In Roman times, wild animal training reached its apex when big cats became such a vital part of the politically motivated circus games. The early circus had two state schools for wild animal trainers, their students promising youngsters from the countryside who were brought to the government-run schools for training. The Mansuetarius School was designed to teach training methods where the animals learned tricks similar to today's performing animals. The Belluarius School taught gladiators to fight with wild-caught lions, tigers, wolves, bears, and other animals brought from all over the empire.

The Roman Government had a requisition order requiring a minimum of so many animals be shipped to Rome every year. The gladiators did not often survive the battles, which were bloody and often deadly. The animals were trained to attack humans once they had recuperated from the ordeal of being transported and put back in shape. The natural instinct of wild animals is to run from humans. In order to achieve the desired affect for a good performance, human flesh was introduced into their diets, flesh of prisoners of war or slaves. The methods used by the Romans, hot irons applied to move the animals from their cages and whips to work them in the arena, were grossly cruel and torturous. Both schools utilized the whip in training as the extension of the trainer's hand. The cracking sound became the cue to perform. A whip does not make contact when it cracks and therefore does not hurt the animal. A properly handled silent whip becomes a precision instrument.

I eventually learned to use the three basic types of circus whips, horse, elephant, and big cat, all of which look deceptively simple to the public. However, it takes a long time for one to master proficiency without loosing an eye as did my late friend, lion trainer Terrel Jacobs. Famous in the fifties and sixties, Jacobs, who performed a fighting act, lost his right eye in a self-inflicted accident.

To develop precision and elegance required dedication and lengthy practice. When I worked the greyhounds, I used the small *chambrière,* a very long, slender, lightweight whip designed to work with small horses. The method was to work from the center of the ring, usually 39 feet or 13 meters in diameter, to reach the horses or other animals circling the arena. In working horses, or in my case the greyhounds, the accuracy of the *chambrière* was vital with a light touch directing each motion. The animals were trained to feel the whip and react, be it either to turn to the left or right, to stop, or to rise up on hind quarters. The entire performance was choreographed at first by the light touch of the *chambrière* and later by the motion only. After lengthy training, it is possible to work the animals without a whip, simply by duplicating the motion with the arm.

With images of whips and a crowd-pleasing performance of tigers in an innovative, original act, I began my search for the large cats. My first acquisition was from the Birmingham Zoo in Alabama. There was an animal importer named Fred Zeehandelaar in New York, who maintained a computer listing of animals available all over the world. Fred never actually came in contact with the animals, but could locate any species of animal sought by an individual or zoo. He had imported the last pair of wild Siberian tigers from Russia before the U.S. Government banned any further importation of tigers from the U.S.S.R. The Russian Government also put a halt to further capture of the tigers in Eastern Russia due to near extinction of the beautiful endangered species.

The snow tiger is the giant of all cats and the original habitat for the species is extremely cold climates. Zeehandelaar placed the two tigers in the Birmingham Zoo to be housed and displayed while the animals were offered for sale to the worldwide zoological market. The Zoo Director, Bob Truett, had been assistant director at the Lincoln Park Zoo in Chicago under Marlin Perkins and I knew Bob well. The zoo in Birmingham was named after the city mayor, Jimmy Morgan, whom I had met. Morgan was not at all knowledgeable about animals, but was responsible for creating and supporting the zoo.

I traveled through Birmingham and stopped to visit Bob, who showed me the tigers. He told me that his keepers had witnessed breeding in the adults, and I expressed interest in purchasing some cubs. While the mature tigers were the property of Zeehandelaar, the zoo in Birmingham had obtained the rights to sell any offspring.

When four cubs were born, I returned to Birmingham and was immediately and totally captivated by them. They were the most beautiful animals I had ever seen. There was one male and three females. I paid for them on the spot and even named them, as directed by the International Stud Book, using Russian names. I named the single male Manchu after Manchuria, the country of origin for the Siberian. I named the females Doutchka, Tara, and Lena. Lena is the name of a huge river running through eastern Russia.

I left Birmingham with the understanding that I'd pick up the cubs on my return at the end of the tour. I completed the engagement and returned to find three of the cubs paralyzed in their rear quarters and the fourth showing signs of a similar paralysis. I had paid $6,000 for the cubs and was expecting healthy tigers.

I requested an audience with Mayor Morgan. Our meeting was a sad commentary. Bob Truett was present while I listened to what Mayor Morgan offered as a solution to what he felt was a serious problem with another animal at the zoo. They had recently acquired an adult hippo. Mayor Morgan expressed concern with complaints from the public lamenting the fact that the hippo was not visible much of the time when submerged in his water pool. When Bob asked the Mayor what he should do about the situation, Morgan answered, "Drain the water." I learned later that when Bob followed the directive, the poor hippo nearly died from sun blistering. The demonstration was a clear indication of what I was up against.

Morgan insisted the crippled cubs were mine and that his associates would aggressively continue medical treatment to counter what he felt was a temporary paralysis. I sadly left without the tigers and without my $6,000. I kept in touch with the zoo and monitored the progress of prominent vets brought in to treat the cubs. The cubs finally recuperated and I picked them up, satisfied they had been cured. The early paralysis later manifested in serious subsequent medical problems that plagued them for years.

I continued to search for good stock, importing two Siberian tigers from France through an animal dealer there. One of the tigers had been captured in North Korea. The two were about seven months old when they came to me. I ultimately acquired 12 tigers that I brought into Florida to begin the training process for the unique act that I had visualized for over a year.

With the many animals becoming part of our entourage, I needed to expand and find a facility I could purchase. Charlotte's family located property in Center Hill. When I saw the 20 acres of pasture land, a huge oak hammock in the center, I knew I had found an ideal setting for permanent quarters. However, from the very start there were mysterious vibes associated with the property ownership as well as resistance to my purchasing the land.

The property was surrounded by three homes on adjoining properties all owned and lived in by Charlotte's relatives. The Maddox Family had become accustomed to using the property to graze animals and grow tomatoes, cantaloupe, and other produce on the rich soil. They weren't at all happy with their cousin Charlotte being involved with a damned foreign hooligan who was infringing on "their territory." I had never met people who held such a narrow view of outsiders, but I was definitely an outsider and I was infringing.

There was an old shack in the center of the massive hammock, the only building on the property with a hand-pumped well located close by. A hermit had lived in the shack, an old boy considered to be a local drunk, who was struck and killed by an automobile while walking home from the Beville's Corner Bar and Liquor Store. I continued to search for the owner but drew blanks wherever I went.

In my search, I poured over the archives at City Hall and discovered that the property had an interesting history. Located four miles from Bushnell, it was the location of a major Indian massacre years before and named the "Dade Battlefield." Seminole Indians purportedly attacked a column of U.S. Army soldiers moving north on foot from Fort Hood in Tampa. The fighting lasted two days, and all but two of the soldiers were killed. The two who survived reported that on the second day of battle the Indians were all in a drunken stupor and turned black slaves loose to finish off the soldiers. Twenty-five soldiers, wounded and seeking shelter, built a rough pine-tree barricade. The slaves went through the barricade and brutally butchered the defenseless soldiers using axes and knives, and taking many scalps. There is a monument marking the battle scene and documentation in the archives proving that the marauding slaves lived on the property near Beville's Corner. Named Camp Abraham, this was to be my temporary quarters until I could locate the owner.

The old hermit's demise left the overgrown jungle-like property and shack uninhabited. With Charlotte's father, George Hansler, helping, I transformed part of the old shack into animal quarters. We also did some fencing, cross-fencing, and minimal clearing. I did not want to invest too much time or money in property that might be only a temporary compound. I continued to search for the owner when time permitted, but I had so many other obligations.

We stayed with Charlotte's parents in Center Hill where we shared a two-bedroom sleeping quarter in the house. I was decorous in not sharing Charlotte's bed while staying in the Hanslers' abode and got along very well with both her mother and father, who seemed happy to have me as a guest.

George was a hard-working, hard-drinking tough guy who worked for the county running a road crew of about 20 with an iron fist. He had no formal education, which thwarted his promotion potential. Often he'd come home from work having been assigned a problem to solve, to seek Charlotte's and my expertise in calculating an amount of gravel or some other critical work-related specification that was beyond his mathematical capability.

George became one of my hunting companions, although his approach was rarely successful in bagging any game, and he lacked respect for the animals and natural terrain. He was a better than average shot when it came to doves and quail, but the deer hunt was less than successful most of the time. He would seek a tree stand in the Ocala Forest, begin to smoke like a chimney, and coughed loudly as he reached from time to time for the flask in his back pocket to enjoy his vodka. The results were predictable as the deer seldom came his way. Occasionally, a buck, chased by one of the hunting dogs, would get into George's range, but by then exposure to the cold, wind, sun, and vodka would result in a clear miss.

With George and the "good old boys" surrounding me, I recognized clearly that I was in an atmosphere where a prevailing attitude and way of life was quite different from what I had been accustomed to enjoying. However, there were too many positive aspects about the central Florida location to let the human population dispel my intentions. I continued to seek the owner of the magnificent oak-filled hammock so ideally suited to my needs.

When I had the animals settled in and Charlotte and some good help in position to watch over the quarters, I actively pursued a new enterprise. In addition to maintaining the training of leopards and greyhounds as well as working with the tigers, I formulated an idea to import rare and exotic wild animals to form my own collection. I did not at the time consider the new business to be for purposes of breeding or selling, but wanted to introduce to the States a collection never before seen in one location. I was naïve in this initial concept, not realizing that in many cases I could not acquire one or two animals. In the case of ostriches, I had to import 75 as the minimum shipment available through a broker in South Africa. The ostrich purchase was just one of many lessons to be learned as I began what would become a highly complex endeavor requiring much preplanning and extensive travel to set up the necessary network. With quarters to contain many different species, I directed my search to countries where French was spoken by the professionals who would be key players in facilitating the capture, deportation, and legal requirements to make such a venture feasible.

All sorts of animals fascinated me. Here an Albino Rhesus monkey.

My first trip to begin the new business was one of many that began with a flight to Paris as usual, then I would catch a commuter plane or train to Rennes to spend three or four days visiting family — and always Simone. My visits home gave the opportunity to spend time with Gerard and my parents and always included dining out in a very fine restaurant and attending some sort of special entertainment in the city.

I was missing Gerard's growing up with only yearly trips to France.

Gerard was a bright young man having been taught, as I was taught, to read the newspaper at four years of age. Mother informed me that Father was honoring my request of no physical punishment. Now a preteenager, they were concerned about the friends he seemed drawn to, the rebellious students in his school and in Rennes. Apparently, there were disturbing behavior patterns forming. I did not understand the problems, nor could I influence Gerard from so far away or during my brief visits. I could only hope that time and maturity would produce in him a positive desire to improve and elevate himself.

I knew that Odette visited each year to spend at least a month with the family. She enjoyed the ocean crossing and made a lengthy holiday of each visit. But her chosen lifestyle, like mine, did not easily accommodate children. She was determined to stay in the States and have a career which left Gerard in France to be raised by elderly grandparents. It would have been so different if Odette had chosen to remain in France, or to have Gerard join her in the States, or if I had decided to be a full-time parent. But I never chose to marry or to be a father. As long as I was involved in the training and performing business, which required a Gypsy lifestyle, I never considered moving Gerard. I thought that my parents' influence, the constancy of the environment in Rennes, and the educational opportunities available in the university city were vital to his development. I had so many business ventures in the works I barely had time to think of anything else. I was also closer to gaining the much sought-after respect of my father, who was obviously impressed with my financial status. My goals were securely set.

I was, however, concerned about the boy and desired for him to mature in a responsible way. It hurt me to think that my parents were struggling to raise a child when they deserved freedom from such profound responsibility. I asked Mother if she thought I should give the green light to Father to administer physical punishment. She was always against any sort of violence, and we both knew Father's temper could flare and be damaging. The boy wanted for nothing materially. I sent money routinely to pay for his care, but that obviously did not bury the sense of abandonment he may have felt, manifesting itself in rebelliousness.

While in Rennes, before returning to Paris for my journey on to Africa, I always met with Simone. We condensed as much conversation and love-making into whatever time was available.

When I left Paris, it was to fly to Cameroon or the Congo, to Zaire, North Africa, Madagascar, to Iran, Turkey, Yemen, Djibouti, Somalia, or South Africa to lay the ground work for the network and later to acquire more species. Initially, I had to find individuals to be in charge of overseeing the many details required to operate a smooth and successful capture and transfer of animals.

As the network formed, it comprised an amazing group of people. Many were expatriates removed from France for political or criminal reasons. Called the *interdit de séjour,* they were either officially engaged in labor under the auspices of the French Government or French-speaking people who worked for the local government or even in private enterprise. Many could have been guillotined in France, and all were banned from ever returning to their homeland.

A major factor in safe transport of animals was the crating. I was in contact with managers of huge forestry operations. On a trip to Gabon my mission was to find the Okoume tree, a huge 300-foot tall, symmetrically-formed tree that stood above the double canopy of the rain forest, a magnificent tree of light wood providing the finest plywood in the world. The director of the operation was a tall, dark-haired, good-looking, well-educated Frenchman from Normandy, who lived with his family on an island two hours from Libreville where I was met, picked up, and flown by small plane to the area being harvested. My host and his family lived in a comfortable house utilizing a generator for power. There was no television and very little communication with the outside world except by radio with limited range. There were several other white families living on the island, connected to the native villages or "*Case*" along the river bank by two small bridges. For the white inhabitants, who returned to France every three years, life in Gabon was remote and unique.

The process for harvesting the wonderful tree was to fly over the forest in search of the distinctive Okoume, map out the area as a guide, then with trucks and bulldozers set in operation and natives successfully encamped, the forest rape began. It was disturbing to me to watch the brutalization of the precious forest as the natives were directed to bulldoze a broad swath in order to make way for the truck to enter and retrieve the felled tree, downed by a huge hand-held chain saw. I was enormously impressed by the conditions surrounding the sad demise of the tree. The spectacular crash of the centuries-old giant was followed by an eerie, sad, complete silence as if the entire rain forest was paying respect to the departed. The tree loaded on the bed of the truck was then removed from the forest and carried, upon leaving the rough, dense terrain, at 70 miles an hour down the paved highway to the processing plant. The natives demonstrated little regard for either safety or maintenance of the mechanized equipment. Ironically, parts for the beleaguered dozer came from the caterpillar plant in Jacksonville, a close-to-home bit of civilization so far removed from the rain forest in Gabon.

When I registered shock at the total disregard for the environment in acquiring the lumber, the manager admitted his guilt in perpetuating serious destruction of the forest floor, but had a job to perform and company directives to follow. I, too, was aiding and abetting the process when I asked to be directed to an individual who would build animal crates. The wealthy man, described as a *déporté de séjour*, had arrived years earlier from France with nothing but his life and freedom and proceeded to use his education, realizing the local officials could be bribed and manipulated, to amass a fortune. He lived in Libreville operating a large manufacturing company that produced coffins for the entire country in addition to other finished wood products.

Prior to the man's arrival and enterprise, the natives performed a simple ceremony at death to bury their deceased in the local village. When the French Government moved in, there was a demand for a precise census and a need for accurate accounting, which obviated the casual burial procedure. Laws were enacted whereby all deaths were to be registered and burial formalized and "civilized," creating the need for coffins. The process to change centuries-old ritual was slow, but the entrepreneur went from village to village persuading the native leaders that unprotected burial was no longer proper nor was cannibalism. He sold coffins as the preferred method for disposing of the departed.

The French forestry director, however, told me of a continuing problem with cannibalism. He said that when the census was taken each year, there would be discrepancies in the tally with four or five teenagers unaccounted for. The teens had been killed and consumed in sacrificial ritual. The natives resisted change. His disclosure brought to mind something I'd heard in France in the late 1940s before leaving for the States. A black senator from Cameroon addressed the respected Paris Senate as he orated, "In spite of the fact that my grandfather was a cannibal, I'm now very well-educated and I want to do something for my people." He actually divulged, quite openly, the truth of what was still occurring among the native tribes in Africa in the 1960s, and I thought at the time the confession rather revealing, but the continuing ritual was now confirmed.

It was confirmed again on another trip to Gabon when I saw firsthand evidence that indeed cannibalism still thrived. Word came through the Government radio notifying all Europeans to stay put, cease all travel. Natives were responsible for killing a Catholic priest just 25 miles from where I attemped to set up my network. Within 48 hours of the warning, a detachment of French paratroopers appeared. I met the captain in charge of the company and introduced myself as a former member of the French army. The captain apprised me of his mission to investigate the murder of the priest. Since my safari was put on hold, I expressed an interest in joining his company to observe the maneuvers. He said that if I wanted to go along it would be in a strictly nonmilitary capacity and without his authorization, and he would not be responsible for my safety. He went on to say he enjoyed talking to a fellow soldier who could educate him on what I had experienced firsthand in Normandy — sweeping across the French countryside, into Paris, and then Germany years before beating back the German oppressors.

The priest had been killed near the village of D'njole. Two days of marching along a river to gain our destination provided the opportunity to share experiences with the officer. We arrived at dawn, and the troops were ordered to surround the village and open fire on the native huts. When the firing began, I hit the ground realizing the grave danger from random open-fire in the dim light of daybreak in what was a volatile and highly ill-conceived tactic. The natives knew of our imminent arrival and had abandoned the area earlier. The soldiers were sent from the village in every direction with one platoon returning to report sighting the remains of the priest about a mile from the village. We found the remains of a savage ritual symbolizing respect and adulation for the departed. In consuming even a small portion of the body, the natives would integrate the priest's powers and his goodness into their own being. One half of the body gone, the other half was hanging from a tree above a recently abandoned campfire in what appeared to be an attempt to smoke the uneaten portion to preserve it for later consumption. It was a grizzly sight, and I hoped and prayed never to be so revered.

While in Libreville I was fortunate to find someone whom I could revere. The coffin man was a highly professional and successful entrepreneur, who had imported woodworking equipment used to manufacture coffins and also finished work used in the building trades. I met him and drew a rough draft of what I required in an animal crate. The following day he had the crate manufactured to my exact specifications. I was immediately impressed with the rapidity of his production as well as the quality of workmanship. Every detail of my sketch was included with double flooring and a removable tray. I ordered crates to be available when the first animals to be shipped were gathered and cleared for export. The gentleman invited me into his home where I met his staff of servants, all creole or local natives including light-skinned children. I imagined the natives catered to all of the man's needs. I left Gabon with arrangements finalized to have crates sent in the future to other countries where crating was not available.

There were a myriad of details to work out. I taught methods for feeding orphaned animals with special formulas and educated individuals on the different diets and proper care for mature animals of various species. There were weeks spent searching for local hunters living in the middle of the rain forest where I remained for a week or ten days, not daring to drink the water. I always managed to get bitten by insects of various description and arrived stateside in an exhausted condition, sometimes with serious, mysterious symptoms that required professional medical diagnosis and care. It took three years and many trips to set up the network with ultimately 40 principals working in my employ.

When I was close to having animals sent, I concentrated my efforts on finding the owner of the property in Center Hill. As I continued to search the archives, I realized that the Maddox Family possessed tremendous political clout in the county and were determined that I should not be successful in purchasing the property. Finally, I found the owner through a doctor friend in Eustis. He had mentioned the situation to his retired butcher. The butcher informed him that his brother, also a butcher, retired and living in Miami, owned the parcel. With the precious name and phone number in hand, I called Miami.

"I've been looking for you, sir, for a long time. My name is Robert Baudy. I'm in show business and own a number of performing animals, which are at this very moment located on a piece of property in Center Hill, which I understand belongs to you."

"Oh," he replied, surprised, "how did this come to pass?"

"Well, my family, Mr. and Mrs. Hansler and the Maddox's, told me that I could put the animals there."

"I was not even aware of that. The Maddox's don't have the right to give you permission to move your animals in, but obviously it was not your fault. You sound like a man of good faith."

"Well, I would be interested in buying the land." He was far more amenable to dealing with me than were Charlotte's family.

"Well, I don't even know the value of the land in Sumter County at this time. I've been retired for some time in Miami, but I'll tell you something, why don't you research that."

"Sir, I've already researched the value. The part of the land in the hammock is overgrown."

"Yes," he said. "I've been preserving the property because the trees are so unique. They're probably the largest trees in Florida."

I continued, "It's uncleared land and it's going to take a lot of money to clear, fence and cross-fence and dig another well."

"I know what you mean," he agreed. "What's your offer?"

I was candid. "Land in that kind of shape is worth about $150 an acre."

His reply was just what I wanted to hear. "I think it's a good offer. Why don't you go ahead with the paper work and I'll sign it."

I quickly retained a local lawyer who drew up the purchase agreement and went ahead with the purchase, relieved and elated to finally own the wonderful parcel. My immediate neighbors did not share my enthusiasm.

When the final sale was legally registered, I began to clear the land and move some of the oak trees. Some of the huge majestic oaks measured 40 feet in circumference. I saved as many of the old beauties as possible since I planned to put a tiger building in the middle of the hammock. As we labored to remove trees, we found .45 calibre lead bullets and imbedded in the roots some octagonal rifle barrels that would be the very same weapons used by the Army, slaughtered in the massacre years before, conclusive evidence of the battle.

As work progressed, we continued to live while in the area at

Charlotte's parents' home using the new property to house the animals and as the training area.

At that time it was legal to contract privately to have a building constructed. I was not a contractor, but I did have friends and acquaintances in the business who advised, "Why don't you build it yourself? You're going to save about 30 percent of the cost."

George had previously been in construction and was well-acquainted with local building subcontractors. I drew the original blueprint, which was to be the tiger housing in what would be strictly an animal complex. I had in mind eventually building a house somewhere on the property away from the animal area. The foundation was put in place and a mason hired to build the actual housing when Charlotte came forward with an idea that changed my plans.

"Robert, if nothing happens to either of us for the next 20 years, we're not going to be in this building, and the tigers are not going to be in this building while we're touring. A separate house would not be used except for six weeks out of the year, and you'll be paying heavy taxes on what would be uninhabited property for most of the year."

Her thinking made good sense as she pointed out, "If we don't have someone living in the house permanently, the house will be broken into, and your bronzes, paintings, and antiques vulnerable to theft. The place could be vandalized."

I approached the head foreman on the job and told him that I decided to change the layout of the plans. We decided to extend and convert the west end of the project so that an apartment could be built adjoining the tiger containment areas. This created complications with the original slab which was now totally inadequate. It would have to be broken to allow for new drainage and a new foundation poured before we could begin. The actual building was redesigned to be under a roof 145 feet in length and 45 feet wide.

I ran into many labor problems doing much of the work initially, hiring and firing people due to ineptness and drunkenness among the itinerant laborers. I even had some near physical confrontations during the long and tedious process which would ultimately take several years before the building was completed. We continued to live at Charlotte's parents' home during the short periods when not on the road.

26

BACK ON TOUR
Retour en la Route

*I*n 1958, I signed a contract for the greyhounds and monkeys and the uncaged leopard acts to appear in Cuba. The three-week engagement was to begin in mid-December and run through the first week of the new year. The trainers and other performers went by air, the animals by ship out of West Palm Beach. The show was held in a huge, new, flying-saucer-shaped building called El Coliseo des Deportes located 45 minutes from Havana by Cuban transport, which was fast and reckless. Baptista was the man in charge at the time. The show was a success and Havana was, for me, a refreshing location away from the stereotyped arenas in the States and Canada and even Europe.

The tropical setting surrounding the city, a city reminiscent of Las Vegas with its many casinos, provided a holiday atmosphere, and we became caught up in the fun and games. We joined the happy Caribbean revelers moving to the "cha-cha" beat. During the night of New Year's Eve, Charlotte and I spent time after the show at the bar and in the lobby amusing ourselves with one-arm bandits and mingling with friends.

On that fateful night, I downed a few glasses of champagne with Errol Flynn who, I recall, was extremely intoxicated on straight whiskey drunk from a bottle carried from table to table as he moved about the casino. I played a dollar machine and hit the $10 Jackpot. I still have the Cuban silver dollars in my possession and have refused to sell them over the years to collectors. They symbolize to me the unpredictability of life itself.

We planned to sleep late the following morning, but that was not to be. I was awakened by violent knocking on the door. I got up to answer as Charlotte slept soundly, Coco, her toy French poodle snuggled in her arms. Lola Dobritch, a member of a flying act, stood in the hall, upset and screaming in heavily Rumanian-accented English.

"Robert, they are killing each other and burning the hotel down."

Since I sleep nude, I did not dare follow her into the hallway. She left as I stood in the doorway, the smell of smoke pungent and threatening. I quickly moved to the window facing the main street and could not believe what I saw below! Gambling machines stacked on the sidewalk against the hotel were burning fiercely. I wakened Charlotte.

"Get dressed. Forget about packing. Let's get the hell out of here."

She got up, we dressed quickly, and using stairs from our second floor room, ran to the lobby. Charlotte clutched Coco in her arms. The lobby, only hours before a scene of revelry, was filled with debris like a bomb had dropped through the ceiling. The uniformed body of a bellhop was lying on the floor, head bashed, brain and blood spilling around it. We moved across the cluttered floor, and I stepped out to the street telling Charlotte to remain behind. I was immediately in the middle of a war zone. Baptista had fled the country in the early morning while uniformed troops exchanged gunfire with the pro-Castro mob. Bullets flew and the few cars blasted their horns continuously in the clamor and confusion of a city in convulsion.

The front of the hotel had huge stone columns, and as I stood beside one, I tried to flag a car to take us to the Coliseo or any other place away from the burning hotel. The drivers laughed and threw insults. I took a couple of $100 bills from my wallet and waved them at a moving cab. The car screeched to a sudden halt. I went back to the lobby, told Charlotte to follow behind and hit the floor of the cab, which she did, but in the process Coco flew from her arms. Only her sudden response, grabbing him by the leg, kept him with us as the car sped away at maximum speed, tires screeching against the pavement, bullets coming from both sides. Our route followed back roads; the driver waved a small black flag as some sort of protective signal.

Only half the people connected with the show were in the huge Coliseo. Many of the performers were still stranded downtown. The show officials stayed at a different hotel situated a mile from our hotel. They did not leave fearing a potentially murderous ride to the Coliseo where no sleeping accommodations were available. They remained under their beds for three days while the mob ransacked the hotel. Among those remaining were Mr. Tom Packs, owner of the show, and the show's director Mr. Jack Leontini, both very good friends of mine. We felt fortunate to be in a building which seemed like a safe haven, but we sensed the unrest and felt totally threatened by what was occurring downtown.

We were fortunate to escape from Cuba.

My major concern was the animals' safety. I had managed to get rice, which I hoped would sustain them. With memories of the French liberation of 1945, I told Charlotte we had to prepare for the worst. I felt we had to find food since we might be detained for a lengthy period. All stores were closed or pillaged and moving from our location was impossible. The second night while most of the show people who made it back to the building were sleeping, we broke into the storeroom of the Coliseum restaurant. We packed food in several cardboard boxes and took them to an empty room on the third floor.

The next day the first of Castro's troops appeared. I was immediately impressed by the soldiers, two of whom were tall and obviously not of Cuban origin. One spoke with a Bronx accent. Their weapons were U.S.-made .45 Colts and Thompson submachine guns as well as U.S. paratrooper light machine guns. They wore olive fatigues, their demeanor calm and at first polite, but reserved in their ignorance of where our loyalties lay.

Within two days the empty Coliseum became crowded. Unknown to us at the time, the building was to become the main "People's Tribunal." Castro's commissars began to set up court in the many offices as the show people were segregated in a small isolated area. Soon we saw prisoners being escorted into the offices, many displaying evidence of severe beatings and some wounded by gunfire. The trials were brief with most of the detainees ordered out to flatbed trucks, hands behind their heads. Castro's men were on the flatbed, their backs against the back of the cab facing the rear of the truck, directing submachine guns at the prisoners, many bloody and beaten. All day long the same trucks arrived, then left to return again, always empty except for two or three soldiers aboard. We learned the majority of the accused were taken directly to the moat of the Havana prison and shot.

As the days passed, the guards made it imminently clear to us that any transgression would be punished severely. The threats, accompanied by a daily scene of tortured prisoners being shoved and pushed through the hasty trial period and then taken off at gunpoint, only heightened anxiety. Our fellow performers were out of food and daily rations of beans and white bread became our sustenance. Perhaps it was just as well we could no longer get to our stashed cache. I had not told Charlotte of the very real danger of being discovered harboring food. The penalty was possibly interrogation under torture and maybe a firing squad. While it was obvious the Castro militia had been ordered to go easy on the Yankees, I was not so sure of their instructions concerning Frenchmen.

After two weeks of a deteriorating situation, everyone's nerves were tighter than a tightrope. One of our compatriots, Pat Anthony, an exparatrooper in his thirties who performed a lion act in the show, was unfortunately displaying signs of imminent nervous breakdown. I was afraid he would say something or physically threaten the soldiers. At one point, as the men were talking about our plight, a wild shot rang out. Pat hit the floor, hands covering his ears, he turned deathly pale and began to shake violently. It took hours to calm him down.

We were all desperately concerned about survival. Eisenhower was President at the time, and we wondered if he might send in the Marines. If so, incarcerated in a building nearly impossible to penetrate, we were vulnerable as hell. We would be the first foreign casualties of such a commando effort. Fortunately, either by design, indecision, or just plain luck, Eisenhower never intervened militarily. After a couple of weeks, some of our group were permitted to leave. Charlotte and I made two trips to the airport hitchhiking in a Wallenda truck, but could not get on a flight either time. On the third attempt, we finally got aboard an overloaded plane with Coco in tow.

Blessedly we touched down safely in Miami leaving the danger behind, but wondered what fate would befall the animals. Fortunately, they arrived in West Palm Beach within days by ship, weak and upset by the lengthy incarceration. I have never returned to Cuba since that dramatic and appalling take-over. From what I have read, not only have they ceased doing the cha-cha, but the Castro regime has tragically depressed and ravaged the economy and the spirits of a former lively and enthusiastic citizenry.

After a brief stay in Center Hill where routine and other work was performed on the new compound, we again took to the road to fill engagements showing the leopards and the greyhounds now fully recovered from the Cuban debacle. When we left the compound for what would be months of touring, the tigers went with us. Part of their training was to become accustomed to the many sights and sounds that accompanied the tour and the all-encompassing performance arena. Also, I wanted to continue working them. It was important to expose them to the music and the people, to be loaded on and off the trailer, and to experience all the nuances of a live performance. Cats, dogs, or any animals for that matter trained exclusively in a secluded compound will arrive in the ring and freeze or bolt. The discipline I wanted to achieve took daily, rigorous training sessions.

The leopard act continued to be well-received. Charlotte, with a helper, pushed the cages into the arena where a steel frame was in place. I had designed the frame containing a number of steel prongs to support the collapsible wood-decorated pedestals, each spaced at precisely the same distance apart. It was imperative to perform the cats in exactly the same routine for every performance. The cats were released from their individual cages and then commanded to jump onto their four-foot high pedestals. The two spotted leopards and the black assumed a pose, seated majestically, obediently waiting for Charlotte to begin the performance by commanding one of the cats to do a plank walk. The cat jumped from his pedestal to a lower stool supporting a narrow plank and proceeded to walk from one side to the other, then turn and walk back again to sit and posture, awaiting the inevitable applause.

The leopards also jumped on cue through blazing rings of fire in a display of great courage. The finale of the act when I appeared, which was for most of the performances, had the black leopard, seated elegantly on his pedestal, waiting for my command. He then leaped 17 feet through the air to my waiting arms. Since I was bare-chested and braced for impact, the finale, unusually dramatic, always startled the audience. The unique routine was met initially with a gasp and then applause as I swung around holding the black, snarling animal in my arms.

The act, like all animal acts, required enormous concentration of training and discipline. The cats, like the greyhounds, did not naturally want to stay put. They were inclined to leave the arena if not kept constantly in control with the whip cracking overhead and audible signals and commands directing every motion. It took thousands of hours to achieve the exacting discipline. All other cat acts up until that time had been performed in cages, the cats captive in the ring or on leash. The cats on pedestals with the audience close and unprotected was a dangerous act and one where absolute control was essential at all times. One deviation and all hell would prevail.

My cats were so well-trained that in all the years of performing I never had any break away. As a matter of fact, in one instance they even impressed me with their integrity. We were in St. Louis where the act was accompanied by a pig act on one side and a Doberman on the other. Pigs are natural prey for the cats in the wild, and I knew the unique placement would be a testing ground. On one performance day, the Dobermans cut loose and began to leave their area; the trainer had lost control. Some of the large dogs ended up in the leopard ring. The leopards amazingly sat on their pedestals like statues, seemingly impervious to the melee enacted at the base, as the pigs squealed and ran in circles with the dogs in hot pursuit. Only then did I realize that as a trainer I did indeed possess unique ability.

I continued working with the tigers as they slowly matured. We moved from one engagement to the next showing the grey-

Charlotte worked with me performing the leopards.

hounds, monkeys, and leopards. When the winter season ended, we headed back to Florida where I resumed work on the housing and continued the tiger training. It was always a welcome relief to pull off the road and leave the vigors of the tour behind, in spite of much work to do with ongoing training and chores necessary to complete the compound. When I found some rare leisure time, I particularly enjoyed hunting, diving, and fishing in the semitropical wilderness. Central Florida had many undeveloped areas and we enjoyed the isolation and quiet of our very special hammock. However, work on the house was slow and frustrating with a labor situation rife with dilatory help.

When I needed to get totally away from the frustration, Charlotte would drop me off at Weeki Wachee Springs, about 30 miles from the compound. I proceeded to skin dive the nine miles to the Gulf. She'd be waiting for me in her station wagon at the wilderness area where the fresh spring water flows into the endless gulf waters. I surfaced usually with eight or ten pounds of

Off the tour provided time for fishing.

fish. We'd build a fire, cook the fish, and enjoy the solitude of late day as the sun slowly disappeared, swallowed by a thin line that soon gave rise to a magnificent sunset.

Charlotte was a proficient fisherwoman using a simple cane pole and out-fishing most men using sophisticated gear. We shared many precious outings in the pristine natural beauty of our surroundings, abundantly enhanced by the oak hammock. Everything confirmed the wisdom of our move from the Northeast.

There was much about the land in Sumter County that fascinated me. I found then and still find the natural attributes quieting and therapeutic. On the compound, the ancient wild grape vines 18 inches in diameter and giant live and water oaks, some 140 feet in spread and 50 feet in circumference, provide a serene beauty almost beyond belief. As I became accustomed to taking a nightly and early morning walk, I found them silent but eloquent testimony to the endurance of nature against all odds, in spite of enormous scars engraved by countless lightning strikes, hurricanes, and tornadoes.

The oak-filled hammock would hold much life-and-death drama in the years to come. But it was home and I felt as one in this hallowed place filled with varied bird life, many flying and common squirrels, and giant eight-foot-long chicken snakes all living in the oaks and demonstrating the importance of such old natural reserves to the preservation of species. My greatest joy became the return from touring to settle in the hammock and work with the animals in the pristine natural setting.

I worked the tigers as we crisscrossed the country and continued their daily methodical training on the compound. It was an extremely hot day during a routine session when I recognized that something had gone wrong. For six months the training of each of the eight tigers had taken place individually, almost like an assembly line. From sun-up to sun-down, each animal was gradually trained first to recognize his permanent pedestal, and then go to a specific location in the center of the 40-foot steel arena. The session lasted about 15 minutes per specimen. Then my outside helper would open the door and within seconds send another cat through the entrance door. The next step was to rehearse two animals at the same time. When the two were absolutely synchronized in their routine, a third cat was then introduced, and then another and another and so on.

On this fateful day, September 20, 1960, which was, by the way, my thirty-seventh birthday, three seconds of life crystallized in my memory and will follow me to the grave. Boris and Chilly, two enormous Siberians, were my present students. Chilly, for some unknown reason, refused to do the return jump from one pedestal to another 17 feet away, so I prodded him gently with the tip of the whip, which was the extension of my hand. It is impossible to have direct contact with a mother-raised specimen due to potential violent reaction and danger ever present.

As I watched Chilly, I knew that he was out of control. With no warning, he suddenly turned and 500 pounds of ferocious tiger leaped straight at me, dilated eyes full of fury, his mouth wide open showing four enormous ivory fangs. As our bodies met, the impact floored the two of us in a mortal embrace. In the next second, I realized that my left hand was paralyzed, the animal's claws imbedded in it. Simultaneously, the first crushing bite went through my right wrist, immediately followed by another massive attack on the forearm, and a third broke through my biceps. I heard skin, tendons, muscle, and bone being torn and crushed like paper and yet, felt absolutely no pain. Survival instinct made me scream the animal's name, "Chilly," and, almost miraculously, the furious predator released me only to retreat to the other side of the arena where he began to pace back and forth, neck expanded, growling ferociously. As I slowly arose, I searched for the steel training fork and hickory stick. I looked down at my left hand — it had been brutalized — scalped — the lacerated skin hung over the forefingers. My eyes watched the pacing, enraged animal as I groped and finally found the wood stick laying on the ground to the right. My right hand felt absolutely numb. A quick glance

Sometimes being careful wasn't enough.

revealed the extent of mutilation. The forearm had been broken, the lower part hanging useless with the two major bones protruding from an open wound — the section artery squirting a powerful stream of blood.

    When I entered the arena, I had a helper outside the exit door. The huge 300-pound fellow, according to his references, had worked as a doorman for Clyde Beatty. A quick look over my shoulder to the door revealed that the helper was gone, which meant I had to try with my crippled left hand to operate the vertical double-latch bar controlling the exit door. Facing the tiger, I slowly backed away from the bloody center of the arena, dropped the stick and finally managed to open the door halfway, struggling with my back to the exit, my eyes constantly on Chilly. When half my body was through, the tiger sprang again leaping wildly through the air, and hitting the door like a Mack truck, sending me flying backwards, and miraculously closing the self-locking device on the gate. The whole time the treacherous attack was taking place, the pacing and growling of a crazed Chilly, and then my slow and stealthy escape, Boris remained on his pedestal and never joined Chilly.

The next thing I knew I was lying on my back, on wonderfully tender grass, looking at the other side of a huge level plain covered by magnificent, vivid blue Florida sky. I knew that my period of grateful meditation should end promptly since I was loosing blood fast. I located a short piece of rope and, with my scalped left hand, made a hasty tourniquet tightened around my upper right arm. I then struggled to get into the car to drive myself four miles into Center Hill to Charlotte. The rest was routine emergency admission to the Leesburg Hospital 18 miles away: treatment, stitching, injections, and a brief pause to let the healing process proceed.

A few weeks later, I was back in the training cage with Chilly as a new outside man stood close by. The cat proved to be a very fast, reliable, and extremely dramatic performer that died of old age at the compound in 1975.

But that is getting ahead of the story, writing Chilly's obituary when there are many more acts to perform and many years of majestic elegance to enjoy.

27

TIGERS AND OTHER ANIMALS
Les Tigres et Autres Bêtes

When the tigers were ready to show before an audience, I arranged some rehearsal dates at local schools. I was paid nothing for the performances, but took advantage of the highly popular appearances that provided the cats with the necessary experience of applause and screaming which we solicited from the young, enthusiastic crowd filling the auditoriums. We also showed at some small fair ground facilities to give the tigers a taste of the outdoor arena and important exposure to the loud marching bands, bright balloons, and noisy clowns: the three major distractions that spooked animals.

When I was satisfied that the cats were ready for the road shows, we accepted our first professional contract to appear in St. Paul at a Shrine Circus presented in a huge building, not unlike other facilities where the greyhounds and leopards had performed many times before. We did not realize that the structure, a huge cave-like edifice, produced acoustical echoes, nor did we realize the effect the reverberating sounds would have on the tigers.

Doutchka had been well-trained to perform the globe routine using her legs to propel and ride on the large, decorated, rolling prop. She also did the hind leg walk to my commands, snapping a whip above my head as she walked backwards, growling menacingly. She became stressed in the echo-chamber, would not eat, and began to pace back and forth. She was terrified of the building environment and had to be removed from the performance.

I called a local vet to diagnose her behavior and administer care. A squeeze cage was used to examine Doutchka. I carried the cage as standard equipment to be used for emergencies, and we definitely had one on our hands in St. Paul. The back wall of a squeeze cage is moveable and pushes the cat to the front, reducing the space and prohibiting the animal from moving or reacting to treatment. It also reduces danger to the examiners. It was impossible to perform an animal demonstrating symptoms of stress. Unpredictable and potentially dangerous, an animal could be prone to attack the trainer or initiate an altercation with another animal. Manchu and another tiger used as an alternate also showed symptoms of stress.

After the diagnosis, I used the time between shows to wheel the containment cages into the big arena and gradually work with the affected tigers, cracking the whip and then sitting with them for hours, slowly putting them through their paces to induce acceptance of the unusual noises. The tigers were also put on antibiotics to ward off possible secondary infections caused by stress-induced lowering of resistance. My knowledge of medical problems and procedures was further enhanced with each episode when veterinarians were summoned or where professional help was not available and I had to resolve problems on my own. It became an ongoing, valuable education.

After five days, the stressed animals seemed to be over the trauma and, along with the animals not adversely affected, were able to complete the contract, performing in peak condition. The audience reception and acceptance of the tiger performance, as it had been originally conceived and rehearsed, was fantastic and more exhilarating than any previous performance by any of my animal acts. As I rode Boris from the ring, I heard the thunderous applause and returned to the arena to several ovations. The demonstration of audience acclamation, excitement with the drama, and the precision of an act that was one hell of a debut for the tigers, as well as for me as trainer and originator of the unique act, was extremely gratifying . It was the beginning of a love affair with the dangerous, powerful animals that would last a lifetime.

With the new act and immediate publicity in the media as well as through the "Network," word spread quickly and thoroughly throughout the industry. I began to receive many substantial contract offers. One agent, Al Dobritch, had booked me many times into various arenas. The tremendously successful agent had an interesting story to tell of his own. It was Al's wife, Lola, who had alerted us to the hotel fire in Cuba when we so narrowly escaped the Castro revolution. I had met Al and Lola years before in Europe when Al performed in a high-flying act, done rather clumsily, the worst act of its kind that I had ever seen. Al was an uneducated, rough character struggling to make a living when I first met him. Under Lola's influence and in partnership with her, he became a successful and innovative agent who operated his business out of offices in New Jersey, and then from Chicago, and finally from Las Vegas. He had an exclusive contract with Ed Sullivan to supply all the circus and variety acts for the Sullivan shows, a rather monumental coup for an agent.

I had a contract at the time to perform for Al through his Midwest office. He was the exclusive booking agent for *Circus Circus*, the TV show produced in Chicago featuring Mary Hartman as hostess. Mary was a gorgeous blond endowed with the most beautiful breasts, and I enjoyed working with her and watching her move through the performances.

One evening after completing the show, Al asked me to accompany him to his apartment where he had an unsigned contract for me to sign to appear at a fair the following year. When we arrived at his luxurious high-rise apartment, he mentioned that Lola was entertaining a dinner guest. Before entering, Al asked me to remove my shoes.

"What for? Don't you have a vacuum cleaner?"

He whispered, "No, no, please do as I do."

As he removed his shoes, he held a finger to his mouth in a gesture of silence and then led me on tiptoe through the foyer back to his office. The large apartment was divided elegantly by heavy decorative drapes separating the living room from the dining room, and I could hear from behind the drapery low conversation and provocative laughter, obviously not to be interrupted. We secured the contract and left the apartment as quietly as we entered. In the cab Al explained that Lola was intimate with the producer, who was her dinner guest, and it was vitally important that we not disturb the important tête-à-tête.

Eventually Al and Lola divorced, and Al moved his base of operation to Las Vegas where his contract with *Circus Circus* called for many animal acts to fill the extravaganzas. He became involved with the mob in the gambling city, an involvement which would prove fatal. There were showgirl friends and a poorly calculated order to have one of his body guards beat up a young man who was sexually involved with one of "his girls." The young man just happened to be related to Sam Giancana, a don in the Chicago mob. Al had overstepped his bounds and was told that if he wanted to live, he would have to go back to Czechoslovakia, and remain in his homeland, never again to return to the States. Al talked to me after receiving the threat and said that he had no alternative as he explained, "They are giving me a headache and I'm going back to the Old Country because they said they are gonna do a job on me."

Al did return to his native country, but did not remain long enough. He was involved with a special lady and also had money to collect both requiring his presence in Vegas. He sneaked back into town (so he thought), but was not successful in keeping his presence secret. The mob worked swiftly and assuredly to terminate Al Dobritch. A girl was used to lure him into the Mint Hotel, where they rendezvoused in a room on the eleventh floor. The next morning his body was found splattered on the sidewalk outside the hotel. The job was done well; no fresh finger prints found and the double-locks secure from the inside of the room.

As an aside, a few years later I read with keen interest that Sam Giancana, Chicago's boss of all bosses, was found shot dead in the basement of his armor-protected apartment despite all the bolts secured from the inside. The newspaper article questioned the mysterious entry and exit by the murderer. It seemed more than coincidental that the same perfectionist had committed both murders, that of Giancana and Al Dobritch years before.

In all the years of travel with so much work to perform, our retinue of employees changed almost as quickly as our locations while we swept from one engagement to the next, from one part of the country to another. There was a tremendous amount of labor behind the scenes caring for the animals and cleaning up after them. There was much that was not glamorous, and there were many humorous as well as tragic incidents and people to savor and to suffer.

One employee stands out as providing much in both categories. His name was Fernie. We were showing at a beautiful resort at Pontchartrain Beach in Louisiana with an exotic restaurant as part of the complex. We kept a snow fence around the area where the animals were contained to keep the public from walking up to the cages. I began to notice a small, dark man with shaved, pointed head, big nose, and large ears that stuck straight out. A most unusual fellow who wore an immaculate white outfit in sharp contrast to his swarthy complexion, he looked at the animals every day. We did two shows a day, and the weather was extremely hot and humid. I left each performance sweaty and thirsty and went directly to the restaurant, in costume, to order a large glass or two of fresh lemonade, a great thirst-quencher. We played in Pontchartrain for ten days and toward the end of the engagement, I spoke to the strange little man who looked so adoringly at the tigers.

"I see you watch the cats all the time!"

He answered with a whiny stutter, "Oh, y-yeah, I, I l-love t-t-tigers."

"I can see that."

As I looked down at the little man, his hands holding onto the top of the fence, his spotless white apron over pure white shirt and pants, my gaze quickly returned to his hands. They were repulsive in contrast to the cleanliness of his clothing, weathered and filthy with long curling fingernails black with crud under the nails and in all the creases. I asked if he worked in the restaurant, hoping for a negative.

"Y-y-yea!"

I hesitated but then asked, "What's your job there?"

"O-Oh, I, I f-f-fix the l-l-lemonade!"

I looked deeply into his innocent face, at his hands and then closed my eyes and shuddered at the thought. Then I made a proposal. I hired him on the spot, not to fix my lemonade or even to save others from such a fate, but we were always looking for helpers to clean up the manure, and I knew that I had before me a man who had the hands to do the job. It was a tough, demeaning position to fill, and we were always losing whoever was employed in the shitty labor. Fernie joined our entourage.

In his thirties, Fernie did not seem to know where he was born or to whom. He was slightly retarded, but able-bodied and soon proved to be a hard worker. He worked like a robot until we directed him to another job. He loved to eat and drink with complete abandon and required monitoring and discipline just like a child.

Hubert Castle was the agent-producer of the *Don Ameche International Showtime* Television Show. I was signed to perform all of my acts on the popular and innovative circus theme show to be included in one taping session. I was booked to perform the greyhounds, the uncaged leopards, and the tiger act. In order to fulfill the engagement, we had to travel from Springfield, Massachusetts, where I was currently showing, to Los Angeles to tape the show produced on the West Coast. I was to be paid more for the single show than any other previous appearance on TV. The exposure would be great since Ameche had garnered a large audience for the colorful and unique format.

I had known Hubert as a performer working years before in a slack-wire act. In his prime, the dangerous low-wire somersault had never previously been performed except by the Mexican-born Con Coleano 30 years earlier. Coleano possessed tremendous talent of grace and elegance in an act that seemed less impressive than the high-wire acts, but was a potential killer. In the somersault, if the performer misses just once without landing properly on the low wire, a severe and usually fatal head injury occurs. As an old-timer, Hubert obviously survived his performance career and knew the business well, having the contacts to gather a fine array of talent for the Ameche Show.

We were nearly finished in Springfield. Typical of the end of every run, with thoughts of packing 85,000 pounds of equipment and animals in preparation for the long haul across country, there was a certain lack of concentration on the immediate performance. It was at that time that most accidents would occur. I was doing a matinee performance with Charlotte, as usual, outside the cage conducting the behind the scenes performance absolutely vital to the success of the act in the arena where each animal had to enter on cue and in proper sequence. If, for any reason, the animals entered the cage out of their planned and coordinated order, fights could ensue and the whole performance put at risk.

On that particular afternoon in Springfield, the performance had gone smoothly with me working each animal individually while the others sat on their pedestals. As a part of the act, I walked close to the tigers to invade their territory and induce a roaring reaction. I knew well that when a cat's territory is violated, they will react predictably; and I knew that some tigers have a more closely defined territory than others. Some would react at two feet while I could snuggle up and touch others. There were two tigers in the arena, Cobra and Python, both possessing hot tempers. They were not the original tigers purchased from the Birmingham Zoo, but animals mother-raised and quick to respond. In my haste and lapse of absolute concentration, I got about three inches too close to Python, who quickly reached out with his paw and hooked my right hand. Python was not the kind of tiger that you wanted to be hooked to for long. I reacted in a way that I knew was wrong and dangerous. Instead of relaxing my hand to give him the opportunity to release his paw, I pulled away quickly and in so doing the hand was torn brutally by imbedded tiger nails.

I was working the act bare torso wearing a necklace of tiger claws. I had completed about two thirds of the act with five minutes left. Somehow, as blood started to spurt and with a finger dangling, torn from the joint, I was able to hold the whip in three fingers and continued to hold the hickory stick in my left hand. Everything happened so fast I didn't feel any pain at first and continued, cool and in control, to circle the whip above my head as I continued giving commands and putting the tigers through their paces.

The blood was gushing by this time, falling on my torso, costume, and the floor of the arena. I became aware of the stir in the crowd speculating if the blood was real or a dramatic prop to heighten the dramatics of a dangerous and threatening performance. The tigers were excited by the blood, and Charlotte and my helpers called to me to get out of the arena fearful that the tigers could go wild at any moment. I knew that I must continue to perform as if nothing unusual had occurred. I knew that if I exited abruptly as Charlotte was demanding, the tigers would have gone wild for the blood and thrown the entire arena into complete chaos and danger.

I had wonderful coaching over the years by Alfred Court and Paul le Royer and knew that I had to maintain absolute control in spite of the profuse blood loss. I went through the final routines commanding the tigers out of the arena, leaving Boris in position. As soon as I threw the whip into the air, he jumped from his pedestal, me holding the dagger with three fingers, he coming

The potential for injury was always present.

menacingly close and kissing me. I kissed him, mounted him, and rode triumphantly and bloody out of the ring. The audience went wild. Charlotte had called for an ambulance. I returned to the arena for a standing ovation, and then, while waiting to be taken to the hospital, noticed Boris, secure in his cage, calmly licking my blood from his paws and cheeks.

While Boris continued to cleanse himself, I left to have my hand repaired. Knowing that I had an important engagement to fulfill on the West Coast, I informed the attending doctor that I could not tolerate any invasive surgery. I knew that I had to maintain use of the hand and asked the doctor to put the finger back in joint and stitch the hand with a drain in place. It was standard medical procedure to stitch wounds tightly. I knew from experience that in sewing wounds imbedded by a dirty cat's claw nearly always induced infection and possible gangrene. Whenever I had any injury, I always attempted to point out to the medics that the wound needed a drain to allow for blood and bacteria to escape. When the doctor, after listening to my suggested treatment method, repaired the hand in the traditional manner, I refused to leave the hospital until he released several stitches and placed a drain in position.

With drain, a full bandage and protective cover in place, I painfully managed to help supervise the packing for the trip to Los Angeles. The morning we were to leave Springfield dawned cold and drizzly. As we approached the grounds, I spotted Fernie crossing the main highway to return to his job. He was supposed to stay with the animals around the clock. He had an army cot close to the animals and was protected, fed, and given time off; but when he was on duty, he was not to leave. It was a rule that I thought he understood, particularly with a liquor store directly across from the grounds. Charlotte drove the car.

"Look, that's Fernie coming out of there," I said as I pointed to the liquor store. We waited for him to cross the highway. I called, "Fernie, what are you doing out of the compound so early?"

He was wearing a black raincoat and was obviously startled and shaken by our arrival.

"N-nothing, M-M-Mr. B-Baudy, n-n-nothing."

"Well, you are supposed to be with the animals. You are not to be across the street!"

"W-W-Well, I had m-m-my b-breakfast . . ." was his whining excuse as he pointed back toward the liquor store muttering something about a little joint down the street. I got out of the car and looked down at him.

"You never told me that you got your breakfast there. Now it's raining and cold and miserable, and . . ." as I spoke I noticed some bulges under the raincoat clinging damply to his small frame. "Fernie, what are you carrying?"

"I-I c-c-carry n-nothing" was his coy attempt to conceal contraband.

"Fernie, now . . . move ten feet, will you please."

As he moved, I could see that he was carrying something and I repeated, "Look, I want to see what you have there!"

He squealed excitedly, "T-t-this is a-a f-f-free c-c-c-country."

"It's a free country all right, but I'm in charge of your welfare, and I want to see what you have under that raincoat."

He was using his hands to hide the bulges, but I insisted he show me what his coat concealed. The pockets were filled with a dozen miniature bottles of whiskey.

"Fernie, give me those bottles!"

He cried out, "I-I c-c-can't do that, I-I- I'm on m-m-medica-ca-tion and I-I n-need them."

"You may be on medication, but this is the wrong kind of medicine. I want those bottles and I want them right NOW."

I took the bottles and Fernie turned quickly to cross the street. I watched him go and saw by the outline of the damn coat that he had more bottles in his back pockets. We did not have time to retrieve the remaining bottles and returned to the hotel to gather our personal belongings, then drove back to gather Fernie and the animals. We could not locate the little man.

I was exasperated. "Jesus Christ, what happened to that sucker!"

We began to search the area and finally found Fernie sitting on the ground next to a telephone pole, his face covered with blood. I ran to him, drunk and jabbering incoherently as he sat on the cold gravel. I pulled a water hose to him and began to flush his face of clotted blood. As I washed his face, I detected no injury from a cut or scratch. I checked his scalp, around his ears, and then his hands. One hand was folded behind his back. I pulled it forward and saw immediately that a finger was missing. Apparently in his drunken stupor trying to suckle the injured hand, he had moved the bloody stump all over his face.

We helped him up and into the building where Charlotte cleaned and wrapped his hand. He would not communicate how the accident occurred, but we were able to reconstruct the scene as we took Fernie to a doctor. We decided that in self-pity, seeking solace from his beloved tigers and too drunk to realize the danger, he got too close. Often unsuspecting fans were tempted to put their fingers between the cage bars, spaced two inches apart by design to avoid accidents, unaware that the seemingly docile animals cannot resist human stupidity. We eventually found Fernie's missing finger inside his glove, too late to save. It would be the first of three similar accidents over a period of three years when trusting humans got too close to a cage.

We were encountering serious delays on the important trip west. When finally packed and ready, Fernie rode with me in the back seat of the Cadillac. Charlotte drove the semi with the animals and handlers aboard. With still no interstates but narrow two-lane roads, the trip was long and tedious. I knew Fernie was developing a serious infection in the hand when he stopped eating and his head felt extremely hot to my touch. Enroute I sought medical attention to have his hand examined and a stronger antibiotic prescribed. As we continued our journey, we stopped for gas. A young man came to the car to fill the tank and in a wise-guy swagger asked, "What happened to you? What got you?" as he pointed to my heavily bandaged right hand.

"Oh, I got chewed up by a tiger."

He looked at me in obvious disbelief and then continued to fill the tank as he looked into the back seat where Fernie sat, injured bandaged hand raised above his head. The attendant directed his next question to Fernie, "And what got hold of you?"

"O-oh, a-a-a t-t-tiger got m-me!"

The kid looked at Fernie, then at me, and I could see he was of the opinion that he'd run into two smart asses. I explained that what had occurred was due to my profession working with tigers, but I don't think I came close to convincing him.

When we arrived at the studio on the West Coast, the first order of business was to find space for the large rigs that had arrived previously. The studio lot was inadequate. The logistical problem solved, I had to set up and work the acts with a heavily bandaged right hand, 45 stitches in place. I controlled the whip with my injured hand. It was difficult and painful, but very necessary, as the tool that commanded the animals and directed every move throughout the acts. I was in constant pain as I rehearsed and went through the pretaping routines. I practiced every routine except the final leopard leap, knowing fully that the impact of the cat flying into my arms would further injure the hand.

When I felt ready to do the final taping, we performed and taped all the routines right up until the leap, knowing it would literally be the finale, at least the final performance until the hand had sufficient time to heal. I took prescribed antibiotics and amphetamines, which countered the infection and dulled the pain; but I was weak and went through the entire performance knowing the catch was going to be damned tough and also excruciating. I cued "Rama" in preparation for the leap as the cameras continued to role. Charlotte and the technicians watched from the sidelines. The black leopard took to the air; I braced myself for impact, which I immediately broke by whirling around, gracefully catching the 145-pound cat. I felt the shooting pains in my hand as the stitches tore apart. I turned to face the camera for a close-up, smiling broadly and then, taping completed and blood seeping through the bandage, I nearly passed out. Back to the hospital for me.

Fernie continued to be a part of the team for many years. He was a hard worker who would perform a job so thoroughly that we had to supervise him closely. I swear if I told Fernie to sand the railroad tracks heading east from Chicago, he would work feverishly until he was out of sandpaper. He was childlike in many ways and often sat for hours counting his fingers beginning with his left hand and pointing as he repeated, 'O-o-one, t-two, three, f-f-four, f-five' and then would begin with the other hand, always disturbed when he could not count to ten due to the missing finger.

Medical problems were a disturbing but compelling part of the tour. On one occasion when Doutchka became ill, I located a vet who diagnosed the cat as suffering from a vitamin A deficiency. The vet told me that a tablet would not be sufficient to raise the levels, but to bolster her diet with plenty of eggs. I went to an egg farm and bought eggs by the gross, cracked, bloodshot, and sold primarily for animal consumption. I kept the eggs in a building on the fairgrounds. Every day I gave three dozen eggs, vitamins, and milk to the ailing tiger. Doutchka was suffering from just one of many health problems that continued to plague the tigers bought as infants from the Birmingham Zoo.

I began to notice that the eggs vanished faster than I dispensed them. I looked around for tracks near the egg crates, feeling that as an animal man I could trap the predator, be it a possum or a raccoon or whatever. There were no strange tracks. One night, taking a flashlight, I drove from the hotel to the fairgrounds. I saw light through a crack in the door to the building housing the eggs. A check on the animals found them all settled in their cages. I tiptoed to the building, opened the door slightly, and saw Fernie sitting in the dirt, his back to me, completely surrounded by cracked shells. The scene brought a flash of memory to a henhouse in the south of France and a little boy sucking eggs, then his grandmother appearing with a handful of nettles to whip his bare behind. I entered the building and admonished, "Fernie, don't you know that you could get cancer from those eggs? Do you know what cancer is?"

Startled by my intrusive entrance, he cried, "O-oh, oh, y-yes, c-c-cancer is ba-bad."

"It sure as hell is and you better not touch any more of those eggs!"

While Doutchka's medicinal eggs were off limits, I did let Fernie assist whenever I had to do either minor surgery or autopsies. I made him soak his hands in a strong bleach solution and then while performing the procedure I commented, using medical terms. If we were in the slaughterhouse, I pointed out various organs and any telltale signs of physical disorders of the liver, lungs, or the kidneys, etc.

One day while cleaning cages, Fernie was my helper and he came up with a surprisingly good suggestion which alludes me, but I remember well complimenting him on his good idea and asking how he came to think of such a wonderful shortcut. He gave a wide, toothless grin, pointed to his head and told me pridefully, "Mr. B-B-Baudy, I-I h-h-have w-watched you and th-th-this t-time I u-u-used my rectum!"

Fernie was always consistent. Usually filthy, he willingly

Whether Charlotte had to care for Fernie or a cat in distress, she was a trooper.

cleaned up the manure, was a diligent worker, and a unique character. We were his family. Charlotte treated him with kindness and tolerated some unpleasant episodes in a motherly way. I was particularly impressed with her forbearance when Fernie accompanied her in the semi as we moved between New York and Chicago on one horrendous occasion.

We were booked to play a Shrine Circus. I drove ahead in the automobile; Fernie rode in the semi cab with Charlotte. The weather turned foul with cold and rain that created extremely hazardous conditions. They were to leave right after me, but with the deteriorating conditions, I knew their trip would take longer. However, I became concerned when they didn't arrive in Chicago hours later. I waited, fearful of an accident. Finally, the rig pulled into the designated meeting place, and I ran to welcome them, relieved they had made the trip with no apparent problems that I could detect from the outside of the semi.

When I opened the door, a pungent, sickening odor escaped and engulfed me. Fernie slipped quickly from the cab and took off. I questioned Charlotte.

"What the hell is that smell?"

She explained that Fernie had developed diarrhea right after they left New York, and she stopped every fifteen minutes for him to relieve himself. Charlotte went on to describe how she stopped to buy him medication, but Fernie insisted that what he really wanted and needed were sardines. Charlotte told him she doubted very much that sardines would solve his problem. He continued talking about sardines in an unceasing, childlike stuttering until she relented and bought some cans of the young pilchards just to quiet him. As he ate the sardines, he became quiet and possibly did not want to admit that the unusual remedy was not working. He made no further requests to stop but continued to mess in his pants all the way to Chicago.

Fernie, like most of my helpers, carried pliers in his back pocket along with a holstered butcher knife, both implements a "must" on the compound. One day I lost my own pair of pliers and noticed that Fernie didn't carry his that particular morning. I went to his quarters to borrow his pair. As I moved a pile of clothes on top of his cot, I felt something hard inside a very dirty sock. I was flabbergasted to find a loaded .22 calibre derringer residing in the sock. The gun was rusty with two live bullets practically welded inside the barrel. I had no idea in the two years of employment that he carried a loaded weapon. I discussed the situation with Charlotte, and we decided that we should keep the gun for the time being. About three weeks later Fernie, disconsolate, came to me.

"Fernie, what's the matter with you?"

"M-Mr. B-B-Baudy, w-we b-b-better be c-careful w-with our s-s-stuff around h-here. S-S-Someone s-s-stole one of m-my s-s-socks."

I had completely forgotten about the gun and did not react until I fully realized what Fernie was really lamenting — his missing weapon.

Fernie couldn't read or write and had difficulty using the proper word. If he spoke of a miracle, it came out mackerel. But we could read him well and always got a big laugh out of his misnomers. He seemed to genuinely enjoy that he had created such joviality. Fernie was a cheerful guy most of the time, content to take care of his precious charges and always kind to most animals. However, snakes and spiders terrorized him, in spite of the fact that most species living on the compound were quite harmless. Even though I gave implicit instructions to my workers to respect the small insects and reptiles, I continued to find chopped-up body parts of the useful and beautiful creatures that enjoyed the run of the place until Fernie captured them. It would take years for the indigoes and chicken snakes to thrive again and then only after Fernie left the entourage.

We were in Chicago for a show that included a chimp act worked by two homosexuals, who seemed to take a particular liking to Fernie. They engrossed him in conversation everyday and when it came time to leave Chicago, Fernie was nowhere to be found. I never saw him demonstrate any interest in girls, but then I never saw him interested in anything other than tigers, food, liquor, raw eggs, and counting his fingers. What I imagine happened was the two gays required someone to clean up after the chimps and they may have kidnapped Fernie. He simply disappeared, and then we heard through the network he was working with the chimps. Two years later we learned that he was back at Ponchartrain Beach. He had provided much amusement and had worked hard for us for years. He left us with some vivid memories of a most unique character, the little man with the filthy hands. I will never again drink lemonade without thinking of Fernie.

28

NEW ANIMALS, NEW MARRIAGE
Nouveaux Animaux, Nouveau Mariage

*B*efore the Florida compound was completed, I formally incorporated The Rare Feline Training Center, establishing a whole new business venture. I knew there were many people who wanted to perform animal acts, ex-acrobats or other performers who hadn't any experience in dealing with animals, but wanted to remain in "the business." There were also people who wanted to break into the business who didn't have the money, time, or skills required to purchase animals and train them. However, my brilliant scheme was short-lived. I didn't anticipate the many inherent problems. As an example, I broke a bear act to be sold. Interested parties came to watch me perform and then went through the arduous paces working the bears to emulate my example. All went well at the compound with me overseeing and helping the neophytes. The new act left to go on tour. Three weeks later I had a phone call from the new owners requesting I bail them out. They were stuck in a remote Midwest location; the bears refused to work.

The call demonstrated what I had learned years before; there is an innate talent involved in working an animal act. While animals will learn to perform for one trainer, they may not necessarily perform for another person unless that individual is similarly imbued with that certain something so well detected and respected by the animals. Many animals will take advantage of a trainer not in full control. Even with all attributes being equal, the new owners had to be prepared to spend at least six months working everyday with me to duplicate as precisely as possible every motion, every expression, sound and behavior. Even with that effort, they were able to obtain only about 80 percent of the master control during what was a demanding and inglorious time of tedious work. I learned over the years that every person and every animal has a different personality. All of my animals knew who was boss. I worked hard on discipline to achieve the control that was the key to the success of any and every act I ever worked. It simply had to be. I was willing to put in the hours, months, and even years that it took to produce a complete and highly disciplined performance. I had a drive, a determination to succeed, and I knew just what was necessary. I never took a shortcut nor was I impatient with the animals. I knew it took time and dedication, and I'm certain much of the determination was induced by Father's initial contempt for the business. However, he had changed his opinion to some degree when he realized how much money I was generating by my various business ventures.

As I traveled back and forth to Europe, Africa, and other foreign countries to build the import business, Father finally verbalized that he recognized the viability of the business. That was a long sought-after goal. I finally achieved financial stability, which obviously elevated my position in his mind to a legitimacy, which in turn was tremendously rewarding to me. No matter how small his acknowledgment, it served to deepen my resolve.

I changed the name from The Training Center to The Rare Feline Breeding Center. There were more and more trips abroad to educate contacts and formulate a tightly knit network to perform as a team in each country. There were also many sources in the States to satisfy animal acquisitions both for me and for others. I joined the prestigious American Association of Zoological Parks and Aquariums (AAZPA). Whenever I played in a city where there was a zoo, I always met the director and began to receive mailing lists of animals available from the approximately 360 zoos across the country offering captive-born animals for sale. I had many national contacts and continued to smooth the foreign network into a cohesive, professional, comprehensive export network.

There had been many trips prior to the one in 1963, flying into Paris, then on to Rennes to spend a few days with my family before going on to other countries on the continent or to Africa to secure and educate the many contacts. These key people were involved in the multifaceted venture to deal with the safe capture, proper care, and professional handling of the animals. They also helped me to understand and cope with the red tape of government policy.

When I arrived in Rennes in 1963, I was met with many signs of discontent. Father was totally frustrated with the volatile job of raising a rebellious 16-year-old. I quickly saw that my parents were losing the battle. Gerard continued to run with a rough crowd, and it was becoming an impossible burden for them to bear. I tried talking to Gerard, but his reaction was evasive. I could not get a commitment from him to do better. I had absolutely no influence on the boy.

I left Rennes upset and feeling helpless to resolve what was an increasingly difficult situation. I didn't have the solution. I flew to Africa and became immersed in the business at hand, which was to finalize arrangements for a shipment of gorillas for the federal government. There was a growing need for a variety of animals to be studied by authoritative groups interested in origins, habitats, and life cycles of rare and not-so-rare animals, and the government at that time had five primate research centers devoted to the study of the species in captivity. I was involved with the Delta Primate Research Center in New Orleans.

While other species of animals always interested me, gorillas were my primary target on this particular importation. I went to markets and saw dead gorillas and gorilla parts (arms, hands, feet, etc.) The mutilated animals had been carried out of the jungle on long poles slung over the shoulders of native hunters. I saw rare mangabeys and many other extremely beautiful species. Africa has possibly 250 to 300 different species of monkeys with the most beautiful coming from the West African forest. I saw species that I never in all my travels saw in captivity nor read about in books. There were snow-white monkeys that looked very much like colobus monkeys with long, long-haired tails.

The natives knew in their tribal language the type of monkeys they were selling, but they could not translate to me in French, German, or English the names of the different species. As far as they were concerned, it was all *bouf*. I told the natives that I would give them three times the price of a dead monkey if they would capture the animals live. They were not equipped to do that.

They hunted with poison darts or in the case of the so-called professional hunters, at least one or two in each village, they used double-hammer shotguns. I had to reeducate them to a market for live animals that could be very lucrative.

I must interject that the gorilla has always held a special place in my esteem as an animal of extreme intelligence used pathetically as food by many of the West African tribes. Protected on paper by the German, French, British, and other colonial governments over the years as well as by many countries on the continent where the species originated, the protective efforts did not thwart the natives in their quest for meat. While in a village in the rain forest, I asked one of the older natives who spoke French why they killed the gorillas.

"Because, it's good meat . . . it's almost as good as man meat, but more chewy."

Whenever a female gorilla was either darted or hit by a bullet, she ran away until succumbing to the wound or poison. When found, she often had a baby still hanging onto her remains. Since colonization, the natives, realizing that the baby did not provide enough meat for an adequate meal, would use the live baby to exchange for sugar, salt, or precious shotgun shells from missionary traders or other individuals. Even the late Dr. Albert Schweitzer, at his hospital on the Lambarene River, reputedly had a number of young, tame, orphaned gorillas running freely around his medical compound. I was within 25 miles of the hospital intending to meet the great defender of life, human, animal, and insect, when a violent storm made travel impossible.

Before the Endangered Species Act of 1973, the orphans could be placed at various zoological establishments throughout the world; but since enactment, this is no longer possible. Fortunately, captive breeding is partially successful in saving the species. However, sadly, today the orphan babies are now consumed along with the mother, and there is every evidence that gorillas are still being killed at a rate of up to 500 per year — a sad commentary on present-day practices and government ineptitude.

When I found the hunters and brokers who would be my source, I made arrangements for light plane transportation of the animals out of the jungle and to the different debarkation points where the special crating awaited, built to my specifications for the various species and sizes of animals involved. My planning and research, ongoing for several years, produced the methods for crating and also the discovery of many rare species to be shipped when all the complicated export requirements were satisfied.

The animals shipped by plane would take no more than a day in transit if everything went according to schedule. However, there were instances to be anticipated where an animal in a crate designated for Tampa was incorrectly placed on a flight to Chicago. I had to make arrangements for the continuing flight and for care and handling during the unplanned delays and detours. I knew that each animal had to be kept in separate containers with a receptacle inside each cage for food. The food and hay or straw had to be removed before the crate was loaded aboard the plane for the flight to the States. The USDA was strict about food and plants, so newspaper replaced the straw. When the animals arrived I would alert my contact to be on hand to meet flights to make sure the animals were given proper food and liquid as they were moved from one flight to the next on their journey to The Rare Feline Breeding Center. There were two trips I recall when I actually flew with young gorillas who would not accept their baby bottle of sugar, milk, and wheat mush from anyone but me. If I had not been aboard and given the animals water, they would not have survived the trip.

There were many idiosyncracies. Every animal was separated even if a family of animals was captured and shipped. I knew that if placed in a common crate or cage, the animals would fight. The circumstances of their capture and removal from natural habitats under totally unnatural conditions produced extreme stress as did the noisy flight across the ocean. I had prepared the compound to handle the incoming animals for a period of time to acclimate them to their new surroundings before being transferred to buyers in this or other countries. I was even sensitive to the need to release the animals in the same order in which they were crated and shipped. Important relationships with other animals had been formed in transport, and even the continuity of using their original shipping container became an element of safety and privacy as it sheltered them from the trauma of transfer into a totally new environment. Leaving the original crates in their new cages became a necessary and comforting addition to the compound.

NEW ANIMALS, NEW MARRIAGE

We celebrated the completion of our new home.

As the animals began to arrive, the breeding process on the compound was expected and became my primary thrust toward preserving endangered species. It also enhanced my collection, creating excitement among other collectors and breeders. Among the many rare species, I imported the first pair of African linsangs, a small animal similar to an otter and never before seen in the States.

My new business venture was stimulating and consuming with every trip into Africa a learning experience. But I always looked forward to the portion of the trip devoted to a coveted rendezvous with Simone. In 1963 she joined me for two days and two nights of heaven in Paris. I had been in touch with her while in Rennes, and she planned to meet me in Paris as I returned to the States.

I met her train at the Montparnasse Station as I had years before, and we went directly to a fine hotel where we thoroughly and intimately shared the hours in total and complete loving. We did not want time to pass as I held her and felt the love between us. I was deeply grateful for the abiding constant in an ever-changing and complex panorama. She fully knew the pain I felt in what was occurring in Rennes. She was a compassionate listener and the love of my life. After the precious time passed, I took her to the train station, then left Paris to return to Florida with thoughts of my parents and Gerard filtering through the wonderful emotion of loving and having been loved. I knew that the increasing problems in Rennes would soon have to be addressed.

We had worked for nearly four years on the compound adding animal containment areas. When the tiger housing and our apartment was complete, it was cause to celebrate. As I traveled back and forth to Europe and Africa, Charlotte had taken full responsibility for supervising the ongoing construction. It had gone through many difficult phases being performed by a crew of up to 50 subs from time to time. I give her a great deal of credit for seeing the completion of the project to the bitter end, which in retrospect was not so bitter once we were able to move in. The oak hammock became our home and soon home for orphaned gorillas.

All animals entering the country today go through either New York or Miami for customs purposes, but at that time arrangements could be made for them to be flown into Tampa where I met the flight with a semi, prepared to handle the heavy cargo of caged animals of varying sizes. My agents had been taught well to crate each animal individually for the long passage. The feeding of the animals in transit was vital with government regulations adhered to to the letter. These strict regulatory policies were set by both the United States Government and the government of the country of origin. There were so many details to consider in the highly complex importation process, but the rewards justified every complexity. With the shipment of gorillas came animals with so many human qualities, we soon felt we were adding children to the compound.

Charlotte and other employees helped care for the new residents. There was a period of adjustment, although the babies had become accustomed to living in homes with my agents in Africa after their capture, often having been abandoned or orphaned when their mothers were killed. Some were toilet-trained; others wore diapers until they became trained. We let them into the house during the day where they entertained us; they spent their nights in separate containers outside where toys were furnished to amuse our "children."

Living with them and watching as they interacted with us and with their new surroundings was quite extraordinary. They added a whole new dimension to the compound which had taken on a family atmosphere with Charlotte's 13-year-old twins sharing our living quarters along with the gorillas. As we became totally captivated by our foundlings, it was satisfying to realize we were saving them from certain death if left in Africa.

We were soon caught up in preparation to leave the compound to go on a lengthy tour that would take four months and cover approximately 45,000 miles. When we had the rigs packed and everything ready to load the animals, Charlotte announced that she was not leaving Center Hill. I could not believe what I was hearing. I sensed an edginess in her attitude ever since we moved into the compound and even before when we stayed at her parents' place. But I was caught off guard by her pronouncement and questioned, "You're not leaving? Why?"

Mr. and Mrs. Robert Baudy — a Baudy original oil on the wall.

"Well, you know we have been talking about marriage for a long time, and I think the time has come. This is it." I looked at her, questioningly, as she went on. "I'm going to stay here and look after the animals for you for about a month, and then you'd better make some other arrangement."

I hardly knew what to say or do. I was well aware of the sentiments of her parents and relatives in the central Florida Baptist Bible Belt, where the grave sin of illegitimate relationships, particularly one involving an imported Catholic Frenchman, held deep resentment. Many locals chose to ignore me and turned their backs when I appeared. I also knew that Charlotte adored her daughters and wanted the legality as well as security of marriage as much for them.

Charlotte knew my habits well and knew that monogamy would not be possible. But I loved her and I respected her although none of my feelings translated into marriage. I didn't want to marry Charlotte or any woman other than Simone, and I could not nor would not resist sexual temptation during the many months on the road living the Gypsy life, meeting good-looking and fascinating ladies. Marriage was the farthest thing from my mind, but Charlotte brought it instantly into focus. I could not evade the issue, and I knew full well that I had to act swiftly if I was to fulfill the contracts that had been signed and were just waiting for Robert Baudy and Company to appear and produce.

I was presented with yet another contract which did not appeal to me. I asked Charlotte what arrangements she had in mind.

She explained that a local minister could perform the ceremony and do it quickly. I knew the guy she was talking about, a wino who lived with his wife in a dilapidated trailer near Center Hill. She said, "We just have to go there, and he will marry us." In the back of my mind, I figured that the impromptu religious ceremony would be a temporary fix and not legally binding, but at least would serve to ameliorate Charlotte's desire to be a wedded wife. I compared the situation to the French custom where tradition dictates a trip to City Hall where the mayor, dressed officially in formal sash, pronounces you husband and wife followed by a religious ceremony that holds no clout. My resignation in what Charlotte proposed was my belief that it would be harmless enough to go see the drunken minister, get the deed done, and get the show on the road.

We went to the trailer and with only the minister's wife as witness took our vows and received the piece of paper declaring us husband and wife. We then went on tour; Charlotte seemed happy — she was victorious. I must confess in all honesty that the ceremony did nothing to change my feelings for Charlotte or for the other women who drifted into my life in the months and years to follow.

As a matter of fact, I changed nothing in my emotional

response or lifestyle and was totally shocked to discover six years later that the little paper delivered to me for 20 dollars in the old trailer in Center Hill was indeed legally binding. I went along with the program living an illusion. To Charlotte's parents and family, she had become Mrs. Robert Baudy. That was fine with me. I continued to love Simone more than any woman in my life, and I continued to find pleasure with other ladies. However, the demands of the many different business ventures did occupy me, and I found the years of marriage to Charlotte quite satisfying and stimulating in the many engrossing involvements that we shared on and off tour.

29

MR. AND MRS. BAUDY ON TOUR
Monsieur et Madame Baudy en Tournée

*W*hen the tour went smoothly and the weather cooperated, life was quite pleasant and rewarding, but tranquility and ease were luxuries not to be expected or taken for granted. The winter tour was particularly brutal when the temperature dipped below freezing and even more brutal and life-threatening at 20° below.

We were playing a Shrine Circus in Madison, Wisconsin, in January; our arena was the coliseum at the fairgrounds. The temperature was below -20°, and the diesel-driven semis couldn't function. Some of the contracted performers weren't able to get through. Fortunately, I had taken into account the diesel fuel problem. It gels in extreme cold, putting the vehicle out of commission. I learned the lesson from my war experience. At the time I ordered the rigs, I had them equipped with gasoline engines in spite of the potential danger from fire. With that foresight, our rigs rolled, and we arrived on schedule in Madison to perform according to the contract.

However, getting there was not so easy on the animals. We had to use crowbars just to open the doors to get into the trailer to feed and water them. When we stopped at gas stations to get water, it froze by the time we carried it out to the animals. The condensation of their respiration created an ice build-up on the bars of their cages so that we could barely see the animals and their daily meat ration froze. The conditions were unbelievable, but we survived.

We continually thought about the Florida compound bathed in warm sunshine. It was insane to be where we were, doing what we were doing, but we had commitments to fulfill and had to press on.

At completion of the engagement in Madison, the weather turned even colder. I didn't think that was possible. I told Charlotte I was going to drive the semi due to treacherous conditions; she was to drive the automobile. I got the motor running on the rig and stepped on the gas peddle. The peddle broke in half. That was a shock. A mechanic came to install a new peddle, and I hoped it would survive the deep freeze.

As we continued the trek across country, I'd occasionally play an engagement close to where Virginia deBoner was performing, and I always found time to visit with her. If we could meet for several hours between performances, it was always cause for celebration. If our meeting was in the evening at the end of a strenuous day, I opened a bottle of champagne to share while we discussed mutual tour experiences. Virginia thought my animal importation business was fascinating; I related all that was happening in the quarters in Florida. She related to me her news from Las Vegas or Los Angeles or one of the hot spots where she'd performed with many show business luminaries. We often capped the evening with a romantic interlude before parting. It was often months before I saw Virginia again, but we always enjoyed the rendezvous and looked forward to next time.

I tried to be discreet, never flaunting the relationship, but I'm certain Charlotte knew what was going on. My pattern of traveling to some engagements without her gave the chance to meet special friends from the past. It did occur and she knew my history and my habits well. I hadn't changed since the marriage vows were taken. Our relationship was good; the team effort was truly a grueling, demanding partnership. I was making a great deal of money, but I was earning all of it. There was so little that was easy or relaxing on tour, and every moment of leisure to escape the rigors seemed absolutely essential, even justified. A beautiful female companion seemed a well-earned and wonderful diversion.

During the years as a star performer, in addition to the large indoor circus events, there were many TV engagements. I appeared several times on the *Jackie Gleason Show*. Jackie was a multitalented genius. His show featured a chorus line of spectacular dancers choreographed by June Taylor. I enjoyed meeting June and watching her work while the gorgeous, leggy girls went through their routines over and over again to achieve the high quality performance expected by the perfectionist. June had several lines working at that time, and I imagine they played the Music Hall and the Roxy as well as Gleason's show. It was a glamorous time, a pretty heady time, and I felt privileged to be watching and working with the likes of Gleason and Taylor. Jackie treated all of his employees and fellow performers like family — I was one of them.

I was on the *Ed Wynn Show* with the greyhounds and leopards. The TV studios were not large enough to accommodate the tiger act which required a 38-foot long cage to transport the animals, and then each tiger in its own cage on wheels. The tiger act required ten men to move the animals from the semi into whatever housing was provided, and then from there into the show ring. It was a massive act designed and suited for the large circus arena.

After several months on tour, we returned to Florida and soon welcomed a visitor from France. Mother came to meet Charlotte and to spend several weeks with us before we went back on the road. Her first trip to the States had been years before when Odette and I were quartered at Swan's Woodborn Farm. On that occasion, Mother accompanied us to several engagements in the Midwest and Texas, where she heard the coyotes howl all night. She had been cool on that trip and was not prepared for the Florida heat.

We took her to see all the local attractions for tourists in central Florida: Cypress Gardens, Six Gun Territory, and Silver Springs. She seemed to enjoy watching me put the animals through their routines and she enjoyed Charlotte. She suffered the high temperatures, but tolerated living with gorillas. I'm certain her report to Father after the first trip held much that was strange and unbelievable. The second trip topped the first, and I could almost see him shaking his head. He knew I was making a success of the animal business, but he didn't know that I had gorillas sitting at my table, drinking my champagne, and even using my commode. To say that the trip to the Florida Compound was an eye-opening experience is not an exaggeration. Mother seemed to enjoy the adventure, but I'm certain that her return to Rennes was, for her, a return to sanity. Perhaps she needed that although she indicated that the situation with Gerard was deteriorating and yet she didn't want him to leave her. She adored the boy; she'd raised him. But in loving him so, it must have been particularly painful to witness the rebellion and feel the hurt that his disrespect demonstrated. She was such a gentle, loving woman, and I'm sure she suffered greatly what must have seemed like failure in raising Gerard.

Soon after Mother left, I began to focus on a tour with Don Ameche. It was touted as being an extraordinary opportunity. Because the television audience reception to the *International Showtime* program had been wonderful, Don decided to take the show live cross-country to large cities. I was included in the cast to show either the leopards, greyhounds, or tigers in different designated cities.

The tiger act required a semi to move it from one show to another.

Ameche felt with the publicity achieved from the television exposure that advertising was not necessary for the road shows. Reality painfully demonstrated the fallacy of his thinking. With no planned promotional material nor appropriated funds toward any sort of advance notice of "our coming," first to Memphis, then Toledo followed by St. Louis, we played "cold turkey." It turned out to be a real turkey — no audience. No one seemed to know that we were arriving or had arrived, and few came to find us. It was bleak performing to near-empty arenas.

On one occasion we were booked into Providence. I arrived with my cats ten days ahead of the scheduled opening performance. Hubert Castle arrived several days later and came to me.

"Robert, this thing is dying."

I agreed with him. We were all getting paid and showing up for each of the previously scheduled bookings, but Ameche was going bankrupt in the process.

"Why don't we do something to help him?" Hubert continued. "Do you think you could turn one of your cats loose in the building? We call the media and then you capture the wild beast."

I thought it was plausible to create a stir, but we encountered a problem right from the start. When I opened the cage to release Sabu, he didn't want to leave the safe confines. I had one hell of a time coaxing him out. If his reluctance had been witnessed by the media, the plan of letting a dangerous, ferocious animal loose to ballyhoo our presence in town would have backfired. Finally, Sabu emerged, obviously suspicious, and slowly began to investigate his surroundings. He was given free reign of the arena during the night. The media was called the following morning to come see the empty cage and take down the details of pending terror.

"Dangerous cat loose and threatening . . . with great difficulty Mr. Baudy captured the cat and returned it to the confines of its cage," read the article in the paper the following day.

It actually took very little time for me to get Sabu back into his cage. When I became intent on the finale of my performance before the press, I even managed to illicit some growls and good action before persuading the leopard to re-enter. We milked the hell out of the publicity and drew a packed house. The newspaper article elevated me to a fearless hero able to capture the cat with merely a masterful use of persuasion and without the use of drugs. The publicity cost Ameche nothing, but every performance for the run of the show was sold out. I celebrated by giving myself a handsome reward for an exceptional performance — a three-carat diamond ring.

I had been away from the compound for six weeks. I had accepted an engagement to show the tigers, languishing in the Florida sunshine, and not rehearsed during my absence. With all that was going on and all that I had to do to prepare for leaving again, there was no time to work the animals before packing them into the semi along with my retinue of helpers.

Off we went with a big question mark as to whether the cats would perform well. We arrived at the designated arena, a large building never before worked by me. The act was performed with absolutely no time to rehearse. I faced the performance with trepidation, never before having shown the tigers without a practice run. It all turned out amazingly well. They went through the whole performance without missing a beat, like a finely tuned clock. The key to their successful performance, under the most extraordinary circumstances, was their retention of every orchestrated move. I believe this was largely due to the fact that I always kept them in separate cages while at the compound. They were never permitted to romp together, which would cause them to lose the discipline and the mind-set necessary to maintain and perform a synchronized act. It was a tribute to their intelligence and also to my diligent training.

As I traveled, I constantly met people interested in wild animals and professionals knowledgeable about certain species. I continued to make contacts with people who knew of The Rare Feline Breeding Center, and many became clients, and some became lifelong friends.

I was playing an indoor engagement at the Indianapolis Fairgrounds when Doutchka became ill. I called for a vet. There was no veterinarian available, but one of the show organizers called a friend, Dr. Ed Schaffer, a local orthopedic surgeon. I appreciated Ed's ability to treat the tiger by taking a stool sample and after analysis prescribing the appropriate antibiotic. Dr. Schaffer's keen interest in animals led to a pleasant, ongoing exchange of information and an instant bonding. When I completed the engagement, I continued to be in contact with Ed who became not only a friend but, over the years, an avid collector of wild animals which I provided. He contained them on a 47-acre farm outside Indianapolis. Ultimately, Ed had camels, llamas, giraffes, and zebras at his farm. He was just one of many in a developing client list of individual trainers, collectors, and even zoos. It was becoming imperative that I make yearly trips to the continent to perpetuate what I had begun in the breeding center.

On the trip to Europe in 1964, I received alarming news. The adventure was unexpectedly interrupted by a conversation with Father's surgeon, who had performed exploratory surgery and reported he'd found prostate cancer. He'd given Father radiation treatments, but the cancer was diagnosed as terminal and had metastasized. Continued radiation therapy was contraindicated. The doctor felt Father would not live for more than a year. Mother had been fully assessed of the condition, but the surgeon chose not to inform his patient. I was stunned and saddened by the revelation.

The trip on to Africa that year was shortened and distracted. When I returned to the States, I became more diligent in contacting the family following the shocking prognosis. Whenever I called, I was relieved to hear their voices declare that he felt well, and I sensed that both Father and Mother were being honest with me. Father was also being honest in his assessment of Gerard's continuing abhorrent behavior. I was frustrated with the situation and with my inability to effect a change. Mother seemed more determined than ever to have the boy remain in France. I imagine she lived everyday with the knowledge that Father's condition was terminal. She was going to loose her husband and couldn't face loosing Gerard as well.

When I visited in Rennes the following year and the year after that, I was elated to find Father in seemingly robust health, his weight and color good, enjoying his pipe, his daily dose of reading, and three glasses of wine. It was a blessing to realize the doctor's prognosis was wrong. But I knew something had to change where Gerard was concerned. He was more of a problem than grandparents deserved, but Mother adored him and I felt stymied in finding a solution.

After visiting the family both in 1965 and 1966, I traveled from Paris to Madagascar. I'd read an article in *National Geographic* about the ancestors of the de Heaulme Family, expatriates who had escaped France during the Revolution. They'd settled on an island off the southeast coast of Africa and soon became one of the most prominent families residing there. They amassed extensive property and enterprise in the south near Fort Dauphin — Dauphin "heir to the throne." The family empire ultimately consisted of thousands of acres of land cultivated in the succulent plant from which sisal rope is manufactured. In addition, the family owned and operated a large and prosperous automobile dealership and had extensive mining interests. They were also dynamically involved in the preservation of rare species of animals, with lemurs in great abundance on their private preserve.

I'd written the family and received replies to my correspondence that were cordial in accepting my request to investigate their well-stocked reserve. I was particularly interested in the importation of lemurs. I had also contacted reptile authorities and other individuals and organizations to further enhance my collection.

On the first leg of the journey, I flew to Antananarivo, capital of Madagascar. On the approach from 20,000 feet, I saw graphically the unique problem of the once heavily forested land. The island was bleeding to death. The reddish-orange *alluvions* originating from the many rivers flowing west into the Mozambique Channel, extending almost 75 miles into the sea. When man arrived less than 2,000 years before, the island was completely covered with luxuriant forest. With the exception of rugged coastal areas, massive deforestation had scalped and laid bare the majority of the landmass, 85 percent of its unique flora devastated. In the process, the rich superficial humus had washed to the sea. Nowhere did I see such a vivid testimony to what Father had prophesied: "We are the cancer of the earth!" The obscene process is still under way today. I had studied about the island, and knew that for millions of years species and subspecies prospered on the island, and I was eager to participate in a visual feast and hoped to acquire some rare species to add to my collection for breeding purposes.

My first stop was Orstom, a French Research Center sponsored by the French Government. I met members of the staff who were helpful in getting importation permits signed and cleared. The paper work became a three-day project.

I went by archaic train from Antananarivo to Perinet. It was astonishing how well the stodgy, old, smoking contraption negotiated the grades and curves through the remaining east-coast rain forest. The purpose of my initial visit was to see the extremely rare and beautiful Indri Lemur protected in a state reserve. From the terminal in Perinet, I took a cab to the northernmost trail requesting the driver to pick me up six hours later at the same precise location. There was a guide riding with us, but I persuaded him that I wanted to explore alone and not to worry about me. Since his explicit job was to worry about me, I had to pay him extra to allow me to do the excursion solo.

I proceeded in a straight, northerly direction for nearly five miles. With every step I was consumed and impressed by the majestic beauty of rugged, misty, mysterious Perinet forests and peaks. I finally picked a hiding place under a canopy of huge umbrella-shaped, prehistoric-looking ferns. It was midmorning and I waited for the Indris' calling sounds, a piercing cry that carries for miles. Soon I heard the primitive, raucous cacophony and, cupping my hands, returned an acceptable imitation. Absolute silence followed. I waited, then heard a single cry closer. Again I responded, and through absolute immobility finally observed from my damp hideout a beautiful varicolored male Indri perhaps trying to locate the "new kid on the block."

I was completely fascinated as I watched the large, magnificent male, hardly noticing that my face and arms were covered with small, half-inch-long, bright green arboreal leeches. I didn't come this far into the Perinet reserve, successfully attracting a wonderful specimen of Indri to within sight, to bother with a few leeches. I remained immobile. Suddenly, I heard the all-too familiar crackling of dead limbs on the forest floor, and the Indri vanished. I was instantly angered by the intrusion. The noise grew closer, then a man materialized through the huge fronds. I saw first a battered pith helmet and then light-reflected gold-rimmed glasses.

A very distinguished gentleman about 70 years of age broke through the underbrush, carrying a long stick terminating in a hook. The man was busy looking at gigantic and gnarled jungle trees. I stood, nearly knocking him off his feet, and greeted him, "*Bonjour.*" He fell back, then recovered as I introduced myself. His reply came in clipped British. We curiously eyed each other. I was covered with tenacious green leeches, his pith helmet askew. We started to laugh and explain the reasons for our presence in this remote enchanted forest.

He was a Madagascan orchid collector who possessed a book listing 1,000 orchid collectors throughout the world. He informed me that he made a fine living shipping the unique plants to individuals and nurseries. He also told me about the "bloody leeches" which I was pulling from my skin as he spoke. He lighted a cigarette and touched one with the lighted end; the burrowing parasite dropped to the ground. He explained, "When you pull them with your hands, you leave the head under the skin, and I'm afraid that tomorrow you will suffer some inconvenience." He was obviously well-acquainted with the subject of leeches in spite of the typically British understatement. After my return to guide, driver, and Antananarivo, I developed a fever and many abscesses

Lemurs would become residents in the compound.

where I'd pulled the leeches from my body. Several hot showers and a vintage bottle of French Sauterne and I was ready to return to Perinet armed with cigarettes and a lighter.

Following the successful Indri sighting, the next stop was Fort Dauphin, 600 miles by light plane to the south. After settling into a hotel, I was soon met by members of the de Heaulme Family. I enjoyed a tour of their reserve where many ring-tail lemurs were evident in a natural habitat. The ring-tail is a ground animal, while most other species of lemur are arboreal or tree inhabitants. I watched closely as they lifted and looked under stones for food. They were protected in the reserve and demonstrated absolutely no fear of their fascinated audience.

I left the de Heaulmes ready to do some exploring on my own, to hunt for radiated tortoise. The unique tortoise is a beautiful specimen living in the desert and gaining an average weight of 30 pounds. The de Heaulmes had directed me to a driver with a station wagon who knew the country well. The land journey took hours before we arrived at the ideal location for spotting and catching the rare tortoise. I left the man in the station wagon and told him to blow the horn periodically to alert me of his location. As far as the eye could see was sky larger and bluer than any I can ever remember. The dramatic horizon was drawn by xerophyte, a low brush which gave the appearance of dead foliage. I soon found that to be a mirage. Xerophyte is lethal and very much alive with three-inch long thorns. The flat plain was occasionally broken by magnificent prehistoric baobab trees reaching 150 feet in the air. It was an incredible sight.

With little rain in the area, the tortoise do not migrate except when the rain drives them from their shelters. I searched for the distinguishing path that would lead to a specimen. I soon found five tortoise that I returned to the station wagon before departing in search of a large specimen which had left an impressive track. I followed the trail through bush for hours, scratched by the cruel thorns, until I became disoriented. By this time, the sky had filled with clouds, no longer was the sun a source of direction. I'd heard that other explorers had died from lack of water and exposure when they became disoriented in the semidesert, and it certainly seemed that I might receive a similar obituary. I wandered for two days listening for an automobile horn.

As I continued moving in search of the man and station wagon, I saw wonderful species that I'd never seen or even heard of before. By walking in ever-widening circles, I finally found my way back to the original location and to the driver, who had gone to Fort Dauphin and back in my absence.

I had a permit to collect 50 tortoise, but I didn't fill my quota on the first trip to Madagascar. However, I ultimately brought 60 of the large reptiles to the States, including five different species. Twenty-five of them were sold to the New York Zoological Society; the society in turn released them on an island off the Carolina coast. I am proud to say that thanks to my getting lost in that damned forest in Madagascar, the tortoise are doing well and continuing to propagate off our eastern shore.

While on the island, I also had in mind bringing back an egg of the largest bird that ever existed in historical time, the *aepyornis*, which became extinct a thousand years before. When man arrived on Madagascar, they killed the huge, 1000-pound birds that grew to 11 feet in height. The eggs, measuring nearly two feet, are still found occasionally after a heavy rain. I was not successful in finding a whole egg but managed to dig some shells, remnants of ancient eggs.

I returned from the trip with many species of lemur never before seen in America. I found fat-tail lemur, for which the Lincoln Park Zoo was a customer for two of the rare and unusual species. I found dwarf lemur, and at night I hunted for some of the smallest primates in the world, the mouse lemur. The tiny lemurs lived in holes of trees, and I was given permission to find the microscopic monkeys on a state preserve. I was not familiar with the terrain, but knew where to search for the hidden specimens and wandered from tree to tree in the dark. When I found a habitat hole, I used a wire, similar in diameter to a coat hangar, and, wearing gloves, worked the wire into the potential nest very gently, until it hit the soft, thick hair of the creature. Twisting the wire slowly and carefully into the hair, I was able to safely extricate the monkey out of the hole and into a waiting burlap sack.

I took many trips abroad to acquire different species. The natives, always curious, stayed behind.

After the successful hunt, as dawn broke, I noticed a piece of blue material on the far side of a 60-foot wide river that ran very close to where we'd been hunting. My guide informed me that a child from the nearest village, six miles distant, had accompanied her mother for water to be carried back to the village. A crocodile savagely attacked and ate the child leaving a remnant of her clothing as the only evidence of the grisly assault that had happened just days before. I just shook my head. I had no idea the Madagascan crocodile was so close and so menacing to our nocturnal hunt. It was chilling as the native related statistics on the 18-foot crocs. Originating on the African continent, they had found their way to Madagascar where the species prospered and became larger and meaner than their continental cousins. My informant said they were not only very fast, but also very aggressive.

I had been in contact with Dr. Roland Albizanc, a French scientist who published a paper on the captive breeding of a very rare animal called the fossa fossa. I was aware of the research paper and fascinated by his accomplishment as the first person to breed the unusual animal that looked like a small puma. Weighing 70 pounds at maturity, the fossa fossa possessed the characteristics of different species of animals similar to the mongoose or cat with retractable claws, but a breeding system like a civet or dog. The fossa fossa, the color of the puma, was a predator that savored chickens, threatening the farmers' inventory. Dr. Albizanc told me that he could have some fossa captured for the breeding compound. In retrospect, I should have taken him up on his offer, one of many that I didn't accept for species never before seen in the States. There were just too many animals arriving regularly at the compound. Orders were received from clients all over the country as I sought the rare and near-extinct, but I couldn't handle every species no matter how tempting.

While in Madagascar I received disturbing news. An American expedition, apparently with the permission of the local Government and with knowledge and supervision of the United States Embassy, was conducting a lemur hunt to provide species for a southwestern zoo. The directors of the project conscripted the services of natives from a village in the northeast portion of the island. The only weapons utilized by the crudely equipped hunters were sling shots. The planned strategy, to knock the lemurs out in the hope that they would survive, developed into a massacre of the frightened primates. Many monkeys didn't survive, and news of the bestial capture incensed authorities and animal advocates on the island. The de Heaulme Family staunchly and vocally opposed the atrocity.

After each of my trips abroad, I returned to the States always exhausted but stimulated by the unique adventures and in the company of some wonderful, exciting specimens, or with the knowledge that many wild species would be arriving on the compound soon. My return to the reality of life at home also took me back to family. In December, 1966, I received word that Grandmother had died. She'd survived Grandfather by 11 years, the last of which were spent living like a hermit in the old monastery. I thought back to the early years, to my childhood and of the love she so generously offered, to the wonderful example she set for my mother. My thoughts turned to Mother, in Rennes suffering not only the loss of a mother, but living with an aging, tyrannical husband diagnosed with cancer, and together struggling to raise and supervise a grandson who was clearly out of control. My chosen lifestyle had not offered much solace to either Grandmother or Mother, and I felt remorse and guilt, but also deep love and compassion for the women who bore so much pain and still had the capacity to give love unselfishly.

I did not return to France for the funeral. There were contracts to fill as well as animals arriving on the compound. The pace was hectic with many different demands pulling at me, and I began to realize that the tour was taking a toll both physically and emotionally. It was becoming tougher to maintain the pace, impossible really, and a drastic change was needed.

30

GERARD

I was totally immersed and focused on business when the message came. Father called from Rennes to say he was putting Gerard on a plane for the States. He explained the reason for the sudden expulsion. The boy had taken a job with the postal service in Rennes. He worked the night shift where wine was consumed against regulations during working hours and arrived at the apartment drunk. Father went on to relate that on two occasions Gerard had wrecked automobiles. Once he'd been forbidden to take the vehicle. Father said that he could no longer tolerate the boy's rebelliousness. Gerard's flight would arrive in New York, and Odette had also been contacted. I was caught off guard by the sudden turn of events and lost little time calling her. We had much to talk about.

Odette had married Ed Swan in 1961. While I knew that she'd married, I knew nothing of the details. Apparently Odette and Ed had formed an attachment while I was still married to her, while we winter-quartered at the Swan horse farm in Bucks County in the early 1950s. She went on to describe what I knew to be an affluent lifestyle. There were several houses located on the Bucks County property. They resided in one until 1964 when they purchased a 75-acre estate which included a large house built in 1760. She also told me that before she married Ed, she was showing the dove act comprised of 30 doves and had actually owned as many as a 100 birds at one time. There was much to learn of my first wife, after years of no communication.

My trips to France didn't include contact with her family, and I had been raised by a father who advised, "Do not dwell on the past but concentrate on the present and get on with the future." I naturally heard of Odette's remarriage from my parents, but I didn't retain much of the information, choosing instead to focus on the business at hand. And there was never any time for gossip or listening to lengthy dissertations unless they had to do with the animal business or something equally compelling.

Odette and Ed met Gerard's plane and took the boy back to their estate. After five days, they put him on a flight to Tampa. Gerard was 19 years old and arrived with an attitude that could best be described as guarded. He'd been expelled from France by a furious, frustrated, and terminally ill grandfather and an equally frustrated, but adoring grandmother. I'm certain he was filled with resentment and fear, excitement and anticipation, and many conflicting emotions as he traveled for the first time to the States to be with parents who'd been too occupied with new marriages and careers to know him well. And he'd heard over the years about life on tour and the many exciting, life-threatening adventures of an animal trainer father. He'd never been effusive, but in the present circumstance I had to initiate all conversation. I think he was embarrassed, and I'm sure he was overwhelmed by the rapid turn of events which would so completely change his life.

As we drove from the airport to the compound, he was noticeably surprised by the central Florida landscape. I explained to him, as I pointed to a huge expanse of natural wilderness, that it was a green swamp that contained bears, Florida panther, and alligators. He was reacting typically, as most Europeans did, to witnessing the wilderness and the wild animals that so naturally abound. Most foreigners have no concept of central Florida. Instead of beaches and tropical growth, it reminds them more of Africa in its vastness and habitation.

Gerard met Charlotte and the 15-years-old twins, Leida and Linda. We had two bedrooms in the apartment: one used by the girls, the other by Charlotte and me. A small separate apartment in the back was designated as Gerard's. Gerard had been well-educated and spoke some English. Spanish and Latin were other languages that were familiar, but he seemed most comfortable conversing in French. The language barrier would prove to be one of several problems complicating and clouding his relationship with Charlotte. As time went on, he was more vocal with me when we were alone after the initial shyness, but he remained reserved with his stepmother. I knew from the beginning that his presence could create serious conflict.

We did not discuss the episodes in France that resulted in his expulsion. It was not going to serve any purpose to dissect or analyze past history, but I knew well what his behavior had been, and I knew that he had a drinking problem, which he tried to hide from me.

The first weeks with Gerard were spent sightseeing throughout the area. I wanted very much for him to become comfortable with his new surroundings, particularly with Charlotte, and I hoped that in sharing some local adventures and having some fun I might succeed in breaking his reserve, but I was not successful in that. I must say that Charlotte tried to provide a normal home situation. When we were at home, she did the cooking and she did very well. I had trained her to cook French cuisine, and she took to the process readily.

A positive aspect of Gerard's presence was the opportunity, finally, for me to be his full-time father. I was determined to give it my best shot. As a matter of fact, I took more time off the tour and enjoyed staying at the compound. As the animal import business increased, I cut back dramatically on the road trips. I had become more selective in signing only contracts for the big circus performances and the more lucrative TV shows. I made more money with less work and less travel. There were engagements where I was booked to show all three acts together. The Shrine Circus in Texas was an example of a huge extravaganza, where 60 different acts were signed to perform. It was a wonderful contract for me that required all the animals going in one direction, rather than the complicated multicity tour with each act going to separate locations. On the occasions when contracts pulled us away from Florida, Gerard and the girls remained at the compound with Charlotte's parents and relatives supervising the three teenagers in our absence.

As the weeks and months went by, I attempted to demonstrate my training methods to Gerard. I wanted to share with him and educate him in what I had chosen as my profession, but more than that I wanted to penetrate his innermost thoughts and emotions. However, from the very beginning there existed a wall between us that I hated but could not break through. The only times he really opened up was when he'd had too much to drink. Then his thoughts and his behavior were unfocused, and it was painful to see that he needed alcohol to more freely express himself; but even then, I didn't feel that he was being honest with me or himself. He was obviously a troubled young man.

Charlotte and I tried to include Gerard in our leisure activities. We loved the outdoors and enjoyed natural pursuits. I loved to hunt and often dove for fish or hunted for game to be shared with friends. Gerard was a city boy, obviously repelled by the outdoor activities and uncomfortable in such surroundings. He watched me working with the animals and became aware of the dangers associated with the many animals on the compound as well as those in the wilds of central Florida. He couldn't understand my desire or my pleasure in any part of the occupation. As I related one incident and he witnessed others, I'm sure he thought me quite insane.

One close call that I recounted to him involved diving one evening for mullets. I was using a mask, snorkel, and spear quite intent on capturing enough mullet to feed five or six guests for a barbecue. As I worked my way through the tall reeds close to the bank, suddenly, out of nowhere, appeared a huge fang-filled mouth open to clamp down on any intruder. I pulled back just in time to escape being savagely bitten by a large female gator protecting her nest. I quickly retreated without being hit, which was a miracle. The attentive mother gator wanted me out of her territory and very effectively demonstrated that desire. I laughingly related the incident to Charlotte and Gerard, but could see that he was horrified by the perilous event. He saw no humor in the story and was even repulsed by the violence described.

He did say to me one day, "I want to do everything you did in your life." I was stunned, even flattered, by his revelation. He obviously had heard the war stories and of my show business experiences over the years, but had never once demonstrated the least interest in any of what I expressed. He never asked any questions. I was totally surprised when he wanted to follow in my footsteps. I was also profoundly touched by his words, but knew it was folly to think that he could perform as an animal trainer. I told him that I found it difficult to believe that he wanted to emulate me when he never even expressed the slightest interest in animals, that he never wanted to go hunting with me, to train animals, or even to have them as pets. I went on to try to explain what I felt was good advice.

"Look, Gerard, if you want to do something with your life, you speak three languages fluently, you're good-looking, you can make a career in a field that would be more in common with what you have."

It was all so nebulous. When I was his age, Father had tried to guide me with little success, even though he was with me and a part of my life since I was a little guy. How could I think it different for me as a father trying to guide a son who had rarely been with me physically or emotionally — a son who was floundering badly. I wanted to help him, to reach him, but I was making no headway. I continued to try to reach out for his sake as well as mine.

He'd been watching me go through the routines with the tigers and leopards, dogs and monkeys. I let him handle the babies born at the compound, but he was awkward and frightened by the mature dangerous animals. He did not possess the innate instincts of an animal person nor were his hands, or his body, or his vocal capabilities strong enough to work the animals and command their respect. The animals sensed the weakness which created further possible danger in the arena.

I was attempting to be a father to Gerard when in June, 1967, I had word that my father was failing rapidly. I was scheduled to go to Africa for three weeks to arrange for a shipment of gorillas, but the situation in Rennes took priority. Immediately on arrival, I saw a man withered from the terrible cancer. When I talked to his doctors, they advised me to remain in Rennes; the end was near. Mother was stoic, but I knew she needed me, and I wanted to be there for her, but also for a father who had denied my success almost to the end. He had been a successful entrepreneur adamantly opposed to my choice of profession when I went to work at Paul's compound with a pregnant wife, and he'd gone into a violent rage when I declined his final offer of the meat market in Le Vesinet, preferring to be an animal trainer. He expressed dogmatic refusal to ever again offer aid or assistance — I was on my own. He had been tough and always refused to attend a perfor-

Father holding my gift to him — a toy poodle. Mother in center with a friend.

mance of the greyhounds and monkeys as the act toured Europe and gained the esteem of a broad audience of my peers. He remained staunch in his denial of my chosen profession until I showed him the contracts that came to me in America and as he received the money that I sent to care for Gerard. But still it was difficult for him to admit that I had indeed found success in the animal training business.

Now as he lay on his death-bed, he was a reduced man both physically and mentally, and he asked that I talk about horses. Father loved his horses. He had ridden for years and owned horses and knew that I had land in Florida and owned horses. He even expressed the desire to visit the compound, but now it was too late.

As I sat by his bed, he asked, "Please tell me about your

horses." I described to him the horses that I bought when I first obtained the land in Sumter County and then went on to vividly detail the horses born on the compound. I was grateful to witness the peace and pleasure he derived in listening. He didn't have the strength to focus totally and would occasionally make comments in French, then revert to Latin, which I did not fully understand. I recognized it was a natural process for the highly educated, dynamic man who had been my tutor and my guide — the one person from whom I wanted acceptance and acknowledgment.

He finally uttered the words that he had been wrong — I was right. I had found success and he was proud of me, although he amended his comments admitting that I had been an exception to the rule. It mattered not that his assessment was amended — he had finally offered what I waited years to hear, and I was deeply touched as I sat, tears stinging my cheeks, watching and listening to his final words before he went to sleep.

The following day I witnessed what was like the gates of heaven opening and the wrath of God being spewed against a wicked world with enough symbolism to incur a spiritual rebirth. I remember well Mother coming to me very upset.

"What's the matter?" I asked.

"Oh, Robert," she cried, "something bad is going to happen today!"

I attempted to sooth her, "Mother, something bad and something good happens every day!"

She continued, "But I saw the crows on the window sill."

"I see them every day. You know I feed them."

"No, no, something bad is going to happen."

There was no placating her on this dazzling, clear vivid-blue-sky day in such complete departure from the grey dismal days that preceded it. At two o'clock in the afternoon, the air turned heavy and the sky quickly turned to inky thick clouds filling the atmosphere with dampness. Father called for his medicine. Just as he alerted us to his breathing difficulty, the power went off. In the darkened apartment, we could not find a flashlight nor could we find his pills. Mother became hysterical as Father gasped for breath. The double windows in the sitting room suddenly blew out, spewing glass noisily across the floor as the powerful wind swept billowing curtains, like violent intruding ghosts into the darkened apartment. Furniture was lifted and moved in what appeared like a science fiction scene. The sudden, foreboding events were in strong contrast to what had been a bright, calm, beautiful afternoon. We finally found father's medication and took the pills and some water to him. He anxiously took the pills and swallowed them.

As suddenly as the onslaught came, the storm abated. As I stood next to Father's bed, holding his hand, he died. At the very same moment, a look of calm came over his face, and I heard a terrific crash. The steeple on the old Catholic Church, just a hundred yards from the apartment, fell to the ground decimating cars parked below. Within minutes the sky cleared as if a blanket of blue had been drawn across. Father lay peacefully in his bed.

The following days were spent in preparation for the funeral. The families had been notified and many came on Father's side whom I had never met. Uncle Gauthier's strength was missed. He had died of a heart attack years before. Relatives from Niévre, Mother's side of the family, were not able to make the long, arduous trip. Mother, devastated, maintained a veneer of strength through the ordeal; the days were shrouded in grey. She was left quite alone with her Emile gone.

When the family dispersed, she was left with me, and I knew that I could not stay with her for long. I discussed the possibility of her returning to the States, but she preferred to remain in Rennes and within days of Father's passing was again embroiled in volunteer work which had been ongoing since they moved into the apartment located just two blocks from the Catholic Hospital. She had taken on the responsibilities when they arrived from Fegreac. The work was the constant in her life which kept her sane through the trauma of Gerard's behavioral problems and Father's illness and would now be her mainstay with both Gerard, whom she had raised and idolized, and her Emile gone.

I left her to fly on to Africa, although my time there would be far less than originally planned. But at least I knew that Mother was in good company with the nuns at the hospital and the patients who adored her. The many hours spent at the hospital had been a source of discontent to Father, who was of the opinion that she could perform the very same work at a government facility as a salaried employee and also enjoy the benefits of retirement. Mother never performed any duty with the thought of remuneration. She was a "Mother Teresa" filled with love for the people with whom she worked and cared for; the hospital, the nuns, and the patients were the nucleus of her existence. In that I knew she was needed and that need alone would sustain her. I flew directly back to the compound from Africa.

My arrival home was met with many emotionally charged relationships and undercurrents that were eroding what I had envisioned as my permanent quarters. With me so dynamically immersed in a new business demanding more and more of my time, it was becoming difficult to maintain any semblance of what I tried to achieve. There was no outright unpleasantness between Charlotte and Gerard, but there was tension. Charlotte complained that she found it almost impossible to communicate with the boy. There was much she didn't understand about him — one puzzling phenomena that she brought to my attention was the way he perspired so heavily even when the weather was cool. The perspiration was caused by tension and also excessive alcohol consumption. I was concerned about many facets of Gerard's physical, as well as psychological being. I was upset by several episodes when he became drunk and withdrawn.

When I felt the need of a break not only for me and Charlotte, but for Gerard as well, I bought a ticket for him to return to Pennsylvania to visit his mother and Ed Swan. Apparently, a car had been purchased for him to use when he stayed with the Swans. He was extremely proud of the fact that he had his own vehicle. It was a used car, but equipped with all kinds of electronic gadgetry. In a way they were pampering him, but they tried to be strict. When he arrived in Bucks County, the law was laid down. Gerard was told that he was not to drink any alcohol and he was not to bring "home" undesirables. He was even given a curfew. Although the room in the mansion, handsomely decorated just for him, was designed to make him feel at home and the car was an extravagance to further demonstrate caring, the rules were too severe and beyond Gerard's capacity to fully appreciate the reasons why. In his youthful, rebellious mode, he overstepped the bounds, wrecked the automobile, and came back to Florida sooner than either Charlotte or I wanted.

He'd been spoiled in France by too much leniency and the

absence of strong parental influence. He had left his grandparents in turmoil, had upset the Swan household, and was not able to come up to what he perhaps saw as my example. Obviously, the boy was suffering many inner demons and hurts and I tried to be patient — tried not to put too much pressure on him. For too many years Odette and I had been only yearly visitors who, while loving him, did not spend the time needed to guide, direct, and mold a young life. How could we expect respect or adherence to discipline when he was thrust into our lives after the pattern of his behavior was set. We were naïve to even think we could change him and were ill-equipped to fully understand all of what he was suffering. It was too late — disaster was in the making. I only hoped that somehow, someone or something would change the pattern. We had failed the boy in our acquiescence to Mother's desire to raise him. It really seemed the best for all concerned in the early years — particularly with careers in the making. Now as he shuttled back and forth from the compound to Bucks County and felt the underlying rejection and disapproval that his antisocial behavior created, his ambivalence deepened. He searched for a way to escape or at least discover a means to prove himself, but he was losing ground on all fronts.

  He applied for a green card with the ultimate goal of becoming a citizen. It reminded me of my legal harangue years before when I sought freedom from George Hamid. George had threatened at the time that I'd never work for anyone else in the States and that he'd block any and every attempt at my becoming a citizen.

  When I was finally legally admitted, I lost little time investigating how to become a citizen. I obtained the book of requirements from the Immigration Service and began to study the history of the country and also to improve my English. I even had thoughts of changing my name. I'd resented the American pronunciation of Baudy (Bawdy) which gave it a vulgar connotation; I preferred the French version pronounced Beaudé. I studied American History as I toured and worked my way across the country fulfilling contracts, expanding my career, and establishing my reputation. It was soon apparent that my name was gaining popularity and recognition obviating the need to change it. It was five years after the Hamid days when I made final preparation to take the oath. I passed the stringent physical examination and added

Bray as a middle name in case I wanted to drop the Baudy, but I never did. I was sworn in along with 50 other inductees in the Federal Court in Tampa on April 3, 1958. Thirty-five years old at the time, I was living one hell of a life, at the pinnacle of my chosen career, and making more money than I ever imagined.

But times had changed; so much was different when Gerard made application. There were no common denominators. He was soon visited by an Army recruiter who informed him that in view of the Vietnam War any foreigners applying for a green card had the choice of either signing up for military duty or having their application filed away for an indeterminate period. This policy applied only to those individuals who qualified to serve in the armed services; Gerard was a prime candidate. He made the decision to sign into the army for three years without consulting me. It was either sign or return to France. I knew that the service would be brutal. He was not accustomed to discipline, and I knew in the military he'd be overdosed on that. He would either become a man or be buried under the regulations.

Soon he was sent to North Carolina for basic training. It was not long before he was expelled from the camp. I was upset by the treatment received, as he explained it, excessive and intolerable. I hated that he was dishonored in such a way, particularly since he'd volunteered; but I was not assessed of the severity of his misdemeanor, which I'm sure was committed in hopes of being discharged. However, the Army had other plans. Instead of a discharge, he was sent to a second training facility in the swamps of Louisiana, where the training and the discipline were more severe.

He somehow stayed the course and toughed it out. With the swamp training complete, Gerard became a full fledged PFC and returned to the compound on leave. He was handsome in uniform, but demonstrated a totally negative attitude toward the military. His grandmother came to visit before he left on duty. The visit was highly emotional. She had not fully recovered from Father's death and now her beloved Gerard, who had been put out of Rennes by his grandfather, was going off to war. I felt so much love and compassion for the gentle, loving woman who was my mother, who had become Gerard's mother. The men in her life had given her much heartache. Thank God, her faith was sustaining, but I could sense and see the pain she carried.

My concern for the boy was also great. Thus far, the military had not influenced him except in a negative way. He was embittered and told me the camp was pure hell. I said, "I tried to prepare you for that... this American Army is much stricter than the French Army and the basic training is very serious." He agreed but was cynical.

"I sure as hell found that out, but it's not as tough as the French Foreign Legion."

I found his attempt to put down my comments and also belittle the American military to be imma-

Mother came to see her grandson in uniform.

ture. I knew the training had been brutal, but what was ahead was going to be far worse. He'd taken on a false bravado, and I could feel the crash coming. He sat at dinner one night after drinking too much and in a display of bravery in front of guests announced that the Army was trying to break him, but they couldn't do it. As he spoke, he pushed a lighted cigarette into the palm of his hand to the horror of all who witnessed the brazen, drunken performance. I was quite disgusted by the alcohol-induced act.

When Gerard went off to Vietnam, I hoped and prayed that he would not be buried there, but felt no optimism. I knew enough about the horrors of war to know that if a soldier is troubled before he gets into battle, he is certainly not going to come away any less disturbed. And I knew nothing of the logistics and horrors of a war in Asia with the updated weaponry utilizing gas and germ warfare, not to mention reportedly rampant drug use. He was soon placed in an artillery battalion and in hell.

It was not long after Gerard went off to serve his new country in a devastating role, when a call came from Paul le Royer announcing that his son, Christian, had committed suicide. The news was shocking, and I knew it would be a blow to Gerard who considered Christian a friend and confidant. I had introduced the boys years before and as their relationship developed, Gerard visited Paul and the boy at the compound in St. Mande whenever he went by train to Paris to visit relatives and friends. Christian was perhaps an inspiration to Gerard as he watched his young contemporary work with animals. They both had in common fathers who were animal trainers. The boys were a year apart but may have shared many common emotions as I think back. Gerard was not raised in the atmosphere of the ring as was Christian, who knew no other occupation. But Christian was forced by a headstrong father into training and even performing animals against his will.

The handsome, delicate young man was given an uncaged leopard act to perform professionally at the age of 16. Paul explained to me that while working the leopards, Christian fell in love with a showgirl at the Moulin Rouge Nightclub in Paris. The girl was married; Paul opposed the relationship. Paul completely forbade Christian seeing the girl, and there were violent outbursts that nearly came to blows. Apparently the girl had gone off to work in Belgium, then returned to Paris, and told Christian she did not want to continue the affair. The boy became despondent over the lost romance and the ongoing pressures of an insensitive father. Paul was nearly inconsolable. He said he was devastated but also felt another emotion, one of disappointment as he philosophized, "Life is a war, everyday a battle — and my son has deserted."

I felt badly for Paul, but there was little I could say or do to change any of it. However, I did know that I would never, could never, force Gerard to become an animal trainer if he did not want it for all the many complex reasons a person wants and needs to work with animals. I have referred to it as a virus, latent within. It is a physical and emotional need and commitment that cannot be willed or hoped for. It's an innate response that cannot be denied and surfaces naturally with the animals sensing and feeling the rapport. It cannot be forced or hold any pretense.

Ultimately, there were extraordinary coincidences associated with the date of Christian's death. They involved his two leopards, Pantherou and Rina. April 22 became prophetic not only as Christian's birth date in 1948 and then his death on his twentieth birthday; but Pantherou died of old age at Paul's compound on April 22, 1970, exactly two years to the day after Christian's suicide and Rina expired from natural causes on April 22, 1972, four years after the tragic death of her owner.

After Paul's call, I thought a good deal about the boy and about Gerard. I didn't want to convey tragic news, but I felt it had to be shared. I had recognized very early in Paul a domineering, tough, narrow viewpoint that would have applied tremendous pressures on his son. I was not with Gerard during his formative years enough to affect any strong example, nor did I feel I was in a position to make demands on him as he was growing up. All of that was left to grandparents, who were not capable of providing what the young man needed. When Gerard arrived in Florida, I watched him interact with the twins and with other females, and I had the feeling that he was uncomfortable, even denigrating females. I tried many times to draw him out, to have him express some feelings, but I simply could not break through the barrier. He hadn't made it easy to understand him, and yet he wanted more than anything to be understood. He was crying out in his own way, but I didn't fully listen to the pain. Now he was in Vietnam and the news of Christian's death would only serve to give more pain.

My attention was riveted to the demands of the compound. I could never dwell for long on any one drama with so many occurring every day. The breeding of animals did not wait until I was in the breeding business. It had become a part of the daily labor, even while we were on tour and in the middle of performing. There were baby black and spotted leopards that joined our entourage as well as some Siberian tigers born en route which only added to the excitement, complexity, and drama of the tour. I ultimately had over 100 separate complexes built on the compound to contain the many different species as they began to arrive from Africa and other parts of the world, as well as from zoos in the States that offered particular species that interested me to enhance my breeding stock. It took some species four years to mature before the breeding process began, particularly in the case of animals from the wild. Most animals in zoos today are captive-bred. After the first generation in captivity, the process becomes easier. Only one or two pair out of ten animals wild-caught such as

North Chinese Leopard babies Ling and Ming.

ocelot, margay, and clouded leopards will breed successfully in captivity. The combination of stress from being restrained, the change in diet and climate, and in some cases the species being joined to a new mate, all conspire to create difficulty, if not failure in breeding. It became a very complex and challenging process with many disappointments, as well as some very exciting and exhilarating results. New life as well as death on the compound became frequent occurrences.

I was successful in mating a pair of North Chinese leopards. There are 24 subspecies of true leopard. I purchased the Chinese leopards separately, and they were the first rare subspecies of cat that bred at the compound. There were vets nearby whom I used when I needed help to solve medical problems with the animals, but when I had a tough problem with a rare and costly animal, I took the patient to Gainesville, where the University maintains a veterinarian school. The finest doctors were available to perform autopsies and surgeries at the facility, and I became well-acquainted with the staff. Some of the professionals became involved in the Florida Panther technical work in which I, too, would participate eventually. Another feature of the Gainesville facility was the "no charge" policy, mutually beneficial to me and also to young students gaining excellent exposure to rare and exotic animals. The university services were a godsend because a vet bill rendered on a rare animal could run into the thousands. I worked with the doctors at the school and witnessed as well as participated in some of the procedures. I also enjoyed the post-op sessions where, over dinner or lunch, many erudite discussions took place to further enhance my knowledge and to share some of my varied experiences, which the doctors seemed to find entertaining as well as educational.

31

MANY DRAMATIC CHANGES
Beaucoup de Changements Dramatiques

When Gerard left the compound and the country, our lives seemed to return to normal, at least to what had been normal for Robert and Charlotte Baudy and Company before Gerard's arrival. We continued to accept bookings, but our road schedule was greatly reduced.

In 1969, I made the usual trip abroad to visit Mother and to participate in the ongoing search for endangered species. On this particular trip, my business dealings were in Iran with a stop in Istanbul. My pretrip research revealed that a rare subspecies of leopard, the Anatolian, was on display at the Istanbul Zoo. Sadly, the zoo was highly disappointing. The facility, small and less than pristine, contained leopards, not African but of a different subspecies than the Anatolian.

I left and flew on to Tehran. I was on the mailing list of the most highly respected zoological publication: *The International Zoo Yearbook.* I had established contact with the director of the Tehran Zoo, Prince Dovlatshahi, who was related to the Shah, still in power at that time. The scientific director of the zoo, Dr. Mostofi, introduced me to the zoologist, a German ex-Nazi named Arnulf Johannes, the man most knowledgeable and helpful in guiding me through my desired hunt and capture of a Persian leopard. I should amend that: my hoped-for capture of a Persian

The rare and very beautiful large leopard living in the mountains northeast of Tehran is called by the scientific name of *Panther Saxicolor*. There were only three or four of the rare leopards in captivity at that time. When I saw what were reputed to be authentic Persian leopards in Germany and Holland during many years of travel, they did not appear to me to be purebred. My desire was to introduce good stock into my breeding.

Mr. Johannes was in charge of the four-acre zoo, and he put a jeep, driver, and guide at my disposal. However, he neglected to adequately advise of the pitfalls involved in attempting capture of the Persian. We took off heading north for the snowcapped mountains, driving through low-lying, semiarid brush that filled the terrain leading to the mountains, where shepherds tended their flock and complained of the leopards killing the sheep. I quickly became educated in the method used for dealing with the predators by shepherds not armed with weapons. The Shah didn't want his subjects armed.

The shepherds had some tough dogs trained to kill cheetahs and other predators such as snow leopards and Persians. When a leopard appeared, the dogs attacked in hot pursuit and continued running, even occasionally catching and killing the marauders. I knew the hunting process was going to be extremely difficult. It would be necessary for a leopard to be treed in order to tranquilize the specimen, and the dogs were not trained to tree their prey. My idea was to return to Iran at a future date with some helpers and dogs from Sumter County, specifically trained as hunters to tree cats such as bobcats and puma. It would be costly to take an entourage to Iran, but it was perhaps the only way that I'd successfully capture the elusive Persian. I returned to Tehran empty-handed, but not totally disappointed. The trip provided enough enlightenment to fulfill future hunting forays.

With days left before my scheduled flight home, I spent them at the zoo where I witnessed many interesting sights such as villagers carrying a hog-tied cheetah, a beautiful beige-colored specimen. I also saw some baby Syrian bears. As an animal trainer, I was particularly fascinated with the Syrian, the prized bear of all trainers. They are more intelligent than other bears, while not achieving the enormous size of other species. They average 250-300 pounds at maturity, and their light brown coat from a distance takes on a magnificent silver sheen.

While in Tehran I also went to the red-light district. Most cities have one, and I tried to be a tourist whenever, wherever I traveled visiting the finest, exclusive sections as well as the ordinary and seamier districts to sense the culture on all levels of society.

When I was ready to leave Tehran, Prince Dovlatshahi seemed embarrassed by the outcome of the leopard search, and he may even have felt guilty in not having me better informed of the extreme difficulties associated with the hunt. He gave me a handsome eighteenth century dagger from his personal collection as a memento. It is one of many such weapons that I greatly value in my collection. The trip, while not successful in its original intent, was highly educational. I met articulate professionals in the zoological field to further enhance my knowledge and did not feel it wasted in the least.

Soon after returning home, I was feted by the Circus Hall of Fame and presented the Award Of Excellence For A Wild Animal Act. The prestigious annual award honored the finest wild animal act in the business. The ceremony took place in the Hobard Arena in Sarasota and was hosted by Bill Cosby. I worked the tiger act before receiving the award and was deeply touched by the honor and merit cited by my peers. It seemed a rather auspicious time to accept the acclaim and face up to reality; the award came at a time when I had to retire from the arena. I was leaving on a high note. But, quite honestly, the high was not always naturally induced.

There were many reasons for reducing the road activity. I wanted to concentrate on the Rare Feline Breeding Center. With many animals in the compound and the wonderful sources I had for rare and endangered species, my goal for creating a real and successful breeding process was becoming a reality. There were many species in the far reaches of the world that were becoming extinct in an atmosphere of uncaring governments and ignorant human behavior, and I felt compelled to help perpetuate endangered species. It became my passion.

But there was another reason that I had to contend with in preparation for the day when I could no longer perform in the show ring. I was nearing my fiftieth year, and the tour had taken its toll. It had been brutal. There were many contracts over the years that required driving two nights and three days nonstop with no time for sleep or even rest until I had set up and rehearsed the animals and then put on a performance. When I was starting in the business, I handled the extreme demands, but as time went on, it became more difficult, even impossible. It was quite common with show people to use drugs and I had easy access when I wanted or needed them. I began to take speed and other amphetamines in the early 1960s to induce energy and ward off sleep while driving from one city to the next, one circus to the next booking. I also used the speed to stimulate a dynamic performance when exhausted. For years I'd worked under excessive pressure, successfully maintaining a high performance level and feeling fine until I began to notice that my hands were starting to shake. I experienced pains in my chest and my appetite was diminishing. The warning signals were impossible to ignore.

Many portions of the acts demanded split-second timing and accuracy, particularly in the leopard act where the leopard leaps through the air; a fraction of a second could bring disaster. I noticed when I caught the black leopard that I was dislocating my back. I never once missed catching the cat, but my body was catching hell. I had never experienced the problem before taking the amphetamines, and the body seemed to assimilate the drugs with no apparent side effects when I was younger and possessed inexhaustible stamina. But I was on a high just waiting to crash.

With the drug-induced heightened energy level, I began to misstep and miscatch the leopard, putting me out of commission and even in bed for three or four days after a performance. In order to overcome the pain or to perform in spite of the injured back, I took pain killers. I was caught in a vicious cycle of addiction: one of speed-induced pain killed by another drug to enable me to perform, which caused further injures, producing more pain. The damaging cycle placed my career and even my life in jeopardy.

Leaving the show ring was not going to be a hardship. Long ago I'd become detached from the audience. I always demanded of myself and of Charlotte and the animals a well-trained, disciplined performance that was masterful and obviously well-received by the audience, but I worked harder to please me than the anonymous mass that filled the arena and applauded the effort. It was the training that had always fascinated me, and I realized that I could be very happy without the audience if I could continue to work with animals to perpetuate species and save rare animals from extinction.

The compound was a beehive when I decided to hang up my whip in 1970. When I was not present, traveling in the States or out of the country, there were shipments of animals that arrived at the Tampa airport to be picked up by employees. It had become a frequent occurrence resulting from my travels to fill orders from zoos or collectors for animals that I had either captured or sought both domestically or from far-off lands. The animals arrived crated and then had to be processed and acclimated before being sent on. It was obvious that retiring from the arena would not reduce my workload. It simply redirected the demands and priorities and eliminated the pressures of the tour. Retirement would also provide an opportunity to get off the drugs.

Sadly, there was disillusionment with the new venture. Over the years as I became more involved with supplying zoos with animals, I became more knowledgeable about the business and realized that most zoos were no better or different than glorified circus arenas. The purpose seemed to cash as many gate receipts as possible with the welfare of the animals secondary. I witnessed some vile conditions that rightfully inspired the animal rights activists to picket and demand legislation to correct many ills. However, it must also be recognized that often government regulation is counterproductive in the paper shuffling and funding required that often takes precedence over the intended impetus of kinder treatment for innocent victims — the animals.

When the decision to retire was *fait accompli,* I looked forward to spending more time at the compound with Charlotte to enjoy the freedom to devote full-time effort to the import/export business. But there was no peace at the compound. Perhaps the animals were interacting and adjusting to life in the oak hammock with more success than the human inhabitants. While I was going through drug-withdrawal symptoms, Charlotte was going through menopause and also dealing with the trauma of teenage daughters rebelling against boarding school and agonizing over boyfriends, who were not welcome at the compound. I felt it too dangerous to have people come into the hammock who were not involved in business. The liability was too great. In addition, I was working damned hard and was edgy with all the female turmoil plus my own inner demons.

When the girls arrived for weekends, there were vicious

arguments between mother and daughters. I demanded they do their fighting out of my range. I discovered that when I appeared in the house, all conversation ceased, but the level of tension increased. Charlotte reacted by arguing with me and began digging up the past, accusing me of being promiscuous and indulging in affairs in spite of our marriage. I could not deny her allegations, although I hadn't been sexually involved with anyone else for quite some time. I resented her sudden demeaning diatribe and found the whole atmosphere untenable. I was totally intolerant of the accusations and bickering, ready to explode when a provocative phone call offered promise to at least relieve the tension temporarily. I do not mean to lessen Charlotte's case against me. She had justification to be frustrated before the phone call, but I should have realized that Charlotte was in no mood for what I innocently initiated onto the compound. It was going to be the final straw.

The call, from a local farmer, inquired if I would be interested in purchasing a two-year-old, six-legged bull. I could not readily see any immediate use for such a freak, except to give us something unique to talk about. I told the man to bring the strange beast and I'd take a look. On examination I found the poor thing quite tame, in good physical condition, but with a ring in its nose. The extra legs, each two feet long, originated at the top of the withers, the knees and hooves in perfect proportion, odd appendages hanging and dangling as the bull moved. I bought the animal at the current price of beef on hoof and put it to pasture in a fenced area abutting Highway 48. Very soon we began hearing screeching tires as vehicles ground to a halt, their unbelieving occupants startled at the sight of the freak. After several accidents, the sheriff requested I remove the bull from view due to the highway hazard. I moved "Ferdinand" into the center of the hammock where most of the big cats were housed. He was now surrounded by tigers, lions, and leopards, completely riveted by the unorthodox potential prey. The cats spent hours staring at the bull. I left one day to pick up a horse, placing Charlotte in charge. She was out attending to some of the animals' cages while "Ferdy" peacefully grazed nearby.

When I returned, I immediately saw that minor damage had been done to several lemur cages, and I went to look for Charlotte. I found her in the apartment exhausted, dirty, and totally stressed.

She described what had happened. The bull had gone berserk for some unknown reason and chased her from tree to tree for 45 minutes. I quickly realized the reason for the nose ring! I went out to locate the crazed bull, but he found me first, and I had to run for my life by climbing the closest tree. Some employees were able to corral the bull after diverting him, freeing me to help in the capture. We loaded him in one of the trailers and drove to Central Packing four miles from the compound, where his arrival commanded complete cessation of activity.

However, the activity back at the compound did not cease. The allegations continued until one day Charlotte packed all her belongings into one of the two Oldsmobile wagons. I did not attempt to stop her. It had been hell in the hammock for several years ever since Gerard's arrival, but his leaving did not return peace to our abode. And with all the smoldering emotions continually erupting, our relationship, both business and physical, ended. She left with the girls and their "things" plus some of the possessions which we had declared to be of joint ownership. I was relieved to see the loaded vehicle pull down the drive and out through the gate.

In the following weeks, there were some curt telephone communications. After a month, Charlotte called and the conversation was conciliatory. She contended that our relationship had been good for so many years and that we had worked well together while on tour and never really had any major problems. She was willing to come back if I'd have her. I felt some hesitancy but I, too, felt that we'd been a wonderful team. She had wanted the marriage in spite of knowing completely what my background had been, and it never seemed to have been an issue. We shared so many common interests, and I was willing to work out the current problems knowing that each of us was capable of putting past accusations and bitterness behind. We could work and live together in the compound as mature people engaged in a fascinating and necessary occupation of raising and breeding animals without the pressures of the tour. And we had removed the irritants: Gerard, the girls and the six-legged bull.

Charlotte returned. I welcomed her and the station wagon filled with her "things," which indeed appeared as though she intended staying. But very soon I noticed that while we did not

The jaguars knew they were loved by Charlotte.

have any disputes during the day while actively engaged in work, she began to argue when we went to bed. This was a strange turn of events. Prior to her leaving, we'd done all the arguing during the day. When we went to bed we were either not talking, or if it had been a good day, we occasionally made love, although the desire for that between us had become rare. I could not quite understand the new pattern. I argued back and perhaps said things that were unkind, but I was working hard all day and in no mood for the fight when all I wanted was sleep. She kept dredging up past history and making accusatory, scandalous allegations. Finally, to placate her I began to agree with her if only to stop the unceasing harangue. I found her behavior bazaar, but in my mind I marked it up to menopausal symptoms.

    I left the compound for a week of business in the Northeast. When I returned, Charlotte was again gone and this time I felt it was final. She had taken everything that she felt entitled to and soon an attorney contacted me with the news that she had filed for divorce. I went to see my attorney to ask if he would represent me in a divorce action. He accepted the case. He was in touch with Charlotte's lawyer and came back with a shocking report.

"Robert, you are in bad shape!"

"Oh, yeah?"

"Oh, yeah. When you let her come back, somebody wired that reading lamp of yours . . . that thing over your bed."

I was astonished, but remembered that one of the girls had been dating a young man who worked in electronics and I imagined that the guy came in to bug the bedroom.

"You're kidding me . . ."

"I'm not kidding you and, oh boy, Charlotte's got the tape at her lawyer's. I went there and heard it, and you are in bad shape."

I was shaken by the revelation. "What are we gonna do?"

"I don't know . . . but I think you will have to settle the case."

"What does she want?"

He paused for a moment and then dropped the bomb.

"She wants the farm."

32

WOMEN
Les Femmes

My primary business had become the importation of animals. I'd made many contacts while on tour to support the business well. However, Charlotte's desire for a divorce and laying claim to the compound put a freeze on my assets. The terms of the divorce stipulated that no one could come into the compound or leave under the guise of doing business. Animals continued to arrive, but under court order were not to be sold. I was surrounded on all sides by Charlotte's relatives, who had never in fact accepted me as anything but an interloper. I knew I was being watched for any infringement of the terms of the injunction. I was forced to seek surreptitious means to operate to remain viable.

Enter another angel of mercy. Gladys Lewis had moved to Florida when her husband Joe retired. They lived in a beautiful home on the shore of Lake Panasoffkee where Joe, as former prominent member of the labor movement, routinely hosted top brass from Washington and also members of the mob. I never met Joe Lewis, but heard many stories about the powerful man who commanded respect from Washington inner circles as well as the leading Mafia dons of the day. Gladys was widowed shortly before I met her. She had enjoyed a full and involved social life as hostess to many visiting dignitaries. All of that stopped when Joe died, and Gladys was casting about for a new interest to occupy empty hours. When I met her and introduced her to my working partners, the leopards, tigers, panthers, lemurs, gorillas, and all the other characters that filled the oak hammock, she became enthralled and expressed a keen interest in helping me.

Gladys, a petite blond, always impeccably coifed and dressed, soon became my savior. She was financially secure, and I was able to go to her for financial aid in addition to making her my temporary partner. She took over the bookkeeping and the paper work processing the sale of animals through her residence on the lake. She kept me afloat for the 18 months before the divorce was settled. Without Gladys, I would have lost the business.

During the period when Charlotte and I were not communicating, I could not understand the delay in the divorce settlement. Our attorneys were evasive. I wanted the final papers drawn, and I knew that Charlotte wanted to get on with her life. I eventually received information which revealed the reason for the delay. Our attorneys were involved in a mutual commercial real estate venture and had accepted the divorce case in conflict of interest, making them vulnerable to disbarment if the illegality was divulged through a court battle. It was imperative that the divorce be settled out of court and the delay was designed to force such a settlement, which is just what occurred. When we signed the papers, Charlotte received $35,000, which did not make her happy, particularly when her attorney took most of that as his fee. My attorney kept telling me that as a friend he was not going to charge a fee. I received his bill for $2,000. Ultimately, the legal harangue cost me nearly $200,000 in lost business and legal expenses.

Life on the compound during the embargo was not dull. There were several occasions when bullets were shot at the property. Once as I stood next to the house, bullets came within inches of me, knocking out a rather substantial piece of concrete wall on the south side of the building. I could never prove who the marksman was, but I had my suspicions. There was a great deal of bitterness during the lengthy legal delay and for years after the settlement. All during the battle, Gladys Lewis was friend and confidant and also mother to many of the small offspring born at the Breeding Center. She nursed the babies in her house on the lake and found a fulfillment in the activity to the complete exclusion, by choice, of her prior social commitments and involvements. She became a wonderful helpmate and mentor, a vital presence when I needed her.

The compound continued to hold interesting events. As a

A lucky tiger cub found a mom in Gladys.

complete departure from routine, a *Playboy* magazine editor contacted me to arrange for the use of a snow leopard and the oak hammock for location shooting. The planned project as it was explained, required months of preparation in training the cat. I signed a five-month contract with the magazine after a cameraman was sent to examine the locale to select the very best site for the shoot and determine the perfect lighting and atmosphere. They wanted a misty portrayal of the animal in his natural environment, inhabited by a beautiful nude model, not exactly common to the oak hammock. The cameraman described the action, and I went to work preparing for the unique adventure.

The animal selected was Tora, a three-year-old male snow leopard and the first leopard bred on the compound. Tora had to be leash-broken first, then trained to climb a specifically designated tree, one leaning at a 40° angle. I used fishing line to tether the cat without giving appearance of any restraint. I used sand bags as props to emulate a human until I had the cat comfortable enough with the training and procedure to have some of my employees pose, letting Tora walk over them. Some of the people, working with the cats on a daily basis and knowing how dangerous they are, were skittish about having a snow leopard brush its furry face over human prey, but the cat was well-trained by the time I introduced humans into the performance, and he obeyed and performed beautifully to every command, every motion.

On the day of the shoot, a gorgeous brunette model wrapped in mink appeared along with three cameramen, a director, assistants, and a handsome, silver-haired, well-dressed gentleman who was covetous of the beautiful lady. I was captivated by her looks, and when I spoke to her, she smiled sweetly, but referred to the gentleman for translation. He was her guide and interpreter and informed me that she did not understand English.

I replied innocently, "Well, you have a very lovely import . . . where did she come from?"

He answered, "She came from Paris."

I laughed and began to speak in French. We got along very well from that moment on.

All was in readiness for the actual shoot, the model instructed to take her position, nude, lying on the large limb of the oak. We had cleared the central compound of the many camels and llama that ordinarily inhabited the area, driving the two herds to the back of the property. The cameramen were on the ground poised to begin rolling; the girl was tense.

I explained to her, "You have seen the cat performing, you can see that the cat is well-trained and as an experienced trainer, I guarantee that you do not have anything to worry about . . . now . . . I would like to direct your reaction. As you lie here, think of someone you love . . . think only of that person and maybe that you are about to have sex with your lover . . . think of the pleasure you are about to feel." Finally she was smiling and relaxed, even demonstrating a look of ecstasy.

I began to walk the cat through its planned and orchestrated performance, to navigate the length of the limb which was about 35 feet long, and then to carefully step over the naked girl, lounging in a most seductive pose. I must admit to enjoying the labor immensely.

Tora reached the languishing nude and stopped, his attention diverted to something in the distance behind me. The cat and girl were five feet off the ground above me and the cameramen. I turned to look at what had captured Tora's intense interest. Suddenly, in one massive move, the cat was airborne, tearing the fishing line from the tree limb and out of my hands. He hit the ground, then took five enormous leaps to pounce on a stray llama.

As Tora leaped through the air, it was quite unbelievable to watch him seemingly fly in an astounding demonstration. It was just beautiful. The Florida panther or puma had been considered to be the best jumping cat in the world with 29 to 30 feet recorded in the longest leaps from a sitting position. When I later measured the leaps that Tora took in his pursuit of the llama, I was amazed to measure 41 feet exactly for each of the leaps. I had read in Russian wildlife journals, translated in Israel, accounts depicting the snow leopard from eastern Siberia jumping from rocks to rocks achieving distances of over 40 feet, but now I could see the capacity of the animal in a captive-born specimen. It was truly incredible.

Tora's final leap put him on top of the llama, his teeth slashing the throat of the unsuspecting animal, as the model, cameramen, and assistants watched in utter horror. I ran to the animals knowing the cat wore a camouflaged collar made of chain and knew as well that once the cat had hold of its prey, it would not respond to any sort of direction or discipline. Once the killing process begins, the cat's senses are totally and wildly focused and cannot be broken or distracted. It is innate in every type of cat, even a house cat, to kill; and once the desired prey is captive, there is no way to save the victim from a frantic, crazed predator. Tora's eyes were dilated; his front paws embedded in the flesh of the llama with his hind claws ripping the guts of the struggling, screaming victim.

I caught hold of the chain at Tora's neck. I knew drastic measures were needed, but I hesitated hitting the cat in the head and risking death of a valuable animal. I twisted the collar as hard as I could, hoping to cut off his air supply. It seemed like an eternity before my effort broke Tora's savage grasp. Tora finally gasped for breath, pulled his paws away and, turning in the process, caught my left hand with his paw. One claw went through my hand.

I kicked the llama to the side and removed my right hand

from the collar, not wanting Tora's fangs to go through my wrist. He had me by the left hand as I began talking to him in the friendly snow leopard sound that is a deep and lyrical muffled growl from the throat. Slowly, he began to respond. His eyes returned to normal. As he relaxed, I kept talking. I pushed my hand toward him hoping that in so doing he'd retract his claw, like a tiger or jaguar would ordinarily do; but I learned that snow leopards cannot retract their claws so easily. I kept talking and he, too, began making sounds to me as I slowly reached for the claw, a risky move because cats do not like their claws touched. I did not want to put him into a killing mode with my throat so close to his face. I gently took his paw, but recognized a threatened look on his face, so I continued talking. I finally removed the claw from my hand and miraculously felt no pain as the adrenaline flowed through my body. An employee threw a piece of rope which I slipped around Tora's neck, simulating the training that he had been through for the shoot, and calmly walked him back to his cage like nothing untoward had occurred.

There was no need to go to the hospital. I had a big hole on the top of my hand and a smaller opening at the bottom. I took a long needle and a piece of twisted gauze, which I pulled through the opening to act as a drain. Finally, I took 250 milligrams of ampicillin, a double scotch, and relaxed after a tough day on the compound surrounded by the Playboy crew and the beautiful model. There had been enough filming to fulfill their requirements before the attack. The model returned a week later for some conversation in French, and also a rather intimate episode, which helped aid the healing process immeasurably.

Another woman came into my life when I badly needed someone to fill the loneliness. I had driven to Tampa to pick up a shipment of animals. Stopping to have the station wagon filled with gas, I saw a beautiful blond dressed in a nurse's uniform walking into the station. She was stunning, a girl in her early twenties, who looked distressed. I approached and asked if I could be of assistance. She said her car broke down a block away from the station. I immediately offered my services.

"Well, if you trust me, I will be more than happy to help you. I'll pay for my gas and take you back to your car."

She agreed and seemed to trust the stranger, who was com-

Chimps were a popular attraction on the compound.

pletely taken with her good looks. I took her to the car where I jumped the battery and got the engine running. We talked briefly. She explained that she was on her way to school where she was in nurses' training. She was divorced and living in a small unfurnished house near the school with her two children. I told her that I was in the animal importation business. She expressed the desire to visit the compound to see the animals and to entertain the children on a very special outing. I knew she had no concept at the time of just how extraordinary the outing would be. We set a date for the following weekend.

    I drove to Tampa and brought Diane to the compound. She came alone the first time and was obviously impressed with the oak hammock filled with animals of every description and the man who lived in its center. She returned to the compound several times with the children, and within three weeks of our meeting, Diane and the children moved in with me. Matt was three years old and Kelly a year older. I inherited an instant family. It was quite an experience from the start.

    Diane had been attempting to toilet train the boy. This was something I'd never been involved in, yet it didn't appear so different from training the gorillas and chimps. I had Matt using the toilet within three days of settling onto the compound.

The children shared the blue room, and Diane shared my bedroom, quickly becoming a valuable and reliable helpmate and lover. Gladys was not happy with the addition of Diane to my staff and into my private chambers, but she knew that I needed a woman to care for me, to keep the apartment in order, and to help run the business.

There was much as usual to be done. With the divorce finally settled, more animals arrived to remain or to be acclimated before being shipped to various clients, business returned to normal. At least as normal as it ever got at the compound. The level of normalcy or sanity depended directly on the behavior of the animals and the people who daily interacted with them, cared for them, came to film them, and to be filmed with them. There were many foreign as well as domestic adventures that, like the years on tour, become a blur of activity impossible to keep in order. I had two women in my life to help maintain a semblance of order. I left them in charge while I went off on my yearly trip abroad.

After the usual visit in Rennes, I flew to Brazzaville in the Congo. The country at that time was completely under control of a Marxist system of government. On landing I saw first a huge banner containing the communist slogan *"Proletaires* of the World Unit" picturing a huge clinched fist. I was immediately impressed by the lack of automobiles and the roads filled with pot-holes. It was a sad commentary on the regime.

I'd been in contact with the director of the zoo in Brazzaville, who was to help me acquire a collection of pygmy chimpanzees and some other animals including gorillas. The director, an articulate Negro educated in Paris at the Museum of Natural History, described a problem facing him the very day I arrived. The night before natives had broken into the zoo and left with a baby elephant and a pygmy hippo, which they killed and ate. The director had reported the incident to the government, but received little satisfaction from the Chinese Communist authorities. All the animals in the zoo were in poor condition, and I quickly realized that the trip was probably wasted. However, the director made an arrangement for me, along with a guide, to visit and examine the native pygmies.

Pygmies comprised the most primitive of African tribes known at that time and had no contact with the tall Negroes, who had previously captured the little people and sold them into slavery. The pygmies had escaped into remote areas and moved from place to place following the animal vital to their existence: the elephant. My guide had gained favor with the pygmies as a former trader and was accepted by them and therefore, I, too, was accepted. When introduced, I looked down at the five-foot-tall males, shorter females, and very small infants. They wore no clothing and lived their nomadic lives worshipping their gods: the elephant, the sun, earth, moon, fire, and water. I spent two weeks in the company of 25 natives watching them perform their simple rituals. It was one of the most fascinating and incredible experiences of my life.

As the tribe moved, they stopped for the night and built crude shelters of large fronds from the natural foliage supported by small skeletal structures made of small tree limbs. I was impressed with their unceasing laughter. While their culture was narrowed by self-imposed isolation, the hunting skills I witnessed were basic but effective. They used either poison darts or poison spears to fell prey. The darts were hand-crafted, and the metal spears were traded from the tall natives living on the outskirts of the Ituri Forest. The natives left the spears at a designated location where animal skins had been left by the pygmies.

I was particularly privileged, realizing that the pygmies maintained absolutely no contact with other humans. Another ritual that served to fascinate me was the elephant hunt. A small boy, perhaps 17 years of age was chosen, and a different boy was sent each time a hunting foray was initiated. As I watched, I felt transported to prehistoric times. The young hunter first covered himself with elephant feces then, taking a spear, left the tribe to follow the herd located usually five or six miles from camp. The boy climbed trees from time to time to sniff the wind. All pygmies possess flat noses with large nostrils that provide an incredibly keen sense of smell. I could not follow through the entire process as my presence would disturb the furtive quest, but the guide explained that when the hunter found the herd, it would consist of a few to as many as 20 elephants.

The boy would wait until the middle of night when the elephants were all leaning against trees in slumber, the males snoring loudly. Due to his body-cover of dung, the boy wasn't detected and quickly approached an elephant in the center of the herd thrusting a spear from under into the gut of the huge mammal. A piercing scream from the victim wakened the herd, initiating a thunderous stampede in every direction as the boy leaped safely into a tree. I knew that when the pygmy was in a tree, he could jump from one to another with agility and natural poise. I had witnessed this ability as they harvested fruit, moving through the trees in silhouette against the sun reminiscent of apes gently swinging from one limb to another. Darwinism seemingly confirmed.

When the two weeks were up, I hated to leave the little people whom I'd grown to admire deeply. But it was time to return to Brazzaville to await my flight for home. There were four days before flight-time, and those were spent at a hotel with very few tourists present. Since the Communist take-over, only Chinese were in evidence. It was strange to take my meals in a huge majestic hall served by ten waiters with no other diners present. I ate wonderful food served on Limoges china. One evening I received an invitation to take a tour of the kitchen facility. I turned down the tour due to an unfortunate incident, regrettably brought to mind, that occurred on a previous trip — one to Douala, Cameroon.

In Douala, my hotel had been the du Commerce where I spent several nights. The manager was an ex-convict, a congenial gentleman, whom I engaged in conversation. We both enjoyed using our native language. The menu included wonderful French cuisine and one dish reminded me of my favorite meal at home: hare cooked in civet. Mother cooked hare often as I grew up, and it was always memorable. I honestly proclaimed the food in the hotel to be as good as what I remembered from my childhood. I knew that hare was not indigenous to Africa, and when I invited the manager to join me at the table, we spoke of food and also of France. He explained that the meat was not hare, but a good substitute, a midget deer called a *duiker.* I didn't tell him it was also the name for the 50 species of small deer. The manager went on to explain that he purchased the animals from local hunters. As the conversation continued, I was invited to visit his kitchen. He was anxious to have me see the food preparation. I said that I'd be delighted.

Immediately upon stepping into the kitchen, I was sorry that I'd accepted the gracious invitation. There were 20 men staffing the food preparation areas, all victims of leprosy. Each of them, upon closer examination, was missing either a finger or in the most horrifying case, a part of the face had been eaten away. Some had only a hole in the center of the face where the nose and part of the cheek should have been. Some had one eye and others had tremendous growths in evidence. It was like a scene in a horror movie or a dark comedy, a depraved depiction of food handlers that sickened and stayed for years in my nightmares. Everyone in the kitchen seemed friendly; all were anxious to speak at one time, some without mouths. The manager explained that the men were the only educated people he could find in the city when he first arrived. He'd gone to the Catholic Mission where lepers were cared for and the Reverend in charge explained that if he was seeking good employees who spoke French, the patients had been taught to cook and would be ideal for behind-the-scenes work. That was just fine for them, but I decided never to go behind the scenes again.

As I traveled back and forth through Africa on the many expeditions, I picked up bugs and infections and returned to the States never quite feeling well. After the trip to Douala, when symptoms lingered, I imagined that I had contracted leprosy. I became a regular customer for check-up and testing at the clinic in Lakeland to have blood work and a profile performed. Waiting for results, I worked myself into a highly emotional state many times suspecting the absolute worst. However, I always came away with an excellent report and soon the symptoms disappeared.

One time I was back at the compound three weeks after a trip to Madagascar, taking a hot shower, when a big worm crawled out of my toe. Apparently, I'd been bitten by a fly and an egg was deposited in the foot. There were many bizarre symptoms to be tolerated, but I obviously survived them all. However, the complications and problems associated with the import business would prove minor compared to the ensuing people problems soon to develop on the home front.

It was not long after returning from the Congo when news came of Gerard. He'd returned from Vietnam. There had been letters from him, which I answered in an attempt to bolster and support his effort, but my positive thoughts never seemed to influence the young man. His written comments continued a barrage of antimilitary condemnation, and I knew that there was absolutely nothing positive gained from any aspect of the tough tour of duty. He didn't even express his good fortune to have survived. He'd been thrown into an inferno along with thousands of others and the antiwar demonstrations on the home front did nothing to encourage or support those serving on the battlefields and jungles in Vietnam. Obviously, I had no way of knowing just how brutal the reception was from a country of people so strongly opposed to the war; but if I hoped for some mature introspection on Gerard's part, I was sorely disappointed. He spoke of spending leave time in Thailand. That was the only positive.

When he returned to the States, he went first to the Swan estate in Bucks County. He returned stateside with no outward signs of the scars that he carried within, but they soon surfaced. He was unsettled when he went to the Far East, and there his problems had deepened.

One day the local Postmaster phoned Odette requesting a private audience with Mrs. Swan. The Swan Family had been residents in Bucks County for years and were highly respected and obviously protected from the possibility of scandal. The Postmaster felt he had to divulge some information to Odette under utmost privacy. Odette met with the solicitous gentleman, who advised that a package had been received from Vietnam addressed to Gerard Baudy containing a substantial quantity of illegal drugs. The Postmaster did not want the information or evidence leaked to law officials or to the press. He was attempting to circumvent an investigation and possible criminal charges, which would lead to an ugly court case, media notoriety, and almost certain imprisonment for Gerard in a scandal that would be embarrassing to the family. The Postmaster was articulate in expressing that if any similar parcels were received, he would not continue the subterfuge and an arrest would be forthcoming.

Odette and Ed had welcomed the boy home and even had a car waiting for him. The car did not satisfy Gerard, so another car was purchased. With the ongoing trauma created by Gerard's presence, the Swan household was thrown into turmoil and Odette's marriage placed in jeopardy. I didn't witness the crimes, but I could imagine the chaos created by the ex-soldier addicted to drugs, and harboring a huge grudge against the military and every other segment of society. Odette was in contact with me all during this period of time, keeping me better informed than I cared to be, but I wanted to be supportive where our son was concerned.

Gerard became involved with a young French girl from a well-to-do politically influential family in Brittany. Martine was employed by a wealthy American family when she was notified of an inheritance, the equivalent of $60,000, left to her by a relative in France. Gerard and Martine returned to their native country to claim the money and proceeded to spend it quickly on purchases that would deplete the windfall and leave very little in her dowry. After they had their fling, they returned to Bucks County where a marriage took place to accommodate Martine's pregnancy.

I continued to talk to Odette from time to time, but I knew little of the day-by-day details of Gerard's life. I was well occupied with my own life, a new lady named Diane, and a new scheme involving the compound.

33

SAVAGE KINGDOM
Le Royaume Sauvage

I'd been importing animals for several years, and the breeding process was well-established. The compound was full of many different species that had grown into what I knew was a fine and varied collection, ideal to share with the public. I had acquired the usual stable of zoo animals with elephants, giraffes, bears, zebras and some white rhinos.

The white rhino is the largest species of rhino, and I took a male and female on breeding loan. We had a large collection of lemurs from Madagascar, the showy precursor of the monkey and very unusual. My trips to the island off the African coast had been fruitful in importing the unique species along with giant tortoise. We also had chimps. In grazing stock there were rare antelope from Africa and red deer, western, and fallow deer. We ultimately had over 200 deer and over 400 different animals on display.

I installed a huge glass enclosure for giant snakes including anaconda, Indian python, Burmese python, and boa. The smallest snake was 15 feet in length, and some of the snakes weighed over 250 pounds. There were ostriches, camels, and llamas. We housed rare gorillas, difficult to handle and very dangerous, in addition to nearly a hundred cats of many sizes and species.

I had imported eight lions from Cameroon to work in an act. They were all male babies six months of age when they arrived and were absolutely gorgeous specimens. Only the male lion is adorned with the thick, luxurious mane which takes about three years to fully mature. The lion is not as intelligent as the tiger. I had been working with them daily, training one animal, then another, and another repetitively, ten times per day for nearly a year before I felt I had a workable act.

During the year, I was also in the process of breaking a camel act. I had purchased six camels from various zoos around the country and was concentrating extra effort on one particular camel to have it carry a snow leopard on its back. The camel training required tremendous patience due to their low level of intelligence and inability to react to commands or any kind of reinforcement. They are also extremely vicious. Another vicious and challenging animal was a killer elephant that I took in from the Cincinnati Zoo. I eventually had the elephant trained to give rides to children.

All the animals required daily feeding, and the gathering, slaughter, and distribution of food was an enormous task, which kept me and a full crew occupied seven days a week. I decided to open the display to the public and recover some of the ongoing expenses in gate fees. I planned to open three days a week from Saturday through Monday to attract some of the thousands of people attending the Flea Market in Webster that opened during the winter season and drew from all over the state and even out-of-state. There was much labor involved in setting up the Savage Kingdom, and Diane was one of my ablest and most reliable workers.

In addition to working the animals, there were props to be built requiring 14 to 16 hours a day of non-stop labor in order to prepare for opening. I knew that if we were just a zoo without animal acts, we wouldn't gain the attention or appeal to an audience large enough to justify opening to the public. It was a gamble but the acts would be a vital part of the attraction, particularly when the limited acreage did not permit the inclusion of mechanized rides, such as those offered at Busch Gardens and other similar large facilities. Our claim to fame would center around the lion and camel acts and other unique features, such as a chimp trained to walk along with me shaking hands with the customers.

I fenced off ten acres for the animals to graze freely. I bought a wagon with a team of midget mules and called it the "Cheetah Express." The wagon ride, driven by a black man through the veldt where rhinos, giraffes, zebras, and deer grazed, gave a good viewing of a damned authentic mini reproduction of the African Plain, cost just $1.50 per customer.

The lions were featured entertainers at Savage Kingdom.

A good friend operated a nursery in Opopka where he grew exotic plants. He also imported plants from all over the world. I had many rare orchids and other showy flowering plants spotted throughout the hammock as decorative pieces. Bromeliads were mounted on driftwood and attached to the outside of cages. The Bromeliad bares a spectacular vividly colored bloom that lasts for months. However, the flower fades after several weeks, but we learned if we spray-painted the faded bloom it maintained a look of original beauty for up to two years.

My plan for the lions was to use them at the end of an educational talk on the history of wild animal training based on facts, documents, and writings preserved from early Roman times. The lesson concluded with a demonstration of the whip, explaining that the whip is not an instrument of torture as the humane society and animal rights activists seem to imply in their castigation of its use, but merely as an extension of the hand and used as a tool to direct and guide an animal in training. Obviously, the whip has been misused by some as a weapon to injure, but I used it to direct and command certain moves. I demonstrated my accuracy and prowess by flicking some paper cups, cutting them in two, and scattering them in every direction.

When the talk was complete and the cups scattered, my help opened a sliding guillotine door located seven feet above in the fork of an oak tree. Four lions entered, one at a time, jumping over me and over the whip held like a hurtle, and then each moved to its respective stool made of cypress logs. All of the props in the huge enclosure were of native materials to further enhance the atmosphere and authenticity of a jungle setting. During the act, I approached each lion to violate its territory, eliciting ferocious roars from my pupils. The lion act became a highly popular attraction at the Savage Kingdom, gaining a large audience of all ages, but appealing particularly to children.

I imported macaws as part of a wild bird exhibit. The colorful parrots were used to decorate and enhance the compound with their vibrant plumage. Hollow-log birdhouses were set in the trees, each with a roof for protection, and I placed a male and female in each tree; that became "their" tree. The birds had free access to the compound as they moved freely through the trees.

The winged inhabitants included peacocks. I was given several pairs by various zoos that were overpopulated with the colorful birds. I bought three white peacocks that quickly adapted, along with the more common species, to the natural environs of the compound and thrived. There were ultimately over 200 of the beautifully plumed birds roaming freely through the hammock, much to the delight of camera buffs.

When it first opened, I had not fully advertised the Savage Kingdom and business was slow. I should have learned my lesson from the Ameche *International Showtime* tour which was not properly promoted and played to nearly empty arenas until I let Sabu out of his cage, and the newspaper articles caught the attention of the people of Providence. After the escape and recapture, they came out to see the "wild cats" of Robert Baudy and filled the arena for every show. Inspired by the lesson, I leased several billboards on the highways surrounding Center Hill and had color brochures printed. I designed the advertising and painted lion and tiger heads on the large signs. My early art training came into play and I immensely enjoyed the artistic deviation from training and manual labor.

Soon people discovered us as word of the wonderful animal

Brochures, pamphlets, and other marketing tools drew animal lovers.

adventure began to circulate, and we ultimately became a major Central Florida tourist attraction. As our reputation grew, we began to receive unsolicited publicity from newspapers focusing a spotlight on the business, and we gained much attention from many different sources. We began to receive requests from the motion picture industry for animals to appear in unique roles. Famous fine artists contacted me to request permission to use animals as subjects for their works. The days were filled with a constant parade of requests and people from many fascinating and diverse professional backgrounds. We also became the recipient of stray animals. The activity level at the Kingdom rarely slowed. With many different wild and dangerous animals contained and those roaming freely, the potential for accident and injury was a daily concern.

One day, a Tuesday, I had to leave the compound on an

errand, leaving Diane in charge. She was able and willing, but she was not an animal person; she did not possess the "virus." Not many of my employees were imbued with the rapport and love that I held for the animals. I had on the compound a large buck deer that I'd purchased to change the blood line of the Florida deer which I'd been raising by incorporating new blood to improve the quality of offspring. The man who sold me the buck warned that the deer had been raised as a pet, but the 300-pound animal was not dependable and could be dangerous. At the time I bought the deer, it had dropped its antlers. When the huge antlers grew back, the animal was impressive. I returned to the compound and found Diane staggering in a daze, her bare breasts exposed through a torn and blood-soaked blouse. She had been savagely attacked by the buck. It was a miracle that she survived. With some help, I rounded up the buck and shipped it back to its owner. Diane was traumatized by the attack, which didn't enhance her feelings for animals.

Soon after the new business was well-established, I received a fatal blow. The U.S. Government passed the Endangered Species Act designed to protect animals being imported from countries where many species were becoming extinct. The result for me was that it became nearly impossible to import any animals listed on the mandate, which included gorillas and big cats. Lions were an exception, but lemurs were also listed, which dashed my hopes for acquiring the coveted Indri, the largest species of lemur and the only species that walked on its hind legs. I had also wanted to import the wild dog of Tasmania, the Tasmanian Devil, but it, too, was on the list. There were records of the dogs being spotted in the wild in the 1970s, but the Government Act halted any hope of capturing and breeding in captivity. The Government Act listed many species that weren't endangered, but due to lack of scientific field surveys, many animals were included as a result of the overreaction to the powerful Washington lobbies, quick to sue the Government to support their rantings. I had to refocus my original concept for the Rare Breeding Center.

At the same time, good news arrived. I was advised that I'd become a grandfather. Gerard and Martine were the parents of a baby girl named Samantha. I had not seen Gerard since his return from overseas, nor was I aware of all that had transpired in the young man's life since his discharge. But I was invited to attend

We all hoped that wife and child would provide positive reinforcement and happiness to our boy.

his Catholic wedding orchestrated by Odette and Mother to satisfy the firmly held belief that the young parents were not legally married in spite of a civil ceremony months before.

I flew to Pennsylvania to witness the event and to meet my granddaughter. I also wanted to be assessed of Gerard's activities since being discharged from the Army. I'd heard about the parcel of drugs, but not much more. He had apparently arrived at the Swan residence accompanied by an unsavory fellow ex-soldier, who was tolerated for several weeks before Ed asked the man to leave. Ed talked to Gerard and convinced him that he should enroll in Bucks County Community College. Mother had arrived from France to see "her boy" safely returned from Vietnam. At that time, Odette and Ed flew to France to purchase Odette's family home in Guilvinec, leaving Mother and Gerard for a month. It was a good time for Mother with her boy. It was during that time when Gerard met Martine. I didn't see Mother on that particular trip, but it was a special time when she could enjoy Gerard before the downhill slide began.

Now Mother had returned and she accomplished what was important to her: a Catholic church wedding. Martine's background, descendant of a communist family, initially created a natural aversion to a church wedding, but Mother's persistence paid off, and we all met for the happy occasion. It did seem like a positive move.

They even came to Florida for a visit before Mother returned to France and the young family returned to New Jersey. Ed Swan was instrumental in finding a job for Gerard at the Johnson and Johnson Company caring for animals used in research. I do not know what occurred to sever the job relationship. I was back working 18 to 20 hours per day at the compound when Gerard, Martine, and baby Samantha arrived. Gerard needed a job. I arranged to move a double-wide trailer onto the grounds to accommodate the family. I told Gerard that if he intended staying with me, he'd have to behave like every other employee — no drinking on the job and no drugs at any time.

I tried hard to be tolerant. However, Gerard didn't attempt to set an example for the other employees. He continued to get high, which was totally unacceptable where dangerous animals were involved. Martine spent most of her time in the trailer. I continued to talk, to counsel Gerard. Some of the discussions became heated. He could not be reasoned with when he was drunk or on a drug-induced high.

I was disgusted with the arrangement, but felt stymied. I'd welcomed them, provided a place to live, and a job. I'd tried to help the man, but he wasn't doing his part. I left the compound on business after again reminding Gerard that he was dealing with animals that had to be contained and were lethally dangerous if they became loose. It was imperative he stay sober. My warnings, as usual, fell on deaf ears. I was gone a week. When I returned Diane told me, and other employees confirmed, that Gerard had turned some of the tigers loose. The report even had Gerard going into a cage with Martine and Samantha to take pictures. They had escaped injury on that occasion, but I could not abide his continued pattern of erratic behavior with so much potential danger imminent.

After months of virtually no change, we had an altercation which seemed the climax to our relationship. The tension had been building for years. I cannot say that I am guiltless where my son is concerned. I know that there is much that I could have done and perhaps should have done during his formative years, but I did try to understand the boy when he came to the States. He maintained his hurt and increasing ambivalence toward a father and mother caught up in the world's adulation, which he refused to embrace.

Our words were strong, and his drugged response was to grab my dagger and hold it at my gut. He was not physically a match for me in his stupor, and I wrestled the knife loose, but was badly shaken by the incident.

Gerard contacted Zerbini soon after the encounter, and in a matter of days he left the compound taking Martine and Samantha with him. I knew nothing of his arrangement, but imagined at the time that he'd made a proposal for a job with the Zerbini Circus. The Zerbinis, Gypsies from France who came to the States in the mid-sixties, performed a lion act with the Hiller Circus. It was my practice, while on tour, to befriend foreign performers newly engaged in working this huge and intimidating country, to offer assistance and guidance. It was also an opportunity for me to get caught up on the latest news of the European Tour, as well as the politics. I could communicate in French with Zerbini, which was always something special.

The senior Zerbini was a tough man, who worked the lions along with his son, a tall, handsome young man of about 16. I recall one time when I was in Zerbini's trailer sharing a bottle of wine and some conversation. The boy entered and obviously wanted to sit in on the conversation while the activity of packing to move on was taking place outside the trailer. The old man asked the boy if he'd rolled up the electrical cables. The boy confirmed he had done the task when another employee came in and said the cables hadn't been secured. I was shocked to see Zerbini's verbal and physical rage that seemed excessive, but also demonstrated the toughness of the old man.

When the senior Zerbini died of a heart attack, the son took over the lion act. There was one lion that was mean and had it in for the kid, who had many close calls confronting and working the dangerous lion. He eventually replaced the bad lion and went on to train the animals to perform a comedy routine. Depicting Tarzan wearing a loin cloth, the boy rode into the arena on an elephant, jumped off, then put the lions through some humorous routines. Young Zerbini performed under contract to Hubert Castle for years, then went on to produce his own show and today is one of the most prominent circus producers in the United States.

When Gerard contacted Zerbini, I'm certain he had no trouble getting a job. Zerbini knew me well. I was the only man working a tiger act years before, and he had a great deal of respect for me and my performance and training expertise. Gerard was hired to care for the lions; he was going on tour. I was relieved to have him off the compound. He'd been a thorn in my side and had done nothing for the morale of the other employees. Gerard was out of control. It was better for both of us that I not witness his continuing performance.

With the young Baudy troop gone, life returned to normal, and I could react to and focus on all that transpired each day in the compound. Things were never dull. One day I had a call reporting an animal sighting and a request, "Mr. Baudy, you must come to investigate this strange animal." There were always many calls and many incidents involving animals, but this particular one brought back a bit of the past.

It had been two years since we received a particular shipment of wild-caught chimps, that were totally untrained. It was at a time when I received shipments routinely. One of the chimps, weighing about 75 to 80 pounds was about four years old. He came in a crate that had not been designed according to my specifications. I always specified that animal crates be equipped with sliding doors, not doors that swing out. In order to transfer the animal from the shipping crate into a cage, we could not join the two containers to meet flush. I had some heavy nets put into place to fill the gaps at the top and around the doors to contain the animal. I had four men standing by to help open the door and secure the nets during the transfer. The chimp, very intelligent and obviously realizing his options, broke through one of the nets and took off like lightning. An 80-pound chimp possesses the power of three grown men, and there was no stopping the frantic, determined escapee. He took off toward the trees, a big black ball with white face running 20 miles an hour, and then jumping into the lower limbs of a tree and, just as in the jungle, swinging from branch to branch and from tree to tree as we hurried to keep him in sight. He was busy swinging and screaming chimp insults to his audience below.

I told the men to watch the agile chimp while I went into the house to load a tranquilizer gun. Loading takes time with many

СССР
МИНИСТЕРСТВО СЕЛЬСКОГО ХОЗЯЙСТВА
Главное управление ветеринарии

Пограничный контрольный ветеринарный пункт № __114__   JFK 0 05 1

ВЕТЕРИНАРНЫЙ СЕРТИФИКАТ № __34__

о происхождении и здоровье животных (птицы)

Я, нижеподписавшийся государственный ветеринарый врач _____
_____ Каспарова Т. И. _____
(фамилия, инициалы)

удостоверяю, что после проведенного мною осмотра __22 января 1968 г.__
(дата)

животные (птица) __сибирские рыси__ в количестве __2__ голов
(вид животных)

номера животных _____
(номера животных могут быть указаны в приложении к сертификату)

принадлежащие __Зоообъединению__
(название хозяйства, владельца, название населенного пункта, района,
области и республики)

отправляемые __Флорида / США /__ через Нью-Йорк
(страна и пункт назначения)

№№ вагонов или название парохода (рейс самолета) _____

перед отправкой содержались в месте происхождения под ветеринарным наблюдением в в течение 40 дней и признаны здоровыми и свободными от заразных болезней.

Животные (птица) выходят из района, хозяйства, благополучного по заразным болезням и что в течение 6 месяцев ни в месте происхождения, ни в соседних пунктах (в радиусе __40__ километров), ни в местности, через которую животные (птица) прошли до места погрузки (железнодорожным путем, на пароходе и др.), нет случаев заболеваний чумой, повальным воспалением легких крупного рогатого скота, ящуром, оспой овец, чумой свиней или птицы и другими заразными болезнями, свойственными животным, в отношении которых выдан настоящий сертификат.

One of many certificates: this is from USSR for two Siberian lynxes.

determining factors to be considered. There are no books written to adequately cover the process, which I learned from years of experience in dealing with many different species and sizes of animals. The temperature is one factor to be considered. When it's very hot, the tranquilizer can be lethal. The type of drug used for a chimp would be different than for a cat. The weight of the animal is another factor. If the dosage is not enough, it will not affect the animal, and if it's too strong, it will kill. It took me about 25 minutes to load three darts before returning to the hammock and hopefully close enough to the chimp to end his spree.

I returned armed to find my people scattered in the compound in search of the missing chimp. No one was able to tell me where the black ball of fur had gone. I became upset. It is understood in every case where an animal gets loose, that someone, somehow, keeps the animal in sight for darting. I didn't know where to look, and my helpers were no help at all. I didn't scream chimp insults; instead they heard words that needed no interpretation. I knew the chimp could be very dangerous, and I knew that I had to go through bureaucratic paper work with a three-page report declaring the wild animal missing. I chose instead to continue the search.

We looked for hours without finding a trace of the escape artist. I felt certain within a couple of days we'd get a call, but even the neighbors did not report as they so often would by phone, "Mr. Baudy, something strange just crossed the road in front of my place . . ." My neighbors were accustomed to sighting many different animals, and whenever they saw something that was not native to the area, I was always called. (Fortunately, that didn't happen too often.) I put my helpers off their routines to search for the chimp. I had all 65 trees on the property climbed — no chimp. After several days, I called off the search, wrote the report, and eventually stopped thinking about the elusive Houdini.

I'd long since forgotten the incident when the call came from the lady who lived seven miles north of the compound. She lived in a small house on the south side of a huge tract of land comprising about 10,000 acres of natural growth. On one edge of the property was a lime rock road. Over the phone she explained, "For the past year, we have seen a number of things happening around our place, but we never saw who done it . . . some dishes have been moved and some other things . . . but we've never seen anyone . . . but this time we saw it!"

"Oh, yeah? Do you have any idea where the animal is now?" I asked, not thinking of the missing chimp.

"Yeah! When I picked up my kid from school, we saw him cross the road."

"He crossed the road in what direction . . . north or south?"

"He's on the south side."

I knew the property well and knew that it contained a small hammock. If the animal went into the wild growth of the vast acreage, we'd never find him, but if he was in the hammock we might succeed. The lady described the animal as a strange looking bear, but it didn't move like a bear.

"I left my little boy sitting by the road to watch it."

I acknowledged that to be a brilliant idea. I got three of my helpers and gathered several tranquilizer guns, short as well as long range. One of the men was a young Frenchman, who was strong, agile, and climbed trees well.

When we arrived at the designated location, the little boy was sitting just as his mom directed, watching for the animal. It had been an hour since the call. He said to me, "Last time I saw it . . . it was on that large oak," pointing to a tree in the hammock near some tall pines. We hadn't had time to contact the owner of the property, but we jumped over the fence and with field glasses began scrutinizing the trees. I noticed in one of the pine trees a large bulky nest, similar to that of an osprey. I had a .30-06 rifle with me, and I figured the nest could be a likely hiding place. I shot a bullet into the trunk of the tree beneath the nest causing all sorts of birds and debris to fly out. The noise was loud enough to alarm any creatures and suddenly, about 50 feet away from the pine, a chimp jumped from another tree. I knew immediately what we were pursuing. As the chimp moved with lightning speed from one tree to another, I couldn't get a bead to shoot the gun. He was leaping, arms extended, and I was impressed with the distance he carried, over 50 feet in one leap from the top of a tree to a lower branch.

As he continued to move, he alluded my sights, but I could see that he was tiring. He kept watching me; whenever he stopped and I raised the gun, he immediately leaped to another tree. This went on for three hours as the sunlight began to fade on the drama in the hammock. I requested that my people collect four or five neighbors, hunters, as quickly as possible and asked that they bring their high-powered rifles. Soon the crackers arrived with their guns and their dogs, but I said that dogs were not necessary. I was immediately rebuffed, "I don't go and my gun don't go no place where my dog don't go!"

I explained to the men that my idea was for them to shoot systematically at trees and drive the chimp from tree to tree toward a smaller clump where we could quickly fell two small pines to block him from returning to the main cluster. I fired the first shot in the pine tree about six feet below the monkey and, sure enough, he left heading away from me. The other shooters were positioned on the other side of the chimp as we successfully drove him onto some pine trees and then felled other trees to prevent their use as his bridge back toward the forest. I loaded a short-range projectile, a handgun, and directed the young Frenchman to climb the tree to shoot the chimp. The guy was shaking as he looked up at the screeching, teeth-bearing chimpanzee, who had enjoyed two years of freedom and resented the hell out of his exposure and imminent capture. He was raising a ruckus that reverberated through the hammock and could be heard for miles.

The property owner arrived, saw what was happening, and became an avid and supportive audience as daylight began to turn to dusk. The Frenchman, obviously shaken by the assignment, darted the chimp, who was exhausted by hours of frantic leaping, and we all watched for 20 minutes as the tranquilizer took affect.

It's quite amazing to watch the transformation of a tranquillized animal. I held the field glasses watching as his expression changed from fear and anger to peace and tranquility. His actions and expressions took on the appearance of a happy drunk. The instinct for survival is strong, and the chimp would not turn loose of the limb even as he was losing equilibrium. Finally, hanging upside down holding on with one hind foot, he lost the battle and fell into a waiting net. We loaded him in a shipping crate with a sliding door and transported the slumbering chimp back to the compound.

I waited until the next day to research the area where he'd been encamped. We had the authorization of the property owner to remove the nest, when we found it set in the top of a pine tree. His engineering and building skills were astounding. He had built a perfect round nest, the bottom made of woven limbs each about the diameter of my small finger. There was a covering of Spanish moss over which was another layer of intricately woven limbs on top of which was a padding of natural vine leaves. I removed the structure and took it back to the compound to display next to the chimp to demonstrate the cleverness and adaptability of the wild animal. The chimp was ultimately sold and delivered to a client in Mexico City.

With so many animals in residence and employees working, everyday held adventure. Whenever one episode seemed to draw to some sort of conclusion, I knew that another would occur. There were never any dull moments at the Savage Kingdom. One time I had to fire a worker for neglect, and the embittered man returned later in the day and opened a cage containing three large western pumas that had come to us from British Columbia. When I heard the call, "Puma loose," I ran outside to look, but saw no sign of the large cats. Within an hour, a call came from a neighbor reporting one of the cats on the north side of the property. Another neighbor called to report a cat on the south side of the compound and then, by following tracks, I located the third on the east side.

The pumas had split up, but when I knew where the three were located, I assigned two people to each of the three locations to watch the cats, while I went to the house to begin the process of loading darts. One of the pumas was a female; the dose would be less than for the two males. I accomplished the loading rather quickly, climbed into a vehicle, and drove to the first puma, up a tree and being observed by my employees on the ground. I darted the female and then returned to the vehicle, made a u-turn heading to the second location nearly a mile away. I shot a dart into the second puma then, leaving two people to watch as the tranquilizer took affect, I again returned to the vehicle, and drove to the third puma.

The last cat was a bit more challenging. It was a male and on the run. I waited until he stopped before I drew a bead and squeezed the trigger. When I returned to the first puma, she was already groggy and was soon returned to her cage. The second puma was already asleep when I found him. The third was also successfully lifted and returned to his cage, all within little more than an hour of beginning the frantic search. It was an amazing accomplishment to capture three pumas loose in three different directions in such a short period of time.

The phone call was shocking. It came from Omaha, Nebraska. Gerard, drunk and slurring, was pathetic.

"Samantha got hurt . . ."

"How did she get hurt?" I asked.

"She got hurt by a lion." I listened to his voice as he rambled. "She may not live . . . rushed her to hospital . . . condition guarded . . ."

I could barely understand him and asked if I could speak to Martine. There was no response. I asked him to call the next day to inform me of Samatha's condition. I sat for a long time thinking about the innocent child and what sounded like a brutal attack. I thought of the past neglect and disregard for danger associated with the cats on the compound. I felt helpless, angry, and hoped that the following day would bring news of a positive prognosis issued by a sober Gerard.

The next call from Gerard gave news that the baby did survive, but there would be ongoing surgeries performed to rebuild and repair her face. Gerard spoke clearly, "Martine was carrying the child . . . she walked to the lion chained to a stake outside the arena. It was a tame lion, but when they got close, the lion went after Samantha." He continued to describe the brutality of the attack. "Martine and Samantha became hysterical as the lion continued to savagely bite the baby's face and head. When workers hearing the screaming arrived, they freed Samantha, but her head and face were caved in. She was still in a guarded condition due to bones fractured and the brain possibly affected by fangs penetrating through the skull . . . the bottom fangs broke into her palate."

As I listened, I again thought of the lack of attentiveness on their part in preventing such a needless accident. I knew that life on tour was demanding and difficult enough without medical emergencies. I asked if there was anything I could do. Gerard said he would let me know.

Although there was never the luxury to dwell on any one tragedy for long in a business that held life and death on a daily basis, I couldn't help but think of Gerard's situation knowing that his life continued to be hell. His war had not ended with his return from Vietnam; it was being fought on a different battlefield. I felt pity for him and for the baby, but I could do little to alleviate the pain and suffering, particularly when so much of it was self-inflicted.

My hands and life were also full. There was enough pain and suffering at the Savage Kingdom. However, there was also humor, fascinating people who came to visit, and such a diverse retinue of employees. Good help was always needed with so much activity at the Center and to perform all that was required in my absence. Earl Simons arrived at the compound at a time when I needed him badly. Earl came from Ohio seeking a warmer climate. He was nearly six feet tall with blue eyes, red hair, and a mentality that reminded me of Fernie. He was a powerful man and proved quickly to be a good worker, except he needed alcohol everyday, and we soon learned had a passion for goats. In spite of strange amours, Earl became a trusted employee to help Diane when I left the compound.

34

MOVIES AND OTHER DRAMATICS IN THE KINGDOM
Le Cinéma et les Drames Au Royaume

*T*he Rare Feline Breeding Center and The Savage Kingdom were contacted frequently to furnish animals for a number of film productions, whether the filming was performed off the compound or in the central Florida location. My responsibilities as an animal trainer and owner of the unique performers went beyond leasing the animals or renting the portion of the compound utilized. I became, in some instances, joint director of the event as the only person on the set who could predict the behavior of the animal or animals. As a trainer, it was not a problem to train an animal to perform in a certain way, but the unusual circumstances presented by each demand was quite different from the nightclub or circus act, which remained fairly consistent. There were always challenging problems to solve and often funny incidents surrounding a serious endeavor.

Marlin Perkins, whom I'd met in 1951 when he was director of the Lincoln Park Zoo, remained a friend over the years and was engaged in hosting the popular television show *Mutual of Omaha's Wild Kingdom*. I'd purchased Rama, a young black leopard, from him years before and trained the cat, the super star of the leopard act, to jump 20 feet into my waiting arms. Rama performed the dramatic leap for 11 years without a single miss. Marlin phoned to ask a favor that had nothing to do with leopards.

Marlin and his entourage had gone to India to film the

behavior of Bengal tigers to include as the finale, the capture of a live Bengal. The crew filmed reels and reels of authentic Indian jungle scenery, but the tiger never materialized to take the bait. It had become a very costly and unfulfilled project which Marlin hoped could be completed at the compound. He suggested using a professional set decorator to duplicate an Indian motif on the compound if I would furnish not only a tiger, but also appropriate bait — fresh calf.

When the contract was written and signed, Marlin's experienced crew appeared to perform the preliminary set building, light testing, etc. After their initial investigation, I arranged to lease a portion of a hammock located across the highway from the compound. The owner of the property was Mrs. Hunt, and the agreement was to perform the shoot in two days with an open end if the weather didn't cooperate.

I had my own crew of five men assigned to help under the supervision of black foreman, Lamar Worthey. The crew built an invisible wire net fencing ten feet high, snaking through the hammock containing two acres. Two tigers, unfortunately Siberian instead of Bengal, were wheeled in transport cages to the set. The trap manufactured in India by Perkins crew consisted of a huge cotton net spread on the ground, the bait tethered to a wood stake deeply grounded in the center of the 30 foot netting.

The plan was for the net to be sprung as soon as the tiger took the bait, which would coincide with Perkins and his handsome assistant rushing in with huge forked limbs to pin the furious, trapped tiger, while another assistant forced the animal into a wooden cage. I explained to Marlin that I'd inspected the Indian-made net and didn't feel it would restrain an upset tiger for more than two seconds and further that the assistants, Marlin and Robert, faced certain grave risk and possible death.

Marlin assured me, "That's the way they are doing it all the time in India."

The first shooting day arrived. I had the bait tied to the post and ordered the guillotine door of the cage open to release Manchu. Manchu was a huge cat, fed like all my animals, on a natural diet fresh out of the slaughter house. But he was curious and had to investigate the set before going into action. The fresh meat must have been an inviting sight, but Manchu did not rush into the planned script. He continued his slow and deliberate investigation for nearly two hours while all members of the crew stood ready, sweating in the 110° Florida heat.

Manchu closed on the bait. Suddenly, he leaped a distance of ten feet, landing on top of the meat. In seconds, Manchu had uprooted the stake and run off before Marlin or anyone else could secure the netting. Obviously, the escape ended the shoot that day. Fortunately, the crew captured enough footage to splice onto existing material gathered in India. However, Marlin wasn't giving up.

The next day dawned grey. Filming was not possible, but tiger number two was rehearsed with a small amount of cold meat. Meanwhile, Manchu slept well after his heavy meal of fresh calf meat the preceding day.

The third day was spent regrouping and modifying the set. When Marlin appeared, I succeeded in persuading him to fake the actual capture using a prop man covered with a tiger pelt struggling violently in the net to simulate the finale. A distance shot would be realistic enough following the footage of the tiger pouncing on the bait which was already in the can. My suggestion would reduce the risk of using a real tiger. Marlin came to my living room and chose one of three tiger pelts from the floor. He insisted on playing the part of the captured tiger. I kind of thought him obsessive since my men were younger and more able to sustain the rigors of working under the heavy skin in extremely high heat and humidity.

When the cameras rolled, Marlin began his performance depicting a violently fighting tiger trapped in a flimsy net. Suddenly all action ceased. We ran to the trap and found Marlin passed out. The heat had gotten to him, but more than that, so had the content of the pelt. It was a favorite depository of Charlotte's toy poodle puppies, all of which had wet on the hundred-pound pelt numerous times. In the heat, it give off an inordinate amount of ammoniac urine fumes, which overwhelmed the pale and sweating Marlin. We brought him to and then directed Lamar to get another pelt and writhe on the ground under the netting. The filming was completed and Marlin and his crew left central Florida.

Periods of calm and quiet were rare at the Savage Kingdom. One day a male Afro-American from New York arrived at the compound. What struck me first was his t-shirt, which displayed a bloody fist on a bright yellow background emblazoned with "We

Shall Overcome." The lettering was formed by dripping blood. It was a striking artistic rendering. The man of 30 seemed to be articulate and willing, and I hired him to cut meat and supervise some of my ostrich breeders.

Among the 15 ostriches were a male and two females in a five-acre, grassy paddock. The male, imported from South Africa, had a gentle disposition with my Caucasian help and with me. I didn't realize that he had any problems, other than the two females sitting on eggs at the time. I asked the new man to help spread some feed at the end of the paddock.

I was driving the four-wheel-drive pick-up when I noticed the male ostrich showing signs of anger and directing it at my deeply occupied helper. Suddenly the feathers went up and with high-steps, the giant, 300-pound bird made a beeline towards the unsuspecting man. I floored the gas pedal and tried to intercept the mad bird, but the ostrich dodged the truck. I made a u-turn and put the truck at full throttle on two wheels. Again the bird dodged me and resumed his lethal charge. There was no time to warn the man, now in danger. I jumped out of the rolling truck and stood, braced with arms open between the bird and the man standing only a hundred feet away.

This time the bird didn't dodge and slammed into me at full speed. I fell to the ground with a heavy thud. The bird hit me with two enormous feet, terminated by four-inch-long sharp claws, and began to peck at my eyes. By instinct, I rolled my head back and grabbed the ostrich with both hands. In an attempt to prevent it from doing further damage, I pulled its head under my arm, tightening my armpit.

Suddenly, I remembered Father's admonition years before, "Really, the best time to get even with your enemy is when he is down." I hadn't thought of that expression until the bird was actively pecking at my eyes. Miraculously, as I held him in a strangle grip, the animal dropped to the ground next to me and became absolutely still. I felt blood gushing from my left thigh. I yelled to the man for help, only to see the disappearing t-shirt streaking through the hammock. It was a comical sight, but I wasn't laughing — yet.

I was alone and knew that if I released the bird, it might strike again. So, inch by inch, I dragged the ostrich 80 feet to the pick-up, its head still securely under my arm. I slowly moved its head out from under, covered its eyes with my right hand, then crawled into the cab of the truck as I released the bird. I had escaped.

The truck, however, was not so lucky. The old Ford is still sitting at the compound, its grill and fenders destroyed by the frustrated blue-neck male ostrich, and I still carry a scar the size of a silver dollar on my leg. I never saw the man again, and I can remember laughing all the way to the hospital.

I had a client in Spain, a surgeon named Dr. Barbier, who maintained a thriving medical practice in Rabat. Through the Barcelona Zoo, Dr. Barbier had received a copy of my catalogue. He came to the compound and bought many animals over the years. He maintained a private collection at his mansion outside Rabat and decided to invest his money in the building of a zoo near Barcelona. He retained me as zoological consultant requiring several trips to set up the facility and select a herd of camels.

In 1975, I made a fateful journey to Morocco and to France. The trip began with ground-breaking for the zoo in Barcelona and became a camel hunt in Morocco, a fascinating experience dealing with the herders and the auctioneers. I flew into Rabat, then with the doctor in his private plane, on to small villages south of Marrakesh, where the quality of the dromedary camels was known to be excellent.

The doctor had a schedule of cattle sales taking place at various villages. There were 200-300 natives living in mud huts in each village, and our arrival was always cause for frantic running as we circled before landing. The children and women were not to be exposed to foreigners.

When we did land, we were met by the men of the village and then entertained over a ritualistic tea ceremony served as we sat on mats on the floor of their quarters, conversing for hours. I was not so patient with the ritual and tried to hurry the process, but Dr. Barbier informed me that the natives were still living as they did in Biblical times, and there was no shortcut to the main objective — to see the camels.

It was fascinating to watch the natives working with and breaking the camels. The camel is an extremely dangerous animal. I'd heard accounts of the male of the species killing zookeepers during the breeding season.

Camels are known to bite their enemies and then proceed to lay on top of the victim, and rotate the chest in a crushing motion. The male has a horny plate on its chest between its front legs. The camel's teeth, like tusks, are larger than a tiger's and the bite is horrible. Because the teeth are jagged instead of sharp, it is the tearing and ripping that creates so much pain and damage. The Arabs place a ring in the animal's nose and control it by pulling on the ring.

The Moroccan portion of the trip was successful. I acquired 25 camels for the doctor. When I left Dr. Barbier, I went to Rennes to visit Mother.

I immediately realized that she had developed serious memory problems. It was disconcerting to listen and watch as she recalled many details of her childhood, then searched in vain for keys and other objects in clear view. She left the stove on and nearly caught the apartment on fire. She was also extremely impatient and criticized my lack of attentiveness toward Gerard, telling me that I didn't do enough for the boy. She had never said anything like that to me in the past when she seemed intent on raising him. Granted that while I'd provided materially for him, I'd left the physical and emotional security of a home up to my parents and had hoped that the university in Rennes would offer the education and influence that would direct his path toward a profession.

Mother's conversation and behavior were so out of character, but obviously demonstrated deep concerns. I took her out for an evening of good dining, one activity she seemed to covet on all my visits. She was detached, not at all like the wonderful, gentle-natured mother I knew, who had a keen memory and mind. Her mind had been the source of minute detail all through her life, making her the dependable and trusted witness that police sought to supply evidence in criminal cases in Le Vesinet years before.

I contacted relatives and the nuns at the hospital to express my concern. They were aware of her memory loss and promised to be more attentive in looking in on her. I returned to the States knowing that she could not continue living alone for long.

The trip from Nevers to Rennes required several train changes and was lengthy and costly, but nieces and nephews made the trek to visit Mother. Cousin Claire and her husband Maurice were the most frequent visitors. Maurice worked for the railroad and his retirement provided travel benefits. They began to spend a week at a time in Rennes and then write to me. Their letters were not encouraging. Mother's condition continued to deteriorate, and they arranged for a nurse to look in on her daily.

As always there was much to occupy me mentally and physically in central Florida. Diane and the children added to that which required my attention. Diane continued to be a hard worker, but I found her attitude and behavior puzzling, remote actually. However, she did seem to appreciate having a home for the children, and I did treat them like mine. We arranged for a school bus to pick them up, but Matt was unruly on the special pick-up and service was cut off. I didn't hesitate to discipline Matt if he got out of control, just as I would my own son.

Diane kept asking for a raise in pay, but I felt like I was providing for her and the kids, and I didn't meet her demands for more money. My refusal was met by an escalating cost of living reflected in canceled checks from the grocery each month. I couldn't get an accounting from her as to the rising costs, but the pattern continued.

With letters and phone calls from France and Mother very much on my mind, I continued to react to the many engrossing incidents that occurred nearly everyday on the compound. One expression that required immediate response was, "Jaguar loose!" Jaguar always commanded my special attention. Pound for pound, it is by far the most powerful cat in the world. Intelligence coupled with its tenacity made any emergency a unique challenge.

The statement from an obviously distraught helper pulled me from my paper work. Not knowing which jaguar was loose or the circumstances of the escape, I quickly reached for three tools: a .38 Smith and Wesson, which I stuck in my back pocket; a long-range tranquilizer projector; and a .30-06 rifle. Out in the field, I realized the calm and inquisitive animal was a captive-born, large-spotted female formerly used in a Disney movie. I was relieved since my collection at the time included several wild-caught black jags. One, named Macho, captured as an adult in the Mato Grosso, had a history of snatching Indian babies from the local village.

A young helper had accidentally left one door open after transferring the cat from one cage to another for cleaning. I'd noticed that this particular cat, ordinarily demonstrating a gentle disposition toward me and other keepers, always displayed hostility toward the young helper. I immediately ordered all of the keepers out of the animal's sight and proceeded to gently herd the jaguar back toward her cage. In the delicate, slow dance, I stopped when she stopped and resumed my stealthy drive when she responded positively to my friendly jaguar sound. I discarded the .30-06 rifle, but kept the tranquilizing gun as a prod. Moving peacefully, I soon brought the animal within six feet of her open cage door when she turned, threateningly! I glanced over my shoulder and saw the boy she hated, who, against my instruction to remain out of sight, stood ten feet behind and to my left.

With a roar of fury, and from a crouched position, the animal sprang. In a fraction of a second, I threw myself in her path. The jaguar tore at my left forearm, raised in front of my face. I wore a heavy winter coat which helped minimize injuries, but with the proverbial tenacity of the jag, she didn't let go. I felt my hand being crushed repeatedly. I tried to reach the .38 in my back pocket, but it seemed an eternity before I loosed it. The enraged animal stood on her hind legs, embracing me in an unshakable grip. At point-blank range, I shot her six times in the neck and thoracic area. It took an endless five seconds before she fell back in a crouch, blood pouring from her open mouth as well as from my hand.

I turned to go to the house to retrieve a weapon to euthanize the animal after staring at her — smoke and blood coming from her wounds. Before I got to the house, my helpers diverted me and took me off to the Leesburg Hospital emergency room where the hand was rebuilt minus a small amount of flesh swallowed by the jaguar. Life-threatening adventure continued to be a major part of my existence, my life on the compound.

As I continued to be apprised of Mother's deteriorating condition, I attempted to conduct business as usual dealing with the many inquiries for animals, receiving animals, and making trips out of Florida on business. I was in touch with Claire and knew that a trip to France was imminent. When Claire called to report that Mother would have to be admitted to a nursing home, I flew home dreading the deed, but knowing that no one else could perform what was unavoidable.

It had been painful for Mother when she was released from

her volunteer work at the hospital. I talked to the nuns hoping that there was some area of work that she could perform; but I knew, realistically, that it was not feasible. When Mother was lucid, I listened to her lament and tried to comfort and assuage her, but there was little one could say to placate her when she was aware and upset. Then when she withdrew, it did not seem to matter. It was devastating to see someone who had been so good to others all her life reach the point where the kindness and goodness of others did not serve to provide any relief or comfort in her darkened, impenetrable psychosis. And that woman was my dear and loving mother.

The nuns looked in on her, and a nurse was hired to visit each day, but Mother required someone to be with her at all times. She had maintained many characteristics in spite of her mental decline, and she valued her privacy and her surroundings. I even had thoughts of bringing her to the States to live with me. I had agonized over all the alternatives knowing that her pattern, to wander off in Rennes from time to time, would be extremely dangerous if she walked out into the compound and came too close to a tiger or panther cage. She required constant surveillance, and I couldn't trust that it would be successful at the farm.

I met Claire and Maurice at the apartment. Mother's condition had declined profoundly. She welcomed me cheerfully as someone she should have known and gave me a big hug, then admonished me for not coming to visit for years. She didn't know that I was her son. I was crushed, deeply disturbed by her total oblivion. Her lucid moments had disappeared. Maurice had already contacted the state agency, and a meeting was set where procedures were explained and medical tests performed.

The examining doctor told me, "Mr. Baudy, you are very lucky that you got away with this for so long."

I asked him to explain.

"With your mother's condition, she could have caused tremendous problems for her neighbors, and they could have reported you. Under French law you are in charge. I don't care if you are in America. You could be held liable for lawsuits. It is your responsibility to get a sanction from the state to cover your mother's situation."

I was not thinking of my liability or of sanctions, but was

consumed with Mother's condition, the horror of the whole procedure, and what it portended.

Claire adored Mother and was devastated by the situation. She couldn't face seeing her aunt put into a nursing home. We braced together for the trip. It was my duty to make final arrangements and commitment. I called a taxi to pick us up at the apartment. Claire had gathered and packed the few items that Mother could take with her. There were tears shed by my dear cousin as we drove to the home. I remained stoic, but agonized over what was the toughest assignment I'd ever performed.

The grey-walled granite building was depressing outside, but clean and orderly within. I was introduced to the director and listened to words spoken, but my mind was on Mother, anxious and obviously shaken by this strange outing. When the director was finished, we were led to a clinic where Mother would be further examined.

To reach the clinic, we crossed through an outdoor courtyard nearly 300 feet square filled with patients. It was like a return to the prison in St. Mande, with Stunner and Didier in search of Maguy. The elderly, infirm, mentally retarded, and senile patients reached out and called to us; it was truly a scene from hell. I couldn't close it out and saw that Mother was horrified and nearing a state of collapse. I held her and guided her through the pathetic melange, telling her that the people were good, well-meaning, and wouldn't hurt her. I was shaking when I delivered her to the clinic. As I left the home, I knew I would never forget the day that I took her to that place.

I returned to the apartment and cried like a baby. I cried for Mother, for all that I'd put her through, and all that I couldn't change. I could no longer convey to her that I loved her. My thoughts went to Stunner and the horror of him, dead on the battlefield, and I kept crying. I met with Simone. I needed to be with her. She consoled and loved me. And she assured me that she would visit Mother. I knew that if Mother had any capacity to feel love, she'd feel it from Simone.

When I returned to Florida, Odette phoned to inform me that Gerard and Martine had divorced. She also reported that Samantha was receiving reconstructive surgeries to repair the massive damage to her head and face. The accident had taken place at a Shrine Circus in Omaha, and the Shrine was covering the extensive medical care and cost incurred by the ghastly injury. That was the good news. Odette didn't know where Gerard was. Unfortunately, I had to feel at least some relief in not hearing from him, but knew it wouldn't last. I was deeply concerned about the lost soul, knowing too well his pattern. I braced for the storm, and in a sense, thought Mother better off not knowing of the ongoing problems in Gerard's life.

35

EXPOSURE
Sous la Lumière

*T*he Endangered Species Act stunned me when it was first enacted. I did not fully realize the potentially dire repercussions from a law passed without research or knowledge by Federal lawmakers attempting to protect endangered species. The bureaucrats were protecting animals in the country of origin by ending importation, while at the same time encroached on the rights of other governments by insisting they sign the pact. Countries that did not comply were threatened with cessation of foreign aid funds.

I did support the act under the precepts of ending the gross massacre that I witnessed at the hands of mass importers, particularly those engaged in furnishing animals to the pet trade. The abuses were rampant and horrendous. I saw wheelbarrows full of dead monkeys at the Miami port of entry, primates that had not been properly cared for in transport. However, I did not fully realize the impact of the act on the private breeder. In bird importation in the United States, there were at least 6,000 licensed breeders of extremely rare birds, breeders entirely reputable and knowledgeable who had spent a lifetime and their own capital perpetuating and saving species. They were suddenly out of business and totally handcuffed in continuing what had been either a hobby or source of income. I even heard of cases where suicides were committed by distraught victims engaged in an industry devastated by the ruling.

The Federal Government mandate under the U.S. Fish and Wildlife Service listed many species which were not endangered.

The authorities had not done their homework, but had hastily reacted and complied with the demands of powerful Washington lobbyists representing the influentially vocal and financially strong animal rights activists. The lawmakers in their haste to avoid lawsuits were grossly inefficient and overbearing.

I had the dubious honor of being the first breeder indicted under the new legislation. My crime was ambiguous. I had taken black jaguar and spotted-leopard pelts from animals that died of natural causes. I sent the pelts for tanning to Jonas, a taxidermist located in Colorado. I wanted the pelts preserved for educational purposes as well as to preserve the memory of the individual animals.

While the pelts were being treated, a wealthy man arrived at the compound. Craddock owned a huge ranch near Bartow and expressed the desire to invest money in the compound. He informed me that he had a zoo in North Carolina for which he bought some animals from me. He was a member of what we in the trade call the "Trophy Club" — a collector of animals hunted, killed, and mounted as decorative pieces. Craddock used Jonas to perform his taxidermy work, knew that I had pelts at the plant in Colorado being processed, and asked if I was willing to sell them. I said he would have to wait until the pelts were returned to me. He responded that it would be no problem for him to pick up the pelts from Jonas. He gave me a check for which I signed and gave him a receipt.

Mr. Craddock contacted me again with an offer to invest $75,000 against a mortgage on the compound. He had his lawyer draw up the papers, which I took to a lawyer friend who strongly advised me not to sign, explaining there were many clauses in the agreement which would result in Mr. Craddock's owning the whole compound within a year. My informant described one clause giving Craddock the right to foreclose on a Friday.

"What difference does that make?" I asked.

"If somebody forecloses by surprise on Friday afternoon, you would never be able to arrange for financing over the weekend. It's the kind of clause that crooked Realtors use."

Craddock's agreement was two inches thick. I took it to my attorney, had it rewritten, then I signed. It didn't take long for Craddock and Robert to have a falling out. In his anger, the influential Craddock contacted a prominent Washington senator and soon Feds from the Fish and Wildlife Service were all over the compound asking questions. They accused me of breaking the Endangered Species Act and cited me for the sale of the pelts to Craddock. The pelts were from captive-born animals that had died naturally. The case went to Federal Court and took two and a half years to close.

I ultimately made four appearances in court during the lengthy, legal harangue. I had a lawyer friend from Lakeland, Charles Mayer, advise me. Between court hearings life on the compound continued with movies made, clients arriving, and much to detract from the waiting guillotine. When I appeared for the final hearing before a judge in the Federal Court in Jacksonville, the investigators had a file that weighed over ten pounds on Robert Baudy. Apparently, the idea was to make a test case to echo throughout the animal export-import business community. My defense was simple and honest; the Act covered interstate and international commerce, but did not cover intrastate transactions. In our case, both Mr. Craddock and Robert Baudy were Florida residents doing business within the state. There was no case to begin with.

The final hearing lasted two days as I observed the growing impatience demonstrated by the Judge who heard both sides and declared in his closing statement, "Gentlemen, obviously this is one of the first cases being investigated under the "so-called" new Endangered Species Act. I would like to tell you that you have wasted not only your time, but my time and the gentleman's time involved, in addition to taxpayers' money, when in fact you have no case whatsoever. I would advise you not to disturb people's lives, to make them spend money for absolutely nothing when you have no just cause. This case is dismissed, and I don't want to see another like it in my court!"

It took the government years to finally amend the original law granting exportation permits under specific guidelines, but the regulations continued to stifle the breeding and importation of captive-born animals and those not endangered. It was a typical, ill-conceived bureaucratic boondoggle.

During the years of court procedures, there were some comic moments on the compound to relieve the seriousness of Craddock's and the Government's attempt to bury me. Some of the most hilarious episodes involved a man named Martinez from Miami who approached me to furnish animals for Tarzan movies he was producing. The movies were designed for distribution in the South American market. Martinez was working on a lean budget and offered me the role of Tarzan. I told him that unless he had the cash to pay me, I was not interested in involving my time which would take me away from the compound in order to perform in an effort not well-financed and with no guarantee and no commitment. He apparently found another Tarzan for the lead.

A month passed after the first encounter with the producer, who returned to the compound extremely distraught. He sadly explained his plight, begging, "Mr. Baudy, I need your help . . . I'm frantic. I don't know what I'm going to do. I have all the equipment rented and set up, and we are filming just down the road. We're nearly finished filming . . ."

I looked at his glasses, drooping oddly down one side of his nose, the milky white lens sagging too low to help his vision, and barely heard what he lamented in anguished detail:

"We had Tarzan tied to the stake with a smoldering fire of gas and kerosene burning around him. We ran out of fuel so one of my extras went for more fuel. He came back and we ran the fuel again around the circle, threw a match to ignite it, and . . . BLAM! It was high octane fuel and there was a tremendous explosion. I gasped and heard Tarzan screaming. Everyone fled from the roaring flames. I went in to free the man but he was tied so securely to the stake, I could hardly get him free . . ."

Martinez cried as he continued, "Finally I freed him and we got the fire out, but he was badly burned. We have only a few shots left to complete the filming, and you've got to help me!"

"What can I do?" I replied, still looking at the strange glasses.

He quickly answered, "You must be my Tarzan. I have only to film a segment where Tarzan, freed, swings out of the trees and battles the jungle warriors who are taking away his leopard in a cage. You *must* help me."

I told him that I would not play the part of Tarzan, but I would help him to complete the film. He said he needed some natives, the leopard, and a cage for the final scene. He would find another Tarzan.

I went to Little Egypt, a neighborhood across from Big Egypt in Center Hill, where blacks live and also congregate to wait for whatever employment opportunities develop. I described to several of the men the job opportunity. They didn't like the idea of carrying a live leopard even if it was in a cage. I convinced them the job would be safe. I told them I trained the leopard which was tame and would remain in the cage at all times. I also informed that they would be paid well, but only after their duties were fulfilled, which would require several hours of actual filming. Convinced, the men appeared at the Savage Kingdom on the appointed day and were costumed and made up to appear as African natives.

The new Tarzan was a rodeo cowboy, who had never appeared in a movie and apparently had never swung from a tree. Tarzan was rehearsed and the natives were put through their paces carrying the cage with the leopard, which was heavy. The time of day for filming determined by the light in the shade-filled hammock was critical. On the first take, Tarzan clumsily swung down out of the upper branches of an oak tree into the hammock and knocked several of the natives to the ground. It didn't look too awkward to me, but Martinez was not satisfied. He had his Tarzan climb back into the tree for a second take. Again his swing pattern was ungainly as he fell into the natives, scattering and pushing them to the ground. The natives regrouped for a third take and then a fourth.

As the light of day began to recede, the natives were staggering from the abusive attack. One of them came to me and in a pathetic cry petitioned, "Mr. Baudy, this is not exactly what we thought it would be. We want our money. We don't want to keep on doing this." I couldn't blame them. They were being battered and bruised in the assault by an amateur Tarzan. I explained to the pathetic man that the agreement was for them to perform the work and be paid when the shooting was complete. I was getting impatient with the ongoing takes, and the natives were being brutalized. Finally, Martinez approved a "take," and the leopard was turned loose as Tarzan went off into the setting sun along with his trusted companion. The natives from Little Egypt got the hell off the compound, and Martinez, I imagine, got a new pair of glasses.

I hadn't heard from Martinez for a long time when he came to see me again. He had returned from Bolivia where he had been assigned to make a documentary on the shepherds who tend the llamas. The llamas are kept at 15,000 feet in remote and inaccessible areas of rugged mountain terrain and total isolation. The shepherds never interact with or see a human female while they work and reside in small, remote houses on wheels, no larger than a doghouse. Historically, it is an accepted and proven fact that the forced celibacy drives the shepherds to have sex with the llamas. Martinez directed the filming of the native customs which included a graphic segment of the mountain residents performing copulation with the furry white llamas.

I was breeding llamas at the Savage Kingdom at the time, and Martinez was again desperate to have my help. He explained that he shot an enormous amount of footage of thousands of llamas and hundreds of shepherds engaged in their daily activity, including excellent scenes of the herders engaged in intercourse with the animals. The film, as prearranged and stipulated, was reviewed by government censors. Martinez drew rave reviews from the officials exclaiming his documentary a wonderful and honest depiction of life in Bolivia, graphically demonstrating the harshness of the life of a shepherd. While the film was sympathetic to the herders, the censors chose to delete all of the footage showing sexual intercourse. Martinez pleaded for me to help him by duplicating the performance at the Savage Kingdom to salvage the $5,000 investment he had in what he considered an incomplete film.

I said to him, "If you secure the human actors, I will supply the llama and the setting."

The agreement was that I be paid $1,000 a day for the set and animal; Martinez would bring the film crew, the actors, and the native garb. When the crew arrived with Martinez, hot to get his delicate footage, we dressed some of my workers as Bolivian Indians with colorful hats and wool blankets. We drove the female llama into a corral. I had spent two days preparing my people for the filming, me to work from behind a wood blind holding onto clear fish line tethering the llama in position for the actual performance.

The man hired to perform the act of intercourse was a hairdresser from Miami. He was a handsome, dark-haired man and excessively chatty as he told me, "Well, Mr. Baudy, I don't know what the job will entail, but I would like you to know the story of my life." His voice, high-pitched and nervous, continued, "I'm a hairdresser from New York. Business was so bad I had to close my salon, and I've been trying to reopen a place in Miami, but Miami is very crowded. I've spent the money I brought down from New York, and I'm in a tight spot and need to earn some money badly. That is why I am here. Mr. Martinez didn't tell me precisely what my job is going to be . . ."

"Well," I said, "I'm sorry, but I had nothing to do with your hiring, but to the best of my understanding you are supposed to have a sexual relationship with a llama."

"WHAT?" The guy looked at me obviously shocked by my description as he began rattling off a long and excited discourse in Spanish that I did not fully understand. I did understand that he did not care for the assignment.

"Look," I said, " slow down. Let's go talk to Mr. Martinez."

I said to Martinez, "Look, you hired this man and you didn't tell him what he was going to do?"

Martinez countered, "I did tell him, but I said he could fake it."

I knew the man was extremely agitated, and I knew that Martinez wanted as close to authentic a depiction of the act. I was anxious to have the performance completed and the crew from Miami the hell out of the compound. I went into the corral to tether the llama and take my position behind the blind. The cameras were ready to roll. Martinez directed the hairdresser to go behind a tree that he pointed to, to do whatever was necessary to achieve an erection. He further directed that the whole segment would be filmed quickly, with cameras rolling, as he came from behind the tree and walked into the enclosure and close to the llama for a "take."

It was nearly an hour before the man came from behind the tree, penis erect, ready to perform. The cameras were rolling and focused as the man approached the llama. The animal was extremely agitated. When the hairdresser reached out to touch the unsuspecting animal, the startled llama reacted with a sudden kick catching the man sharply in the testicles. The man fell back screaming as he grabbed his crotch and backed out of the corral. Everyone was quite horrified. The man was obviously hurt.

Martinez, seeing his "take" ruined, ran to me and asked if I would talk the man into trying one more time. I had a long conversation with the pained hairdresser convincing him that I did not believe the animal would kick a second time. I promised to hold her more securely and guaranteed he would be safe. The guy obviously needed the money badly. He worked himself into another erection and again approached the llama, held firmly in position while spitting foul saliva at me. As the man slowly, cautiously approached, the llama's leg went up and again caught the hairdresser between the legs. I heard the cry and saw the man disappear. Martinez was beside himself. He could see his investment going down the drain. He came to me pleading for me to perform the act with the llama.

"Damn, you're crazy! I'm holding the damned animal, catching the foul spittle, but I will not have intercourse with the llama."

Martinez looked around and then implored his son, working the camera, "Will you do it?"

"Shit no, I'm not going to do THAT! I'm gonna' stop the camera. I'm disgusted with the whole thing."

Martinez decided he would have to perform if he was to complete the filming. It took seemingly forever before he came out from behind the tree. As he approached the llama the sun was beginning to set on what had become a very long day. He wore a Bolivian shepherd's blanket and colorful hat, his penis erect. He moved close to the white wooly llama's rear quarters. The llama was too busy spitting at me to notice as the camera caught the implied activity — we had a "take."

There were many actors and many performances by various humans as well as animals on the compound over the years. One of the most entertaining characters was Jo Banana, a Western Africa white-faced chimpanzee worth every dollar of the $1,000 I paid to bail him out of jail. Jo had been raised by an orange grove owner outside LaBelle, who treated the chimp like a child and a member of the family. Jo slept in his own crib before graduating to a regular bed. He loved to ride the family pony, the very activity which ultimately created his legal problem.

One day while taking a stroll in the neighborhood, Jo spotted a grazing pony in a pasture. With one athletic leap, he cleared the fence from behind the unsuspecting pony and landed abruptly on the back of the startled animal. Within seconds, the terrorized pony took off at full gallop, ran into a fence, and broke its neck. The owner of the pony was not amused and called the authorities. Since the fatal pony ride was not Jo's only peccadillo, the local sheriff seized Jo, incarcerating him in the county jail. I was informed that during Jo's arrest, he managed to delicately steal one of the deputy sheriff's revolvers. Jo had to be bailed out of jail to the tune of $1,000.

During Jo's stay in the LaBelle jail, a lady friend of the owner took him daily meals at breakfast, lunch, and dinner, service to which Jo was accustomed at home in the grove. I purchased Jo planning to use him as a promotional tool for the compound. I didn't realize at the time that I would be adding to my household. I furnished a cage with an army cot and blanket for sleeping, but Jo spent most of the daylight hours in the house with me or roaming the country in the pick-up truck sitting next to me as he rode nonchalantly, a serious expression on his craggy face, his right arm dangling over the rolled down window. From the day Jo arrived, he was quite a gentleman even after a few glasses of wine, which he enjoyed sipping at my table. He learned to recork the bottle and never broke any glasses either during the drinking process or while carefully washing them in the sink. He enjoyed smoking cigars and tipped his ashes into a waiting ashtray. He used the commode and never failed to flush after sitting for a spell while enjoying a good Havana.

I took Jo to parties with me. For any special occasion, I dressed him neatly in fancy denim pants, white tennis shoes, and a baseball cap. His absolute favorite was inscribed "We shall overcome." He was such a lovable character that even the words on the cap did not create any antipathy in the local Sumter County bars where Jo enjoyed watching the behavior of the homo sapiens while sipping his wine. Jo was also very handy with tools. He used a hammer and handsaw with great dexterity and best of all worked for PEANUTS. What a guy!

I did use Jo for my originally intended purpose as an attention-getter for the Savage Kingdom. He rode up and down on a cable attached from the ground to the tip of a 50-foot pole next to Highway 48.

A trip to France was necessary in addition to business in Barcelona with Dr. Barbier. I visited Mother. She thought I was Gerard. Simone went with me. She was an angel. She had been visiting Mother once a week in the nursing home and even took her out for drives. I loved her for the compassion she so freely and lovingly gave.

I hadn't spent any time in the apartment in Rennes the

previous year dealing with the many household items stored there, but the opportunity to rent it took me back and forced me to disperse the books in Father's personal collection of which there were over a thousand in addition to many fine bronzes and antique furniture. In order to facilitate the rental agreement and clear the apartment, I didn't have time to wrap and ship the many personal items to family members nor to auction in Paris; time was too short. There were friends of Mother's and some of her doctors who had expressed interest in particular antiques, art objects, or books, and I gave them all away. There were some finely bound books worth a great deal of money. In some cases, I regret having so hastily dispersed what I would treasure today. But to those people who so kindly and patiently served Mother, I was satisfied knowing the items would be enjoyed and appreciated.

I returned to Florida where I was less than appreciated and discovered I was being taken advantage of by Diane. Gladys told me that she suspected Diane was stealing from me.

I replied, "Look, the woman may be stealing from me, but I am not paying her enough. I realize that, but at the same time I'm taking care of her kids, kids who are not mine, buying them clothes and toys. When things get better financially, I will pay her better, but for now it's the best I can do!"

But having what I had suspected verbalized by Gladys focused my attention on the situation. I had been giving Diane carte blanche with the grocery bill. I had told her from the beginning to get whatever she wanted to feed the children and me, and I even trained her well in shopping for and preparing food in the French manner using wines and special herbs. But action was warranted. I went to my friend, Eugene Eubanks, director of the bank.

"Hey, Eugene, look at my god-damned grocery bill."

He looked it over. "Well, obviously it's not all kosher . . ."

She was buying $85 worth of groceries and asking that a check for $150 be cashed. Eventually, the monthly bill had gradually escalated to $800. That was one hell of a cost-of-living increase. I confronted her; I even had a statement from the grocery store manager that confirmed her pattern. Diane denied the allegations and made no excuses for the exorbitant increase. I was extremely disappointed in the woman, whom I trusted for many years. Mostly I was disappointed in her inability to face me and tell the truth. But an interesting confession did materialize.

Gladys came to me and confessed that she was the culprit who instructed Diane in "how to get more money out of Robert." Apparently, Diane went to Gladys for consolation from time to time, and I'm certain they had much to talk about where I was concerned. Gladys admitted that she told Diane how she operated as the wife of Joe Lewis.

"Joe was making a lot of money and always carried $3,000. But he was stingy with me and when he got drunk, I went to his pants pocket and took a couple of hundred, and he never missed it. One time we were in Vegas, and the son of gun lost $20,000, but he wouldn't even give me any money. I was furious. I took a couple of thousand that time, and he never missed it." The advice was taken into account by Diane. She never took cash from my pockets that I knew about, but she obviously had her own methods.

I felt like I was in the middle of a soap opera with the two women manipulating me. Gladys valued our friendship too much to let Diane or someone else implicate her in the check-kiting method to extort money which she was guilty of inspiring. With Gladys' revelation, I at least understood better Diane's *raison d'être*. I also realized how damned naïve I was where women are concerned. I had been involved with many women over the years; but I never understood them, and I was becoming less and less enchanted with the conniving and the discontentment that seemed to enter relationships. I was wearying of the battle.

My relationship with Diane changed dramatically. She was too frightened to confess any guilt and probably felt completely justified. She needed the job desperately, and I needed her to be there. I didn't ask her to leave, but intimacy ceased to be a part of the arrangement which became strictly business.

Gladys, a sophisticated lady imbued with a great deal of common sense and compassion, was extraordinary in many ways. I had spent hours and days with her over the years, but we had never become sexually involved. She'd been an angel when I needed her during the lengthy divorce from Charlotte until the final papers were signed. I had so much respect for the lady and fully intended maintaining the relationship as platonic, recognizing her as a very special friend and also a tremendous helpmate who adored and lovingly cared for the animal babies that needed bottle feeding and to be nurtured during their weaning. But, circumstances made that difficult, and as in so many previous affairs, we found ourselves involved.

I'd become accustomed to spending hours with Gladys overseeing the babies while she cared for them in her home on the lake, where we thoroughly enjoyed the unique challenge and gratification associated with raising dependent animals. Her home was elegant, and it was a haven as well for me, sharing drinks and dinner as a guest in the pristine surroundings of the lakeside abode, being treated like a king. I was at the Lewis home one afternoon when a violent storm, which had been forecast, started with heavy winds and torrential rain thundering down in hurricane velocity for hours with no sign of abating. As we watched the rising, churning lake encroach on her property, Gladys panicked. I knew she needed moral as well as physical support.

I placed sandbags wrapped in a protective bulwark across the lake side of the foundation while Gladys drank some hefty scotches to calm her nerves. After hours of intense work, arduous in the slashing rain to preserve her property, I returned to the safe confines of the house and sat, exhausted, to join her in a drink or two. We shared dinner and more scotch as the storm continued to rage; finally we went to bed together. That was the first time that I'd ever shared Gladys' bed. As we held one another that night, we discovered other previously untapped qualities. It was the beginning of a fulfilling relationship initiated as the floodwaters seeped into the house.

When we awakened the following morning, the winds had subsided, but we stepped into three inches of water. The carpeting and much of the furniture were ruined and required a massive effort to remove. Extensive redecorating was called for.

It was predictable that our first intercourse would be the first of many. I stayed to help Gladys remove the water before we even assessed the extent of the damage. I returned to the compound to find trees felled by the storm and much work to bring the hammock back to a workable business enterprise. But through all of the work, Gladys found me to be sustaining as I, too, found her to be special, bringing wisdom, maturity, and a wonderful spirit of fun to our relationship.

Even with the new arrangement, she chose to live in her

home. I stayed at the compound, except for interludes when I spent nights and sometimes several days with her enjoying fishing and relaxing in the beautiful wild environs of Lake Panasoffkee. Gladys was six years older than I and knew better than to attach strings to our relationship. We enjoyed an open, honest, and fulfilling assignation until the day she died.

36

LIFE IN THE SAVAGE KINGDOM
La Vie au Royaume Sauvage

One of the factors which influenced locating my permanent winter quarters in central Florida was the abundance of domestic farm animals kept not only in Sumter County, but in the five adjoining counties. The law of averages made it predictable that large numbers of horses and cows would suffer crippling injuries or accidental death. Consequently, I have been advertising for years "Free removal of crippled horses and cows." The freshly butchered meat was nutritionally important in raising healthy cat specimens. Since I began to pick up the infirm and dead animals, I've collected well over 15,000 animals to supply the enormous amount of food required daily on the compound. During the winter months the feline appetite increases, and it takes 3,000 pounds of meat per day to feed all the animals.

When I finally closed on the property, the plans drawn for animal quarters and our apartment included a slaughterhouse which was a vital part of the installation, particularly when the animal importation and breeding business burgeoned. Located a half mile from the main house, the slaughterhouse was designed with a huge winch capable of lifting a 3,000-pound bull. Once we were called upon to pick up an elephant that had broken a leg at a nearby fair. We were equipped to handle the large mammal.

We maintain to this day a fully operational facility, complete with drain and septic tank, that has performed well to provide thousands of pounds of raw meat required to sustain the animal residents in the hammock. In addition, there is also a smaller slaughter facility close to the main building where small animals are processed.

I did much of the slaughtering for years having had excellent training, compliments of the Germans. My staff worked with me, and I trained each employee in the proper methods of butchering for the feline diet, which is completely different from meat rendered for human consumption. It's important that the hides stay attached to the meat, and in that procedure, I was obviating a lucrative potential market where 50 to 100 dollars was the assessed value of each hide. What was far more important to me was the fact that the hide provided a wonderful high protein content at 98 percent toward a rich nutritional diet for the feline animals.

With all the tools necessary to maintain a huge, fully-stocked compound, the need for meat is extensive, and I attempted always to answer all requests to have animals picked up. The service was and still is offered free, but it has been taken for granted. I received, and still do to this day, phone calls from the highway patrol as well as from sheriff's departments in the counties surrounding Sumter. Calls from the police come most frequently on weekends when there is more drinking and driving. After dark when senses are dulled by alcohol and vehicle speeds are increased, it becomes more difficult to see and avoid a black cow standing in the middle of the highway. I've seen accidents where animals are brutalized by a car or truck, and I've also seen some people badly injured. Whenever there is an accident involving an animal, Robert Baudy is the first to be called.

Over the years, I've developed a unique relationship with the ranch owners in central Florida. Often when a valued pet or animal is injured or ill, I've been called to determine if the animal can be saved. In most cases, the owners know that the animal has to be destroyed. And then, more often than not after picking up the affected animal, I receive lengthy telephone inquiries from the owners as to the cause of illness or death. It's been my policy, as the butchering and autopsy procedures take place, to make an extensive list of what I find to be the problem. Obviously in many instances, it is vital to know the cause to prevent the spread of disease through a herd. In the meantime, I've spent many hours on the phone, in the picking-up process, and in the butchering which costs the animal owner nothing. I get free meat, but they get not only free animal removal, but a professional diagnostic evaluation. For this reason, there are many people in the area who seemingly worship me for the knowledge I offer. I have amassed quite a following and in that, I feel a sense of pride and honor knowing that I do offer a much-needed and legitimate service.

However, many people are under the impression that I'm supported by the county. If I'm called when I'm snowed under and unable to answer immediately, I may have an irate individual ask and even demand that I come or lament, "What am I to do?" I tell them to call their vet. I've had calls when the "favorite horse" died and fell over the septic tank on a Sunday morning. I was dressed in my Sunday best attire, and you can bet that became a damned messy operation, tough on slacks and jacket.

An interesting pattern has evolved over the years. There have been animals picked up and treated successfully that fully recuperated. I have always called the donor to inform them that their animal has survived and can be returned. Only once did I get a positive response. For whatever reason, most people decide that the animal is no longer desired, so I inherited many such animals. There are always horses, cattle, stray pigs, goats, and chickens wandering through the oak hammock surrounded by leopards, tigers, bobcats, and other natural but caged predators.

One day a State Wildlife officer arrived with a question. He asked if I could use some feral cattle that had been pursuing and annoying local hunters in the huge green swamp, part of which is located only 12 miles from the compound. I said that I'd take a look and see if I could capture the wild spoilers. I drove to the swamp in a new, green, four-wheel drive, open-body Ford pickup. I knew from the officer's directions approximately where the cattle were located, protecting "their territory," and had little trouble picking up tracks. I loaded my .30-06 and as silently as possible, tried to snake through the brush to catch a sighting of my prey. I was moving against the wind. The brush became impassable and I sought another route as the wind abruptly changed, blowing my scent toward the wild cattle. I'd hoped to see the enemy before it detected my presence.

Without warning, I heard a thundering charge crushing through the thicket. Instinctively, I looked for a handy tree in case my rifle missed the mark. I was about a hundred yards from the pick-up with several pine trees between me and the vehicle, but none were climbable as an escape. Suddenly, like a rocket, a bull came stampeding out of the dense vegetation just five feet from me. In a blind rage and at high speed the animal went on about a hundred feet before making a u-turn. I turned and jumped into the thick growth using it as cover to zigzag in a detour towards the truck. The massive bull, head down, charged in a straight line after the crunching sounds created by my wild crashing through brush. With seconds to spare, I made it back to the pick-up and jumped onto its protective open end just as the long horns grazed the side of the Ford. In the bull's frustration and rage, he broadsided the truck body with such violence that I couldn't get an accurate bead on his head. After minutes of fierce blows against the metal, he backed away to regain breath, and I dropped him with a single brain shot.

As I settled down to let my pulse slow, I noticed the thorns, briars, and wood shards embedded in my arms (the poison ivy came a week later). I sat for a few minutes to recuperate, stunned by the ferocity of the attack, not noticing an enormous diamondback rattler just five feet from the truck, obviously disturbed as well by all the commotion.

Just as I moved out of range of the snake, I heard the loud rattle of an approaching vehicle. A battered, multicolored pick-up appeared, driven by a Florida cracker, grizzled grey beard and unkempt hair covered by a greasy, torn rebel hat. The man climbed out of his truck holding an old bolt-action, rusty, .22. With a toothless grin, he looked at the bull.

"I'll jes be damned! I see ya' finally got that fuckin' bull. I heerd yur shot, was curious ta see who won. I've ben shootin' at that son of a bitch fur years. I bet its got 30 pounds a' lead under its hide!"

He turned and walked back to the rusty truck, then came back with a full bottle of crystal clear moonshine. I detected he'd already been drinking as he fought, cussing, to open the bottle. He pulled a huge hunting knife from his belt and neatly knocked the neck off the bottle. He amiably offered me the first drink. I didn't want to succumb to glass particles in my intestines after having survived the attack by the bull and declined his offer.

"Well, pardner, don' worry. I'll jes drink fur ya'. Hey, by the way, I woodin' mind if ya were ta give me three pounds of that bastard's back-strap fur my Sunday barbecue!"

I returned to the compound to get help securing the bull. I did the butchering and had the cracker pick up his share of the beef.

On another occasion, I received a call from a gentleman who wanted to dispense of his 30-year-old, *very tame* (his description) mustang. As we were trying to load the uncooperative jug-head in my horse trailer with little success, I suggested that I'd take the lead from the inside of the trailer as the owner coerced the misfit from behind with a switch. Before I knew what happened, the mustang jumped into the trailer knocking me to the floor. The man quickly slammed the gate shut, and the horse proceeded to try to kick me to death. All I could see, lying on my back looking up, was a sweaty belly and flying hooves hitting the metal sides of the trailer. Eyes darting wildly, I tried to move my arms to protect me, and I still don't know how I survived, but the trailer went in for substantial rewelding work the following day. Miraculously, I didn't need repair.

Not all of the adventures at the Savage Kingdom were life-threatening, and some visitors had artistic aspirations. As knowledge of the unique collection spread, I was contacted by various artists seeking source material for their work. The first artist to contact me had approached me years before while I was showing the tiger act in California. From the West Coast, Toledo specialized in animal art utilizing a scratch-board medium, the finest details scratched into a black surface to capture every hair of the particular animal as revealed by the white under-surface. Toledo was a handsome fellow, well-educated and extremely talented. However, his technique did not achieve the acceptance or credibility among collectors and connoisseurs who strongly supported and collected the works of such renowned wildlife artists as Charles Fracé and Guy Coheleach.

After many trips to the compound to study and photograph the cats, Toledo went out of the scratch-board business and into a more lucrative art form for him, that of jewelry design. When he last came to visit, he brought examples of his gold and platinum custom-designed pieces which had gained popularity with many Hollywood celebrities. He presented me with a gold buckle with a lion head handsomely embossed and crafted, the head inspired by one of the cats in my collection.

It was through John Hamlet that I was introduced to Charles Fracé. John was considered the number one expert on birds of prey. He lived in Homosassa Springs, where he performed with trained eagles and falcons and had in his collection many different species. John was in the process of producing a book titled "The World of Raptors," being illustrated by Charles. John wanted me to meet the artist, who flew to Florida routinely from his New York studio to spend time in the bird sanctuary where he photographed, sketched, and studied closely the various birds in their natural surroundings. One day John brought Charles to the compound. The brilliant artist was immediately enthralled by what he saw. He had no idea that such a wonderful collection of cats existed, and an instant rapport developed between Charles, me, and the Savage Kingdom — The Rare Feline Breeding Center.

When Guy Coheleach discovered my cats, he, too, began to utilize the facilities and animals for his paintings. The two men, Fracé and Coheleach, were of nearly equal prominence in the world of wildlife art, both having gained international recognition. I had the feeling they performed on a highly competitive level, and I often felt that a balancing act was needed whenever they arrived at the compound. They came on separate occasions, each with their families, and took motel rooms nearby. While wife and children visited the compound briefly, the artists spent days in research and actual work. Each of them performed magnificent paintings from which limited numbered edition prints were made, and I was always the recipient of one of the first pulled. I also received original art from time to time, all of which I proudly displayed in my living quarters.

When Coheleach was due to arrive for a session, I made certain that his work was prominently displayed, and Fracé's work was put behind the scenes until Fracé arrived, and then his work took precedence. I tried to be sensitive to the artists' temperament, knowing fully from personal experience how real it is and I didn't want to offend either of them. I was playing to my audience, but I also felt the deepest respect for both men.

When Charles arrived with his German-born wife Elke and their two handsome sons, I'd close Charles in a cage with a good cat. He'd have his camera, sketch pad, and materials and would remain in the cage for hours. I always chose a calm animal that wouldn't be excitable and would not bother Charles or feel threatened by his presence. I knew well the animals that could be trusted to perform quietly and calmly through the lengthy sketching and photography sessions. Obviously, when the paintings were reproduced in magazines, books, or advertisements, they had the appearance of having been made on location in the animal's natural habitat, which was the desired and intended affect. And I know that later on there was a good deal of field work involved in their work, but finding a willing ocelot, jaguar, or tiger in the wilds to pose for hours was quite impossible. In a zoo atmosphere, it was also very difficult. I had the cats, the location, and the expertise to supply the necessary subject for each painting. Charles Fracé is considered an absolute master of background and landscape detail as well as in capturing the actual animal and placing it in a setting, which was convincingly authentic. He was a stickler for sure.

On one occasion Charles was completing a painting depicting three young Margay in the desert. It was before he'd become so thoroughly familiar with his newest subject. I was visiting Manhattan on business and stopped by his studio where the work was well under way. I hadn't seen any of the original sketches and immediately knew that Charles had made a critical error that would be picked up by knowledgeable collectors.

"Charles," I said, "people who know cats will know that Margay have only one baby."

He was devastated. He'd been working the painting for three months with a highly detailed, magnificent background completed and the baby Margay perfect except in depicting a multiple birth, which is biologically incorrect. In order to salvage the painting, he transformed the cats to ocelots and completed a wonderful painting.

Twenty-five artists found their way to the compound over the years to do research and to study the cats up close or to photograph the animals, either in cages or on a leash in a setting to achieve natural background affects. The leading cat artist from Belgium flew over to spend two days doing research for future works. Also other foreign artists have made the trek to the Savage Kingdom. After returning to their respective studios, a composition in rough form or more often a highly detailed preliminary rendering was sent to me for critical appraisal to check not only composition but anatomy.

It was also common to receive telephone calls from the office staff members of the various artists requesting information on proper use of foliage and terrain in the background of their paintings. I'd been in so many settings all over the world and knew well the indigenous surroundings whether rocky, desert, cold, sparse of growth, or dense jungle. In the case of a painting of lemurs from Madagascar, I suggested that somewhere in the foreground it might be natural to include a green leech or two. The subject matter brought memories of a hunt for rare Indri lemur and the excitement of finally sighting a specimen while leeches crawled on my arms and face and began to burrow under my skin. It was just one of many truly unique, firsthand encounters that would enhance my knowledge to share with others.

The Savage Kingdom had been operating for nearly eight years, open to the public three days each week. It had become a burdensome activity which, while self-sustaining cost-wise, held many more problems and complications to override the healthy gate receipts. Under Government statute when open to the public, we were required by law to keep the cages spotless, the ground raked and manicured around the enclosures, and the shrubbery trimmed. It required 17 employees beginning work at four in the morning on opening days to fulfill all requirements, and some of the help was less than reliable. I didn't always have a full crew to perform the myriad details. In addition, the routine activities of the Breeding Center were interrupted with no slaughtering of animals possible during opening hours. Since many of the employees were part-time, there seemed to be a definite increase in theft with tools missing and gate receipts depleted if Gladys was not available to watch-dog the entry. I couldn't oversee every area of the compound. And there was much to oversee.

During the years that we operated, we were fortunate that there were few accidents involving the public. The potential was great with many wild animals and huge reptiles filling the oak hammock and pasture land. The animals and reptiles were contained and all went quite smoothly, but occasionally an escaped creature created undesirable emotional trauma for me and for our guests.

The snake exhibit was impressive, and handling the huge

reptiles could be lethal. We had anacondas, huge water snakes from South America reputed to grow in length to 28 feet, although I never owned any that achieved that length. We had African pythons, Indian pythons, and some boas. The glass enclosure was heated, which was absolutely essential to maintain the snakes year round, particularly in the winter months when the temperatures could drop below freezing. I had a male Indian python (*Molurus molurus*) and found a female python measuring 18 feet. The female was at the Toledo Zoo, and the zoo director agreed to send the female on breeding loan.

When the reptile arrived at the compound, the snake and crate combined weighed over 250 pounds. The female was a pretty, gentle snake, and the male seemed to feel just as I did and went about the mating process normally, but our plans were foiled by a faulty electrical system. When the heater broke down and the back-up system malfunctioned during a particularly cold night, I didn't become aware of the problem until too late. I counted on the second system to prevent any loss, but when both failed, the snakes froze to death. Once a snake's body temperature drops below 36 degrees, it will never recuperate. They were brain dead the following morning and died within 24 hours. I had to fill out a report and notify the Toledo Zoo of the loss which was substantial to them, but quite devastating to me in losing all of my reptiles.

When I solved the heating problems, I restocked the snake exhibit. In the process, we relocated snakes arriving on the compound. Snake handling is quite an art, and obviously many people do not care to be involved in the detail, but it is imperative when dealing with a 200-pound boa constrictor to handle it well and with much efficiency.

In order to remove the large snake from its enclosure, I had to throw a piece of burlap over the snake's head and eyes to prevent it from biting me. Thusly blinded and struggling, I'd grab the head with both hands behind its neck, while at the same time two, three, or even four helpers would grab the body. The second most important man was assigned to control the tail. As long as the tail is free to move, the snake has the capacity to constrict and kill quickly. There were occasions when a crippled deer was provided as food for a snake, and it was an incredible sight to watch the snake position itself in order to strike. The striking motion is faster than the eye can see. From a set position, viewed clearly by onlookers, the next view is of the snake wrapped around its prey. No one could believe that a snake so large can move so fast.

I have heard of many deaths by constriction. No one was ever seriously hurt on the compound, but on one transfer a 15-foot boa got loose and quickly disappeared. Snakes can miraculously find hiding places that give refuge from the craftiest hunter. The boa found its way into the attic of the apartment. It was during the summer and made itself at home and kept the attic clear of raccoons, opossum, and rats that occasionally sought shelter in the dark, cool rafters above my living quarters. A snake eats about once a month, and its manners are docile when not hungry and left alone. However, it will become obnoxious when prey is sought or when it feels threatened. Occasionally while entertaining guests, we'd suddenly hear a burst of raucous bouncing from overhead that sounded like a tiger loose in the attic. I knew that the snake had found a meal, but my guests swore that I contained a cat in the upper reaches of my sanctuary. When I attempted to calm them by saying, "Don't worry, that's just a 15-foot boa having its dinner," the reaction was sometimes a hasty exit.

I tolerated the snake for months. It kept the vermin population at bay. But with winter coming, I knew that it could not survive the cold. Foraging for food, it came down to the back room when its lair was barren. I was contemplating its capture, but hadn't acted on the impulse until a reptile authority visiting the compound mentioned that the snake was capable of eating a small child. If hungry enough, it would aggressively go after Diane's youngest.

The time for capture had come. I crawled into the long attic. At 145 feet with many trusses, it was difficult for me to maneuver, but ideal for the snake to gain escape routes and hiding places. I could have followed it into the eaves, but didn't want to be bitten in the face. None of my helpers had the desire or guts to go after the frightened reptile. After several failed attempts, I gave up and waited until, once again, the hungry predator came down into the back room looking for food.

When I heard the telltale noises, I gathered some of my men, and we entered the room. I was the head man and threw the burlap sack over the boa's eyes, then quickly grabbed its head. My men then got hold of the struggling body, one of them grabbing the tail.

Suddenly the tail man lost hold and the whipping tail wrapped around me. Fortunately, a snake cannot constrict with the last third of its body, and the men were able to pull the tail free from its strangulation hold. We carried the boa back to its glass enclosure for the winter.

I experienced for the second time a total loss of snakes due to freezing weather when the heating system again failed. I decided to go out of the snake business. It had become a costly and difficult exhibit to maintain successfully with too many extenuating circumstances involved. I decided never again to keep animals that were dependent on artificial means to sustain life.

Another incident occurred that held extenuating circumstances that I could not control. A group of hippies arrived to tour the Savage Kingdom. I think they must have been smoking pot; they were high on something and having a hell of a good time. One of the members of the entourage had an encounter with one of my Bactrian camels named Chairman Mao. Mao had been the lead camel in an act I'd broken. He was a stud who could be extremely dangerous. Mao did not bite; I'd broken him of that nasty trait. But when male camels are in their breeding cycle (or rut, similar to musth in elephants) they become absolutely obnoxious. They inflate their enormous tongues like a large black balloon, then regurgitate and foam in an ugly display that is also a warning of predictably abhorrent behavior. When Mao was experiencing his cycle, he was not one bit choosey. He'd attempt to mount the horses, the zebras, an elephant, and even a wagon. He damaged wheelbarrows and went after the giant tortoise.

Gladys was in charge of the box office when the hippies entered and began their tour. She told me later, she thought they could be problem guests on the compound, so she made it a point to monitor their behavior. When she saw them enter the camel pen, she alerted me. Someone had left the gate open exposing the hippies to Mao, our 2,000-pound camel, who became enamored of the group when they began to feed the camels in spite of signs everywhere to the contrary. Mao apparently fell in love with one of the long-haired visitors and was in hot pursuit of his latest amour. When I reached the pen, I saw that Mao had knocked the man to the ground and held him using his massive neck to keep the man on all fours, attempting to perform the breeding process on

My friend Mao.

the anguished, struggling victim. The camel kept hitting the hippie in the head. I'd never faced the problem before, but ran like hell to beat Mao away from the man, lying prostrate by this time, and covered with camel saliva. I used my whip to get Mao back in his pen and returned to apologize profusely to the frightened, disheveled, and badly shaken hippie. As the group left the compound, there were words exchanged with Gladys, who went to my defense pointing out the "no feeding" signs that hung throughout the compound.

Ultimately, there was a lawsuit against the Savage Kingdom, which was dismissed on grounds that the man had violated the rules posted clearly and in so doing had placed himself in jeopardy. I doubt the man will ever again feed a camel. After the encounter, I put a ring in Mao's nose with a small cable hanging from it. Whenever he had to be restrained, one of my helpers took hold of the cable, and Mao immediately became docile.

When we closed the Kingdom, there was noticeable decline in activity and return to a more normal routine. We still had the daily care of many animals, but without the added concerns of opening to the public. I felt more comfortable about traveling away from the compound. I left Diane and Earl in charge and flew to visit Mother and Simone. Mother was being well cared for in the nursing home, but her condition remained enigmatic. It was depressing to see her seemingly in a world of her own. At least she was not suffering. Simone continued to be attentive. Simone had problems of her own concerning family members, and it was a time for sharing and comforting one another. Our time together was beautiful, supportive, and sensual.

When I returned to Florida, I was confronted with problems and incidents uniquely associated with running a wild animal compound. Diane was working hard, and I give her a great deal of credit for her work performance for the 11 years she was with me, but it was costly both monetarily and emotionally. Our relationship had deteriorated measurably.

I returned to phone calls from Gerard, slurred and lamenting his ongoing bitter diatribe. I listened and tried to understand, tried to supply answers knowing they were neither heard, understood, nor even wanted. He was my son and his pain and suffering became my pain and suffering. There were conversations with Odette. Martine and Samantha lived close to her; she was involved with her daughter-in-law and granddaughter trying to be caring at a time when she was needed. She, too, heard from Gerard through anguished phone calls. Neither of us knew what to do for the boy, our son, who was no longer a boy, but a man — a tragically confused, sick man.

37

KATHY

During the winter season, the Monday Flea Market in Webster draws crowds from miles around, even from out-of-state. Thousands attend the weekly event. My attendance from the start was to purchase produce to feed the monkeys on the compound. If I made my move late in the day, I purchased what had gone unsold. Twenty-five cents to the dollar looked good to the farmer faced with repacking his produce. It was well worth the trip.

I was at the market when I first saw Kathy. Her parents owned a nursery in Belleview, near Ocala. They took a booth to sell plants and flowers. Kathy worked at the shop and also at the flea market. I was quite fascinated watching her from afar as she waited on customers. She was a dynamo, good-looking, and vivacious. I couldn't resist meeting her. As I talked to her mother, I didn't realize Kathy stood so close behind me. I stepped back and her cigarette burned my hand. I jumped and turned to look at what had stung me. She apologized for being "in my way." I declared that she was a "hot" number. Actually, I was more than delighted to have her in my way.

Our first conversation led to others which soon led to a dinner date. I invited her to bring her children to visit the compound. Kathy was raising three children, a girl named Laurie from her first marriage, and two sons, Danny and Joe, from her second husband who was in the military. She was recently divorced for the second time and living with the children in a rented A-frame in the middle of woods outside Belleview.

When I visited what seemed like an enchanted cottage, I found a charming, cozy, inviting abode with fireplace, inhabited by a beautiful lady who possessed a wonderful sense of humor coupled with high levels of energy and enthusiasm — a delightful individual. I'd not met any woman in recent years who offered so much. Kathy was just what I needed. I began to spend weekends at the house where I supplied the food for cookouts. Kathy and I made love for the first time in the A-frame, which I found to be a wonderful haven away from the cares and tension of the compound. Kathy appreciated me, and her children seemed quite intrigued by the animal man, who began to spend time with their mom. I felt like I'd found a family and a woman to love.

While visiting Kathy one day, I had business to transact in the area. I'd sold some wolves to a couple living near Belleview. When I didn't receive their check, I asked Kathy if she would accompany me to their home to pick up the tardy payment. She had a day off from the nursery and agreed to show me the way to the address. When we arrived, the owners of the wolves informed me they had sent a check for $500 to the Breeding Center weeks before. I was embarrassed by my ignorance and apologized for the error. I was extremely angry when I learned later that Diane had endorsed the check and deposited it in her account in a bank in Leesburg. Diane denied any and all allegations of misconduct while attempting to pad what I recognized as a meager salary. I didn't pursue the complaint knowing she'd been a hard-worker for the 11 years that she and the children had been on the compound. It seemed redundant to broach another misdemeanor.

The hours and days spent at the A-frame with Kathy were a departure from what was becoming an untenable relationship with Diane. While I was, admittedly, guilty of not paying her enough, she solved that problem by manipulating checks and kiting the grocery bills. There were deepening cracks in the foundation of our relationship, but I was not in a position to put an end to it. However, it would soon resolve itself.

After a weekend with Kathy and the kids, I returned to the compound for the night before flying to New York to attend an auction at Christie's to sell several animal bronzes. As was my nightly routine, I made the rounds of the enclosures carrying a .22 magnum derringer for protection just in case I ran into threatening marauding animals or if any of the caged animals were loose. The weather was cold and I wore a sheepskin coat. When the tour was completed, I automatically removed the gun from my pocket and put it away, out of sight of the children before retiring. The following day, I gathered my traveling paraphernalia and left to catch the flight out of Tampa. When I went through security, all hell broke loose — lights flashed and buzzers rang. I was searched and the derringer was discovered in my back pocket, a total surprise to me. I knew that I'd removed it the night before, but it sure as hell was in an agent's hands at the Tampa Airport. I was taken into custody for questioning.

I explained the reason for the gun as part of my nightly routine. I gave the name of my lawyer, Eric Wagner, who had his practice in Ocala. I carried business cards for identification and was recognized by some of the airport personnel, which did lend credence to my alibi. I was released and went on to New York on a later flight. It was a minor inconvenience and an embarrassment blown out of proportion at a time when airports around the world had tightened security in reacting to highjackings and terrorist activities.

Eric ultimately contacted the judge to discuss what became a county case filed against Robert Baudy. I never had to go to court, and Eric managed through persistence to get the gun returned to me, *two years later*. Legally, I was liable for carrying a concealed weapon without a permit. It was a misunderstanding that created a puzzle to me that I felt Diane could solve. I'm not absolutely certain she was guilty, but knew she'd deny any knowledge of how the gun got into my pocket.

When I returned from Manhattan, I was relieved to have Diane's announcement that she was leaving the compound. She'd been dating a man who drove a fancy convertible, and I suspect she had an offer she couldn't refuse. She departed with the children, leaving the apartment quite empty, but it wouldn't take long to fill the void.

Kathy and the three children moved in. Kathy's arrival brought a new energy, laughter, and fun to what had become a serious, dour atmosphere. She was a wonderful addition, but she also brought complications.

Kathy had been receiving alimony payments from both exhusbands. From her description, the two men hated each other for obvious reasons. But when I became involved with her, their hate became galvanized and focused on my intrusion, and they united for convenience sake to build a case against me in their attempt to legally end their alimony. They sought evidence that maligned my character, to further demonstrate the unacceptability of the compound as home for the children.

I was called into court many times to defend my position and to prove that I was not guilty of the charges of child-abuse, which became a part of their ammunition. The hearings were made public, and my reputation muddied badly by false accusations. Kathy had become a very special and important lady. I loved her and hated to see the pain she suffered over the fear of loosing her children.

I went to friends and professional acquaintances, who knew me well, to be character witnesses against the heinous allegations. The first court case concerned Laurie. The judge met with the 11-year-old in his private chambers. The outcome was a decision granting the father custody of Laurie for six months, after which another hearing would determine the ongoing fate of the girl. At the second hearing, Laurie requested that she be permitted to return to her mother.

The legal battle continued to rage as life went on at the Breeding Center. Another battle was about to commence. Gerard arrived, and he needed a job. It was history repeating itself. I couldn't see how it would play any better the second or third time around, but I was willing to try. He stayed for two weeks. It was impossible.

When he left the compound years before, I'd found over 200 empty cold medicine bottles discarded behind some cages on the perimeter of the grounds. It was a frightening testimony to his need and desperate search for a high. His addiction was slowly destroying any vestige of self-esteem and prevented him from holding a job. What he needed was professional help. He left for Tampa.

He worked many jobs in the area before settling for a period of months working in a plant that manufactured vertical window blinds. Gerard approached me with the idea of him opening a similar business with my backing. I investigated the possibilities. I hated to discourage honest industry and enthusiasm, but upon inquiry found the blind business in Tampa saturated with little growth potential. I didn't have money to blow, and he'd never demonstrated even a modicum of dependability since his return from Vietnam. Sadly, I couldn't back a business run by a man addicted to drugs. I hated to turn him down, but I wouldn't gamble, and he was sorely disappointed with what must have seemed another indictment of his character. He soon quit his job.

There were months when his rent was not paid, and I had to write a check to keep Gerard's apartment. For a while, he lived in an apartment provided for veterans, but that was only a temporary arrangement. He was evicted for violation of rules. Whenever I arrived in Tampa, whether on business for the Breeding Center or to aid Gerard, I always took him to dinner and always found him in the company of strange, unsavory companions. Kathy and I began a monthly routine of driving over to look in on him. She was supportive and compassionate. She saw a young man, diminished in self-respect and struggling to sustain a lifestyle that didn't have any semblance of stability or promise of future gain. He drifted out of focus, and I couldn't get a bead on what I could do to change the pattern, the hurt — the impending doom.

Gladys was a mentor. I could talk to her and gain support as well as an objective opinion, but she was also hurt by my apparent need of other women. She thought it was a mistake to take Kathy and the children in. I admitted that with three children, there were complications. When the legal hassles developed, it was difficult and painful. The price I had to pay for having Kathy share my life and help run the compound, which she did willingly and efficiently, was high. She was a wonderful woman, who kept the apartment in order and provided so much pleasure in the intimacy of my bedroom. I also discovered that spending time with the children was enjoyable. They found life at the Breeding Center very exciting. It was a unique environment for everyone concerned. Their contentment with the arrangement made the court procedures, where they were being jerked around by fathers, attorneys and judges ignorant of the facts, needlessly, and inexcusably damaging to the innocent victims — the kids.

Gladys told me many times after our first sexual encounter that she realized that I loved beautiful ladies and that her age was a factor in our relationship. I didn't feel that age had any bearing on my feelings for Gladys, but I didn't want what she wanted: marriage. She said that if I'd marry her, she would be quite content to remain living in her home on the lake raising the baby leopards and tigers and she'd even tolerate my need to have a woman living with me on the compound. She loved me and I loved Gladys, but I knew that marriage would only complicate an arrangement that she seemed to find fulfilling and which I found to be extremely satisfying. I'd been stung twice. I knew that wedding vows led to commitments difficult to break and painfully binding. I couldn't, wouldn't tolerate another marriage.

I was called to bail Gerard out of jail in Sarasota. He'd been arrested for shoplifting. When I spoke to the public defender, he explained to me that Gerard was just one of many like him, "Young men totally messed up by the Vietnam War."

I wanted to tell the lawyer that I appreciated his analysis, but in all honesty I knew that Gerard's problems began before he went into the service. The hoped-for mature growth in an atmosphere of harsh discipline had not materialized. I'd been naïve.

Gerard was jailed for 30 days and then released. It was one of many incidents, where he was picked up and locked up for weeks, then put into rehabilitation before being released.

When I visited Gerard in the treatment facility in Tampa, I learned that he was being given methadone as a palliative. That was anathema to me. I couldn't see the wisdom or a far-reaching cure gained by administering more drugs. I had to assume the pros knew what they were doing to somehow, in some way, cure the boy, or at least set him on a path to stay clean and initiate a positive, productive mode. But my hopes were not high.

Bonnie worked as a county employee in a community service capacity. She met Gerard during one of his incarcerations and became his confidant, his friend, and I imagine, his lover. A petite, attractive woman, she seemed to adore Gerard. From a family in Tampa who seemed devoted as well to Gerard's cure, she was the best influence to stay the course with him. He seemed to care deeply for her.

When Kathy and I visited, Bonnie joined us for dinner, and it was evident that she loved Gerard and was good for him. She didn't live with him, but saw him through many episodes of abuse, jail, and recuperation in the Tampa rehab facility.

However, in spite of Bonnie's presence, I continued to receive slurred phone calls soon after Gerard's release from jail or rehab and calls from lawyers representing him when he was arrested.

It became a continuation of bad news and painful contacts. There seemed to be no end in sight, and I was becoming emotionally drained and sickened by the tragedy of one man's life — my son. He reached out for attention and I responded, but it wasn't enough. It never held the answer or seemed to address the problem.

The Seventh Day Adventist Church maintained a zoo on the grounds of a camp north of Gainesville. Camp Kulaqua was set in a magnolia hammock that held a beautiful natural spring in an idyllic setting that attracted children from all over the country. The camp managers were church affiliated, and they came to me to purchase animals for the small zoo. I'd worked with the managers and met many of the sponsors of the camp, one of whom was Earl Smith, a prominent and highly successful businessman and entrepreneur in central Florida.

One day I told Earl about Gerard's troubles and he said, "Look, Robert, if Gerard wants to help himself, I'll get him a job at the camp. He will be furnished with a nice bungalow, but there is one thing . . . he's got to quit drinking and quit smoking pot. If he's willing to do that, to clean up his situation, he will have it made."

I felt if Gerard took the job he'd be in an atmosphere of deeply religious and caring people, who might provide the inspiration, or at least set an example of living totally different from anything he'd experienced previously. I went to Gerard and impressed upon him what rules were imposed on what I thought was a positive employment opportunity. Gerard accepted the position to care for the animals in the zoo. I knew he had the background to handle the job well.

Within three months, I had a call from the manager asking that I drive to Gainesville; the man wanted to talk to me about Gerard. I made the drive knowing before I arrived that it was another strike against my son. The manager was candid. He said there was evidence that Gerard brought liquor onto the camp grounds, that he'd seduced some of the teenagers, that he was bringing pot onto the grounds, and even growing the weed in a plot near the animal housing. I offered to talk to Gerard, but the manager explained that the problems were beyond any possibility of conciliation. They would not keep Gerard under any circumstances. They didn't want to hurt or embarrass me, nor did they want to do anything to upset their financial supporter, my friend

Earl Smith, but Gerard was dismissed.

I confronted Gerard with the allegations. He was defensive and suggested that he was totally unsatisfied with the position. He said it was no better than being in jail if he couldn't have his beer and his freedom. I pointed out that he knew well the terms when he accepted the position and if he couldn't amend his behavior in order to keep a job, I was washing my hands of him. Too many people tried to help and were hurt and disappointed by his denial, his inability to take responsibility. I told him he was on his own, and I was damned tired of bailing him out of self-induced trouble. I included the many incidents that had occurred since he left the compound with Martine and Samantha, when he began his decline into oblivion. I condemned his need for drugs that kept him a captive, threatened and threatening persona. I wondered aloud where it would end. We parted and I felt that I never wanted to see or hear from him again.

It was impossible to understand Gerard. Why he lacked the willpower or desire to quit the drugs and get on with his life was beyond me. I had suffered withdrawal from the amphetamines years before. I knew what the pain of withdrawal was. At the time, I'd approached many doctor friends who were willing to put me on methadone; but I knew that in taking the interim drug, I was only introducing another addictive agent into my system. I chose, in spite of the hellish time weaning myself, to take some wine early in the day that helped to calm me.

Why couldn't Gerard pull himself together? If he needed attention, he had it from me. But I resented the constant intrusion, the bad news, the anguished phone calls for help. I was torn and I hated it. I was so damned busy at the compound with complicated demands placed on every waking hour, animals coming and going, supervising the operation as well as interacting with professional authorities who called or came for advice and to share their knowledge in the ongoing species enhancement programs. I was on the run most of the time just to acquire enough food to maintain the animals. I lost tolerance for Gerard's pleadings as he lost favor with his mother and stepfather in Pennsylvania and almost everyone else who tried to listen and help.

Even Earl Smith came to Gerard's aid again. He set up a business, run by his own son, to produce clocks made from Cypress tree stumps cut, sanded, and polished as backing for the clock mechanisms. Earl attempted to establish two young men in an independent, self-sustaining business venture, and I wished them luck, success, and everything good.

With Kathy at the compound and so efficiently able to run the facility and supervise the help, I was free to travel to France. Mother had been in the home in Rennes for several years before being moved to a home in the country. She had devoted many years to the elderly, the poor, and the infirm in Rennes, who knew her well and revered her for the kindness. She was treated exceptionally by the nuns and other staff at the nursing home. When she was moved to the country, her reputation preceded her, and the staff was most kind and considerate.

When I arrived to visit, the staff was most solicitous. When I approached Mother, a smile filled her face and she held her arms out and gently called *mon petit* (my little one). Knowing that she was so tenderly cared for made her confinement tolerable. When she was no longer ambulatory, the attentive care did not cease, but it became intolerable to visit. I escaped the torture by burying myself in work.

There were many trips in those days out of the country as well as within the States. If I couldn't take Kathy along, I directed her to call "Doc" if any problems arose that she couldn't handle. Doc was John Gabler, whom I'd known for years as a fellow member of the American Association of Zoological Parks and Aquariums. John, a practicing physician, also had a small private zoo. He'd sold the zoo and closed his practice to retire to Florida in 1977. We'd kept in touch and had developed a close bond as small independent zoo operators trying to represent similar operations as members of the AAZPA, whose members were primarily large metropolitan zoos. As a matter of fact, it was John's opinion, and mine, that the snooty association was always setting rules and regulations and shitting on the small independent owners. We attended the annual meeting and tried hard to fight for the rights of the private sector members.

I valued our relationship and even sought John's expertise as a medical man. He became my doctor, and there were several occasions when he'd be called to help solve a problem on the compound. When a snow leopard got out of its cage while I was away and Kathy was shorthanded, she called John. He drove over from Eustis and found the leopard 150 feet up in the far reaches of one of the oak trees. John prepared to dart the cat and did so. He was and still is a friend and confidant — someone I value greatly. He always answered an SOS; but I must say that when I left Kathy in charge, she demonstrated common sense in meeting most problems and I knew I was leaving the compound in good hands. However, I enjoyed very much taking her along with me when I had enough help to leave behind to tend the animals.

I took her to Tulsa when the museum was experiencing financial difficulties and all the treasured art was for sale. I purchased some wonderful animal bronzes on that occasion. Another trip took us to New York. It was Kathy's first trip to the big city, and she was enthralled with the adventure.

One evening while in Manhattan, I took her to dinner at a favorite French restaurant on the West Side. The charming eatery was located in the cellar in an atmosphere of intimate authentic ambiance where the cuisine reminded me of home. It had been one of my haunts during the years I lived in the Northeast. I was well-known by the owners and welcomed royally.

Kathy was not acquainted with French tradition and obviously did not recognize the *rillettes* as something to be shared. The pâté came in a tureen along with delicious toasted garlic bread. I was busy talking to our hostess, sipping wine, and chatting about old times, paying little attention to Kathy, but noticing that our waitress was looking aghast at Kathy. When I looked she was putting the last bit of *rillettes* into her mouth. How could she know that the four pounds of pork pâté were to be shared with every guest in the restaurant. I was embarrassed, but didn't want to upset Kathy. I excused myself and took the hostess aside apologizing for the innocent gluttony.

"Oh, Mr. Baudy, do not be upset. You know these Americans; they do that all the time. They don't know any better."

When I explained to Kathy what she'd done, we both laughed out loud and continued to laugh often after that special night whenever we recalled the visit to Manhattan and her pâté dinner.

Kathy was a wonderful asset in running the Breeding Center. She was accustomed to dealing with clients and handled them like a pro. She enjoyed people and life, and it was abundantly evident.

The animal bronzes in my collection were either acquired at auctions or in my travels. This signed Barye is one of many by the French sculptor that I treasure.

I had the utmost confidence in her ability. When a wealthy friend from England called for help, I knew that Kathy could handle the Florida business while I traveled abroad to aid Mr. Aspinall in his moment of need. I left her in charge along with Earl, who'd become my right-hand man.

Mr. Aspinall owned two zoos in Kent in addition to gambling casinos in London and other business enterprises in Great Britain. He had been a customer purchasing many animals since visiting the compound previously, when Gladys gave him the grande tour.

The British Government began proceedings to close his zoos after two zookeepers were killed by tigers. Aspinall called on me along with Al Oeming from Canada and several other recognized animal experts to act as expert witnesses to supply evidence and testify on his behalf.

He flew us to Canterbury, all expenses paid, where the trial was conducted. Aspinall didn't want the tigers destroyed nor his operation closed. I gave my deposition to several lawyers informing them that the law was written making illegal the destruction of any endangered species under any circumstances. Tigers were on the list. Based on my testimony and full knowledge of the law, the case was dismissed, the tigers saved, and the zoos remained open. However, within a year two other zoo employees were killed by elephants. Obviously, there were serious problems that needed to be addressed.

When I made the decision to sell the collection of giant tortoise, I was contacted by a Japanese conglomerate planning to open a zoo south of Tokyo. The Japanese delegation made an appointment to visit the compound. After talking business and showing them around, I asked Kathy to take the VIPs on a tour of the area. I owned a new, white Lincoln, which Kathy drove to squire them through Disney World and other popular attractions. She showed the clients a wonderful time, which was ultimately rewarded by a $75,000 purchase.

In thinking back, I realize that it was during Kathy's time on the compound when I made the most money in animal sales. It was also during her four years that I enjoyed the luxury of a woman whose capacity for pleasure added so much pleasure to my life in spite of the ongoing legal harangue, which came to a dramatic conclusion in 1986. The year held two emotionally devastating occurrences.

On February 21, I received the telephone call from France. Mother had died. The call was shocking, but at the same time relieved some of the pressure of keeping her in a nursing home imprisoned by a mind gone blank, and me in knowing that her mind took her into another world and out of mine. While I could visit and see her, I didn't have her. Placing her in the home had been the most difficult decision of my life. Words are inadequate to fully express what I felt seeing the deterioration. It had been doubly painful in the realization that nothing could reverse it. The hopelessness, the fact that she had been extraordinarily aware and alert and so keenly passionate in serving the needs of others all her life. How sad to die oblivious to the world and caring that surrounded her. Many thoughts washed over me as I thought back on a life so well lived in the service of man.

I flew to France. It was blanketed in snow and the mist-filled air lent a somber, colorless shroud to the occasion. Relatives on Father's side from Brittany attended the funeral held in a beautiful modern church in Rennes. Many friends and hospital staff members were present. Mother's family attempted to reach the snowed-in city, but were stranded en route. The long journey from Nevers and Paris was impossible with transportation closed down. Mother was laid to rest in the cemetery beside Father. We all stood and watched as the casket was lowered into the frozen ground, the wind whipping damp cold mist, and the temperature dropping on a miserable, foreboding parting that stood in such strong contrast to the warmth and tenderness of her love.

Simone was with me. We shared one wonderful evening in the romantic atmosphere of a river barge, just the two of us — the barge transformed into an elegant restaurant. Simone had been so close to Mother. She'd treated Mother as her own, and I loved her for that. Our parting was emotional. I didn't know when I would see her again.

I did not remain in Rennes for long. I went to Paris for the flight home. The airport was closed and all flights canceled until the snow had been removed. I went to a favorite bar off the Champs Élysées. It was a popular drinking establishment, where Americans congregated along with Parisians, and I knew some of the waitresses who had worked there for years. When I finally caught the flight out of Paris, I was not home 24 hours when the newspapers reported a terrorist bombing at the bar in Paris severely injuring 17 people.

Kathy and Earl had watched over the compound in my absence, but her status was soon to change. The child-custody case was reopened. When the final ruling was announced, it provided that Laurie could remain on the compound, but the boys had to leave. The legal battle continued to create angst for Kathy who faced loosing her alimony and her sons if she remained with me. She couldn't fight any longer. The vindictiveness of husbands spurned was an emotion I'd never before witnessed, so damaging to highly impressionable progeny. Kathy and I faced what neither wanted — we were forced to separate.

There was more upsetting news. Gerard was in jail in Gainesville. Earl Smith had tried in vain to save the boy. I was called to bail him out. Through Earl's connection, I was granted a private hearing with the judge along with a lawyer for Gerard. I pleaded, as I had many times before, to have Gerard freed knowing that he'd only be back again in a similar lockup. His life had become one misdemeanor after another.

My impassioned plea to the judge was, "When this kid left France, what he wanted to do was somehow duplicate what I did by serving with the American forces, but what I did was quite different. I wanted to free my country. He came here as a French citizen. He wanted to become an American citizen, and our government made him an offer he could not refuse. They said, 'If you want to become an American, you have to fight in Vietnam.' This was a Catch Twenty-two: They told him he could go back to France, but he didn't want that. He wanted to be an American, and I advised him that he should volunteer, so that he would at least have the option to choose the service he preferred instead of being drafted. When he left, he was a clean-cut gentleman who spoke three languages very well, had the finest education money could buy, and that's the way he was when he went to serve. When he came back, he was a ruined man!" I had covered for Gerard again.

As I spoke I watched the man's face, tears coming down his cheeks, and then he spoke, "Mr. Baudy, I heard enough. My son went to Vietnam, and he came back just like your son. I will do something I have never done before, I will order the release of your son before Christmas."

Gerard's drama was played against the ongoing manipulative activities of jealous, vindictive husbands as well as jealousy demonstrated by Gladys over Kathy's presence. There was much material for a real live soap opera, and I was grateful for the compelling demands made by the animals to provide an escape from the human drama.

The animals provided drama as well. Greek mythology describes the cyclops or one-eyed giants. The compound was inhabited by many rare and unique species in pristine condition with no aberrations in all of the many hundreds of births over the years. BeeJay Lester was working for me as a volunteer. We met in 1971, when I was working in Jacksonville. She saw the tiger performance, introduced herself to me after the show, and we remained in touch. When she came to work, she fulfilled her great and abiding love for animals. BeeJay was highly excitable. She screamed in delight at the birth of every baby, and her outbursts always startled the hell out of me in spite of their frequency. We were having babies born every week and sometimes daily.

I eventually became accustomed to the emotionally induced trumpets and did not react too strongly when I heard her scream, "Robert, Robert, come quickly. We have a cyclops!"

The distance between us and wind blowing against her bellows kept me from understanding the words.

I called, "What the hell are you yelling about now?"

A shocking birth on the compound.

When I got to her side, I looked down to see the birthing of a western puma and saw the shocking forehead of the baby with one large eye in the center. I had never experienced the medical phenomena firsthand and will admit it was traumatic. I'd say it was one of the most dramatic events on the compound. The baby lived only three days. But life and drama continued.

When Kathy left, she moved back to Belleview. She told me we must try to forget one another. The situation was impossible and it simply made no sense to continue the relationship if we had to live apart. It was extremely painful to suffer Kathy's absence. I'd found a happiness and contentment with a woman that I'd never experienced before. We were totally compatible on every level and thoroughly enjoyed every aspect of the relationship. We had discussed marriage, but I knew that it would not solve the problems with her husbands. A marriage would only deepen their resolve to take the children. I had been accused of not only child abuse, but neglect in not encouraging and supervising their religious training. The accusations cited the danger from the animals on the compound, as well as from the calibre of people employed in addition to an evil Robert Baudy. We'd been living with an onslaught of cruel defamations placing the children in a hellish vice, and we had to sacrifice our chance for a shared life to protect the innocents.

With court proceedings behind, Kathy moved out, but my love for her had not changed and to realize that she was so close and yet so far was torture. I went to see her. Her second husband hired a private investigator, and it became dangerous to continue further contact. Her absence was like death. Kathy was gone. Mother was gone. I had lost two women whom I loved deeply.

The judge in Gainsville was good to his word, and Gerard was released from jail one week before Christmas. He returned to the compound for the holidays. There seemed little to celebrate. Gerard left soon after and within three months was in jail in Sarasota.

The compound, while full of animals, seemed very empty.

Gladys was my staunch ally and source of comfort. She'd seen me through the divorce from Charlotte and was well aware of the pain I felt in Kathy's absence. I needed Gladys and she needed me.

Gladys suffered an asthmatic condition for as long as I knew her. She smoked heavily and continued to do so in spite of breathing problems. I began to spend more time with her and heard the coughing at night and each morning upon awakening.

I suggested she see a doctor. She was defensive. She said she knew that there was a serious lung problem, and I agreed with her. When I felt her chest and listened, I knew she was experiencing pain that indicated a cancer. We were candid with one another about the prognosis. I took her to see Doc and he confirmed our fears. John consulted with us and felt that due to the asthma, surgery was not advised. He asked Gladys to amend her habits: if not give up, at least reduce smoking.

Gladys was a realist and a brave lady. Some would think her foolish if they didn't know better. She told me that in spite of the doctor's warning to the contrary, she fully intended to enjoy the remaining months or years of her life and had no desire or intention of giving up either her cigarettes or her J&B scotch whiskey. John estimated she had about two years to live.

With the dire prognostication, Gladys became more deeply and caringly involved in the nurturing of the baby leopards, tigers, pumas, and ocelots that she took into her home. She bottle fed them and lovingly tolerated their destructive behavior through several redecorating projects. She'd been performing as surrogate mother for years and had become particularly attached to all her babies.

One pair provided an unusual result. Most of the babies were ultimately sold and left the compound. Others matured and remained for breeding purposes. But a baby leopard as well as a baby jaguar did not sell. They matured and romped together, and I built cages for them that fit into Gladys' garage. It is not uncommon in captivity for a male tiger to breed a female lion or a male lion to breed a female tiger. The production from such hybridization is called a *tiglon* or a *liger*. Leopards and jaguars had never to my knowledge hybridized, and so we were all surprised when Gladys' female jaguar became pregnant. We soon had *lepjags* on the compound, two of which were sold to Siegfried and Roy.

In spite of her illness, Gladys continued to nurture babies and me. She loved the babies, she loved life, and she loved me. When she decided to live out her final years on her terms, I told her I'd be there for her for whatever time was left.

I curtailed the trips to Tampa to visit Gerard. Kathy had been wonderful about suggesting we look in on him and take him to dinner. Her compassion was one of many fine traits, and she had a talent for making our visits pleasant and supportive.

Gerard came to the compound to visit occasionally with friends tagging along, friends who were not desirable influences. They'd arrive high on drugs or alcohol, and I did little to encourage their visits or their stay. Phone calls from Gerard made little sense. He was still seeing Bonnie, but his appearance and conversations were that of a dissipated, cynical, haunted individual, and I wanted to close my eyes to him. I wanted him to leave me alone. I was frustrated and felt helpless and guilty in my inability to help or to love him as a father should.

Gerard's continuing trauma was more than upsetting and seeing Gladys suffer with the cancer was painful. During a tough time, I was fortunate to find pleasant diversion and haven in St. Petersburg. I met Dr. Ed Popick and his Austrian-born wife Siggy through Pepito, a photographer friend from Tampa. Pepito announced one day that he was bringing friends to meet me and to explore the compound. The Popicks lived on the Gulf Coast, where Ed was engaged in many diverse business enterprises including several Humana Medical Clinics. The entourage arrived in a chauffeur-driven limo, one of many Ed owned and hired out.

The Popicks invited me to visit their home after touring the animal-filled hammock. When I took them up on the offer, I was impressed with their magnificent residence in Madeira Beach and the several apartments they owned overlooking the water. I began to spend weekends in their paradise and was given a key to one of the apartments to use whenever I chose. I found the visits therapeutic in the serene atmosphere of a handsomely decorated apartment overlooking the vast Gulf shared with Ed and Siggy living the good life.

Siggy was younger than me by about ten years, but she remembered well the conditions in Austria after the War. When I was involved in the final months of the War in Berchtesgaden, I was close to where she was born and raised. We talked by the hour about our youthful encounters and experiences during and following the War. The friendship became very important to me, and I in turn introduced the Popicks to Gladys. They embraced her as well. Siggy was full of fun and willing to share her largesse. For Gladys' birthday, Siggy appeared at the compound in a limo with driver to pick me up and then Gladys to fete her on her special day. We all had a wonderful time, Gladys enjoying a taste of the high life she'd known with Joe during their Washington days. Sadly, the good times were not to last.

I was aware that Siggy and Ed were experiencing serious marital difficulties, but I was shocked one day while sitting on the beach with Siggy when she announced, "Monday I'm going to file for divorce." I immediately tried to talk her out of the drastic action, knowing that Ed didn't want the marriage to end. I knew him well enough to know that he had the power and finances to fight any challenge. I knew she'd be hurt badly by an ugly divorce and I tried to dissuade her. She didn't listen.

I'd grown to love both Ed and Siggy. I couldn't take sides, but I knew that when the proceedings began, their paradise would explode, and I'd lose a sustaining relationship with two wonderful people. I hated to see it all come to an end.

Once the allegations began, the marriage deteriorated rapidly into a burgeoning, costly divorce action with Ed losing some of his business holdings and Siggy losing a lifestyle, which had been grand. They both paid dearly for the break-up, and I lost my haven on the Gulf.

38

HONORS AND RECOGNITION
Les Honneurs et la Reconnaissance

*F*or almost ten years I worked gratis for the United States Fish and Wildlife Service on a plan to preserve the Florida panther. The government sponsored and supervised plan, called the Recovery Plan For The Florida Panther, included ten committee members, nine of which were employed by the government. I was the only non-paid member filling the stipulated position of respected, experienced cat breeder. I was recommended by the Audubon Society as a most knowledgeable breeder of cats. It took ten years of field work and meetings to hammer out and finally submit a finished plan to the Florida Game and Fresh Water Fish Commission.

The many meetings over the years were held at various locations around the state from Tallahassee to Miami and in parks, swamps, and offices, discussing the animal and searching out specimens in remote areas where panthers had been sighted. There were field trips by helicopter in teams as well as lengthy discussion sessions, all of which gave me a good inkling about how the bureaucrats work — a frustrating and laborious process.

There were thought to be about 200 Florida panthers alive when we began the survey, and I recommended early on that we must initiate a plan to begin captive breeding immediately if we were to be successful in perpetuating the very existence of the species. I verbalized my feelings, pulling no punches.

"While we are doing this study, and it is obviously going to take a great deal of time, more cats are going to disappear, are going to be shot by poachers, and/or die of attrition and disease.

We ought to collect a few animals, start the breeding program, and then go into the field to do the theoretical work."

My recommendation was heard but outvoted nine to one every time I broached the absolute need to get on with captive breeding.

The field trips were informative and quite fascinating, and gave access to remote areas that I would never have experienced if not for the survey. There were many trips in search of the elusive panther, but one was unforgettable. It was a trip to the Fakahatchee Strand located in south Florida below Alligator Alley and connected to the Big Cypress National Preserve. The swampy area is the last strand of large trees holding Royal Palms and other unique vegetation not logged into extinction, reputedly unmolested by man, and a natural and safe haven for panthers. I was one of 15 predators walking through the strand in waist-deep water, cold and pure as it moved against our bodies. We were wearing work clothes, but no wet suits or boots to protect us against snakes or alligators. Our leader on safari, a member of the Department of Natural Resources and an expert on the particular habitation unique to the strand, was Ken Alvarez.

Ken was a powerfully built man, well-educated, erudite, and quite dignified as he described in wonderful detail the trees, flowers, orchids, and even animal life in the Fakahatchee. We were a fascinated, captive audience as we moved through the water, looking up and around. I took photographs with my trusty Nikon. As I listened to Ken's account, I suddenly realized that his voice had ceased in midsentence and, looking ahead, saw ever-widening ripples where Ken should have been. We were all surprised and watched for him to surface. We waited a matter of seconds with no sign of Ken, alligator, or any unusual activity in the water. I was about to go under for a look when Ken appeared, 20 feet away, looking like a swamp creature with algae and other swamp growth clinging to his ears and face. We all laughed and then went on. As we proceeded, several other members of the party suddenly fell beneath the surface into sinkholes. I managed to keep my head above water and continued to snap pictures.

On another field trip, I joined a small group flown by helicopter along with machine-gun armed guards into an area of Big Cypress possibly containing panthers. We questioned the need for artillery and were told that the last time they entered the swamp, they interrupted a drug drop and were fired upon. I continued to hammer my suggestion to begin captive breeding, but was repulsed again and again. It was clearly evident that the panther population was diminishing before our eyes. They were down by nearly 50 when the survey began, and some of those were killed by our own efforts. In some instances, we ran the panthers down using hounds to facilitate tranquilizing in order to attach radio collars to monitor migratory patterns and behavior. I was against the method as disturbing the population and running the cat into areas where they were further threatened by crossing highways to escape human predators.

After the original plan went to Washington, the State Department of Natural Resources, the Game and Fresh Water Fish Commission, biologists, and other field workers realized that my initial recommendation was indeed the only hope for saving what was fast becoming an extinct natural resource. A new agency was formed by the state called the Technical Advisory Council designed by the government and comprised of three experts to guide the Game Commission in performing the actual work. I received a phone call from Governor Graham asking me to serve on the newly formed council. I was flattered and most anxious to get on with the field work, which would eliminate all the paper work and discourse of bureaucracy and finally produce solid, positive results. As in many government-organized and supervised efforts, whether state or national, the people chosen to perform the breeding were not always the most capable or even authoritative where cats were concerned.

When I began an active role in the panther survey, I did my own research, and I discovered that the only place where I could find purebred Florida panthers was at an attraction called Everglades Wonder Gardens in Bonita Springs owned by the Piper Brothers. I visited the attraction and met the Pipers, who knew of me and of the Breeding Center. The Pipers had four pairs of panthers. One pair was old at 27 years and beyond breeding age, but the others, younger, had been taken from a mother shot by hunters. The Pipers had been successful in breeding panthers previously, but had discontinued the process. I made arrangements to borrow their animals, one pair at a time, to attempt breeding at the compound. They agreed to cooperate with me if I performed the process at my cost and returned a certain number of offspring to them.

The first pair adapted well to the compound after overcoming the initial fear induced by the scent of natural predators — tigers and leopards. When they had adjusted to the environs, they began the breeding process. The female cycled and the male mounted, but there were no offspring. I found the situation strange and took some sperm to the University in Gainesville for analysis. An abnormality was detected. It was decided that the animal should be tested.

I took the caged panther, the youngest male, to the School of Veterinary Medicine where Dr. Chillet specialized in Sperm Research. Chris Belden of the Game Commission and several other researchers were present when the procedure was performed. The panther was contained in one of my squeeze cages, tranquilized and then electro-ejaculated by inserting a vibrating probe into the rectum and applying electrical current. This induced artificial masturbation, which in turn produced a sperm specimen to be examined under a microscope. The spermatozoid was moving very slowly, which the participating experts felt was indicative of a problem. I made a suggestion.

"You know the animal is tranquilized. Don't you think the effect of the drug sedating the host is not also sedating the sperm?"

My colleagues found my analysis very humorous, so I asked, "Why do you find that so funny?"

"Because that is not the way it works in cats!" Most of them had worked exclusively with house cats.

I returned to the compound with no solution to the problem and no conclusive diagnosis. I kept the pair housed together. In a month, we heard the sounds of babies crying under their den. We had broken through the barrier for no apparent reason. There had been no change in routine or diet. I named the firstborn *Uno* and gave the others names in proper order *Dos, Tres, Quatros,* and so on. We ultimately had over 120 panther cubs born on the compound, some of which have been turned loose in the wild.

In spite of the millions spent by the Game Commission collecting animals in the wild and dispersed to breeders, there has not been a single captive-born animal produced, to my knowledge, other than mine, that has been returned to its natural habitat. While this feat has not been acknowledged by the authorities, I feel a great deal of pride in the accomplishment. That is only one of many accomplishments over the years in addition to honors bestowed.

As an art collector and also an art student, I enjoyed being associated with the famous artists who have come to the compound seeking source material and adding to my collection. In 1987, I was honored as an invited guest by the City of Atlanta to attend a retrospective exhibit of Charles Fracé. I was asked to speak at the special gathering on the subject of endangered species and presented with a handsome plaque engraved, "Charles Fracé Twenty-fifth Wildlife Art Anniversary in appreciation of your support — Charles Fracé to Robert Baudy." I shall always revere the honor and the plaque. But more than that, I cherish the friendship that evolved with the extraordinary artist who spent so many hours at the compound studying, photographing, and sketching my cats.

It was also in 1987 that I received two round-trip tickets to attend the opening of the zoo in Tokyo where the giant tortoise were displayed. I was invited to bring a guest and asked to give a talk on endangered species at the inauguration of the new facility. I wanted Kathy to make the trip, but that was not possible. I didn't want to go alone.

Fay Francis was a client who owned a bathing suit business in Melbourne selling custom-designed French bikinis. She'd purchased several cats from me and came to the compound from time to time always with a beautiful model or two accompanying her. When I went to her place of business, there were gorgeous women on the premises who modeled the bathing suits. One day Fay said to me, "Boy, do I have the girl to go to Japan with you!"

I'd told Fay about the trip and lamented that Kathy couldn't join me. Fay introduced me to a tall blond model in her early twenties, a lovely looking girl with a sweet personality and a wonderful body. She was anxious to take a trip to the Far East and I knew that the whole adventure would be enhanced if shared by the beauty.

The flight from Tampa cross-country and over the Pacific went smoothly. When we arrived in Tokyo, our plane was met by a press corps directed to film and interview me. When we deplaned, the model walked ahead of me, a tall, leggy, blue-eyed beauty with long blond hair — a knockout of a girl who stood out dramatically from the short, dark-haired Orientals. Well, I was nearly forgotten as the press went wildly after my companion. Their cameras and attention totally focused on the lovely lady. I was accustomed to being upstaged by beautiful women and magnificent animals and got a big kick out of the performance.

When I was finally recognized, I gave an interview and from that time on was treated royally by the Japanese hosts, who showed us many wonderful attractions in Tokyo and its environs. However, wherever we traveled my blond companion was the center of attention.

Upon returning to Florida, I became instantly caught up in compelling, dramatic life-and-death occurrences, both human and animal, that filled the compound. Gladys was filling her hours surrounded by babies, while the Popicks were embroiled in a nasty divorce.

There were phone calls from Odette concerning Gerard, pleading with me for an answer that would serve each of us in the dreadful, lethal slide which seemed only to be gaining momentum. With so many tragic situations, I made a determined effort to bury myself, gratefully, in the business at hand, running an animal-filled compound bursting with new life. In addition, I received solicitations, as well as visitors, from foreign countries as well as natives, seeking expertise and source material, all of which lent credence to what I was about and provided some solace from the hurt.

To help buffer the pains and to share and enjoy the ongoing births on the compound, Angelie Blesse came into my life. I was introduced to the extraordinary lady through an acquaintance in Bushnell. Angie was a horsewoman seeking employment. I spoke to her first over the phone and then interviewed her. I was immediately impressed with her credentials, not the least of which were her extreme good looks. The tall, lithe, athletic body, beautiful face and long blond hair only enhanced her love of animals. She came from a fine family. Her father was a decorated Vietnam veteran, who retired from the service as General after working at the Pentagon. Angie's sister was still in Washington working in the White House. Soon after Angie joined us, there were calls from Washington that added a certain excitement to the central Florida compound. Angie was exceptionally intelligent and quickly picked up the routine, handling the animals instinctively.

Angie didn't live on the compound. She found an apartment

in Bushnell, where she had many friends and acquaintances. She was imbued with the special animal virus and became so comfortable in the oak hammock that she began a routine that I warned her about as something professional trainers never do. After she'd been around the cats for a period of months, she went into their enclosures with buckets full of raw meat and fed the cats by hand. Trainers and handlers know that at feeding time animals will occasionally fight over the food, and the danger of injury to an intruder is great. She survived and the animals loved her. She learned how to discipline the cats and quickly became a wonderful asset to me.

Angie raised many babies and loved riding my horses at full gallop through the hammock. I had a dozen horses at the time and some were outlaw horses that she handled with firm discipline and even broke. She was a strong-willed woman, very sure of herself, and she didn't take lightly to anyone crossing her.

One day I looked out the apartment window as I heard screaming. I saw Earl running as he cleared a four-foot fence pursued by Angie carrying a two-by-four and she, too, cleared the fence like the fine athlete she was.

I went out, loudly admonishing, "What the hell is happening?" Apparently Earl had done something to one of Angie's favorite cats and reacted to her objection with some commentary that infuriated her. She was really hot, and I think she would have killed Earl if I hadn't stepped into the fray to calm her.

In her free time Angie and her friends enjoyed going to the bars in the area. She'd been dating a local cowboy named Billy. The way I heard it, when the romance broke up, Billy was upset to have lost the best-looking woman in Sumter County. One night soon after they split, Angie went into one of the watering holes with a girlfriend. Seated at the bar was Billy along with some buddies. He attempted to talk to Angie, who tried hard to ignore his presence. He persisted. Angie had a couple of drinks, then got up to leave. As she walked past the bar, Billy said something ugly. She turned and asked him to repeat what he'd said. When he did, she pulled her fist back and hit him in the face, knocking him off the barstool. She regained her composure, turned, and left the bar. Up until that time Billy had been considered one of the toughest cowboys in the county.

When commercials were shot on the compound, Angie took

the place of the professional models who, more often than not, were paralyzed with fear by working with tigers and leopards. When the director and crew saw Angie, they were delighted to use the beauty who willingly posed caressing an unleashed cat, demonstrating complete relaxation and naturalness, and helping to achieve the desired effect.

Angie raised many baby cats during the four years she worked for me. She enjoyed taking some of the young cats off the compound to attend picnics or to visit friends. I did not approve of the activity as permits were required whenever a cat is removed from the Breeding Center. I could have been fined, but I had little influence over the willful, determined beauty. She possessed an intrepid streak which I presume she inherited from her father, the General. She was quite fearless, but was also fun, and she possessed a wonderful sense of humor. She had so much going for her. I felt incredibly fortunate to have her services for the four years, and I hated to see her go when she married a man who lived out of state. She left the compound and I began to search for someone to replace her. I knew it wasn't going to be easy.

A shopping center had opened in Bushnell in the early 1980s. It was a boon to the small town and became a busy and successful hub. I frequented the large grocery store and often dined at the Pizza Hut. I don't like to cook for myself and enjoyed getting off the compound to meet friends and share a meal. I also found restaurants to be a good source for future employees.

On one of my evenings out, I noticed a very pretty dark-haired girl with soft brown eyes, who was also a fine waitress. I struck up friendly conversation. I knew that if a girl was a hard worker and had the added bonus of loving animals, I'd found the combination that best suited my needs. Lily Lehman's mother owned a pet shop outside Tampa where Lily grew up in the company of many different animals. She'd had quite a lot of experience raising baby birds by eye-dropper and had handled other pets. I invited Lily to visit the compound. She came to work soon after Angie left.

Lily was married at the time and lived in a home overlooking the Withlacootchee River. Her husband worked for a cable network company, and she had her own transportation to get to and from the compound. I trained her from the start on the proper methods for handling baby cats and also worked her into a full and comfortable knowledge of the care and handling of mature cats and animals. She adapted well.

Soon after Lily's arrival I had visitors, a group of inspectors from the USDA. After making their tour, I was ordered to raise my perimeter fencing to eight feet. I was further informed that if the job was not completed in ten days they would close me down. I found out later that the requirement was excessive and not legal, but at the time I couldn't investigate legal ramifications knowing I'd have a hell of a time just complying.

I contacted a contractor friend in Webster, who'd come to my aid on many occasions. The man was a black contractor who employed local blacks. As a matter of fact, he owned about half the black community in Webster. His business enterprise consisted of crews transported to Georgia and to other farming areas to harvest watermelon and other crops. He also maintained crews to perform heavy-duty repair work after a hurricane, when wind and tornadoes toppled trees in the hammock. Strong men and heavy equipment were needed to cut up and remove felled oaks, and the same crew was needed to perform a fencing miracle. We were talking about fencing 42 acres, requiring thousands and thousands of dollars worth of material to say nothing of the cost of manpower. With less than ten days, we estimated that a crew of 15 was necessary.

One of the men working on the fence was named Samuel Lee. I had in my employ at the time a man whom I wanted to fire. He'd been sent by Gerard, and I took the chance of hiring the ex-con with a lengthy prison record, but it was a mistake. He was dishonest although I had him butchering, and I couldn't do without a man in the position.

I'd talked to Sam's boss about the need to fill the spot, and he recommended Sam as being a good worker and an honest individual. He even encouraged me to ask Sam if he wanted to work permanently on the compound. When I approached Sam, I told him he could come for a trial period, and then we'd make a final decision based on his ability to handle slaughtering animals. It's not for everybody, but is a vital position at the Breeding Center. Sam began work in 1989 and proved to be a valuable employee. He became the main butcher, and after thorough training and adjusting to the conditions, he could process a cow in less than 20 minutes, which is excellent.

I felt fortunate to have both Lily and Sam on the busy compound where the breeding process continued in a constant, ongoing perpetuation of species. There was much to accomplish and no such thing as a holiday or even a vacation. Everyone stayed busy all the time. I must admit that I've been a taskmaster in a business that gave no quarter.

39

BREEDING
L'Élevage

When the Endangered Species Act abruptly terminated many of my original plans for the Breeding Center, I refocused my original intent. Trips to Africa and to other far-flung places in the world to search out rare and endangered species were no longer practical nor was importation of animals on the list possible. I had developed a strong and efficient network and maintained a compound filled with animals for perpetuating and selling domestic as well as those rare and endangered species already in my collection acquired before the Act went into effect.

I concentrated my efforts on the breeding process. My list of clients required 4,000 brochures mailed twice a year describing the animals bred in addition to surplus animals available. The original mailing piece went to zoos and private collectors and was then copied and further circulated to curators, such as those working with mammals, reptiles, and birds, as well as to other interested and knowledgeable authorities. This gave me a broad, worldwide base from which inquiries came through the mail, by telephone, and even through personal visits to the center.

Whenever a purchase was made and the shipment completed, particularly in the case of a zoo purchase, the event received media coverage which further spread the reputation of Robert Baudy and the Breeding Center. My name and reputation were well-established. To this day, I receive calls every week, as well as visitors from all over the world, seeking to talk to Robert Baudy, to see the collection, to pick my brain for research projects, to sketch or photograph a certain species, or to interview me for a newspaper or magazine article. There are still sales of animals in spite of strict government import-export regulations, which only serve to complicate each and every transaction.

From its inception, the business of supplying food, feeding, and caring for the animals required labor beginning before sunrise and lasting well after sunset everyday.

There have been thousands of births over the past 30 years. The first breeding on the compound occurred with the working leopards that I used in my act. When I began to accumulate rare species, the North Chinese leopards bred as well as hyenas, lemurs, foxes, peafowl, ostriches, llamas, and horned animals. I eventually had over 200 exotic felines including snow and clouded leopards, African and Asian leopards, black and spotted jaguars, ocelots, Siberian lynx, bobcats, pumas, and white and normal tigers.

In the breeding of cats, whether it be the large cats (which breed primarily during the daytime) or the smaller cats (that tend to be nocturnal), it was imperative that the process be monitored and supervised in order to protect the animals from harming one another. That's a rather idealistic view. Once the mating process begins, the cat assumes an attitude, a totally focused resolve which cannot be disrupted or violated without serious consequences.

When the female is in season, more naturally during the winter months, she will become very vocal, and begin rolling on the floor of her cage. In breeding of pumas, the piercing scream of the female is like a human female reacting to violence. The high-intensity scream is designed to attract the male. This usually elicits the male's mating call. In the case of jaguars or leopards, the calls sound more like a raspy handsaw cutting wood.

In order to be successful in the breeding process, it is imperative that the male and female, of whatever species, accept the chosen mate. Without compatibility, they will fight and kill each other when placed in a common enclosure. For that reason I always contained the two animals to be bred in adjacent cages for a period of adjustment. In some cases where animals from the wild were being prepared for mating, it required over a year of close proximity for the adjustment period. When the two cages were placed together, I reinforced the heavy, sturdy large mesh wire with a finer mesh to prevent claws coming through and injuring the other cat. I heard many sad stories over the years of breeders, who did not provide the extra protection, where claws and ears were mutilated so badly that animals had to be destroyed. I've had to repair many cages when the fine mesh was torn and ripped by impetuous, amorous animals, but it was worthwhile in time and energy to preserve safety and lives. However, even with the extra protection, I did lose some specimens.

Before the government ban on importation of wild animals, between the late 1950s and early 1970s, I received hundreds of animals, among them, 15 clouded leopards from Indochina, leopards from Burma, and many other diverse species from other parts of the world. Naturally, the wild-caught animals required more time to adjust to their confinement and to all the nuances to which a captive-born animal was already accustomed.

Once the breeding pair is adjusted to the sight of one another, the next consideration in the early stages is smell. When the male and female are finally ready to breed, they are placed in a common cage designed to be controlled from without by a guillotine door, which makes it possible to move an animal from one section to another if separation becomes necessary at any time during the mating process. By using this mechanism, we place the male in the female half of the cage and vice versa where each animal sprays the other's domain. The male performs like a tom cat, spraying backwards. The spray serves to intermingle scents, which enhances acceptance into sacred, unmolested territory.

After spraying, the animals are placed together, and an audience is present to observe the activity, even of the nocturnal small cats. We found the spotted leopards to be more discrete, desiring the privacy of night to perform, but we had to record the date of the initial mating as well as the number of times of mounting. Mounting of tigers and leopards occurs ten to 15 times per day and continues night and day for four or five days or until the female has ovulated and been impregnated. In some cases, it took eight days to achieve the desired ovulation.

The actual act of mounting has always been dramatic to witness as well as to hear, due to the possible danger to either of the mating pair. The male approaches from behind grabbing the female's neck in his mouth as he mounts her — her tail receptively aside as she crouches on the floor ready to receive the penetration of the penis, which, by the way, is surprisingly small in an animal of such enormous size and power. As the male penetrates the female with eight or nine thrusts in order to achieve orgasm, there is little noise until he ejaculates, then the male emits a tremendous roar, which is accompanied by the female turning on her back and slapping the male with her paw.

We had a unique problem to solve when breeding the rare North Chinese leopards. We'd gone through the process of placing a male and female in adjoining enclosures and having them snarl and scratch at one another to get the nastiness out of their systems. When the cats seemed more friendly toward one another, the male was released into the female's cage. The spraying had taken place, and we thought they were ready to mate, but we were not prepared for the brutality of the male grabbing the female's neck. His fangs injured her fatally. The loss of any animal is upsetting and totally against my principles unless absolutely necessary or in life-threatening circumstances. I could see that the male leopard had the potential to destroy every female placed in a common enclosure for mating.

I talked to Doc about the problem and he thought of a unique solution. He suggested getting rid of the fangs. We knew we couldn't pull the teeth because they go too deeply into the head and that would produce other problems. John suggested we tranquilize the male and take him to John's dentist in Eustis for surgery. The dentist was willing to perform his first leopard dentistry. We had him cut the fangs near the gum, perform root canals, and make caps for the projecting teeth. The sight of the leopard, sitting asleep in the dentist's chair was hilarious and worth a photograph. When he returned to the compound, he recuperated well and did mate successfully.

It is not cruel to utilize advanced medical techniques on animals. Obviously, if they are not able to run as they would in the wild, their claws grow long and require trimming, just as hoofed stock needs to be shod. I never declawed an animal and never applied any treatment that I felt would hurt the animal. However, using various expert medical and surgical techniques has solved many life-threatening problems, enhanced, and even saved lives.

Wild-caught animals required the most watchfulness during mating. When it was necessary to break up fights by tranquilizing a fierce animal, it could take up to 15 minutes, and by that time one animal could easily kill the other. When we had to break up fights, we used gimmicks that I'd learned years before from Alfred Court and Paul le Royer. There were simple props that startled animals and diverted their attention. One such prop was a fire extinguisher. I kept some handy, but they were not always reliable if they'd gone flat. The most trustworthy prop was automobile hub caps tied together at the end of a steel pole. The sudden clanging metal created such an alarming clatter that it always distracted the animal.

I remember watching as a trainer was being attacked by a tiger, years before, in a European arena. One of Court's workers ran to get the metal noisemaker, which did alarm the tiger momentarily. The animal turned the trainer loose enabling him to escape.

But an animal diverted from the heat of battle or attack will not be diverted long. If the escape is not swift, the animal will very quickly return to its prey. In one case I entered a cage to save an animal from being mauled to death, only to have the victim turn on me. A predator moves swiftly and well-trained outside helpers are vital in order to accomplish a successful escape.

All of my cat enclosures are designed with a guillotine door which closes off the den from the outer portion of the enclosure. When an animal is hurt, it often wants to retreat to its den, which is generally open at night and closed during the day. When an injured animal seeks its den to escape further attack, it is important that the door be opened and closed quickly to contain and protect the injured animal. If the separating process is not done quickly and assuredly, and the attacking animal gets into the den, there is no way to separate the two. Death to one or both nearly always follows.

Uno was the first captive-born Florida panther bred on the compound. He has since grown to be over 150 pounds. When he was a youngster, I trained him to perform to my commands. We used Uno's photograph to publicize the work being performed in the field to save the endangered native panthers. Most early pictures published by the Game Commission showing Florida panther are of Panthera Uno. I had him climbing trees when he was 18 months old. We took him off the compound routinely, turned him loose, and filmed him in what would be his natural habitat. He responded like a pet dog to my cue and very obediently returned to me when I called.

When Uno was three, I began to introduce him to some of his half-sisters to begin breeding. I watched him daily and realized that he had achieved a good deal of weight, which was beginning to strain the chain collar fastened to his neck. The collar had to be enlarged. Ordinarily, I'd use a squeeze cage to contain an animal to cut a collar and extend it, but I felt that time was pressing due to another commitment and decided to bypass tranquilizing and work on him in the enclosure. Fortunately, I had an excellent crew working with me on that particular day.

BeeJay Lester was working along with a burly 200-pound man, who did my carpentry, plus another young man of about 20. I warned them, "Look, this cat is looking at me strangely; but if we put him in a squeeze cage, we're talking about three hours of work. I don't think we need to do that. I'm going to go in with the cat and take the small bolt cutter with me." (The collar was put together with a clip that had rusted so it had to be cut apart.)

Uno growled from deep inside his chest, and I was wary. "He has never made that noise before." I told BeeJay, "You'll be in charge of the door." The cage had an outside swinging door. I told her, "You open the door for me to go in, and be prepared to open the door to let me out. I'll be facing the cat at all times, and I don't expect any problems, but watch closely."

Because Uno had never made that noise before, and had a strange look on his face, I turned to the carpenter, "In case there's a problem, and he pins me, I want you to move in ready to hit him."

The guys were damned tough, and I felt like I had good back-up if Uno pulled anything unexpected. Fortunately, it has been my policy that each and every employee on the compound, whether hired to rake leaves, do carpentry or whatever, be well-trained by me to handle every kind of situation. They have been exposed to the animals under many different circumstances, and it is imperative that they not panic, but know exactly what to do.

I went into the cage with Uno, and like a flash he jumped at me. He caught me by the leg and threw me into a corner of the cage. His teeth went through my boot and into my leg. He grabbed me in a bear-hug as he moved toward my throat. Training and natural reflexes caused me to raise my elbow. Fortunately, because of the cold weather, I wore a sheepskin coat — a sturdy thick

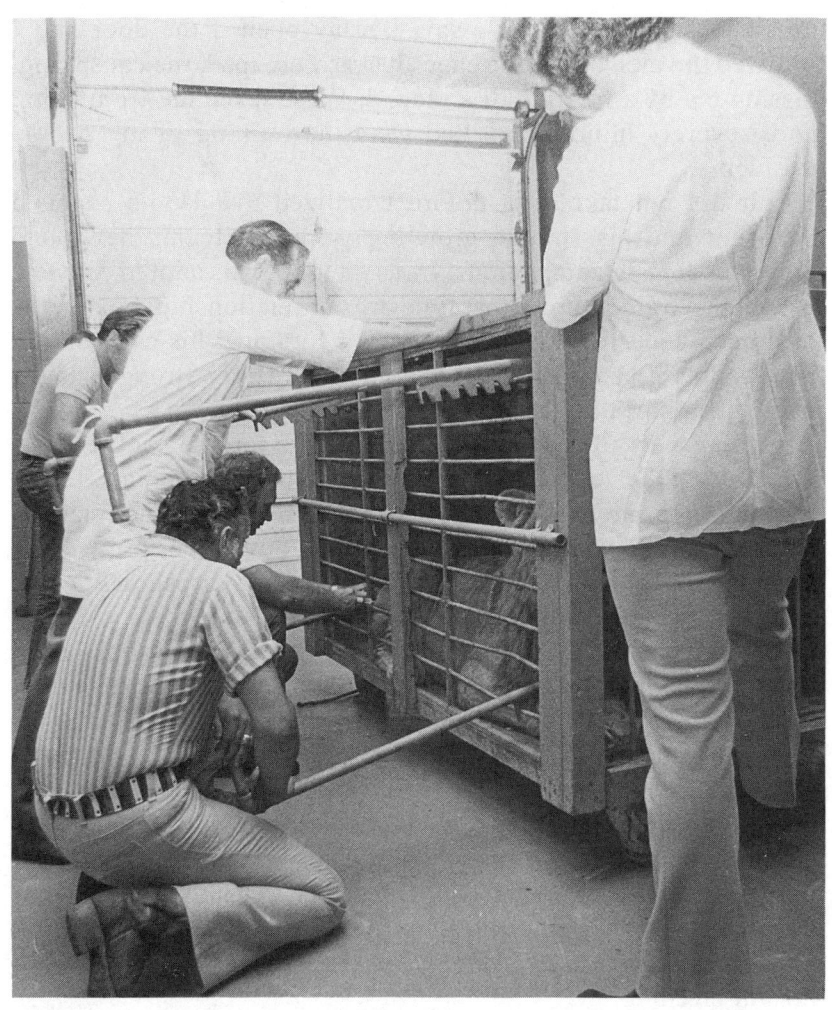

Over the years the squeeze cage was invaluable for safe handling of animals.

protection against claws and teeth. I struggled to a standing position in the corner of the cage facing the cat on his hind legs going for my jugular. I called to the men who had cautiously entered the cage, "Hit to kill!"

The carpenter wielded a shovel with all his might, and clobbered Uno with the flat part solidly on the back of his head. Uno turned loose, and I broke away. BeeJay opened the door and I followed the men out of the cage. Just as I escaped, the cat sprang, missing me by a fraction of a second. What saved me from being more severely injured or killed were the training of my people and luck.

It did not take long before I realized that Uno's changed demeanor and his strange growling were due to his newfound interest in female companions. I was no longer his adored, trusted, and obeyed trainer. From that time on, our relationship took a very different stance. To this day, whenever I go near his cage during the breeding season, Uno roars and indicates very strongly that if given the opportunity he would go for my jugular. We have a well-defined, respectful admiration and tolerance for one another.

During the years that I've been involved with animals, I have been surrounded by helpers who had their assignments well-planned and orchestrated if an emergency occurred, but I never wanted any of them armed with guns. I have employed sharpshooters, but knew that in the heat of battle with an attacking cat, there is a great deal of movement in the struggle. The risk of me being shot during violent attack was too great. Many people living in the surrounding area of Sumter County were dead-shot hunters, but I never trusted anyone to draw an accurate bead on an attacking animal. I preferred to train my people to remain calm and to startle the animal, but I never wanted a gun aimed at a vicious battle.

In the wild, the life-span of a large cat is probably not longer than ten years. There are too many predators. In captivity, when they are protected, well-fed, and given medical attention to ward off parasites, a cat will live 17 or 18 years. I have seen jaguars 25 years old still breeding.

At the Cincinnati Zoo, there was a paralyzed jaguar that had lived a long, full life. At age 25, in spite of age and infirmities, he did not want to give up what he enjoyed so well, and for so long — mounting females. That was quite extraordinary, but I must admit to admiring the old boy whose instinct so universally practiced and enjoyed was still intact.

For the past 15 years, zoos have been attempting to artificially breed rare cats. The process continues with a very low rate of success, mainly because it takes many copulations to cause the female to ovulate. With artificial insemination there is only one implantation. There have been some offspring produced by this method, but it is rare and there is usually only one baby produced, seldom a normal litter of three or four.

Interestingly, the small cats do not produce more than one or two offspring. I found the small cats particularly fascinating. Very few zoos are involved in breeding the smaller felines. I had wonderful success with the Asian golden cat from Malaysia, but there were never more than one or two babies, and it is for that reason that I had to quit breeding the small cats. Economically, it was not feasible. The labor involved in maintaining them was the same as for the larger cats that bred more frequently and produced multiple litters. The smaller cats breed once a year. The large cats have the potential to breed three times with the gestation period of 95 to 100 days. If the litter is removed from the den, the female recycles within three to six weeks and is capable of again breeding. I never did attempt to breed the large cats three times a year, but I knew the capability was there.

Another small cat I imported and studied was the beautiful flat-headed cat from Asia. This rare cat commonly lives close to water and is a fine swimmer. Unfortunately, like so many other species, the flat-head cat is nearly extinct today.

One animal that I had on the compound, but did not attempt to breed, was the bear. I brought some Kodiaks, the giant of all bears, onto the compound to be sent on to clients. I brokered the bears, but had no intention of keeping them for long. The Kodiak is highly intelligent, but like all bears, is not to be trusted. I'd seen lethal attacks over the years and knew that if Alfred Court and Paul le Royer had suffered injuries, I did not want to place myself in extreme danger. Furthermore, I did not want to incur the financial burden of setting up permanent enclosures for the huge animals. Statistics prove that more animal experts and trainers have been killed by bears than by any other species.

Another fascinating breeding involved the South American maned wolf. The unusual animal is red in color, like a fox, and I was one of the first to introduce the rare species to this country. My contact was through a network of collectors based in Paraguay. Paraguay at the time was controlled by a dictator of German origin, and the country was a haven for Nazis who had escaped from Germany. A group of obviously pro-Hitler, but well-educated German zoologists came to the compound to do research. They told me about the maned wolf, which I decided to import and breed. I imported ten specimens captured by Paraguan Indians and shipped by the Germans.

Along with the animals came a request that I have one of their key men work at the compound for a stipulated period of time. I agreed, but soon knew that I'd made a mistake. The man had been an SS officer. His number was clearly visible on his arm. He possessed a violent temper and displayed sadistic tendencies, which I could not tolerate on the compound. We had some heated discussions concerning the War and concentration camps. I knew the relationship would be stormy and eventually escalate into an impossible, volatile eruption.

The first order of business with the maned wolf was to test for parasites. We knew that every carnivorous animal in the wild is loaded with parasites as a part of their system. In an attempt to perpetuate the species, I tried to worm the infected animals. I began with a small dose of medication to kill the parasites. Knowing that any medication designed to kill the inhabiters could also be harmful to the host animal, great care and thought went into the treatment. There were and are many drugs designed specifically to counter the many different varieties of parasites. In the treatment of tape worms, round worms, or hook worms we use Avomactine — a very effective medication, but one not available when I was treating the maned wolf.

It was also imperative in dealing with a species totally foreign to me, while using a medication that tended to be toxic, that I take extreme care in the dosage, always being cognizant of possible allergic reaction which could lead to death.

After the initial dose, I noticed within two or three days the wolf stood, looking sad, and inactive, and had no appetite. The animal ultimately died. In one case, the parasite actually dug through the abdomen and exited while the animal was still alive. I did perform several autopsies and discovered that the left kidney cavity — never the right — was completely empty of kidney and was occupied instead with a huge worm coiled inside the pouch. The bright red worm was the size of a large pencil. The condition, which pre-existed, apparently did not hinder the wolf, who seemed to survive well on one kidney. Not every wolf had a kidney worm, but 75 percent of the animals that I imported hosted the deadly parasite. From my stock of uninfested wolves, a captive-born population was eventually established and still flourishes today.

After working for months with the wolves, I sold a pair to the Memphis Zoo and several individual males to zoos that had single female specimens. With those animals, I sent a prepared statement stipulating the animals were eating well at the compound and were seemingly healthy, but I went on to describe what my experience had been, and that I felt strongly that each of the wolves could be host to a kidney worm. In most cases, the various zoos did find the parasite and treated the condition, but lost the animals. I documented my care, treatment, and the results, but as in so many similar incidents over the years, it has been my experience that zoo vets do not necessarily believe or trust in my expertise. They have been educated and trained professionally and possess the college degree that establishes their credentials, which they naturally feel excels that of an animal trainer and ex-showman. In many cases, they proceeded to ignore my documentation and treated an exotic animal just as they would a cat, dog, horse, or some other domestic animal. Their experience in dealing with wild and rare species is practically nonexistent, and therefore they often lose the animal.

As I continued working with the maned wolf and the other animals on the compound, the SS officer's attitude and behavior continued to create problems to which I reacted. There were ugly confrontations. After one particularly vituperative argument, I watched him from afar, knowing that his anger would be vented in a perverse way. I had the feeling he'd be capable of extreme harm to me, the animals, and the other workers on the compound. To my horror, he let some cats loose. My fears confirmed, I grabbed my .30-06 and went after the man as he intently watched the cats disappear into the shadows. I was furious, and told him, "I think you have made a mistake coming to work here, and you sure as hell have made a mistake letting the cats loose. This is Sumter County. You see this rifle? I feel like I'd like to kill you, should kill you. Some of those animals may escape from my place and attack kids. Taking you to court will take too much time and will not accomplish anything. I'll tell you one thing, you are going to help me put those cats back. But believe me, I will kill you if you stay. Once the cats are back, you're out of here!" Several of my people helped round up the cats. The following day the German was gone.

I'd imported many gorillas before the Endangered Species Act totally changed my business. The large, dangerous animals brought $5,000 per specimen before the legislation was enacted. Since the act, a young female is now worth $100,000. When I was importing gorillas, it was cheaper to import than to breed them. In order to breed gorillas, a very costly facility was required consisting of large outdoor cage with heated quarters to contain and protect the animals at night and during the winter months. The whole installation required hydraulic controls on the doors, and I estimated the complete housing would cost a million dollars. I sold most of the gorillas that I imported, but I kept several specimens on the compound to exhibit. I even had in mind working a gorilla act. However, the technical requirements obviated the feasibility of such an act. I found that the animals did survive cold temperatures fairly well, but they proved highly susceptible to catching any and all human ailments. They caught colds easily, and other virus-type illnesses, and were not immune to symptoms suffered by the employees.

In order to transport the gorillas properly and safely, an enormous rig with thick glass enclosures, temperature and humidity controlling devices, and other costly features was necessary, which determined the ultimate decision.

Over the years, lemur breeding has been one of the most successful and satisfying of all breeding animals on the compound. As a pseudoscientist, I was fascinated by the lemurs, precursors of human beings 65 million years ago, long before monkeys, apes, and humans appeared, and existing only in Madagascar. They were the first animal that demonstrated characteristics of man. They are called prosimian, which means "before monkeys." I always seek information on the origin of animals.

Many zoos have featured lemurs in their exhibits. The Frankfurt Zoo has a huge collection, and in this country, Duke University sponsored and developed an extensive research program on the lemur. The directors of the University project visited our compound to interview me about the trips to Madagascar and my success in lemur breeding.

Lemurs are seminocturnal. Their habits are to move at early

daybreak for two or three hours, when most of the breeding takes place, or late in the evening. The hammock is shaded during the day and inky dark during the night, which produces ideal living conditions for the lemur. However, those same conditions prevent observation of the mating process. Most of the wild-born animals did not appreciate an audience and would cease mating whenever we were present.

One time a crew arrived from the University of Florida with cameras and sound equipment to film and record the breeding process, including sounds made during copulation. The crews set up their equipment and waited patiently for the action to begin, but the animals, shy and sensitive, did not perform. It was a wasted trip to the compound except for information that I proffered. I learned over the years that it takes years of captive breeding and two or three generations for the wild-learned and practiced habits to diminish and finally disappear.

My cage design for the lemur and the locations of cages were ideal. I had them built with two dens; one to protect the inhabitants from the north side, and one from the west wind. I thought that with the large oak trees I possessed the perfect setting, and I was correct. I still have lemurs that are great-grand-offspring of the animals collected in 1968. The cages are made of wire with plywood dens, sliding doors, and a special heating system that did not use a heat lamp, but instead a heater that screwed into a bulb socket, unfortunately a costly apparatus.

I have 15 red-fronted lemurs, which are descendants of lemurs I captured myself in Madagascar. I soon found the breeding uncomplicated if they were fed a good diet of fresh fruits and bamboo leaves. Fortunately, a huge hedge of bamboo exists just across the road from the compound, in a patch about 300 yards long and 900 feet wide. With permission from the owner, I send my people across to cut and gather the bamboo. In addition, I travel each Monday to the market to acquire fresh produce. The lemurs have been well worth the investment. Not only are they fun to breed, but are a beautiful animal and command up to $10,000 each.

We did discover that monkeys could tolerate the kind of cold experienced during the winter in Florida and actually thrived better without an artificial heat source. There has been so much on-the-job training over the years, so much knowledge acquired living and working with animals. The many successes, and even failures, provided insight, direction, and enhancement of my knowledge. They have reinforced and legitimized my reputation as a source of information valuable to other breeders, collectors, zoo directors, curators, and other interested individuals who contact me for my expertise and experienced assessment.

But still I have to suffer the indignation of government employees at the state and federal level, inspectors representing the USDA who arrive on the compound and impart their uneducated bureaucratic diatribe on how to care for lemurs and how to provide the proper habitat for breeding clouded leopards, and on and on. I listen and then ask the neophyte inspector, "How many lemurs or clouded leopards have you bred and raised?" Fair question.

It rankles me to be the subject of inquisitions, directives, and even fines, when I am considered among my peers to be an authority after years of successful and active work in the breeding process. It is also painful to see government regulations so diametrically opposed to what I know to be sound and correct management of species in captivity.

I am particularly angered when my domain is placed in danger by the incompetents. Any damage or threat to the compound is disturbing and creates real pain and suffering. If that threat is at the hands of nature, I can accept it much better than when it is at the hands of a government bureaucracy.

I feel a great sense of loss when a hurricane or tornado fells one of the oaks. In addition to the loss, there is a significant amount of physical work and great expense sawing and burning the fallen tree. Such major operations confirm and reaffirm the lasting beauty and toughness of what seems to be a symbol of stability and dignity against the sad deprivation at the hands of man.

But the saddest demise of all was when a USDA inspector came onto the property and ordered me to seal some cracks in the concrete pad surrounding one of the giant trees around which we'd built a tiger cage. I tried to explain that the recommendation would kill the 400-year old masterpiece of nature, and the cracks were doing nothing to harm the cats living peacefully beneath the protective canopy of oak. My pleadings were ignored, and the oak tragically fell, as predicted. I keep the stricken giant supported by huge cables to slow its final disappearance — a fitting display of the incompetence of some of the *experts,* who are in charge of state animal welfare enforcement. It would seem that centenarian trees are of no concern to the bureaucrats despite the fact that no animal ever suffered from two-inch wide cracks in the cement flooring.

However, in spite of government intervention, I continue to breed animals and continue to find the process stimulating and satisfying in producing healthy, active, vibrant offspring in a compound that has been my haven for over 30 years.

One of the most satisfying breeding experiences I'd ever had involved hyenas. There are three different species of hyena from Africa: the regular spotted; the brown, which is nearly extinct; and the striped hyena, which is a smaller animal than the other two species. When I came to America in the early fifties, the striped hyena was plentiful in Africa and in parts of the Middle East. Since that time the species has become extinct.

The spotted hyena had been bred in captivity before I began working with them. I was always fascinated by the intelligence of the animal and also by their feeding habits. As scavengers, they enjoyed the leftover meat from the tigers and leopards. I realized very early in the process that the hyenas did not appreciate fresh-cut meat with the bone nicely intact. They preferred to wait for the scraps left after the fresh meat had been consumed by the big cats.

Many zoos contained hyenas during the period that I worked with the species, but the success rate in breeding was very low due to the diet of fresh meat and commercial feed that served to fatten the specimens, but did not encourage successful breeding. With all of my animals over the years, instead of introducing sophisticated feed used for captive-bred animals, I tried to duplicate what a particular species was accustomed to in the wild. Zoos spend enormous amounts of time and money on research to evolve a diet that would produce and enhance the breed, but in almost every case, going back to nature produced the finest results.

While I worked primarily with the spotted hyena, I was the only breeder in the world breeding all three species in captivity at one time and in one location. The hyenas were not dangerous unless cornered and threatened. I'd go into the cage with impunity. What really fascinated me about the species was their level of intelligence and sensitivity.

Hyenas are far more intelligent than cats. In one case, a mother was neglecting her babies, and we had to take the babies and bottle-feed them. I began the nurturing process and then had Gladys and some other helpers take the babies to their homes for care. When the animals achieved a weight of about 25 to 30 pounds, they were returned to the compound. We noticed immediately that they had become human-imprinted and followed whomever raised them, just like a pet dog.

We had some that were kept semiloose in the hammock; and as long as their human *mother* was present, the young hyenas followed and stayed close to her. We even noticed that the hyenas could be used as a kind of "watch-hyena." Their instincts were so keen that when a stranger came to the compound, the hyenas detected the scent, picking it up more quickly than my dogs. They even demonstrated their discovery by making eloquent, guttural sounds indicating various emotional responses.

I also studied the scavenger and hunting instincts in the small, tough animal, which has been documented to have killed lions in Africa. They are not a fast animal, but possess tremendous endurance and are known to trot after prey for miles until the weaker prey finally succumbs to exhaustion. The hyena can trot for 20 miles in pursuit, and along with other animals that form the tribe, the scouts, they readily dispatch much larger prey. When they have finished with the victim, there is absolutely nothing wasted.

I raised the baby hyenas on different milk products. I experimented with cow milk and canned goat milk, and finally settled on a product called Espilac, produced by the Borden Company for puppies. Espilac was a good product except it lacked adequate levels of vitamin A. We did notice that some of the animals developed eye problems from the deficiency, and I enhanced their diet with liver and other organ meats, which solved the problem and produced a beautiful, healthy hyena population on the compound.

Of all the animals that I imported from the wild, less than ten percent of the wild-caught animals successfully bred in captivity. The stress of being taken from their natural habitat, placed in enclosures with dietary changes, and the introduction of humans into their daily habitation, all produced trauma that naturally disturbed and retarded the life-cycle. Eventually, they began to assimilate and eat whatever was presented in order to survive and would then, in some cases, adjust to their confinement. But it usually took time and patience for the trainer-breeder as well as for the animal. I did learn that importing very young members of the species produced far better results and more successful breeding. I advised the commission on preserving the Florida panther that in order to be successful in saving the precious hemispheric resource it would be prudent to gather young panthers.

On one of my early trips to South Africa to establish contacts I realized the potential for breeding ostriches. The large 300-pound, two-toed flightless birds were being bred in captivity in South Africa for over a hundred years. There were large ostrich farms breeding strictly for commercial purposes. I visited the farms and found the process highly educational. Nothing of the animal is wasted. The meat is sold for consumption, the skin tanned for sale to clothing and shoe manufacturing industries, and the feathers plucked and used for a variety of decorative purposes. History books describe the Romans, 600 years earlier, using ostrich feathers as helmet plumes.

I watched and learned the methods for handling the ostrich as they gained maturity. A whip was an important tool to fend off attack by the dangerous males, which are potential killers, particularly during the breeding cycle. I knew well how to use a whip properly, not to hurt the bird, but to establish respect and boundaries when a threatening bird demonstrated signs of wild behavior. The sight alone of the snake-like whip and its motion catch their attention. When an ostrich is going to charge its prey, whether animal or human, there are definite precursor signs, such as blowing its feathers, opening its wings, and doing a dance, which gives very short notice of pending attack. My pattern was to crack the whip in the air before an emergency occurred to demonstrate to the agitated bird that I was in command.

I ordered 75 chicks before I left South Africa. They arrived in Tampa in crates. Each specimen was approximately three feet high and in quite an excited state. I proceeded to dispatch over 50 chicks to various zoos in Canada and in the States from which I'd received previous orders. My mailing list included between 500-600 zoos existing at that time, in addition to roadside zoo facilities dotted all over the continent that were also clients. When I satisfied the demand for ostriches, I was left with about 15 birds.

Originally, I didn't intend to breed ostriches, but as they grew to maturity, enjoying and thriving on ten acres of pasture contained by seven-foot-high fencing and cross-fencing with no barbed wire, I had to rethink and rejustify the ostrich population. The containment alone required specific safety measures to protect the less intelligent species capable of tremendous speeds, and, during the mating cycle, becoming particularly rambunctious.

In the mating of ostriches, I learned from my South African mentors that putting a single male in an enclosure with two or three females produced the best results. I also learned that when the female lays her eggs, or clutch (laid over a period of eight to ten days and containing ten to 12 eggs), if the eggs are taken from the female and put into incubation, the female would lay a second clutch after several weeks. The female naturally will sit on the eggs to incubate them, but I wanted to induce more progeny.

The process in bird incubation is similar to the instinct of cats. Nature causes the female to cycle again when the offspring are killed or taken away. In nature, the female cat will stay with her litter for seven days around the clock, not moving to drink or defecate during the period before leaving to forage for food. In her absence, small predators such as hyenas, wolves, or snakes quite often move in to kill the babies. If unsuccessful in keeping the litter, the mother cat will, in a matter of weeks, go into season again in order to perform the usual breeding process and birth. Nature's design, when simulated under artificial methods and conditions, can produce satisfactory results. Using the incubator with the ostriches produced many chicks.

I had huge incubators for rare birds that I transformed so that each ostrich egg would have a separate compartment. The incubator rotated the eggs just as the mother would. Temperature and humidity control was imperative, and I did so well that the compound became overloaded with baby ostriches. Ultimately, I realized many zoos were breeding ostriches and I wasn't able to charge enough for each bird to cover my expenses in hatching and raising them. I made my own feed requiring a grinder to combine oyster shells, selenium, vegetables, cooked chicken eggs, and cooked meat to form the healthy diet that achieved the wonderful stock. It became quite a labor and, while satisfying in many ways, was not lucrative enough. But I retired from the ostrich business too soon. Currently ostriches sell for up to $10,000 per bird.

The very same miscalculation put me out of the llama business sooner than was prudent. After raising llamas for ten years, I got out due to species incompatibility with camels and other hoofed stock. Within four years, a group buying exotic animals systematically went from zoo to zoo and bought all surplus llamas. The group became aware that the Government was going to end importation of llamas. I wished that I'd been privy to that information. The price escalated to $5,000-$6,000 for a female llama.

When I initially went into the llama business, I acquired my stock domestically from zoos across the country. Most zoos have a petting area nearly always containing baby llamas. The babies are adorable and have a friendly demeanor, but as they become human-imprinted and mature, they lose all respect for humans, and become obnoxious, particularly in the case of a male llama during breeding season. They are from the camel family and share the extreme antisocial behavior of spitting grossly unpleasant spittle, not saliva but the digested contents of their stomach.

In the mating of llamas, the female lays flat on the ground, the male approaching from behind. As the male mounts, there is much conversation between the two as they make all sorts of strange noises. The breeding male llama, like the male camel, is obnoxious and will try to mount anything and everything in close proximity, from humans to wheelbarrows and even vehicles parked nearby.

The breeding process for the *Camelidaes* is similar to the llama, with the female in a reclining position to receive the male mounting from behind. The male camel is extremely vocal during copulation. The female produces only one offspring.

I did have a white camel born on the compound, which was a complete surprise since the male and female were not white. I had seen quite a few white camels on my trips to North Africa with Dr. Barbier, but had never before seen one in this country. I ultimately sold the baby for a substantial price.

The male lions did not produce any offspring, although I'll give them high marks for trying. When the lions matured to the age where, in the wild, they'd be involved in breeding, my lions reacted as would other species under the same circumstances — they began falling in love with one another. In the wild, when the females are in season, there are fights among the males to demonstrate superiority and dominance, and to establish territory. The fights are ferocious. Everything was cool on the compound for about three years until the sexual frustration created a pairing off. The lions began mounting one another and performing copulation. I had a group of homosexual lions that were having quarrels and fights that I had to break up, including one that became so violent and uncontrollable that I left the enclosure to save my life. The lions did survive the battle, and I continued to work with them. The violence took place primarily during the winter months, which would be the normal breeding season. They went through the routines obediently and for the remainder of the year behaved quite responsively and predictably with few problems. When I closed the Savage Kingdom, I sold the lions to various circuses, zoos, and animal trainers.

Among the rare birds acquired, I had imported macaws from South America. The colorful parrots live to be 60 years old, and they bred successfully in their individual birdhouses in the oak trees. They remained a noisy, colorful community from which I sold to other dealers and collectors over the years.

I also bred rhinoceros. The white rhino is the largest of the species which include the Asian, the Sumatran, and the black. The white is a misnomer, that is, the color of the hide is actually grey, similar to that of an elephant. I had acquired a pair on breeding loan from a Cincinnati Zoo. They were delivered by a drive-through safari designed to disperse the large mammals when the zoo could not contain all the animals they'd imported.

Breeding loan is a common practice in the zoo business. I would estimate that 25 or 30 percent of animals in a zoo do not belong to that particular zoo. The arrangement is usually the result of overcrowding or the desire to breed by a zoo to enhance a collection. At the present time, I have over 40 cats maintained by other owners. If there are offspring from any of my cats the agreement is for me to participate in 50 percent of the profit from sales.

In the case of the rhinos, I was anxious to have them in my display at the Savage Kingdom and hoped that mating would prove successful. I knew that water is important to the rhino to prevent dehydration. We dug a large hole and kept it filled with water for frequent dunking. They sought water just as they would in their natural African habitat, then rolled in the mud, followed by drying in the sun. From a distance they appeared light grey, even white as opposed to the black rhino, and hence were labeled *white*.

Curiously, the rhinos are practically blind. They have tiny eyes, but do possess a keen sense of hearing. Their ears are like radar, moving constantly to pick up sounds, and their sense of smell is also greatly attuned. The mating process is similar to that of elephants, with the huge six-foot-high male mounting the female from the rear. I had never before witnessed the mating of the 3,000-pound mammals. As we watched, it seemed incredible how docile both remained during the process.

At one point, we attempted to move the rhinos from one area to another. We did so by exciting their sense of smell using feed as bait. When they stopped or got off track, an employee stung them with a pebble thrown at the hind quarters, and the rhinos would take off quickly. It was humorous to watch the rhinos move in an attempted gallop, more of a trot.

There was an empty enclosure secured by nine-gauge chain-link fencing, the heaviest fencing material available. The door of the concrete-floored enclosure had been left open by accident and the male rhino wandered inside. It was far too dangerous to attempt to lead him out. If he became obstreperous, he could kill anyone entering the enclosure.

I told my people, "Look, let's not disturb him. I don't want to lose my cage to begin with, and I don't want to lose any of you." (Possibly, I had placed my priorities in the wrong order.) "And," I continued, "I'm not about to go in with him!"

When the male realized that he was separated from his mate, he first began to lift the side of the fencing with his horned snout. When that didn't succeed, he went right through the chain link as if it were tissue paper. I had major repair work to do on that enclosure.

The white rhino has square lips, unlike other species that possess an upper lip similar to a small elephant trunk. The common name for the white is the square-lipped rhino. They adjusted well to grazing in the pasture and took quickly to the 20 acres contained by electric fencing. It was quite a sight as travelers on roads surrounding the compound passed by and looked upon the pastoral scene with cows, a bull, and a pair of rhinos that made my bull appear like a midget.

It was an extraordinary day when one of my staff came

running to inform me that a baby rhino had been born. I could barely believe what I heard. When I reached the birthing place in the shade of a live oak, I beheld the new baby, pink as a human baby, and one of the most adorable sights I'd ever seen on the compound. It looked like a cartoon — a miniature baby standing with its mother, the father proudly circling. It was a definite highlight, one of the most satisfying and stimulating events that occurred in all the years at the Breeding Center.

Another event of monumental proportions, requiring a year of work to complete, was the sale of 18 tigers, born on the compound, to the Taft Corporation, owners and operators of two theme parks, one outside Cincinnati and the other outside Richmond. The sale was based on my ability to make the tigers comfortable and compatible with what would be their new home, living in drive-through safari-type open areas. I worked with the tigers for nearly a year to prepare them for freedom. I planned well the logistics for the transfer requiring 18 custom-built containers carried on five separate rigs along with ten employees to accomplish the many details in what was a smooth and successful delivery, precisely on schedule to the appointed parks. It gave me the ultimate pleasure to watch the process, which was testimony to what the Breeding Center was all about. My goals were fulfilled when captive-bred and raised animals found their homes in pristine, well-monitored, and maintained parks and zoos where travelers from all over the world could watch and enjoy animals in safe and secure confines. My greatest satisfaction was in the realization of perpetuity.

There were some failures over the years that were sad and disappointing, but they provided knowledge to prevent future loss, not only on my compound, but at other facilities as well. There can be little success in breeding without risk-taking.

I imported 33 cheetahs, including ten that I captured in Djibouti. The terrain of the small country, located on the tip of the horn of Africa, next to Somalia, is sand and rock with little vegetation. I'd made the acquaintance of a man who owned a restaurant named La Palmeraie (Palm Grove), which struck me as being very funny as the only trees I saw were decorating his restaurant and made of tin. My friend accompanied me on several cheetah hunts, using a jeep to chase down the swift-moving cats as

MODELE No 27 № 00112

CERTIFICAT ZOO-SANITAIRE

POUR CARNIVORE DOMESTIQUE OU SAUVAGE

SERVICE DE L'ÉLEVAGE DU TERRITOIRE FRANÇAIS DES AFARS ET DES ISSAS
POSTE DE DJIBOUTI

I. — IDENTIFICATION DE L'ANIMAL :

Espèce : FELINE   Race : 3 Guépards - Cheetahs (ACINONYX-JUBATUS)

Sexe : 2 femelles - 1 mâle   Date de naissance : âgés de 2 mois

Robe et particularités :

II. — NOM ET ADRESSE DU PROPRIETAIRE : Monsieur ESTIVAL - DJIBOUTI -

III. — PAYS DE DESTINATION : U. S. A.

Nom et adresse du destinataire : Monsieur Robert BAUDY - P.O. Box 132 CENTER HILL - FLORIDA

Moyen de transport : Avion -

IV. — RENSEIGNEMENTS SANITAIRES :

Le Vétérinaire officiel soussigné certifie :

a) Les animaux désignés ci-dessus et examinés ce jour n'ont présenté aucun signe clinique de maladie contagieuse.

b) Ils ne présentent aucun signe de rage.

c) Ils ont séjourné ~~depuis six mois~~ (*) ~~ou~~ depuis leur naissance (*) sur le Territoire où aucun cas de rage n'a été observé depuis deux ans.

* c) Ils ont été capturés depuis plus d'un mois, période pendant laquelle ils ont été mis en observation.

* d) ~~Il a été vacciné comme l'indique le certificat~~ joint.

— Taxe sanitaire : 15.000
— Coût du certificat : 200 F.D.

TOTAL : 15.200 F.D.

Fait à Djibouti, le 18/3/70

Le Docteur Vétérinaire,

TERRITOIRE FRANÇAIS DES AFARS ET DES ISSAS
B.P. 297
Service Élevage et Industries Animales
Le Chef de Service

(*) Rayer la mention inutile.

Testimony to a succesful Cheetah hunt

we drove over the rough terrain. It was quite an adventure and very successful. I acquired other specimens from neighboring regions and South Africa; some came from zoos.

Before the cats arrived, I prepared an enclosure specifically for them. It was 400 feet in length with trees in the center. I felt that I had the ideal setting to promote propagation. What I didn't realize was an indigenous flea infestation that was deadly to the small cats. No matter how often we disinfected the animals, within three days they had thousands of fleas attacking them. We tried flea collars, but the cats were allergic. We began a process of putting them in a squeeze cage, each cat, every other day, in an ongoing spraying application to rid them of the pesky parasites. The stress induced by defleaing, using toxic spray, kept the cats from breeding. They survived the treatments, but did not produce offspring.

I sold three specimens to a businessman in Miami who owned a surgical tool company. I informed the man of the method of caring for the cats and of the problems I encountered. He set up his housing or enclosure on concrete instead of the ground and followed the other procedures I recommended, based on my failures, and ultimately bred the first litter of cheetahs ever born in this country. The babies were born to the female I had captured in Djibouti.

The cheetah, like the snow leopard, is a very specialized animal, requiring a dry, cold climate. We learned through trial and error that the southwest portion of the States is most ideal for breeding and raising the spotted cats.

There were so many lessons learned and yet to learn. In all the years of breeding, one of the challenges was taking the young from their mothers. There are no two cases alike, and many circumstances dictate the time and method. When a client wants a mother-raised specimen, it is left with the mother to be raised. When a tame specimen is desired, we remove the young within three weeks, to be bottle-fed, then vaccinated and shipped at ten weeks of age. Sometimes removal depends on the mother. A good mother, in her prime and taking care of her offspring, may keep the baby or babies for some time although I prefer not to let the newborn stay under the mother for more than ten days. Where felines are concerned, in the wild, they are normally born in the snow, in harsh conditions where food is not readily available. In the den, in captivity, they tend to overeat.

In a recent case, one snow leopard mother was particularly aggressive toward me, and I was afraid that when she began bouncing off the sides of the cage when I approached that she would step on her baby. I asked a helper to assist me — standing at one side of the cage while I got into position to hook or retrieve the baby quickly so that there was no injury to either the baby or the "marauder."

As the birthing process continues, the animal population is in a constant state of flux. The challenges remain ever-present, seductive, compelling, and also life-threatening.

40

LIFE AND DEATH
La Vie et le Mort

As animals continued to come into the compound, many kept for breeding, others shipped on to various destinations, many domestic sources became my suppliers following the Endangered Species Act. Occasionally, I receive a call from a zoo that asks me to accept an outlaw cat that has killed or injured one or more zookeepers. The zoo cannot tolerate the presence of such a dangerous animal, and they know that, by reputation, I have the expertise as well as the facility for handling dangerous animals. Other situations arise where breeders or collectors are forced out of business or for whatever reason can no longer maintain their animals. I have acquired specimens that would possibly have been destroyed if I had not accepted them. In many cases the animals become breeders.

The process continues with many births and much work raising the new babies, caring for the mature animals, and spending time on the telephone proffering expertise or being alerted to an animal that has been injured and must be picked up.

It was business as usual on the compound with Gerard's problems continuing to plague him and me. I had not seen Gerard for months, but listened to his anguished, incoherent phone conversations lamenting troubles and seeking my aid in an ongoing legal battle with the government and the Army. Visiting him had become impossible. To observe firsthand the visible and pathetic decline, and to see the people he called his friends, men and women who were lost and sick, became more painful than I cared to endure. My visits did not seem to help or influence him. The effect even became negative, and I decided that they served no purpose except to deepen the ambivalence.

When the phone rang, it was Gerard pleading with me to aid in his immediate argument, holding the government responsible for his problems, acerbated by the war and his contact with *agent orange*. He sought an additional allotment to bolster his veteran's pension. In addition to his quarrel with the government, he was in and out of jail and constantly being threatened with imprisonment for parole violation. His deepening morass was also shared with Odette through phone calls, accusing her of showing little compassion for his problems. She'd call and we discussed at great length our sorrow with what had become the tragedy of Gerard. We felt totally and painfully inadequate to help him.

On April 30, 1991, the day before his 44th birthday, I received a call of desperation. As usual he was high on drugs or alcohol. His speech was slurred as he described his plight. The authorities were going to pick him up to send him to Raiford for parole violation. He spoke with rambling vindictiveness against the government, the Army, and against the local authorities in his attempt to convince me that he was not to blame for any of what he was accused.

"Gerard, I cannot do anything to help you on the basis of what you are telling me," I explained. "What I need from you is the paper work. I'm sure there is lots of that. And if you will send me that, I'll take it to my lawyer friend . . ."

"I've got a lawyer." He'd interrupt.

"Well, then, what are you calling me for? If you have a lawyer, what more can I do?"

He said something about the case costing a lot of money.

"Don't you have a free lawyer?"

"Yes, I've got a free lawyer, but she doesn't want to handle my case anymore."

My thought was that he had exhausted his legal defense in the futility of the situation. "That's another thing, I need a letter from your lawyer. After I get all the facts on the table, I'll study all the paper work very carefully. Then I will make a decision. I will try to help you to the best of my ability." I knew there was little I could do.

The following day Gerard phoned Odette, and they exchanged a heated conversation. Gerard accusing her, and me, of leaving him in a rut. He said, "You never did anything for me." After the emotional outburst, he finished his conversation. "I hope you will be happy after today!"

Odette called me immediately after the exchange. "I don't know what he's up to, but he called and blamed me for all of his problems for the past ten years."

The next call came from a neighbor of Gerard's in Tampa. The voice on my recording machine indicated grave concern, "Mr. Baudy, something important has happened. Will you please call me?"

There was a name and number. I dialed it, fearing the worst.

"Well, you'd better brace yourself . . ."

I answered, "I have a strong feeling of what you are going to tell me and I'm prepared."

"Your son committed suicide yesterday. A neighbor boy discovered him hanging from a rope on the porch. The police were notified, and there will be an investigation and an autopsy."

There were many phone calls back and forth to the police and to Bonnie. The police could give me no information, and Bonnie was stunned by the death. She had spoken to Gerard the day before and said to me she found him to be cool, not despondent, at least over the phone, and she could not believe that his behavior or his voice indicated suicide. There were calls to Odette and other family members in France.

The body was autopsied. I talked to the police officials and asked them to investigate whether or not the cause of death was suicide. In view of the company Gerard kept and the fact that he was receiving government checks, I was suspicious of foul play. I did not have to make the request. The investigation had begun the day of the death with the autopsy as standard procedure. But they would not divulge any information.

The family wanted the funeral to be conducted at the Bushnell Veterans Cemetery and for me to make the arrangements. My heart was not in it. I didn't want to face the horror of the circumstances, the many people who would come to a service held locally and attended by people in the area who loved Gerard and knew of his troubles, to be witnessed and played out so close to the compound. Nor did I feel up to hosting, for three or four days, the family members arriving on the compound with the potential for venomous outbursts that would only further destroy any semblance of dignity accorded the solemn occasion. I was crushed by the tragedy and also feeling a great deal of guilt, but could not face all the hypocrisy. No one knew Gerard's real story, not even his father.

After more phone calls, the decision was made to have the body cremated and to hold a simple funeral service in Tampa. The cremains were to be dispersed at a later date.

Bonnie organized the service held in a Catholic Church not far from where Gerard had lived. I hoped there would not be a crowd. Bonnie and her family were present — I was grateful for their support. They were fine, caring people who loved Gerard. Their presence in his life during his last years had been significant. They had become his family, and I appreciated them for that role. Odette and Ed arrived by car and took a room at a nearby motel close to the church. About 50 people attended the service. Martine and Samantha did not attend.

I had not seen Odette for years. She had aged markedly, and I felt compassion for her suffering. As the priest spoke soothingly of the fallen soldier, my thoughts went back to the animal compound in St. Mande. I saw us working the animals, laboring hard to survive, and then I saw baby Gerard in his bassinet — blue from near-strangulation and wrapped tightly in a fine lace veil. I could almost feel myself picking up the small, quiet form and firmly patting his back. I had saved his life then.

I recalled at the time that we decided, with so much work requiring both Odette and me in the early stages of a burgeoning career and struggling so hard to survive, that the child would be safer and better cared for by his grandparents. How could we know the decision would end like this?

Then my mind went to a beautiful, young Odette crying as we left Fegreac, leaving the boy behind. I saw quick flashes of the boy as he grew: Visits to Fegreac and Rennes to share my success with the family, not knowing the potential problems. Then I saw him as he arrived in the States, and recognized troubles within the young man who was my son.

As the priest continued the eulogy, speaking of the military service, my mind clearly went to Gerard in uniform going off to Vietnam, and then to the many disturbing incidents that filled the months and years of bailouts. I painfully recalled incoherent conversations which offered little hope. Then my thoughts stopped, as if in answer to the questioning, and I saw the house in Fegreac and me holding Gerard, just a little boy in a wondrous romp. We were celebrating my newfound success. I danced, laughing, and he was laughing in my arms, until his head hit the stair and he went limp. I wondered right after the accident if damage had been done that would affect him permanently. Could all of his problems have stemmed from that sudden, severe blow to his head?

I thought of my parents. Mother who adored and doted on him, and wanted him to remain in Rennes with her. How convenient it was to have the boy cared for in what I thought to be a stable, secure environment, far better than sharing the nomadic life of his father. I wanted something better for my son. And Father: the strict disciplinarian, a man who lived life to the fullest and wanted me to share in every adventure and learn each aspect of every life-enhancing experience. I had failed Gerard in that. I was not there to impart, to share, to instruct, to discipline, to build a man, and I implored my father not to be harsh with the boy.

Gerard remained a little boy, resentful of parents who abandoned him, and he never got over the hurt. He wanted our attention and our presence. He wanted us. In that deprivation, he wanted to hurt back. He succeeded in that. And now the hurt had ended for him.

Following the religious portion of the service, Bonnie had arranged for the veterans to present an American flag to Odette. My thoughts were instantly brought to the present when the flag was delivered to a physically and emotionally drained Odette, who I thought was going to collapse. I, too, was drained and filled with questions. How could it have been different? It was too late.

The Swans left for Pennsylvania and I left for Beville's Corner. I returned to the compound thoroughly shaken by the events of the last few days and by so much that had preceded, so many incidents that we should have recognized as signs of impending doom. I could not get Gerard's life, or his death, out of my mind, as one day, then the next, and the next held many questions. During all the years of traveling the world, caught up in fame and the dynamics of building not only a career, but in perpetuating endangered species, I never thought Gerard was not being well-cared for. Nor did I ever think that he would be better served by being at my side as I moved so quickly through each day and every adventure with little time to think of anything other than the immediate involvement. I truly felt that he had the best chance to mature and develop in the secure confines of a stable environment in Fegreac and then Rennes. And as long as I provided well, monetarily, I felt his chances of developing a well adjusted maturity were well grounded. It was too late to learn, to go back, to do things differently.

When he arrived in the States, his anger and discontent were wrapped in the frustration of his love for his grandmother, who suffered from his rebelliousness. Drinking to absolve guilt and ease his adolescent perception of life only compounded his guilt and created abhorrent behavior, for which he was expelled from France by the people who loved and cared for him. He arrived too full of resentment and fear to heed the newly imposed discipline that came too late. He was, sadly, too immature and troubled to deal with the forming destructive pattern. The complexities of the overriding circumstances were too much for any of us to handle. We all went about living our lives, frustrated by a lack of understanding or communication, which only served to deepen the alienation. The battle had been lost long ago, and now Gerard was gone.

With the demands of the compound always present, I worked through each day physically exhausting myself and grateful for the compelling activity. I was involved at the time in the frustrating problems of completing a delivery of cats that had been arranged nearly a year before.

I was contacted by Madame DeLors, a zoo owner in France, seeking cats for her small, specialized zoo located several hundred miles south of Paris. Madame DeLors' son, Rudolph, involved in the family business, particularly favored large cats. The zoo primarily displayed rare birds, but they did have a leopard and some bears that had appeared in the movie *The Bear*. The DeLors wanted to expand their feline collection. I recommended they visit the compound to inspect the animals and make their decision. Both mother and son made three visits to the Breeding Center. They selected two Siberian white tigers; a male and a female.

As in all animal transactions, stringent government guidelines, regulations, and extensive paper work were required before the transfer could be completed. I retained a lawyer to facilitate the sale. Madame DeLors stipulated the sale and actual transfer be completed for an advertised extravaganza to introduce the new tigers and also to promote the zoo.

The wait for the government permit seemed interminable. As the date for the special introduction grew closer, Madame Delors contacted me expressing fear that the bureaucratic process seemed likely to place the grand opening in jeopardy. I recommended she contact the government to accelerate the process. She was a small, highly motivated, dynamic lady. She caught a plane to Washington and, along with my lawyer, bugged the hell out of the United States Fish and Wildlife Service in Arlington. There was much at stake for her, and for me. I'd been working on the special crating to contain the tigers and had acquired the health certificate and had even made reservations on a flight to France for the animals. Much time, money, and labor had already been invested by both Madame DeLors and me.

The determined lady did prevail, and the two-year-old tigers were flown to Paris, then transferred by truck to the ZooParc de Beauval in St.-Aignan-Sur-Cher. They were advertised as the first pair of white Siberian tigers unique to France.

The new residents found their home in what I saw pictured as a large natural habitat with trees, a waterfall, moat and rocky outcropping. I had investigated, through my French collaborators, the pristine zoo. I knew I had succeeded in placing the tigers in an ideal setting. I was particularly gratified to have my tigers on display in my native country. Madame DeLors invited me to attend the opening ceremonies, but I was too depressed to attend a gala.

While there were many obligations that consumed me physically, my thoughts were still of Gerard. And then another call came. Siggy Popick was dead. I called Ed to offer my condolences in spite of the bitterness of the divorce that I knew had been painful for both of them. It was shocking to realize that a woman so full of enthusiasm and energy, one who lived life to the fullest, was gone. Siggy had been hospitalized for acute hepatitis, treated successfully and released, but suffered a fatal heart attack.

I attended the funeral and was attuned to the emotional outpouring of friends and family. I remembered back to the times when Siggy appeared at the compound, delivered by chauffeured limousine and never without a bottle of gin for herself and wine for me. If she stayed overnight, I was fully aware that she enjoyed her drinks and our conversations. She loved the compound and loved the animals. On the occasions when she spent the night, she'd arise early the following morning and go out to commune with the animals, take pictures, and enjoy the natural setting of the animal-filled hammock. I thoroughly enjoyed her company and admired her zest for life. Now she was gone.

Life and death on the compound with babies born and animals slaughtered to sustain those living were daily events, accepted as normal, ongoing characteristics of the business. Human death was shocking and particularly difficult to accept when it came suddenly and unexpectedly. It was even harder to accept when it came at one's own hands.

Gladys was dying, slowly and painfully, and that was another kind of death, one that I witnessed as I became more attentive to her needs in her final months. She had raised and nurtured babies for me up until a year before she died. She had beaten the odds and outlived the doctor's initial prognosis of a two-year survival following the diagnosed cancer. She was still actively caring for the animals three years after the dire prognosis, but it became evident that she could no longer have the babies with her in the home on the lake.

I'd talked to many doctors and surgeons regarding Gladys' condition. There was never any hope for surgery or other treatment to prolong her life, or even to lessen the suffering with the complication of asthma. She had done just as she'd predicted; she continued living her life, enjoying cigarettes, and her daily ration of J&B in addition to her card games with lady friends. She was a tough lady with a soft and gentle nature. She faced the pain bravely, knowing well the outcome, and suffered without complaining up until the end.

I spent more time with her. Two nights each week I slept on a cot near the couch in the living room. Gladys had two vertebrae welded in her back from a rapidly deteriorating decalcification. She was in constant pain and could not get comfortable in her bed to sleep. She didn't want to go on pain pills.

When she went into a coma, I called an ambulance, and we admitted her to the Leesburg Hospital. She came out of the coma and returned to the house on the lake, but soon realized that she could not stay alone. She knew the time had come when she needed care, so a nursing home was chosen. I made the arrangements for a private room in the well-run luxurious home where she spent her final two months. There, I visited her daily.

Gladys died December 9, 1991. I lost a dear, precious friend and confidant. We'd loved one another deeply, and my profound sentiments were mirrored to a degree in a tribute written by BeeJay Lester which appeared in the January/February L.I.O.C. Endangered Species Conservation Federation newsletter:

Tribute To The Lady of the Lake,

On December 9, 1991, the grand dame of surrogate mothers to wildlife babies died. Gladys Lewis of Lake Panasoffkee, Florida, lost her life to cancer. It is indeed a tremendous loss not only to the wildlife animals, but to those of us who have been fortunate enough to know her.

Gladys was a longtime member of the LIOC, Florida Chapter. She hosted several LIOC meetings in her lakeside home, she attended chapter and national conventions, gave her friendship and support to many LIOC members and wildlife fanciers who visited her. For her work with wildlife and conservation, she received much media coverage.

Living the life of luxury on the lake, Gladys had never raised any wildlife babies prior to meeting Robert Baudy of Center Hill's Rare Feline Breeding Center. Baudy needed someone to raise his captive-born exotic cat offspring; Gladys had the time and desire to assist. The two paired up and with Baudy's expertise, Gladys became an expert. Over the 20 years or so that she volunteered her efforts, she raised many species of wildlife babies born at Baudy's compound.

Gladys was surrogate mom to bears, hyenas, lemurs, foxes, peafowl, and ostriches. Mainly she raised the exotic felines such as snow and clouded leopards, African and Asian leopards, black and spotted jaguars, ocelots, Siberian lynx, bobcats, pumas, and white and normal tigers. According to Baudy, Gladys raised over 400 babies for his compound. She was dedicated to the little ones faithfully keeping them fed, cleaned, and loved.

Unselfishly, this lady of the lake nursed newborns at all hours of the night, giving up her bridge games and shopping trips to care for them. Gladys was a gracious and giving hostess, who kept such a positive outlook on life that she made her friends feel

Surrogate mother to the young: Gladys Lewis

cheerful just being around her.

Gladys Lewis will surely be missed. We all loved her and will always remember this wonderful, kind lady who so deeply touched our lives.

Gladys was gone; Siggy was gone; Gerard was gone. Word

came that through connections in Washington Ed Swan had made arrangements to have Gerard's ashes interred at Arlington Cemetery. I was pleased and supportive of his efforts, but I didn't attend the ceremony, which I did recognize as being the highest honor bestowed a fallen soldier. I could not handle the emotional trauma that would only reopen wounds not yet healed — wounds that would never heal.

I was deeply depressed just after Gerard's death; and as I watched Gladys suffer, I found myself feeling there was little reason to go on. I contemplated suicide. I spent many hours in lethargy, barely able to react, and not wanting to solve the ongoing problems and responsibilities that required my attention everyday. Thank God, Lily was with me, met the challenges, and encouraged and soothed me. She actually kept the Breeding Center and me alive in an understated, but firm hands-on display of compassion, which I fully realize saved my life.

I have perpetuated life in many different animal species over the years. Lily Lehman was responsible in part for the perpetuation of the life of Robert Baudy, and I am deeply grateful to her for being there when I desperately needed her.

As life goes on at the Breeding Center, Lily has since moved on. No one on the compound has ever been able to escape the multifaceted labor demands, and I have always been right in the middle of the activity. I have no alternative, but those people who work along with me come and go just as the animals come and go, in a continuing metamorphosis unique to the oak-filled hammock.

Since Lily has gone from my employ, she does visit from time to time to do much needed paper work for me. However, Margaret Wright, better known as Maggie, has become my right hand. Maggie arrives promptly at 6:30 each morning and tends to the babies, feeding them, and cleaning out their cages. Most recently, I have had six baby tigers living in the house. Maggie has been a wonderful loyal employee who tends to the animals' needs and will even straighten up the kitchen and bedroom when the house is particularly disheveled. Maggie makes a gallant attempt at performing any and all details on the compound, and I would be sorely pressed to manage without her.

At the Breeding Center, each day dawns quietly but always holds the promise of activity so uniquely inspired by my chosen life work. As the years have passed, I am amazed that I have survived so much. I am also flattered to realize that the Audubon Society recognizes me as a leading authority on captive breeding and management of wild cats, of which there are 37 species in the world. I have been successful in breeding 27 species and subspecies known to man and find particular satisfaction in having produced 67 clouded leopards, the mysterious cat from southeast Asia, still enjoyed by the public in many zoos throughout the world.

When the telephone rings, I never know if it's a request to pick up an injured animal or a foreign journalist seeking permission to interview and photograph the animal man. Recently reporters came from Germany, Italy, and France to interview me for articles which appear in such magazines as *Stern, Natura Zoologia,* and France's *VDS,* lending further credence to current as well as past performance.

There have been many requests by government agencies, curators of zoos, other breeders and trainers, and universities to document my knowledge. A book has been germinating for a long time to contain my expertise. The title will be *Management of Wild Feliadaes: A Summary of Successful and Unsuccessful Experiments in Captive Breeding of Exotic Cats in Central Florida.*

Recently, the Audubon Society held its biennial convention in Fort Myers, and I hosted on the compound reptile expert Peter Pritchard and World Wildlife Fund cat specialist Peter Jackson, who called the collection of felines one of the finest existing in the world at this time. In looking back over years of work, his assessment brings the ultimate honor, but it is one of so many in a career that took me from a mud show in Paris to the Medrano, the Schumann in Copenhagen, to Radio City Music Hall, the New York Palace, the *Ed Sullivan Show* and so many other arenas across the North American Continent.

I look toward my 73rd year with one regret: Gerard's death at his own hands. It stood so distinctly apart from what I believed and of that which I spoke and demonstrated so eloquently all through my life: that life is a precious gift and all that surrounds us in nature on this beleaguered planet must be preserved and protected, enjoyed and enhanced — not threatened and maligned. Gerard's adult existence seemed so wasted, so tormented, so lost.

While I suffer guilt over the tragedy that I did not have him participate in life at my side as he grew, I am most saddened by the fact that Gerard was not capable of searching for his own answers to solve what were not unsolvable problems. How wonderful it would have been if he had lived and enjoyed the life that he was given, if for no other reason than to prove that he could in spite of me or what he may have felt about parents who left him to be raised by grandparents.

I still live everyday to the fullest in an oak hammock in Central Florida, filled with over 70 cats that require daily care. I watch with awe and appreciation the perpetual birthing process that provides daily stimulation to what has been my milieu, my place in the sun.

Today, I feel more dedicated than ever to perpetuating that which remains the same, my constant, my animals, in a very special place that is little touched by the outside world.

Robert Baudy

I've loved every one of the little ones. This is a baby Florida panther.
Photo Credit: Photographic Images, Tampa/Pepito.

41

ADDENDUM
By Sandra Thompson

Where do you end the story of a man's life when there is so much yet to live, to experience, to impart? When that life holds much vigor and energy involved in perpetuating animal species which only promises self-perpetuation, it is impossible to write the final chapter.

As the work progressed, I was on the phone early with Robert nearly every day for months. Never once was our conversation exclusively committed to the past, but always included current, compelling activities, whether it be to recapture a cat that had escaped due to carelessness by an employee, or to answer a call from the highway patrol, or a call from a farmer to pick up an animal sick, injured, or dead to be slaughtered. Often there were dangerous circumstances involved in the process.

When Robert was called to gather a colt, killed by wild dogs, he found an overly attentive mare protecting her baby. Robert advised the owner to hold the mare at bay while he pulled the colt free. As he was pulling the dead animal from the corral, the mare bolted and nearly killed him. On another occasion, he was called to pick up a wild pig, and again, narrowly escaped serious injury when the pig attacked.

Due to previous years of drought conditions in Florida, several of the huge oak trees had died. In heavy wind storms, the enormous leafless trees fell into the cat-filled hammock damaging enclosures and threatening not only the cats, but creating the potential for escape. For days Robert, along with a crew of employees, labored extensively to cut up the fallen limbs, heavy branches, and massive trunks, and then repaired the affected enclosures.

On a visit to Palm Beach County to do some proofing and to discuss the progress of the manuscript, he was called, upon arrival, to the telephone to be advised of a dire problem that had developed at the compound in the several hours since his departure. A horse that had been put down by a Sumter County vet, picked up by Robert, and slaughtered to be frozen had, against Robert's explicit instruction, been fed to some of the cats. The cats exhibited toxic symptoms. Robert had been unable to contact the vet before leaving the compound to ascertain the medical diagnosis, indicating the reason for the horse's euthanasia, to confirm the meat safe. It was just another drama unfolding at The Rare Feline Breeding Center.

Seven days after the brief visit, when I finally spoke to Robert, he told me about his week. After discussing with me the summation and other details of the book, then dinner and more conversation, he slept for several hours before arising at 4:00 a.m. to return to Center Hill. He was concerned about his cats, anxious to get back to the compound, and to Lily, where he found six snow leopards affected by the poison.

The leopards had been given neck meat from the butchered horse. When an animal is put to sleep, the injection is administered into the jugular vein, making the neck meat extremely toxic. The cats were semicomatose when he arrived. He quickly prepared them for injection of Atropine. They were quietly left alone, but attentively observed, to either pull out of the coma or expire. He called in a taxidermist to stand by in case the cats died, to preserve the valuable pelts.

In addition to the trauma associated with the potential loss of six animals, work went on in preparation for a show in Wildwood, plus working with colts recently born on the compound. They were to be readied to go to a local lady trainer for sale at a horse auction. As the days passed, the leopards were watched closely by Robert and an idle taxidermist, who sat around smoking cigarettes, waiting for the cats to expire. The sick felines were fed milk instead of water and gradually responded to the antidote. They all survived. The taxidermist was paid for smoking while Robert remained actively engaged in the myriad of details involved in the diverse and compelling events at the compound.

With each phone session, I taped 20 or 30 minutes of material to build and enhance the story of a man approaching his seventies, still facing life-threatening adventure everyday, and maintaining a hectic pace that would defeat most humans. It was such an incredible experience for me to listen to the heavily French-accented voice telling his story. I was amazed by the man and the years of struggle to survive so much adversity that began during the invasion of France, continued through the War years, the tough early years of a forced marriage, and then the fame and prominence gained through the dangerous labor of training and showing animals, all of which became his lifeblood.

A compelling constant throughout the provocative story began to emerge with Robert's introduction to sex by a thoroughly experienced and eager older woman. It became the precursor that set the stage for viable, though illegal, entree to the bordellos of St. Germaine, which only enhanced his appetite for sensual pleasure. The love affair with beautiful Simone added solace to a life on the run from the German invaders and sustained all through his many years of running, not only from the Nazis, but from the burgeoning demands of circus fame and ensnaring marriages. As the story proceeded, there were many involvements with many different women.

Jodi and Ed Schaffer indicated Robert's proclivity for women as a concupiscent presence on the compound, and in his life, in many ongoing arrangements, too difficult to track. In my naïveté I was soon aware and astonished, as the story unfolded, by the number of romantic dalliances. As Robert told of his early sexual arousal and visits to the brothels, I included the incidents as important in coloring the man's story. When Simone became his first love, I was touched by the tenderness of the delicate affair and the tragedy of having to deny it to parents on either side, who were filled with hatred and mistrust for the other. When Robert continued in his quest and became involved with women associated with Paul le Royer, and with women he met as he served time in the army, both in Spain and in Germany during the War, I realized that his desire was indeed insatiable.

During his early circus fame, as he toured with Odette, his marriage seemingly did not provide the depth of sexual or emotional stimulation to satisfy his yearning or to quell the overpowering temptation that came with ardent women who approached the handsome, prominent, successful performer. It became a delicate balancing act that seemed absolutely necessary in order to portray the man in his true and focused involvement, which was to achieve a successful career training outside and showing animals in the arena and then in the breeding of endangered species.

Robert indicated that in all the years after the War of working with animals, there was never a vacation. When he became caught up in the fame achieved with the greyhound act, he was so fully booked and so fully aware that he had finally found a modus for proving himself to his father, that he never relaxed the driving force. Instead, he went from arduous and daily training of greyhounds and monkeys to training Great Danes, tigers, and lions and working with other animals to train and perform in an unrelenting panoply to fulfill his ultimate ambitions. In the consuming work that required unceasing mental and physical concentration, in acquiring the animals, then in the training process, and in transporting various acts from one location to another, there was never time away.

Even his travels abroad were only briefly broken to visit family. The trips were designed to enhance a career and to fulfill the goal of saving endangered animals. The demands of his profession were total and extreme, and romantic dalliance provided release and renewal. However, it was becoming evident that if I were to include every lover, there would be little space left for describing the animal training, performing, and breeding sequences.

My goal was to achieve a balanced portrait to include many varied interests and adventures to maintain credibility. Robert was clearly fascinated by, and involved with, *many* beautiful women, which did not interfere with his consuming quest to succeed in his professional life-choice. When he introduced a woman, then another woman, and another, whether he was married or not at the time, he never revealed the relationship with bravado, arrogance, or conceit. He demonstrated genuine caring, respect, and love for each paramour that belied promiscuity. He readily admitted his full appreciation of every beautiful woman he met, but impressed upon me that he never imposed himself, but allowed natural instincts and desires to work their way into mutually satisfying relationships.

He was a handsome young man who matured as an elegant, successful showman and animal trainer placed in the arena with many sensual ladies. He wanted to marry Simone, but circumstances prevented the union. He was forced to marry Odette, then Charlotte, and in both instances took marriage vows that he had no intention of keeping. I felt that his view of sex and women had little to do with monogamy or the lack thereof, but more with the natural, stimulating aura surrounding the act which gave pleasure to both participants. In that, there was never a hint of associating guilt or sin. There were broken marriages, hurt feelings, and disillusionment; but over the course of his life, Robert has maintained amicable relationships with most of his former lovers. He seems, in retrospect, to feel kindly toward each of the special women who shared his passion. It is with gratitude and even a sense of awe, that he recounts every facet of his sexual prowess. He fulfills the role of French lover unequivocally.

As he continued to divulge his life experiences, I felt sympathy for the harassment he described by a government bureaucracy, run by highly ill-informed appointees and incompetent field workers, and being overburdened with regulations that often were counterproductive to the Breeding Center's main purpose, to perpetuate endangered species. Robert related to me that he knew several animal breeders who committed suicide because of the devastating and totally stifling "Big Brother" bureaucracy.

Robert told me in the early stages of the story that recalling his childhood, his adolescence, and then the War years was his escape from the dangerous and frustrating daily involvements. It became a catharsis for him. It became a captivating and fulfilling involvement for me. Everyday adventure seemed to loom in what would be a never-ending story of one man's life: his odyssey. I did not ever want it to end, for with it would end my *modus vivendi*, which was to question deeply and receive answers that revealed the tragedy as well as the euphoria, the dramatic feats in the arena as well as the happiness and sadness that filled the scenes behind the curtain and stage.

When Robert visited me in south Florida and on my trips to visit him at the compound, he demonstrated an enthusiasm, a verve, a zest for life which belied the pain, the suffering, the depression he expressed feeling, all of which further enhanced the telling and the credibility of his biography. On one visit, he demonstrated the use of the ancient 15-foot Italian leather whip as he masterfully cracked it with precision in a classic performance of the consummate animal trainer.

As the pages were mailed to the compound, I was gratified to hear him say, "You have caught it; you have seen inside me. You are doing one hell of a job."

In his assessment, there was something of great value to me. To have a person reveal his soul and to be a part of the telling, and in so doing, give pleasure, release, and perpetuation to the storyteller is profoundly stimulating and satisfying. How could I possibly want for more?

When Robert spoke of being the first breeder indicted under the Endangered Species Act of 1973, I felt his pain in being accused of that which would be anathema to him and his purpose in operating the Breeding Center. He loved animals and treated them with respect and awe since his early childhood. He never lost a vestige of the early inquisitiveness which ultimately led to the desire to breed and perpetuate animals.

When he divulged the tragedy of his son and his inability to communicate his feelings to Gerard, I knew his pain and guilt were genuine emotions in reaction to the devastation of a needlessly wasted life. Robert was too caught up in perpetuating other life to save that which he never realized was lost, until it was too late.

There was so much in Robert's youthful quest for freedom, and then a career that drove him to the pinnacle of his profession under extremely difficult circumstances, but he never faltered. Only during the incarceration in Aix-en-Provence did he give up hope. Having survived so much adversity, how could he possibly fail?

And how could Gerard know the depth of his father's character formed by life experiences? A father's disapproval drove Robert. And in that drive were many needs to achieve a balance, sought in the arms of women in spite of his married status. The need fulfilled was anathema to wives working at his side in a tough Gypsy existence, where they did not find the same fulfillment. As first one woman, then another, and another, and so on were mentioned and brought into the story, I realized the potential for guilt where a son, not fully included, was demonstrating deepening emotional problems.

Robert Baudy has literally had a tiger by the tail. Nearly everyday of his life has held some sort of adventure involving an animal or animals in an ongoing quest to fulfill his existence. Being so dynamically involved in a stimulating, provocative profession, he sought escape from the very real problems that were looming not only in his son's life, but in the many broken relationships with women who came in and out of his life.

As the story began its final pages, I realize, regrettably, that I have had to judiciously omit the inclusion of so much material in order to include that which painted the most complete picture, albeit without the myriad of details that filled each day. On balance, Robert became a legend in the annals of the Wild Animal Kingdom, legitimately, and through a focused determination that was undeterred by marriages, by being a father, and by the romantic divergences that were only a small portion of the larger picture. And in that unwavering vision, it is only natural that he approaches his final chapters without the permanency of a female companion.

It is prophetic to realize that the man is now quite alone except for a few valued employees and a following of animal lovers and authorities from diverse fields who contact him. He remains with his 70 felines and other animals who exist because he exists. He is left buffered by the creatures that served him well and loyally and were his steadfast companions more easily understood by and obedient to the consummate trainer and lover.

There are more chapters to be written. A recent conversation described the imminent arrival of a young French girl of 21, who has experience working for a prominent zoo in France. She is seeking the experience of working for Mr. Robert Baudy at the Rare Feline Breeding Center in Center Hill, Florida. Robert reported that the girl was due to arrive for three months of training. She will live with Robert, and she will speak French. If he is fortunate, he will have her cook for him in the French manner which he prefers, and she will, in her own way, write another chapter in his life.

So life does indeed go on; and when it has held so much excitement and pathos, it is indeed worth telling and preserving. It has been for me a privileged opportunity to ask the many questions that evoked joyous memories as well as painful emotions.

It is irony, or simply the maturing process, that has produced insight and a balanced, educated, objective view of his world, which has influenced his thinking dramatically. He was adamantly opposed to taking over the meat market that would have occupied him in Le Vesinet and altered his life. It is dichotomous that in repudiating his father's offer to be a butcher, Robert ends up butchering to sustain the animals in his compound. It is also dichotomous that the consummate performer, trainer, and breeder who spent his early years hunting, and his later years training and breeding animals, enters the last quarter of his century expressing opposition to training, hunting, and incarceration of animals.

It is testimonial to his heightened senses to realize that while women played vitally important roles in his life, he nears his 73rd year expressing his passion for perpetuating species, enjoying the beauty that surrounds him in nature, in the arts, and derived from looking at a beautiful woman without the need of sexual involvement. He has come to terms with his singleness and seems quite content to let the memories of past pleasure fill rhapsodic leisure moments of which there are few with so many diverse daily obligations.

Memories fill his free time and provide much to savor as well as to suffer as they flicker in and out of his psyche. He continues his never-ending commitment to his professional expertise — to his animals. He can control the beasts. He understands them well. He derives infinite pleasure in their presence, in filling their needs, and in the constancy of their behavior.

He achieved the ultimate satisfaction by reaching the pinnacle as a performer in the circus arena, both in Europe and in the United States during the 1950s and 1960s. To be acknowledged as one of the world's leading authorities on captive breeding of exotic felines is the crown to climax his final achievement. To have bred over 120 Florida panthers on his compound, more than any other single breeder or organization, is the ultimate accomplishment. He has definitely become a legend in his own time.

And now, as his career comes full circle, he expresses the desire to see all animals freed to roam and breed naturally, unmolested by man. But that may be too late.

There is the promise of a book on captive breeding and veterinary data that has been requested by many different organizations over the years. There is also the need to repudiate much of what has been practiced in the animal training and breeding fields and in the management of zoos, where reprehensible practices have been rampant.

There are many more anecdotes that filled the days of this man's life which were only touched upon in a cursory manner in this volume. There could be a volume devoted to the women in Robert's life. There could be a volume pertaining to employees who've worked alongside Robert in the show arenas and at the compound. There could be a volume describing various animal training methods. There are many stories to tell to close the circle. This is a beginning, and it is with utmost pleasure that I have shared in the telling of the adventure of the French Lover who loved animals, beautiful women and LIFE — Robert Baudy, the Animal Man.

Sandra Thompson

A Great Performance: white tiger, Robert Baudy, and Sandra Thompson.
Photo Credit: Photographic Images/Pepito, Tampa.

About The Author

Sandra Thompson, raised in Sea Cliff, New York, on the North Shore of Long Island, worked for Grey Advertising, Chanel, Inc., and *Redbook Magazine*. She attended Cooper Union Art School in Manhattan on her way to a career as Editorial Artist for the *Fort Lauderdale News and Sentinel,* having moved to Florida in 1961. Sandra married David Thompson, owner of Thompson Office Supply Company in Ft. Lauderdale. They are the parents of sons, Bret and Craig, who join David's two sons, David, Jr., and Richard. When David retired, they moved to Palm Beach County where David spent the years between 1925 and 1954. The decision was made to collaborate on the telling of his Palm Beach years published in 1992 as *Palm Beach From The Other Side Of The Lake*. She is also the coauthor of *Palm Beach & Bar Harbor a la Testa* and currently is at work on another biography. In addition, Sandra spends leisure time on the links and at the drawing board. Life is never dull with so many compelling involvements.

A Great Performance: white tiger, Robert Baudy, and Sandra Thompson.
Photo Credit: Photographic Images/Pepito, Tampa.

About The Author

Sandra Thompson, raised in Sea Cliff, New York, on the North Shore of Long Island, worked for Grey Advertising, Chanel, Inc., and *Redbook Magazine.* She attended Cooper Union Art School in Manhattan on her way to a career as Editorial Artist for the *Fort Lauderdale News and Sentinel,* having moved to Florida in 1961. Sandra married David Thompson, owner of Thompson Office Supply Company in Ft. Lauderdale. They are the parents of sons, Bret and Craig, who join David's two sons, David, Jr., and Richard. When David retired, they moved to Palm Beach County where David spent the years between 1925 and 1954. The decision was made to collaborate on the telling of his Palm Beach years published in 1992 as *Palm Beach From The Other Side Of The Lake.* She is also the coauthor of *Palm Beach & Bar Harbor a la Testa* and currently is at work on another biography. In addition, Sandra spends leisure time on the links and at the drawing board. Life is never dull with so many compelling involvements.